LIEDER
LINE BY LINE

and word for word

Lois Phillips

Charles Scribner's Sons
New York

Printed in Great Britain
Library of Congress Catalog Card Number 79–66633
SBN 0–684–16442–6

Contents

Bamford College
South Hill Avenue
Harrow Hill
Middlesex

Dear Miss Phillips,

It is difficult to put my enthusiasm for your translations into adequate words. This is exactly what students desperately need, an accurate *word* for *word* detail, without which a Lied cannot be coloured vocally. Of course, they should all sit down and do this for themselves, but I'm afraid they never do.

Your project is urgently needed, it is a wonderful idea and I shall be among the very first to buy copies as soon as you have published.

Yours sincerely
Janet Baker

Preface

'Of course what young singers really need when they are studying *Lieder* is a word-for-word translation, with the equivalent English word printed under each German word,' said Roy Henderson during a conversation with Sir Anthony Lewis, Principal of the Royal Academy of Music in 1969.

Shortly afterwards I too happened to be discussing the study and performance of *Lieder* with Sir Anthony, and he repeated what Roy Henderson had said. I was very interested; such translations would indeed by extremely useful, printed together with a version in good, clear prose, which would be essential to disentangle the often unintelligible series of words resulting from a literal word-for-word translation. After some further discussion I was invited by Sir Anthony Lewis to undertake a series of translations for the singing students of the Royal Academy, with a view to eventual publication to enable them to be much more widely used.

Singing in a foreign language presents many problems. Apart from correct pronunciation and emphasis, it is of the utmost importance for the singer to know what the song is about, not merely in the general sense, but in every detail, if a real interpretation is to be achieved. Nowhere in song literature is this more necessary than in German *Lieder*, where at its most demanding, as for instance in any song of Hugo Wolf, the singer – and also the pianist – must understand every word and phrase, so close do the words lie to the music flowing from them.

It is the aim of this book to help the performer to a better and more complete knowledge of the language, and of the poems themselves. It is certainly not intended to save him the trouble of searching out all he can for himself, or even of learning German at all! But most young singers when they begin to study *Lieder* are ill-equipped to deal with the formidable problems that they are likely to encounter in the poems: those of grammar, including the considerable difference in the order of words in German from that used in English; the use of obsolete words and expressions, and of dialect; the often far from easy language of poetry itself, with its special use of words and hidden depths of meaning. No translation is 'the answer'; it can, however, be a valuable starting point for further search and research.

I would like to thank most warmly all those who have been involved in the very exacting task of producing the manuscript; Miss N. Snowden and Frau H. Brinkmann for their intelligent and beautiful typing; Mrs Renate Parsons and Miss Angela Parsons and a team of very kind friends who checked the manuscript at various stages and offered many useful suggestions; Miss Ilse Wolf and Dr Irene Marinoff who generously gave me their most expert help; and Dr Eva Schiff who read the entire manuscript and had countless valuable discussions with me in the most varied places.

I am also grateful to colleagues on the staff at the Royal Academy of Music for their suggestions as to choice of poems to be included; to Dame Janet Baker and Mr Roy Henderson for their interest and encouragement, and to Sir Anthony Lewis for his always ready advice and support.

Finally, I must thank Susannah Finzi for her invaluable collaboration over the prose translations of the poems. It was a great joy to share with her this highly demanding and stimulating experience, which has enriched and deepened our own knowledge of so many *Lieder*.

London   L.P.
January 1979

Notes on
Word-for-Word Translations

To help the clarity of these:

1. Brackets have been used round:

    (a)   reflexive pronouns, where they would be omitted in English.

    e.g. *Drum   sehn' ich mich   nach ihr*
        therefore long I   (myself) for her

    (b)   (little), where a diminutive ending means something like 'dear little', in an affectionate sense.

    e.g. *Geistlein*
        (little) ghost

    (c)   (it) in impersonal expressions.

    e.g. *Es   sass ein Salamander*
        (it) sat a   salamander

    (d)   words in certain common expressions, where the meaning would be unnecessarily misleading if the single words were literally translated.

    e.g. *es   gibt* rather than: *es gibt*
        (there is)   it gives

    (e)   a word that is understood, but not actually there.

    e.g. *Meine alte Katze tanzt wahrscheinlich mit*
        my   old cat   dances probably   with (us)

(f)   certain words of emphasis

```
e.g. Kühl bis    ans    Herz  hinan
     cool (unto) to the heart (up to)
```

2. A dash – has been used in inseparable verbs, where the prefix has no clear meaning apart from the rest of the verb.

```
e.g. stellt ... ein
     presents   –
```

3. Words are written between – and –, where the German words belong together as an expression.

```
e.g. heute Nacht
     – tonight –
```

Ludwig van Beethoven
(1770-1827)

1. *ADELAIDE*
   ADELAIDE (also set by Schubert)

Friedrich Matthisson

1. ADELAIDE

Einsam   wandelt dein Freund im   Frühlingsgarten,
solitary wanders your friend in the spring-garden

Mild   vom   lieblichen Zauberlicht umflossen,
gently by the lovely   magic-light encircled

Das durch   wankende Blütenzweige   zittert,
that through wavering blossoming-twigs trembles

Adelaide!
Adelaide!

In solitude your beloved
wanders in the garden in spring,
wrapped in a soft, enchanted
light, that trembles through
the swaying blossoms, Adelaide!

In der spiegelnden Flut,   im   Schnee der   Alpen,
in the sparkling   torrent in the snow   of the Alps,

In des   sinkenden Tages Goldgewölken,
in of the declining day   gold-mass of clouds

Im   Gefilde der   Sterne strahlt dein Bildnis,
in the fields of the stars shines   your image

Adelaide!
Adelaide!

In the sparkling waters, in
the snow of the Alps, in the
golden clouds of the declining
day, in the firmament of stars
your image shines, Adelaide!

Einst, o Wunder! entblüht   auf meinem Grabe
one day O miracle springs into flower on my   grave

Eine Blume der   Asche meines Herzens;
a   flower of the ash   of my heart

Deutlich schimmert auf jedem Purpurblättchen:
clearly shimmers on each crimson-(little) petal

Adelaide!
Adelaide!

O, one day there will be a
miracle - from the ashes of my
heart a flower will bloom on
my grave; on each crimson petal
will shimmer so clear, Adelaide!

2. *SECHS LIEDER*
   SIX   SONGS

Christian Fürchtegott Gellert

2. SIX SONGS

i. Bitten
  prayer

i. Prayer

Gott, deine Güte   reicht so weit,
God   your goodness extends so far

So weit die Wolken gehen;
so far the clouds go

Du kronst uns mit Barmherzigkeit,
you exalt us with mercy

Und eilst, uns beizustehen.
and hasten us to succour

Herr! Meine Burg,   mein Fels, mein Hort,
Lord my   stronghold my rock my   refuge

Vernimm mein Flehn,   merk   auf mein Wort;
hear   my supplication give heed to my   word

Denn ich will vor   dir beten!
for I   want before you to pray

O God, Your goodness
extends as far as the clouds
above. You exalt us with Your
mercy, and are quick to succour
us. Lord, my stronghold, my
refuge, my rock - hear my
supplication! Listen to my words,
for I would pray to You!

ii. Die Liebe des   Nächsten
  the love of the neighbour

ii. Love of thy neighbour

So jemand spricht: Ich liebe Gott!
if someone says   I love God

Und hasst doch seine Brüder,
and hates yet his   brothers,

Der treibt mit Gottes Wahrheit Spott
he makes with God's truth   mockery

Und reisst sie ganz darnieder.
and drags her wholly down

Gott ist die Lieb', und will, dass ich
God is the love   and wants that I

Den Nächsten liebe gleich als mich.
the neighbour love same as myself

If someone says, I love
my God! and yet he hates his
brothers, he makes a mockery of
God's truth and drags it in the
dust. God is Love, and desires
that I love my neighbour as I
love myself.

iii. Vom   Tode
  of the death

iii. On death

Meine Lebenszeit verstreicht,
my   life-span slips by

Stündlich eil   ich zu dem Grabe,
hourly   hasten I to the grave

Und was ist's, das ich vielleicht,
and what is it   that I   perhaps

Das ich noch zu leben   habe?
that I   still to to live have

My span of life slips by,
I hasten hourly to the grave.
What is it that perhaps I still
must do? Think, O man, about
your death! Do not delay, for
this one thing you must do.

Denk, o Mensch, an deinen Tod!
think O man   on your   death

Säume nicht, denn Eins   ist not.
defer not   for one thing is needful

iv. *Die Ehre Gottes aus der Natur*
    the praise of God from the nature

iv. Praise of God by Nature

Die Himmel rühmen des   Ewigen Ehre,
the Heavens praise of the eternal glory

Ihr Schall pflanzt seinen Namen fort.
their sound spreads His   name forth

Ihn rühmt der Erdkreis, ihn preisen die Meere;
Him praises the earth   Him praise the oceans

Vernimm, o Mensch, ihr   göttlich Wort!
hear   O man   their divine   word

    The heavens praise the glory
of the Eternal; they sound forth
His name far and wide! The entire
earth praises Him, the oceans
praise Him! Hear, O man, their
divine word!

Wer trägt   der   Himmel unzählbare Sterne?
who sustains of the Heavens countless stars

Wer führt die Sonn' aus ihrem Zelt?
who leads the sun from her vault (of Heaven)

Sie kommt und leuchtet und lacht uns   von ferne,
she comes and shines   and laughs to us from afar

Und läuft den Weg, gleich als ein Held!
and goes the way like   as a hero

    Who sustains the countless
stars in the firmament? Who leads
the sun from the vaults of
heaven – the sun that comes and
shines and laughs at us from afar,
and runs its course, like a hero?

v. *Gottes Macht und Vorsehung*
   God's might and providence

v. God's might and providence

Gott ist mein Lied!
God is my   song

Er ist der Gott der   Stärk.
He is the God of the strengt.

Hehr   ist sein Nam'
exalted is His   name

Und gross sind seine Werke,
and great are His   works

Und alle Himmel sein Gebiet.
and all Heavens His domain

    God is my song! He is the
God of might! Exalted is His
name, and great are His works;
all the Heavens are His domain.

vi. *Busslied*
   repentance-song

vi. Song of repentance

An dir allein, an dir hab' ich gesündigt,
to you alone   to you have I   sinned

Und übel oft   vor   dir getan.
and wrong often before you done

Du siehst die Schuld, die mir den Fluch verkündigt;
you see   the sin   that to me the curse proclaims

Sieh, Gott, auch meinen Jammer an.
look God   also my   misery at

    Before You alone have I
sinned; often have I done wrong
before You. You see my sin,
that proclaims to me how cursed
I am. Behold me, God, in my
misery.

Dir   ist mein Flehn,   mein Seufzen nicht
to you is   my   supplication my   sighing not
   verborgen,
   concealed

Und meine Tränen sind vor   dir.
and my   tears   are before you

From You my prayers and sighs are not hidden; my tears are there before You. O God, my God, how long must I endure my woes; how long will You withold Your being?

Ach Gott, mein Gott, wie lange soll ich sorgen?
oh God my   God   how long shall I   to be anxious

Wie lang entfernst du dich   von mir?
how long absent   you (yourself) from me

Herr, handle nicht mit mir nach   meinen Sünden,
Lord deal not with me according to my   sins

Vergilt mir nicht nach meiner Schuld.
repay me not   for my   guilt

God, do not deal with me according to my sin; do not punish me for my iniquity! I seek You, let me see Your countenance, O God of forbearance and mercy.

Ich suche dich; lass mich dein Antlitz   finden,
I   seek you   let me   your countenance to find

Du Gott der   Langmut   und Geduld.
You God of the forbearance and endurance.

Früh wollst du mich mit deiner Gnade füllen,
soon may   you me   with your grade to fill

Gott, Vater der   Barmherzigkeit.
God, Father of the mercy

Fill me soon with Your grace, Lord and father of mercy. Let me rejoice in You, for Your name's sake; You are the One who readily brings comfort.

Erfreue   mich   um deines Namens willen;
let rejoice (myself) for your Name's sake

Du bist ein Gott, der gern   erfreut.
you are one God   who readily comforts

Lass deinen Weg mich wieder freudig wallen,
let your   way me   again joyfully to travel

Und lehre mich dein heilig Recht,
and teach me   your divine right

Inspire me joyfully, to follow Your way, and teach me of Your holy righteousness daily to act according to Your will. You are my God, I am Your servant.

Mich täglich tun   nach   deinem Wohlgefallen;
me   daily   to do according to your wish

Du bist mein Gott, ich bin dein Knecht.
you are my   God   I   am your servant

Herr, eile   du, mein Schutz, mir beizustehen,
Lord make haste you my   refuge me to to help

Und leite mich auf ebner Bahn!
and lead me   on just path

O Lord, my refuge, make haste to help me, and lead me on to paths of righteousness! He hears my cry, the Lord accepts my supplication, and receives my soul.

Er hört mein Schrei'n, der Herr erhört mein Flehen
He hears my   cry   the Lord hears my   supplication

Und nimmt   sich   meiner Seelen an.
and takes care (Himself) of my   soul   -

BEETHOVEN

3. *MAILIED*
   MAY-SONG

3. SONG IN MAY

Johann Wolfgang van Goethe

Wie herrlich leuchtet how gloriously shines	How gloriously does nature shine! How the sun gleams, and the meadows laugh!
Mir die Natur! to me the Nature	
Wie glänzt die Sonne! how gleams the sun	
Wie lacht die Flur! how laughs the meadow	
Es dringen Blüten (it) crowd blossoms	Blossoms burst forth on every twig, a thousand voices from every tree,
Aus jedem Zweig from every twig	
Und tausend Stimmen and thousand voices	
Aus dem Gesträuch from the bushes	
Und Freud und Wonne and joy and bliss	And joy and ecstasy from every heart. O earth! O sun! O delight! O bliss!
Aus jeder Brust. from every breast	
O Erd, o Sonne! O earth O sun	
O Glück, o Lust! O happiness O delight	
O Lieb, o Liebe! O love O love	O love, so golden, and fair as morning clouds on mountain peaks!
So golden schön, so golden fair	
Wie Morgenwolken like morning-clouds	
Auf jenen Höhn! on those summits	
Du segnest herrlich you bless gloriously	Gloriously you bless the green fields - the whole world in its sea of flowers.
Das frische Feld, the fresh field	
Im Blütendampfe in the blossom-mist	
Die volle Welt. the whole world	
O Mädchen, Mädchen, O maiden maiden	O maiden, how I love you! How lovely are your eyes! And you love me!
Wie lieb ich dich! how love I you	

Wie blickt dein Auge!
how glances your eye

Wie liebst du mich!
how love you me

So liebt die Lerche
so loves the lark

As the lark loves singing
in the air, and a morning
flower the fragrance of the
heavens,

Gesang und Luft,
song and air

Und Morgenblumen
and morning-flowers

Den Himmelsduft,
the heaven's-fragrance

Wie ich dich liebe
how I you love

so passionately do
I love you - you, who give me
youth and joy and spirit

Mit warmem Blut,
with warm blood

Die du mir Jugend
that you to me youth

Und Freud und Mut
and joy and spirit

Zu neuen Liedern
to new songs

for new songs and dances!
Be for ever joyful in your
love for me!

Und Tänzen gibst:
and dances give

Sei ewig glücklich,
be for ever happy

Wie du mich liebst!
as you me love

4. *FLOHLIED DES MEPHISTO*
   FLEA-SONG OF THE MEPHISTOPHELES

4. SONG OF THE FLEA
   BY MEPHISTOPHELES

Johann Wolfgang van Goethe
(from *Faust* Part I)

Es war einmal ein König,
there was once a king

There was once a king,
who had a great flea, for
whom his love was far from
small; he loved him as his
only son. He called for his
tailor, and the tailor came:
'Measure the young nobleman
for jacket and trousers!'

Der hatt' einen grossen Floh,
who had a great flea

Den liebt er gar nicht wenig:
whom loved he at all not little

Als wie seinen eignen Sohn.
like as his own son.

Da rief er seinen Schneider,
then called he his tailor

Der Schneider kam heran:
the tailor came nigh

"Da, miss dem Junker   Kleider
there measure to the young nobleman garments

Und miss   ihm   Hosen   an!"
and measure to him trousers -

In Sammet und in Seide
in velvet and in silk

War er nun angetan,
was he now clad

Hatte Bänder auf dem Kleide,
had   ribbons on the attire

Hatt' auch ein Kreuz daran,
had   also a   cross on it

Und war sogleich Minister
and was at once minister

Und hatt' einen grossen Stern.
and had   a   great   star

Da   wurden seine Geschwister
then became his   brothers and sisters

Bei Hof auch grosse Herrn.
at   court also great gentlemen.

Now he was dressed in
velvet and silk, he had
ribbons on his clothes, and
a cross, and at once he was
made a minister and given a
Star of Honour. Then all his
brothers and sisters became
nobles at court as well.

Und Herrn   und Fraun am   Hofe,
and gentlemen and ladies at the court

Da   waren sehr geplagt,
then were very plagued

Die Königin und die Zofe
the queen   and the lady-in-waiting

Gestochen und genagt,
bit   and nibbled

Und durften   sie nicht knicken
and were allowed them not   to squash

Und weg sie jucken   nicht
and away them to scratch not

Wir knicken und ersticken
we   squash and smother

Doch gleich, wenn einer sticht!
but   at once when one   bites

The ladies and gentlemen
of the court were all greatly
distressed; the queen and her
lady-in-waiting, they were
nibbled and bitten, but were
not permitted to squash them
to get rid of the itch. But we
crush them at once when we are
bitten!

5. *WONNE DER WEHMUT*
   JOY   OF THE MELANCHOLY

5. JOY IN MELANCHOLY

Johann Wolfgang von Goethe

Trocknet nicht, trocknet nicht,
dry   not   dry   not

Tränen der   ewigen Liebe!
tears of the eternal love

Ach, nur dem   halbgetrockneten Auge
oh   only to the half-dried   eye

Wie öde,   wie tot die Welt ihm erscheint!
how desolate how dead the world to it seems

Never cease, never cease,
O tears of eternal love! Only
to eyes that never weep does
the world seem desolate and
dead!

6. *AN DIE FERNE   GELIEBTE*
   TO THE DISTANT BELOVED

6. TO THE DISTANT BELOVED

Alois Jeitelles

i.

i.

Auf dem Hügel sitz ich spähend
on the hill sit I   gazing

In   das blaue Nebelland,
into the blue mist-land

Nach   den fernen Triften sehend,
towards the distant pastures looking

Wo   ich dich, Geliebte, fand.
where I   you beloved   found

I sit on the hillside
gazing into a hazy blue land,
at the distant pastures where
I found you, my love.

Weit bin ich von dir geschieden,
far am I   from you separated

Trennend liegen Berg   und Tal
dividing lie   mountain and valley

Zwischen uns und unserm Frieden,
between us and our   tranquillity

Unserm Glück   und unsrer Qual.
our   happiness and our   pain.

So far am I from you –
mountain and valley lie between
us, dividing us and our
tranquillity, our happiness and
pain.

Ach, den Blick kannst du nicht sehen,
ah   the look can   you not   to see

Der   zu dir so glühend eilt,
which to you so glowing hastens

Und die Seufzer, sie verwehen
and the sighs   they scatter

In dem Raume, der   uns teilt.
In the space   which us divides

Ah, you cannot see the
burning eagerness with which I
gaze towards you, and my sighs
are scattered in the space
dividing us.

Will denn nichts mehr zu dir dringen,
will then nothing more to you to penetrate

Nichts der   Liebe Bote   sein?
nothing of the love messenger to be

Singen will ich, Lieder singen,
to sing will I   songs to sing

Die   dir   klagen meine Pein!
which to you lament my   pain

Can nothing further reach
you – can there be no messenger
of love? I will sing to you
songs that lament my anguish!

Denn vor   Liedesklang entweichet
for before song's-sound vanishes

Jeder Raum und jede Zeit,
each   space and each time

Und ein liebend Herz   erreichet
and a   loving heart reaches

Was ein liebend Herz geweiht!
what a   loving heart dedicated

Before their strains all
space and time can vanish, and
a devoted heart can reach the
one it truly loves!

ii.

ii.

Wo   die Berge   so blau
where the mountains so blue

Where the blue mountains
peer from a misty grey, where
the sun's rays fade, and clouds
float by - there should I like
to be!

Aus dem   nebligen Grau
out of the misty   grey

Schauen herein,
look   in here

Wo   die Sonne verglüht,
where the sun   ceases glowing

Wo   die Wolke umzieht,
where the cloud moves by

Möchte   ich sein!
should like I   to be

Dort im   ruhigen Tal
there in the quiet   valley

Where in the quiet valley
sorrow and pain are still, where
the silent primrose muses in the
rocks, and the breeze so gently
blows - there should I like to
be!

Schweigen Schmerzen und Qual.
are silent sorrows   and pain

Wo   im   Gestein
where in the rock

Still die Primel   dort sinnt,
still the primrose there reflects

Weht so leise der Wind,
blows so gently the wind

Möchte   ich sein!
should like I   to be

Hin   zum   sinnigen Wald
thither to the brooding wood

I am driven to the brooding
wood by the violence of my love
and inner torment. But nothing
would draw me from here, my
love, if you were ever at my
side!

Drängt mich Liebesgewalt,
urges me   love's-violence

Innere Pein.
inner pain

Ach, mich zög's   nicht von hier,
ah   me   draws it not   from here

Könnt ich, Traute, bei dir
could I   dear one with you

Ewiglich sein!
for ever to be

iii.

iii.

Leichte Segler in den Höhen,
light   sailers in the heights

O you light clouds sailing
on high, and you, little brook,
so narrow and small - if you
espy my sweetheart, bring her
a thousand greetings!

Und du, Bächlein   klein und schmal,
and you little brook small and narrow

Könnt mein Liebchen   ihr erspähen,
could my   sweetheart you to espy

Grüsst sie mir   viel tausendmal.
greet   her to me many thousand-times

Seht, ihr Wolken, sie dann gehen
see   you clouds   they then go

Sinnend in dem stillen Tal,
musing in the still   valley

Lasst mein Bild vor   ihr entstehen
let   my   image before her to arise

In dem luftgen Himmelssaal.
in the airy   heaven's-hall

                                   Then, o clouds, if you should
see her, walking pensive in the
quiet valley – let my image rise
before her in the lofty dome of
heaven!

Wird sie an den Büschen stehen,
will she by the bushes to stand

Die nun herbstlich falb   und kahl,
which now autumnally pale yellow and bare

Klagt ihr, wie mir ist geschehen,
lament to her how to me is happened

Klagt ihr, Vöglein,   meine Qual!
lament to her little birds my   anguish

                                   And if you should see her
amongst the trees, that now in
autumn are pale and bare – tell
her of my fate, little birds,
lament to her my anguish!

Stille Weste,   bringt im   Wehen
calm   west wind bring in the blowing

Hin   zu meiner Herzenswahl
thither to my   heart's-choice

Meine Seufzer, die   vergehen
my   sighs   which vanish

Wie der   Sonne letzter Strahl.
like of the sun   last   ray

                                   On your drifting breezes,
calm west wind, carry to my
heart's desire the sighs that
vanish like the sun's last ray.

Flüstr' ihr   zu mein Liebesflehen,
whisper to her to my   love's-beseeching

Lass sie, Bächlein   klein und schmal,
let her   little brook small and narrow

Treu in deinen Wogen sehen
truly in your   waves to see

Meine Tränen ohne   Zahl!
my   tears without number

                                   Little brook, so narrow and
small, whisper to her of my
beseeching love, and in your
ripples truly let her see my
countless tears!

       iv.

                                   iv.

Diese Wolken in den Höhen,
these clouds in the heights

Dieser Vöglein   muntrer Zug,
of the little birds merry   flock

Werden dich, o Huldin,   sehen
will   you   O gracious one to see

Nehmt mich mit   im   leichten Flug!
take me   with (you) in the light   flight

                                   These clouds on high, this
merry flock of birds – they will
see my gracious one! O take me
on your airy flight!

Diese Weste   werden spielen
these west winds will   to play

Scherzend dir   um   Wang und Brust,
jestingly to you about cheek and breast

In   den seidnen Locken wühlen –
into the silky   locks to burrow

Teilt ich mit euch diese Lust!
shared I   with you this joy

                                   These west winds will
lightly play about your
cheeks and breast, and stir
your silken locks. Could I
but share such joy!

Hin   zu dir von jenen Hügeln
thither to you from those hills

Emsig   dieses Bächlein   eilt.
busily this   little brook hastens

Wird ihr Bild sich   in dir spiegeln,
will her image itself in you to be reflected

Fliess zurück dann unverweilt!
flow   back   then without delay

The little brook busily
hastens to you from the hills.
If you should reflect her
image – then flow back without
delay!

     v.

     v.

Es kehret der   Maien, es blühet die Au,
it returns (the) May   it blooms the meadow

Die Lüfte, sie wehen so milde, so lau,
the breezes they blow so gently so mildly

Geschwätzig die Bäche   nun rinnen.
babbling   the brooks now flow

May is returning, the
meadows are in flower, the
breezes blow so gentle and
mild, and the babbling brooks
are flowing.

Die Schwalbe, die kehret zum   wirtlichen Dach,
the swallow   who returns to the hospitable roof

Sie baut   sich   so emsig   ihr bräutlich Gemach,
she builds herself so eagerly her bridal   chamber

Die Liebe soll wohnen da   drinnen.
the love   shall to live there within

The swallow returns to
the hospitable roof, and
eagerly builds her bridal
chamber, for love shall dwell
within.

Sie bringt sich   geschäftig von kreuz und von quer
she brings herself busily   from criss- and from -cross

Manch weicheres Stück zu dem Brautbett hieher
some   softer   piece to the bridal-bed hither

Manch wärmendes Stück für die Kleinen.
some   warming   piece for the little ones

From far and wide she
busily brings soft scraps for
her bridal bed, and to warm her
little ones.

Nun wohnen die Gatten beisammen so treu,
now live   the mates   together so faithfully

Was Winter geschieden, verband nun der Mai,
what winter divided   joined now the May

Was liebet, das weiss er zu einen.
what loves   that knows he to to unite

Now the pair dwells
faithfully together; what
winter divided, May has joined,
uniting all who love!

Es kehret der   Maien, es blühet die Au.
it returns (the) May   it blooms the meadow

Die Lüfte, sie wehen so milde, so lau.
the breezes they blow so gently so mildly

Nur ich kann nicht ziehen von hinnen.
only I   can not   to move from here

May is returning, the
meadows are in flower, breezes
blow so gentle and mild, but
I cannot stir from here.

Wenn alles,   was liebet, der Frühling vereint,
when everything that loves   the spring   unites

Nur unserer Liebe kein Frühling erscheint,
only to our   love no   spring   appears

Und Tränen sind all ihr Gewinnen.
and tears   are all her gain

While spring is joining
all who love, our love alone
knows no spring, and tears are
its only reward.

vi.

vi.

Nimm sie hin denn, diese Lieder,
take them - then these songs

Die ich dir, Geliebte, sang,
which I to you love   sang

Singe sie dann abends   wieder,
sing them then in the evening again

Zu der   Laute süssem Klang!
to of the Lute sweet sound

Now take these songs, my love, which I have sung to you — sing them again in the evening to the sweet sound of the lute.

Wenn das Dämmrungsrot dann ziehet
when the twilight-red then moves

Nach   dem stillen blauen See,
towards the still blue lake

Und sein letzter Strahl verglühet
and its last   ray   ceases glowing

Hinter jener Bergeshöh;
behind that mountain-top

And when the twilight glows on the still blue lake, and the last ray fades behind the mountain-tops;

Und du singst, was ich gesungen,
and you sing   what I   sung

Was mir   aus   der vollen Brust
what to me out of the full   breast

Ohne   Kunstgepräng erklungen,
without artifice   sounded

Nur der Sehnsucht sich   bewusst:
only the longing   itself is conscious of

and you sing what I have sung, that flowed from a full and simple heart, that knows only longing —

Dann vor   diesen Liedern weichet
then before these songs   yields

Was geschieden uns so weit,
what separated us so widely

Und ein liebend Herz   erreichet
and a   loving heart reaches

Was ein liebend Herz geweiht.
what a   loving heart dedicated

then will that which divides us yield before these songs. For a devoted heart can reach the one it truly loves!

7. DER KUSSE
   THE KISS

7. THE KISS

Christian Felix Weisse

Ich war bei Chloen ganz allein,
I   was with Chloe quite alone

Und küssen wollt' ich sie:
and to kiss wanted I   her

Jedoch sie sprach,
yet   she said

Sie würde schrein,
she would to scream

I was alone with Chloe, and wanted to kiss her. But she said it would be in vain, for she would scream.

Es sei vergebne Müh,
it be   vain   labour

Ich wagt' es doch und küsste sie,
I   dared it but   and kissed her

Trotz   ihrer Gegenwehr,
in spite of her   resistance

Und schrie   sie nicht?
and screamed she not

Jawohl,   sie schrie,
yes indeed she screamed

Doch lange hinterher.
but   long afterwards

But I dared to kiss her
in spite of her protesting.
And did she scream? Yes, indeed
she did – but a long time
afterwards!

8. DAS GEHEIMNIS
THE SECRET

8. THE SECRET

I.H.K. von Wessenberg

Wo   blüht das Blümchen,   das nie   verblüht?
where blooms the (little) flower that never fades

Wo   strahlt das Sternlein,   das ewig   glüht?
where shines the (little) star that for ever glows

Dein Mund, o Muse! dein heil'ger Mund
your mouth O Muse your hallowed mouth

Tu   mir   das Blümchen   und Sternlein kund.
make to me the little flower and little star known

Where blooms the little
flower that never fades? Where
shines the little star that
gleams for ever? Your lips,
O Muse, your hallowed lips tell
me of this little flower and
star.

"Verkünden kann es dir   nicht mein Mund,
make known can it to you not   my   mouth

Macht es dein Innerstes   dir   nicht kund.
makes it your innermost soul to you not   known

Im   Innersten   glühet und blühet es zart,
in the innermost soul glows and blooms it tenderly

Wohl jedem, der es getreu bewahrt!"
happy to each who it true   keeps

'My lips can tell you nothing
that you know not in your heart.
A star gleams, a flower blooms in
every heart – happy is he who
faithfully tends it.'

9. ICH LIEBE DICH.
I   LOVE YOU

9. I LOVE YOU

K.F. Herrosee

Ich liebe dich, so   wie du mich,
I   love you   thus as you me

Am   Abend   und am   Morgen,
in the evening and in the morning

I love you, as you love
me, in the morning and at
night; no day passed when
you and I did not share our
troubles.

Noch war kein Tag, wo   du und ich
yet was no   day where you and I

Nicht teilten unsre Sorgen.
not   shared our   troubles

Auch waren sie für dich und mich
also were they for you and me

Geteilt leicht zu ertragen;
shared easy   to to bear

Du tröstetest im   Kummer mich,
you comforted in the sorrow me

Ich weint in deine Klagen.
I   wept in your   lamenting

Shared, they were easy
to bear for us both; you
comforted me in my sorrow,
I wept in your distress.

Drum   Gottes Segen   über dir,
therefore God's blessing on you

Du meines Lebens Freude,
you my   life's joy

Gott schütze dich, erhalt dich mir,
God protect you   keep you to me

Schütz und erhalt uns beide!
protect and keep us both

God's blessing on you,
joy of my life! God protect
and keep you for me – God
protect and keep us both!

Franz Schubert
(1797-1828)

1. *GRETCHEN AM   SPINNRADE*
   GRETCHEN AT THE SPINNING-WHEEL

1. GRETCHEN AT THE SPINNING-WHEEL

Johann Wolfgang von Goethe
(also set by Spohr)

Meine Ruh   ist hin,
my   peace is gone

Mein Herz ist schwer;
my   heart is heavy

Ich finde sie nimmer
I   find her never

Und nimmermehr.
and never more

My heart is heavy, my peace
is gone; never, never again shall
I find it.

Wo   ich ihn nicht hab
where I   him not   have

Ist mir   das Grab,
is to me the grave

Die ganze Welt
the whole world

Ist mir   vergällt.
is to me embittered

Where he is not with me, to
me is a grave; the whole world
seems bitter as gall.

Mein armer Kopf
my   poor head

Ist mir   verrückt,
is to me mad

Mein armer Sinn
my   poor mind

Ist mir zerstückt.
is to me cut into pieces

My poor head is in a frenzy,
my poor mind shattered.

Nach ihm nur schau ich
for him only look I

Zum   Fenster hinaus,
to the window out

Nach ihm nur geh ich
for him only go I

Aus   dem Haus.
out of the house

I seek only him as I peer from
the window; to seek only him do I
leave the house.

Sein hoher Gang,
his proud carriage

Sein' edle Gestalt,
his   noble figure

Seines Mundes Lächeln,
of his mouth smile

Seiner Augen Gewalt,
of his eyes power

Und seiner Rede
and of his speech

Zauberfluss,
magic-flow

Sein Händedruck,
his hands-shake

Und ach, sein Kuss!
and ah   his kiss

Mein Busen drängt
my   bosom presses

Sich   nach   ihm hin.
(himself) towards him (towards)

Ach dürft ich fassen
oh might I   to clasp

Und halten ihn!
and to hold him

Und küssen ihn,
and to kiss him

So wie ich wollt,
so as I   wanted

An seinen Küssen
on his   kisses

Vergehen sollt!
to perish should

His proud bearing, his noble
figure, his smiling lips,
compelling eyes,

the magic flow of his speech,
the touch of his hand, and ah,
his kiss!

My heart yearns for him. Oh,
if I could but embrace and hold
him,

and kiss him as I would - from
his kisses would I perish!

2. *SCHÄFERS   KLAGELIED*
   SHEPHERD'S LAMENTATION

   Johann Wolfgang von Goethe

Da   droben auf jenem Berge
there on high on that hill

Da   steh ich tausendmal,
there stand I   thousand times

An meinem Stabe hingebogen
on my   staff bent over

Und schaue hinab in   das Tal.
and look   down into the valley

2. SHEPHERD'S LAMENT

High on the hill there I have
stood a thousand times, leaning
on my staff, and looking down into
the valley.

Dann folg   ich der weidenden Herde,
then follow I   the grazing   flock

Mein Hündchen   bewahrtet mir   sie;
my   (little) dog protects   to me her

Ich bin herunter gekommen,
I   am down   come

Und weiss doch selber nicht wie.
and know yet myself not   how

I have followed the grazing
flock, my dog keeping watch for me,
and come down here below – but even
I cannot say how.

Da   stehet von schönen Blumen
there is   of lovely flowers

Die ganze Wiese so voll;
the whole meadow so full

Ich breche sie, ohne   zu wissen,
I   gather them without to to know

Wem   ich sie geben soll.
to whom I   them to give shall

The whole meadow is full of
lovely flowers. I gather them,
without knowing to whom I shall
give them.

Und Regen, Sturm und Gewitter
and rain   storm and thunderstorm

Verpass ich unter dem Baum.
miss   I   under the tree

Die Türe dort bleibet verschlossen;
the door there remains closed

Doch alles ist leider ein Traum.
but all   is alas   a   dream

I shelter beneath the trees
from the rain and thundery
storms. Her door over there
remains closed – alas, it is
all a dream.

Es   stehet ein Regenbogen
(it) stands a   rainbow

Wohl   über jenem Haus!
indeed over that house

Sie aber ist fortgezogen
she but is moved away

Und weit in   das Land hinaus,
and far into the land away

There is a rainbow over her
house, but she has gone away, far
away across the land.

Hinaus in   das Land und weiter,
away   into the land and further

Vielleicht gar über die See.
perhaps   even over the sea

Vorüber, ihr Schafe, nur vorüber!
ended   you sheep   only ended

Dem   Schäfer ist gar so weh.
to the shepherd is very so sad

Across the land, and further,
perhaps across the sea. It is
ended, my sheep, all ended! And
your shepherd's heart is full of
grief.

3. *NÄHE   DES   GELIEBTEN*
   NEARNESS OF THE BELOVED

3. THE BELOVED IS NEAR

Johann Wolfgang von Goethe

Ich denke dein, wenn mir   der   Sonne Schimmer
I   think of you when to me of the sun   shimmer

I think of you, when the shimmer of the sun gleams on the sea; I think of you, when the glimmer of the moon is reflected in spring water.

Vom   Meere strahlt,
from the sea   shines

Ich denke dein, wenn sich   des   Mondes Flimmer
I   think of you when (itself) of the moon   glimmer

In Quellen malt.
in springs reflects

Ich sehe dich, wenn auf dem fernen   Wege
I   see   you   when on the distant paths

I see you, when the dust rises on distant paths; in deepest night, when the traveller crosses the narrow bridge.

Der Staub sich   hebt;
the dust (itself) rises

In tiefer Nacht, wenn auf dem schmalen Stege
In deep   night   when on the narrow   bridge

Der Wandrer bebt.
the wanderer trembles

Ich höre dich, wenn dort mit   dumpfen Rauschen
I   hear you   when there with dull   rushing

I hear you, when waters surge with a dull roar; in the quiet wood I go to listen, when all is still.

Die Welle steigt,
the wave rises

Im   stillen Haine geh ich oft   zu lauschen,
in the quiet   wood go I   often to to listen

Wenn alles schweigt.
when all   is silent

Ich bin bei dir; du seist auch noch   so ferne,
I   am with you, you be   even still so far away

I am with you; however far away you are, to me you are near! The sun is sinking, soon the stars will light my way. O that you were here!

Du bist mir   nah!
you are to me near

Die Sonne sinkt,   bald leuchten mir   die Sterne.
the sun is sinking soon shine   to me the stars

O wärst du da!
O were   you there

4. *DES   MÄDCHENS KLAGE*   4. THE MAIDEN'S LAMENT
     OF THE MAIDEN   LAMENT

Friedrich Schiller

Der Eichwald braust, die Wolken ziehn,   The oak trees bluster in the
the oak-wood blusters the clouds move   wood, the clouds are racing. The
                                                   young maiden sits on the green
Das Mägdlein sitzt an Ufers Grün,   bank, where waves break with all
the maiden   sits on bank's green   their might. She sighs into the
                                                   darkness, her eyes clouded with
Es   bricht sich   die Welle mit Macht, mit   weeping.
(it) breaks (itself) the wave with might with
  Macht,
   might

Und sie seufzt hinaus in   die finstre Nacht,
and she sighs out   into the dark   night

Das Auge vom   Weinen getrübet.
the eye from the weeping clouded

"Das Herz ist gestorben, die Welt ist leer,   'My heart is dead, the world
the heart is died   the world is empty   is empty; no longer can it fulfil
                                                   my desire. O holy saint, call
Und weiter gibt sie dem   Wunsche nichts mehr.   your child home! I have tasted
and further gives she to the desire nothing more earthly joys - I have lived and
                                                   loved!'
Du Heilige, rufe dein Kind zurück,
you holy one call your child back

Ich habe genossen das irdische Glück,
I   have enjoyed the earthly happiness

Ich habe gelebt und geliebet!"
I   have lived and loved

Es   rinnet der   Tränen vergeblicher Lauf,   Her tears run their fruitless
(it) runs   of the tears fruitless   course   course, but laments cannot waken
                                                   the dead. 'Tell me, what comforts
Die Klage, sie wecket die Toten nicht auf;   and heals the heart when the
the lament she wakes the dead not   up   delights of sweet love have
                                                   vanished - I, your saint, will
Doch nenne,   was tröstet und heilet die Brust   not deny it you.'
but name (it) what comforts and heals the breast

Nach der   süssen Liebe verschwundener Lust,
after of the sweet love vanished   delight

Ich, die Himmlische, will's nicht versagen.
I   the heavenly one will it not to deny

"Lass rinnen der   Tränen vergeblichen Lauf,   'Let my tears run their
 let run   of the tears fruitless   course   fruitless course - laments cannot
                                                   waken the dead. But when the
Es wecke die Klage den Toten nicht auf,   delights of sweet love have
it wakes the lament the dead not   up   vanished, the sweetest joy of
                                                   a mourning heart is love's grief
Das süsseste Glück   für die trauernde Brust   and lamenting.'
the sweetest happiness for the mourning breast

Nach der   schönen Liebe verschwundener Lust,
after of the beautiful love vanished   delight

Sind der   Liebe Schmerzen und Klagen."
are of the love griefs   and laments

5. *AN DEN MOND*
   TO THE MOON

5. TO THE MOON

Ludwig Hölty

Geuss, lieber Mond, geuss deine Silberflimmer
shed   dear   moon shed your silver-glimmer

Durch   dieses Buschengrün,
through this   bushes-green

Wo   Phantasien und Traumgestalten immer
where fantasies and dream-shapes   always

Vor   mir vorüber flieh'n!
before me past   flee

Enthülle dich,   dass ich die Stätte finde,
unveil yourself that I   the place find

Wo   oft   mein Mädchen sass,
where often my   girl   sat

Und oft   im   Weh'n   des   Buchbaums
and often in the fluttering of the beech-tree
   und der   Linde
   and of the linden-tree

Der   gold'nen Stadt vergass!
of the golden   town forgot

Enthülle dich,   dass ich des   Strauchs mich
unveil yourself that I   of the bush   (myself)
   freue,
   delight

Der Kühlung ihr   gerauscht,
that cooling to her rustled

Und einen Kranz   auf jeden Anger streue,
and a   garland on every green strew

Wo   sie den Bach belauscht!
where she the brook listened to

Dann, lieber Mond, dann nimm den Schleier wieder,
then dear   moon then take the veil   again

Und traur' um deinen Freund,
and mourn for your   friend

Und weine durch   den Wolkenflor hernieder,
and weep through the cloud-veil down

Wie dein Verlassner   weint!
as your forsaken-one weeps

Dear moon, shed your silvery gleam through the green trees, where phantoms and dream-like shapes pass before my eyes! Draw back your veil, that I may find the place where my love so often sat, forgetting the golden town in the fluttering of the beeches and the linden tree. Draw back your veil, that I may delight in the trees that coolly fanned her, and strew flowers on every village green where she listened to the brook. Then, dear moon, draw your veil again, and mourn for your beloved, weeping through this misty veil of clouds, as the one you have forsaken weeps.

6. WANDERERS   NACHTLIED
   WANDERER'S NIGHT-SONG

.6. WANDERER'S NIGHT SONG

Johann Wolfgang von Goethe
(also set by Liszt and Wolf)

Der du   von dem Himmel bist,
who you of the heaven are

Alles Leid und Schmerzen stillst,
all   pain and griefs   assuage

Den, der doppelt elend   ist,
him who twofold wretched is

Doppelt mit Entzücken füllst,
twofold with delight   fill

Ach, ich bin des   Treibens müde!
ah   I   am of the bustle   weary

Was soll all der Schmerz und Lust?
what means all the grief   and joy

Süsser Friede,
sweet peace

Komm', ach komm in meine Brust!
come   ah come into my   breast

You, who are in Heaven,
assuage all pain and grief. He
who suffers twofold, you fill
twofold with joy. Ah, how weary
I am of life's strivings! To what
end, all this joy and sorrow?
Come, sweet peace, O come into
my heart!

7. DER FISCHER
   THE FISHERMAN

7. THE FISHERMAN

Johann Wolfgang von Goethe
(also set by Richard Strauss)

Das Wasser rauscht', das Wasser schwoll,
the water rushed   the water rose

Ein Fischer   sass daran,
a   fisherman sat thereby

Sah   nach der Angel ruhevoll,
looked at   the angle quietly

Kühl bis   ans   Herz hinan.
cool (unto) to the heart (up to)

Und wie er sitzt, und wie er lauscht,
and as he sits and as he listens

Teilt sich   die Flut   empor;
divides (herself) the torrent upwards

Aus   dem bewegten Wasser rauscht
out of the moved   water rushes

Ein feuchtes Weib hervor.
a   moist   woman forth

The water rushed, the water
rose, a fisherman sat quietly
watching his rod, his very heart
cool. And as he sat and listened,
the waters parted, and out of the
swirling stream rose a woman's
form.

Sie sang zu ihm, sie sprach zu ihm,
she sang to him, she spoke to him

"Was lockst du meine Brut
 why entice you my   brood

Mit Menschenwitz und Menschenlist
with human-wit   and human-cunning

Hinauf in   Todesglut?
upwards into death's-fire

Ach wüsstest du, wie's Fischlein   ist
ah knew   you how the little fish is

So wohlig auf dem Grund,
so content on the bottom

Du stiegst   herunter, wie du bist,
you would climb down   as you are

Und würdest erst   gesund.
and would be for the first time well

Labt   sich   die liebe Sonne nicht,
refreshes herself the dear sun   not

Der Mond sich   nicht im   Meer?
the moon himself not   in the ocean

Kehrt   wellenatmend   ihr Gesicht
returns waves-breathing her face

Nicht doppelt schöner   her?
not   twice   more fair back

Lockt dich der tiefe Himmel nicht,
tempts you the deep sky   not

Das feuchtverklärte Blau?
the moist-radiant   blue

Lockt dich dein eigen Angesicht
tempts you your own   face

Nicht her in ew'gen Tau?"
not   here in eternal dew

Das Wasser rauscht', das Wasser schwoll,
the water rushed   the water rose

Netzt' ihm   den nackten Fuss;
moistened to him the naked   foot

Sein Herz wuchs ihm   so sehnsuchtsvoll,
his heart grew to him so full of longing

Wie bei der   Liebsten Gruss.
as at of the beloved   greeting

Sie sprach zu ihm, sie sang zu ihm;
she spoke to him she sang to him

Da war's um ihn gescheh'n:
then was it to him happened

Halb zog sie ihn, halb sank er hin,
half drew she him half sank he there

Und ward nicht mehr gesehen.
and was not   more seen

She sang to him, she spoke to
him, 'Why do you entice my brood
with human wit and cunning, up to
their parching death? If you but
knew how content are the little
fishes below, you yourself would
come down as you are – only then
would you be fulfilled.

Is not the moon refreshed in
the ocean? And the sun – is her
face washed by the waves not
twice as fair? Does the sky with
its deep radiant blue not tempt
you? Does your own face not tempt
you into the eternal waters?'

The water rushed, the water
rose, his feet were lapped by the
waves; his heart was filled with
longing, as from the loved one's
kiss. She spoke to him, she sang
to him, and he was lost for
ever – half dragged by her, half
sinking down, he was never seen
again.

8. *ERSTER VERLUST*
   FIRST LOSS   8. FIRST LOSS

Johann Wolfgang von Goethe
(also set by Mendelssohn)

Ach! wer bringt die schönen Tage,   Oh, who can bring back those
ah   who brings the fine   days   fair days, those days of my
                                                   first love! Oh, who can bring
Jene Tage der   ersten Liebe,   back just one hour of that
those days of the first   love   precious time! Alone I nurse my
                                                   wounds, and with ever-repeated
Ach! wer bringt nur eine Stunde   lament, I mourn my lost
ah   who brings only one   hour   happiness.

Jener   holden Zeit zurück!
of that lovely time back

Einsam   nähr' ich meine Wunde,
solitary nurse I   my   wound

Und mit stets   erneuter Klage
and with constantly renewed lament

Traur' ich um's   verlor'ne Glück
mourn I   for the lost   happiness

Ach, wer bringt die schönen Tage,   Oh, who can bring back those
ah   who brings the fair   days   fair days, who can bring back that
                                                   precious time!
Wer jene holde Zeit zurück!
who that lovely time back

9. *LIEBE SCHWÄRMT AUF ALLEN WEGEN*   9. LOVE ABOUNDS ON EVERY PATH
   LOVE SWARMS   ON   ALL   PATHS

Johann Wolfgang von Goethe
(from *Claudine von Villa Bella*)

Liebe schwärmt auf allen Wegen,   Love abounds on every path,
love swarms   on all   paths   fidelity lives for itself alone;
                                                   love comes swiftly to meet you,
Treue   wohnt für sich   allein;   but you must seek after fidelity.
fidelity lives for itself alone

Liebe kommt euch rasch   entgegen,
love comes you swiftly towards

Aufgesucht will Treue   sein.
sought out wants fidelity to be

10. *HIN   UND WIEDER   FLIEGEN PFEILE*   10. ARROWS FLY HITHER AND THITHER
      THERE AND BACK AGAIN FLY   ARROWS

Johann Wolfgang von Goethe
(from *Claudine von Villa Bella*)

Hin   und wieder   fliegen Pfeile,   Arrows fly hither and
there and back again fly   arrows   thither; light arrows fly from
                                                    Cupid's slender golden bow. Have
Amors   leichte Pfeile fliegen   you young maidens not yet been
Cupid's light   arrows fly   struck? It is fate, only fate!

Von dem schlanken goldnen Bogen,
from the slender   golden bow

Mädchen seid ihr nicht getroffen?
maidens are you not   struck

Es ist Glück, es ist nur Glück.
it is fate   it is only fate

Warum fliegt er so in Eile?   Why does he fly in such
why   flies he so in haste   haste? He seeks to vanquish that
                                                    maid there. Already he has flown
Jene   dort will er besiegen;   past; her heart is carelessly
that one there wants he to vanquish   unguarded. Take care, for he is
                                                    coming back!
Schon   ist er vorbei geflogen,
already is he past   flown

Sorglos   bleibt der Busen offen.
carelessly remains the bosom open

Gebet Acht! er kommt   zurück!
give   heed he is coming back

11. *HEIDENRÖSLEIN*   11. WILD ROSE
      LITTLE BRIAR-ROSE

Johann Wolfgang von Goethe
(also set by Brahms)

Sah ein Knab ein Röslein   stehn,   A boy saw a wild rose
saw a boy a (little) rose to stand   growing on the heath, as fresh
                                                    and lovely as the day. Quickly
Röslein   auf der Heiden,   he ran up to see it, looked at
(little) rose on the heath   it with great delight. Little
                                                    rose, little rose, little red
War so jung und morgenschön,   rose, little rose upon the
was so young and morning-fair   heath.

Lief er schnell, es nah zu sehn,
ran he quickly it near to to see

Sah's mit vielen Freuden.
saw it with much   delight

Röslein,   Röslein,   Röslein   rot,
little rose little rose little rose red

Röslein   auf der Heiden.
little rose on the heath

Knabe sprach: ich breche dich,
boy   said   I   gather you

Röslein   auf der Heiden!
little rose on   the heath

Röslein   sprach: ich steche dich,
little rose said   I   prick you

Dass du   ewig   denkst an mich,
that you for ever think of me

Und ich will's nicht leiden!
and I   will it not   to suffer

Röslein, Röslein etc.

Und der wilde Knabe brach
and the unruly boy   plucked

s'Röslein   auf der Heiden;
the little rose on   the heath

Röslein   wehrte   sich   und stach,
little rose defended itself and pricked

Half   ihm doch kein Weh und Ach,
helped him but no   woe and alas

Musst' es eben leiden.
had to it just to suffer

Röslein, Röslein etc.

The boy said, I'll pluck
you, little rose upon the heath!
The rose said, I'll prick you,
so you'll never forget me – for
I'll not suffer it!

But the wilful boy plucked
the little rose upon the heath.
The rose defended herself and
pricked him, but her moans and
cries were in vain – and she just
had to suffer it.

12. AN DEN MOND
    TO THE MOON

12. TO THE MOON

Johann Wolfgang von Goethe

Füllest wieder Busch und Tal
fill   again bush and valley

Still   mit Nebelglanz,
silently with mist-splendour

Lösest endlich auch einmal
set free at last also once

Meine Seele ganz;
my   soul wholly

Breitest über mein Gefild
spread   over my   countryside

Lindernd deinen Blick,
soothing your   glance

Wie des   Freundes Auge mild
as of the friend   eye   kindly

Über mein Geschick.
over my   destiny

Silently you fill once more
each wood and valley with your
misty splendour; at last my soul
is set free.

Your gentle gaze reaches
out over the countryside, like
the kindly eye of a friend over
my destiny.

Jeden Nachklang fühlt mein Herz
each echo   feels my   heart

Froh' und trüber   Zeit,
glad and of melancholy time

Wandle zwischen Freud' und Schmerz
wander between joy   and sorrow

In der Einsamkeit.
in the solitude

My heart feels every echo of glad and melancholy times. Between joy and sorrow, I wander in solitude.

Fliesse, fliesse, lieber Fluss!
flow   flow   dear   river

Nimmer werd ich froh,
never am I glad

So verrauschte Scherz und Kuss,
so pass away   jest   and kiss

Und die Treue   so.
and the fidelity so.

Flow on, flow on, dear river. Never can I be glad; thus did love and laughter pass away, and thus fidelity.

Selig,   wer sich   vor   der Welt
blissful who himself before the world

Ohne   Hass verschliesst,
without hate turns in on

Einen Freund am   Busen hält
a   friend to the bosom holds

Und mit dem geniesst,
and with him enjoys

Happy is he who can turn from the world without bitterness, and with a friend close at his side, can share the secrets,

Was, von Menschen nicht gewusst
what of men   not   known

Oder nicht bedacht,
or   not   considered

Durch   das Labyrinth der   Brust
through the labyrinth of the breast

Wandelt in der Nacht.
wanders in the night

which unknown and unheeded by men, wander at night through the labyrinth of the heart.

13. LIEBHABER IN ALLEN GESTALTEN
      LOVER   IN ALL   FORMS

Johann Wolfgang von Goethe

13. LOVER IN MANY FORMS

Ich wollt'   ich wär' ein Fisch,
I would wish I were a fish

So hurtig und frisch,
so nimble and cool

Und kämst du zu angeln,
and came you to angle

Ich würde nicht mangeln.
I would not to be wanting

I wish I were a fish, so nimble and cool; if you came to catch me, I'd be there. I wish I were a fish, so nimble and cool!

Ich wollt'   ich wär' ein Fisch,
I would wish I were a   fish

So hurtig und frisch.
so nimble and cool

Ich wollt'   ich wäre Gold,
I would wish I were gold

Dir   immer   im   Sold;
to you always in the pay

Und tät'st du was   kaufen
and did   you something to buy

Käm'   ich gelaufen,
would come I run

Ich wollt'   ich wäre Gold
I would wish I were gold

Dir   immer   im   Sold.
to you always in the pay

I wish I were a gold piece,
always in your employ; if you
wanted to buy something, I'd go
running off to get it! I wish I
were a gold piece, always in your
employ!

Doch bin ich, wie ich bin,
but am I,   as I   am

Und nimm   mich nur hin,
and put up with me   only –

Willst bess're   besitzen,
want   better one to possess

So lass dir   sie schnitzen.
so let to you her to cut

Ich bin nun wie ich bin;
I am now as I   am

So nimm   mich nur hin!
so put up with me   only –

But I am as I am, and you'll
have to take me thus; if you
want someone better, let her be
made to measure! I am as I am,
and you'll have to take me thus!

14. *DAS ROSENBAND*
    THE ROSES-RIBBON

14. THE GARLAND OF ROSES

Friedrich Gottlieb Klopstock
(also set by Richard Strauss)

Im   Frühlingsschatten fand ich sie;
in the spring's-shadow found I her

Da   band ich sie mit Rosenbändern:
then bound I her with rose-ribbons

Sie fühlt' es nicht und schlummerte.
she felt it not and slumbered

I found her one spring in
the shadows, and bound her with
chains of roses. But she felt
nothing, and slumbered on.

Ich sah   sie an; mein Leben hing
I looked her at my   life hung

Mit diesem Blick an ihrem Leben;
with that glance on her   life

Ich fühlt' es wohl und wusst es nicht.
I felt   it indeed and knew it not

I looked at her, and in that
glance, my life was caught in
hers. This I felt, but did not
know.

Doch lispelt' ich ihr   sprachlos zu
yet murmured I   to her speechless (to)

Und rauschte mit   den Rosenbändern:
and rustled with the rose-ribbons

Da   wachte sie vom   Schlummer auf.
then woke she from the slumber   up

Sie sah   mich an; ihr Leben hing
she looked me   at her life hung

Mit   diesem Blick an meinem Leben,
with that   glance on my   life

Und um   uns ward Elysium.
and about us was Elysium

Yet I murmured to her softly,
wordlessly, and the chains of
roses rustled. She awoke from
her sleep,

and looked at me. In that glance,
her life was caught in mine, and
all around us was Elysium.

15. *DEM   UNENDLICHEN*   15. TO THE INFINITE
    TO THE INFINITE

Friedrich Gottlieb Klopstock

Wie erhebt sich   das Herz, wenn es dich,
how raises (itself) the heart when it you

Unendlicher, denkt! Wie sinkt es,
Infinite One thinks how sinks it

Wenn es auf sich   herunterschaut!
when it at itself looks down

Elend   schaut's wehklagend dann und Nacht und Tod!
wretched looks it lamenting then and night and death

My heart is uplifted when I
think of you, the Infinite! When
it sees itself, how it is cast
down! Wretched and lamenting, it
sees but night and death.

Allein du rufst mich aus meiner Nacht, der im
alone you call me   from my   night who in the
  Elend, der im   Tode hilft!
  misery who in the death helps

Dann denk' ich es ganz, dass du ewig   mich schufst,
then think I   it wholly that you for ever me   created

Herrlicher! den   kein Preis, unten am   Grab,
Glorious One whom no   praise below in the grave
  oben   am   Thron,
  above at the throne

Herr Gott! den dankend entflammt, kein Jubel
Lord God who thanking kindled   no   jubilation
  genug besingt!
  enough praises

You alone recall me from my
darkness; You who help in times
of trouble and in death! Then I
know with my whole being, that
You created me, that I might
live for ever. O God of glory,
whether I praise You from my
grave, or at Your throne in
Heaven, no praise can be great
enough. O Lord, You kindle in
me eternal thanksgiving.

Weht, Bäume des   Lebens, in's   Harfengetön!
blow trees of the life   into the harps'-tones

Rausche mit ihnen in's   Harfengetön, kristallner
murmur with them into the harps'-tones crystal
  Strom!
  stream

Ihr lispelt und rauscht, und, Harfen, ihr tönt
you lisp   and murmur and harps, you sound

Nie es ganz! Gott ist es, den ihr preist!
never it wholly God is it whom you praise

O tree of life, blow into the
strings of the harp; let your
murmuring unite with theirs, O
crystal stream! You may whisper
and murmur, harps, but your music
will never suffice for it is God
Himself whom you praise!

Welten, donnert, im   feierlichen Gang, in
worlds thunder in the solemn   course in

der   Posaunen Chor!
of the trumpets chorus

Ring out your trumpets, all
you peoples of the earth! All you
suns in your radiant course,
join the chorus of trumpets!

Tönt,   all' ihr Sonnen auf der Strasse voll Glanz,
resound all you suns   on the way   full splendour

In der   Posaunen Chor!
in of the trumpets chorus

Ihr Welten, ihr donnert,
you worlds you thunder

Du, der Posaunen Chor   hallest
you the trumpets chorus resound

But you peoples of the world
with your trumpet chorus will
never suffice. It is God Himself
whom you praise!

Nie es ganz: - nie es ganz: Gott,
never it wholly never it wholly God

Gott, Gott ist es, den ihr preist!
God   God is it   whom you praise

16. *MIGNONS GESANG*
    MIGNON'S SONG

16. MIGNON'S SONG

Johann Wolfgang von Goethe
(from *Wilhelm Meister*)
(also set by Beethoven, Schumann,
Liszt and Wolf)

Kennst du das Land, wo   die Zitronen blühn,
know   you the land where the lemons   blossom

Im   dunklen Laub   die Gold-Orangen glühn,
in the dark   foliage the gold-oranges glow

Ein sanfter Wind vom   blauen Himmel weht,
a gentle wind from the blue   sky   blows

Die Myrte still und hoch der Lorbeer steht,
the myrtle silent and high the laurel stands

Kennst du es wohl?
know   you it (perhaps)

Dahin! Dahin!
thither thither

Möcht'   ich mit dir, o mein Geliebter, ziehn.
should like I with you O my love   to go

Do you know the land where
the lemon-trees blossom, and
golden oranges glow in dark
foliage; where a gentle breeze
blows from a blue sky, and the
silent myrtle and high laurels
grow? Do you know it? There,
·there should I like to go with
you, my love!

Kennst du das Haus? Auf Säulen ruht sein Dach,
know   you the house on pillars rests its roof

Es   glänzt der Saal, es   schimmert das Gemach,
(it) gleams the hall (it) shimmers the room

Und Marmorbilder   stehn und sehn mich an:
and marble-statues stand and look me   at

Was hat man dir,   du armes Kind, getan?
what has one to you you poor child done

Kennst du es wohl?
know   you it (perhaps)

Do you know a house - its
roof rests on pillars; there's
a gleaming hall, and shimmering
rooms, and marble statues look
at me and say, 'What have they
done to you, poor child?' Do
you know it? There, there
should I like to go with you,
O my protector!

Dahin! Dahin!
thither thither

Möcht'   ich mit dir, o mein Beschützer, ziehn.
should like I   with you O my   protector   to go

Kennst du den Berg   und seinen Wolkensteg?
know   you the mountain and his   cloud-path

Das Maultier sucht im   Nebel seinen Weg;
the mule   seeks in the mist its   way

In Höhlen wohnt der   Drachen alte   Brut;
in caves lives of the dragons ancient brood

Es   stürzt der Fels und über ihn die Flut.
(it) plunges the rock and over it the torrent

Kennst du es wohl?
know   you it (perhaps)

Dahin! Dahin!
thither thither

Geht unser Weg! o Vater, lass uns ziehn!
goes our   way O father let us to go

Do you know a mountain with
a path veiled in clouds? The
mule seeks its way in the mist,
an ancient brood of dragons
dwells in the caves, and the
torrent sweeps over a plunging
rock. Do you know it? There,
there lies our way! O father,
let us go!

17. RASTLOSE LIEBE
   RESTLESS LOVE

17. RESTLESS LOVE

Johann Wolfgang von Goethe

Dem Schnee, dem Regen,
the snow   the rain

Dem Wind entgegen,
the wind against

Im   Dampf der   Klüfte,
in the steam of the ravines

Durch   Nebeldüfte
through mist-vapours

Immer zu! Immer zu!
ever on ever on

Ohne   Rast und Ruh!
without rest and peace

In the face of the snow, the
rain and the wind, through damp,
dim ravines and drifting mists -
keep on! Keep on, without rest or
peace!

Lieber durch   Leiden
rather through suffering

Wollt ich mich   schlagen,
wished I   (myself) to make (my) way

Als   so viel Freuden
than so much joy

Des   Lebens ertragen.
of the life   to endure

I had rather make my way
through suffering, than endure
so much of life's joy.

Alle das Neigen
all the inclining

Von Herzen zu Herzen,
of heart to heart

In the drawing together of
heart to heart, oh, how strange
are the workings of grief!

Ach, wie so eigen
ah   how so strangely

Schaffet das Schmerzen!
works   the grief

Wie, soll ich fliehn?
how shall I   to flee

Wälderwärts ziehn?
forestwards to go

Alles, alles vergebens!
all   all   in vain

Krone des   Lebens,
crown of the life

Glück   ohne   Ruh,
happiness without peace

Liebe bist du!
love are you

Shall I then flee into the
woods? In vain, in vain! Crown
of life, joy without peace –
you are Love!

18. ERLKÖNIG
    ERL-KING

18. THE ERL-KING

Johann Wolfgang von Goethe

Wer reitet so spät durch   Nacht und Wind?
who rides so late through night and wind

Es ist der Vater   mit   seinem Kind;
it is the father with his   child

Er hat den Knaben wohl   in dem Arm,
he has the boy   indeed in the arm

Er fasst ihn sicher, er hält   ihn warm.
he holds him safe   he holds him warm

Who rides so late through
the wind and the night? It is a
father with his child; he clasps
the boy in his arms, holds him
safe, keeps him warm.

"Mein Sohn, was birgst du so bang   dein Gesicht?"
my   son   why hide   you so fearfully your face

"Siehst, Vater, du den Erlkönig nicht?
see   father you the Erl-King not

Der Erlenkönig mit Kron und Schweif?"
the Erl-King   with crown and train

"Mein Sohn, es ist ein Nebelstreif."
my   son it is a   mist-streak

'My son, why do you hide
your face in fear?' 'O father,
do you not see the Erl-King,
the Erl-King with his crown and
train?' 'My son, it is only a
swirl of mist.'

"Du liebes Kind, komm, geh mit mir!
you dear   child come go with me

Gar schöne Spiele spiel ich mit dir;
very lovely games play I   with you

Manch bunte   Blumen sind an dem Strand,
many gay-coloured flowers are on the shore

Meine Mutter hat manch güldnen Gewand."
my   mother has many a golden   robe

'Sweet child, come away with
me! I will play fine games with
you. There are many gay flowers
by the shore, and my mother has
golden robes.'

"Mein Vater, mein Vater, und hörest du nicht,
my   father my   father and hear   you not

Was Erlenkönig mir   leise verspricht?"
what Erl-King   to me softly promises

"Sei ruhig, bleibe ruhig, mein Kind:
be quiet stay   quiet my   child

In dürren   Blättern säuselt der Wind."
in withered leaves   rustles the wind

'O father, father, and do you not hear what the Erl-King softly promises?' 'Be still, be still, my child! The wind is rustling in the withered leaves.'

"Willst, feiner Knabe, du mit mir gehn?
want   fine   boy   you with me to go

Meine Töchter   sollen dich warten schön;
my   daughters shall   you to serve well

Meine Töchter   führen den nächtlichen Reihn
my   daughters lead   the nightly   dance

Und wiegen und tanzen und singen dich ein."
and rock   and dance and sing   you (to sleep)

'You beautiful boy, will you not come with me? My daughters would serve you well; they lead the nightly dance, and would rock you, and dance for you, and sing you to sleep.'

"Mein Vater, mein Vater, und siehst du nicht dort
my   father my   father and see   you not   there

Erlkönigs Töchter   am   düstern Ort?"
Erl-King's daughters in the dark   place

"Mein Sohn, mein Sohn, ich seh es genau:
my   son my   son   I   see it exactly

Es   scheinen die alten Weiden so grau."
(it) gleam   the old   willows so grey

'O father, father, and do you not see the Erl-King's daughters in that dark, dismal place?' 'My son, my son, I see them clearly; it is only the grey glimmer of old willow trees.'

"Ich liebe dich, mich reizt   deine schöne Gestalt;
I   love you   me   allures your   lovely form

Und bist du nicht willig, so brauch ich Gewalt."
and are you not   willing so need   I   force

"Mein Vater, mein Vater, jetzt fasst er mich an!
my   father my   father now   seizes he me   -

Erlkönig hat mir ein Leids getan!"
Erl-King has me   a   harm   done

'I love you, and am stirred by your beauty; if you do not come willingly, I must use force.' 'O father, father, he is seizing me now! Oh, the Erl-King is hurting me!'

Dem   Vater grauset's,   er reitet geschwind
to the father shudders (it) he rides   fast

Er hält in den Armen das ächzende Kind,
he holds in the arms   the moaning   child

Erreicht den Hof   mit Müh   und Not;
reaches   the court-yard with trouble and difficulty

In seinen Armen das Kind war tot.
in his   arms   the child was dead

The father shudders, swiftly he rides, holding the moaning child in his arms. In anguished haste he reaches the court-yard — in his arms the child is dead.

19. *SELIGKEIT*
   ECSTASY

Ludwig Hölty

Freuden sonder Zahl!
joys   without number

Blüh'n im   Himmelssaal
blossom in the heaven's-hall

Engeln und Verklärten,
angels and (the) blessèd

Wie die Väter   lehrten,
as the forefathers taught

O da   möcht'   ich sein,
O there would like I   to be

Und mich   ewig   freun.
and myself for ever to rejoice

Jedem   lächelt traut
to each smiles dear(-ly)

Eine Himmelsbraut;
a   heaven's-bride

Harf' und Psalter klinget,
harp and psalter resound(s)

Und man tanzt und singet.
and one dances and sings

O da   möcht'   ich sein,
O there would like I   to be

Und mich   ewig   freun.
and myself for ever to rejoice,

Lieber bleib' ich hier,
rather stay   I   here

Lächelt Laura mir
smiles Laura to me

Einen Blick, der saget,
a   glance that says

Dass ich ausgeklaget.
that I   finished lamenting

Selig   dann mit ihr,
blissful then with her

Bleib' ich ewig   hier.
stay   I   for ever here

19. ECSTASY

   Countless joys abound in the
halls of Heaven - angels and the
blessèd, so the elders say. O
how I would like to be there,
rejoicing for ever and ever!

   A heavenly bride smiles at
every one, harp and psalter
resound, and they all dance and
sing. O how I would like to be
there, rejoicing for ever and
ever!

   Laura smiles at me, and her
glance tells me my troubles are
over. If I can enjoy such
ecstasy with her, I will stay
here for ever!

20. *GOTT IM FRÜHLING*
    GOD IN THE SPRING

                                      20. GOD IN SPRINGTIME

Johann Peter Uz

In seinem schimmernden Gewand
in his   shimmering   robe

Hast du den Frühling uns   gesandt,
have you the spring   to us sent

Und Rosen um   sein Haupt gewunden.
and roses about his   head   wound

Holdlächelnd   kommt er schon!
sweetly-smiling comes he already

Es   führen ihn die Stunden,
(it) lead   him the hours

O Gott, auf   seinen Blumenthron.
O God   upon his   flower-throne

You have sent spring to us, twining his head about with roses. He is here already, smiling sweetly. O God, each hour leads him nearer to his flowery throne.

Er geht in   Buschen und sie   blühn;
he goes into bushes   and they blossom

Den   Fluren kommt ihr   frisches Grün,
to the meadows comes their fresh   green

Und Wäldern wächst ihr   Schatten wieder,
and to woods grow   their shadows again

Der West   liebkosend, sein tausendes
the west (wind) caressingly his   thousand
*   Gefieder schwingt,*
   feathers waves

Und jeder frohe Vogel singt.
and each   glad   bird   sings

He walks amongst the bushes and they blossom; a fresh green comes over the meadows, and in the woods, shadows grow again. The west wind caresses with his thousand wings, and every bird sings merrily.

Mit   eurer Lieder süssem Klang,
with your   songs   sweet   sound

Ihr Vögel! soll   auch mein Gesang
you birds   shall also my   song

Zum   Vater der   Natur sich   schwingen.
to the father of the nature (himself) to soar

Entzückung reisst mich hin!
delight   charms me   -

Ich will dem   Herrn lobsingen,
I   will to the Lord   sing praises

Durch   den ich wurde, was ich bin!
through whom I   became what I   am

You birds, I will join my song with your sweet strains, as they rise to the Father of all nature. Delight fills me - I will praise the Lord, in whom I have my being!

21. *GESÄNGE DES HARFNERS*
   SONGS OF THE HARPER

21. THE HARPER'S SONGS

Johann Wolfgang von Goethe

i. (also set by Schumann and Wolf)

i.

Wer   sich   der   Einsamkeit ergibt,
he who himself to the solitude   yields

He who succumbs to solitude, ah, he is soon alone; others live, others love, and leave him to his torment.

Ach! der ist bald allein;
ah he ist soon alone

Ein Jeder lebt, ein Jeder liebt
everyone lives everyone loves

Und lässt ihn seiner Pein.
and leaves him to his pain

Ja! lässt mich meiner Qual!
yes leave me to my anguish

Yes, leave me to my anguish! No longer will I be lonely, if I can but once be alone.

Und kann ich nur einmal
and can I   but once

Recht einsam sein,
quite alone to be

Dann bin ich nicht allein.
then am I not   alone

Es schleicht ein Liebender lauschend sacht,
(it) steals   a loving one listening softly

Does a lover steal up softly to listen if his beloved is alone? Day and night, pain and anguish steal over me in my solitude.

Ob seine Freundin allein?
if his   friend   alone

So überschleicht bei Tag und Nacht
so steals over   by day and night

Mich Einsamen   die Pein,
me solitary one the pain

Mich Einsamen   die Qual.
me solitary one the anguish

Ach werd' ich erst einmal
alas will I only once

Alas, only when I lie solitary in my grave will anguish leave me alone.

Einsam im   Grabe sein,
solitary in the grave to be

Da lässt sie mich allein!
then leaves she me   alone

ii. (also set by Schumann, Liszt and Wolf)

ii.

Wer nie sein Brot mit Tränen ass,
he who never his bread with tears ate

He whose bread was never moist with tears, who never lay weeping the miserable nights away – he cannot know you, heavenly powers!

Wer nie die kummervollen Nächte
he who never the sorrowful   nights

Auf seinem Bette weinend sass,
on his bed weeping sat

Der kennt euch nicht, ihr himmlischen Mächte!
he knows you not   you heavenly   powers

Ihr führt in's   Leben uns hinein,
you lead into the life us (into)

Ihr lässt den Armen   schuldig werden,
you let   the poor wretch guilty   to become

Dann überlasst ihr ihn der   Pein;
then abandon   you him to the pain

Denn alle Schuld rächt   sich   auf Erden.
for all guilt revenges itself on   earth.

     You bring us into life, you
let man in his misery transgress,
then you abandon him in his
torment; on earth all guilt
brings its retribution.

   iii. (also set by Schumann and Wolf)

iii.

An die Türen will ich schleichen,
to the doors will I   to steal

Still und sittsam will ich stehn;
silent and modest will I   to stand

Fromme Hand wird Nahrung   reichen,
pious hand will sustenance to give

Und ich werde weiter gehn.
and I   will on   to go

Jeder wird sich   glücklich scheinen,
each will himself happy   to seem

Wenn mein Bild vor   ihm erscheint;
when my   image before him appears

Eine Träne wird er weinen,
a   tear will he to weep

Und ich weiss nicht was er weint.
and I   know not   what he weeps

     I will steal from door to
door, and stand there humble
and silent. Charitable hands will
give me sustenance, and I will
go my way. Every man will
recognise his own good fortune,
when he sees me before him; he
will shed a tear, and I will not
know for what he weeps.

     22. JÄGERS   ABENDLIED
       HUNTER'S EVENING-SONG

22. HUNTER'S EVENING SONG

     Johann Wolfgang von Goethe

Im   Felde schleich ich still und wild,
in the field steal   I   silent and savage

Gespannt mein Feuerrohr,
cocked   my   rifle

Da   schwebt so licht   dein liebes Bild,
then hovers so lightly your dear   image

Dein süsses Bild mir vor.
your sweet   image me in front of

     I prowl through the fields,
savage and silent, my rifle
cocked and ready. Then your dear
image, your sweet image hovers
lightly before me.

Du wandelst jetzt wohl   still und mild
you go   now   perhaps silent and gentle

Durch Feld und liebes Tal,
through field and dear   valley

Und ach, mein schnell verrauschend Bild
and ah   my   quickly dying away   image

Stellt sich   dir's   nicht einmal?
appears (itself) to you it not   once

     Perhaps you go now, gentle
and silent, through the fields
and the well-loved valley. Oh,
does my quickly fading image not
appear even once before you?

Mir   ist es, denk' ich nur an dich,
to me is it think I   only of you

Als in den Mond zu sehn;
as in the moon to to see

Ein stiller Friede kommt auf mich,
a   quiet   peace comes upon me

Weiss nicht, wie mir   geschehn.
know not   how to me happened

It seems I see you in the
moonlight as I think only of you;
over me steals a quiet peace,
and I cannot say what has
befallen me.

23. AN SCHWAGER   KRONOS
    TO 'POSTILLION' TIME

23. TO TIME, THE COACHMAN

Johann Wolfgang von Goethe

Spute   dich,   Kronos!
make haste yourself Time

Fort, den rasselnden Trott!
away the rattling   trot

Bergab   gleitet der Weg,
downhill glides the path

Ekles   Schwindeln zögert
disagreeable giddyness lingers

Mir vor   die Stirne dein Zaudern.
to me before the brow   your dallying

Frisch, holpert es gleich,
briskly jolts   it at once

Über Stock und Steine den Trott
over stick and stone the trot

Rasch in's   Leben hinein!
swiftly into the life (into)

Make haste, O Time - away at
a rattlng trot! The path runs
smoothly down the hill; your
tarrying brings a galling
giddiness to my brow. Briskly
we jolt over sticks and stones,
trotting swiftly into life!

Nun schon   wieder den eratmenden Schritt,
now already again the gasping   step

Nun schon   wieder mühsam   Berg hinauf!
now already again laboriously hill up

Auf denn, nicht träge   denn,
up then not   sluggishly then

Strebend und hoffend hinan!
striving and hoping upwards

Now the breathless pace
returns - once again we labour
up the hill. Up then, not
sluggishly, striving hopefully
upwards!

Weit, hoch, herrlich rings den Blick
far   high glorious around the glimpse

In's   Leben hinein;
into the life (into)

Vom   Gebirg zum   Gebirg
from the mountains to the mountains

Schwebet der ewige Geist,
soars   the eternal spirit

Ewigen   Lebens ahndevoll.
of eternal life   portentous

Wide and high, a glimpse
into Life itself; from peak to
peak the eternal spirit soars,
portent of eternal life.

Seitwärts des   Überdachs Schatten
sideways of the roof   shadow
 Zieht dich an,
 draws you —

Und ein Frischung verheissender Blick
and a   renewal   of promising glimpse

Auf der Schwelle des   Mädchens da.
on the threshold of the girl   there

Labe   dich! Mir   auch Mädchen,
refresh yourself to me also girl

Diesen schäumenden Trank,
this   sparkling   drink

Diesen frischen Gesundheitsblick!
this   fresh   of health-glance

Sideways, drawn by the shadow of a roof – the charming sight of a girl in the doorway – let it restore you! Enjoy this reviving sight like a cool, sparkling wine!

Ab   denn, rascher hinab!
down then swifter down

Sieh' die Sonne sinkt!
see   the sun   is sinking

Eh'   sie sinkt, eh'   mich Greisen
before she sinks before me   old man

Ergreift im   Moore Nebelduft,
seizes   in the moor misty-fragrance

Entzahnte Kiefer schnattern
toothless jaws   chatter

Und das schlotternde Gebein.
and the trembling   bones

Down again, still faster – look, the sun is sinking! – Before it sinks, before the moorland mists encircle me, an old man, with chattering toothless jaws and trembling limbs!

Trunk'nen vom   letzten Strahl
drunk   from the last   ray

Reiss' mich, ein Feuermeer
seize me   a   fire-sea

Mir   im   schäumenden Aug'
to me in the sparkling   eye

Mich geblendeten Taumelnden
me   dazzled   reeling one

In der Hölle nächtliches Tor.
in the hell of nightly   gateway

Seize me, drunk from the last rays of the sun, a sea of fire blinding my sight, so that dazzled, I reel into Hell's nocturnal gateway.

Töne, Schwager, ins   Horn,
blow coachman into the horn

Rassle den schallenden Trab,
rattle the echoing   trot

Dass der Orkus vernehme: wir kommen,
that the Orcus may hear we are coming

Dass gleich an der Tür
that at once at the door

Der Wirt   uns freundlich empfange.
the inn-keeper us cheerfully may receive.

Coachman, sound the horn – on at a rattling trot! So that Orcus hears we are coming, and the innkeeper waits at the door, hospitably to receive us!

24. *DER WANDERER*
   THE WANDERER

24. THE WANDERER

Georg Philipp Schmidt von Lübeck

Ich komme von   Gebirge   her,
I   come   from the mountains (from)

I come from the mountains. Mists rise in the valley; the ocean rages. Silently I wander, seldom happy, always asking in my sighs, 'Where?' always, 'Where?'

Es   dämpft das Tal,   es   braust das Meer,
(it) steams the valley (it) rages   the ocean

Ich wandle still,   bin wenig   froh,
I   wander silently am little happy

Und immer   fragt der Seufzer:wo?
and always asks   the sigh   where

Immer: wo?
always where

Die Sonne dünkt mich hier so kalt,
the sun   seems me   here so cold

Here the sun seems so cold, the flowers faded, life old. The chatter of men is an empty sound; I am a stranger everywhere.

Die Blüte   welk, das Leben alt,
the blossom faded the life old

Und was   sie reden, leerer Schall,
and what they talk   empty sound

Ich bin ein Fremdling überall.
I   am a   stranger everywhere

Wo   bist du, mein geliebtes Land?
where are you my   beloved   land

Where are you my beloved land? I have sought you, dreamt of you, but never found you! A land so green with hope, the land where my roses bloom,

Gesucht, geahnt, und nie   gekannt!
sought   imagined and never known

Das Land, das Land, so hoffnungsgrün,
the land the land so hope's-green

Das Land, wo   meine Rosen blühn,
the land where my   roses bloom

Wo   meine Freunde wandelnd gehn,
where my   friends wandering go

where my friends roam, where my dead come to life; the land where they speak my tongue — O land, where are you?

Wo   meine Toten auferstehn,
where my   dead rise

Das Land, das meine Sprache spricht,
the land that my   language speaks

O Land, wo   bist du?
O land where are you

Ich wandle still,   bin wenig   froh,
I   wander silently am little happy

Silently I wander, seldom happy; always asking in my sighs, 'Where?' always 'Where?' A ghostly whisper echoes back to me, 'There, where you are not, there is happiness.'

Und immer   fragt der Seufzer: wo?
and always asks   the sigh   where

Immer: wo?
always where

Im   Geisterhauch tönt's   mir   zurück:
in the ghost-breath sounds it to me back

Dort, wo   du nicht bist, dort ist das Glück!"
there where you not   are   there is the happiness

25. *LIED EINES SCHIFFERS AN DIE DIOSKUREN*
    SONG OF A SAILOR   TO THE DIOSCURI

25. SAILOR'S SONG TO CASTOR AND
    POLLUX

Johann Mayrhofer

Dioskuren, Zwillingssterne,
Dioscuri   twin-stars

Die ihr leuchtet meinem Nachen,
who you light   my   boat

Mich beruhigt auf dem Meere
me   calm   on the sea

Eure Milde,   euer Wachen.
your gentleness your watching

O Castor and Pollux, twin
stars, you light my little boat,
and calm me on the sea with your
gentle watching.

Wer auch fest   in sich   begründet,
who-ever strong in himself proves

Unverzagt dem Sturm begegnet,
undaunted the storm meets

Fühlt sich   doch   in euren Strahlen
feels himself indeed in your rays

Doppelt mutig und gesegnet.
twice   bold and blessed

Whoever proves his strength
by meeting storms undaunted, in
your light feels twice as bold
and blessed.

Dieses Ruder, das ich schwinge,
this   oar   that I wield

Meeresfluten zu zerteilen,
ocean-waves to to divide

Hänge ich, so ich geborgen,
hang I   so I   in safety (am)

Auf an eures   Tempels Säulen,
on to of your temple pillars

Dioskuren, Zwillingssterne.
Dioscuri   twin-stars

These oars I wield to part
the ocean waves; when I reach
safety I will hang them on the
pillars of your temple, O Castor
and Pollux, twin stars!

26. *AM   GRABE ANSELMOS*
    AT THE GRAVE ANSELMO'S

26. AT ANSELMO'S GRAVE

Matthias Claudius

Dass ich dich verloren habe,
that I you lost   have

Dass du nicht mehr bist,
that you no   more are

Ach! dass hier in diesem Grabe
ah   that here in this   grave

Mein Anselmo ist,
my   Anselmo is

Das ist mein Schmerz!
that is my   grief

I have lost you, you are no
more. Ah, here in this grave my
Anselmo lies - that is my grief.
How we loved each other! As long
as I live, never again can joy
enter my heart.

Seht, wie liebten wir uns   beide,
see how loved we (ourselves) both

Und so lang' ich bin,
and so long I   am

Kommt Freude niemals wieder in mein Herz.
comes joy   never   again into my heart

27. *AN DIE NACHTIGALL*
    TO THE NIGHTINGALE

27. TO THE NIGHTINGALE

Matthias Claudius

Er liegt und schläft an meinem Herzen,
he lies and sleeps on my   heart

Mein guter Schutzgeist   sang   ihn ein,
my   good guardian-spirit sang to sleep him –

Und ich kann fröhlich sein und scherzen,
and I can gay   to be and to jest

Kann jeder Blum und jedes Blatts mich   freun.
can of every flower and of every leaf myself to rejoice

Nachtigall, ach! Nachtigall, ach!
nightingale ah   nightingale ah

Sing mir den Amor nicht wach!
sing to me the Cupid not   awake

He lies sleeping on my breast; my guardian spirit sang him to sleep. I can jest and be gay, every flower and every leaf delights me. Nightingale, O nightingale – do not wake my Cupid with your song!

28. *WIEGENLIED*
    CRADLE-SONG

28. CRADLE SONG

Matthias Claudius

Schlafe, schlafe, holder, süsser Knabe,
sleep   sleep   lovely sweet boy

Leise wiegt dich deiner Mutter Hand;
softly rocks you of your mother hand

Sanfte Ruhe, milde Labe
gentle sleep tender comfort

Bringt dir   schwebend dieses Wiegenband.
brings to you hovering this   cradle-ribbon

Schlafe, schlafe, in dem süssen Grabe,
sleep   sleep   in the sweet grave

Noch beschützt dich deiner Mutter Arm;
still shelters you of your mother arm

Alle Wünsche, alle Habe
all desires   all possession

Fasst sie liebend, alle liebewarm
holds she lovingly all love-warm

Sleep, sleep, my fine sweet boy, your mother's hand softly rocks you. The swaying of the cradle brings you tender comfort, gentle sleep.

Sleep, sleep, in the sweet sheltering hollow of your mother's arm; all she has, all she desires, she holds in the warmth of her love.

Schlafe, schlafe, in der   Flaumen Schosse,
sleep   sleep   in of the down   lap

Noch umtönt   dich lauter Liebeston;
still surrounds you pure   love's-sound

Eine Lilie, eine Rose,
a   lily   a   rose

Nach dem Schlafe werd' sie dir   zum   Lohn.
after the sleep   will she to you to the reward

Sleep, sleep, cradled in down, with the pure strains of love echoing around you. When you awake, she'll give you a lily and a rosebud.

       29. *AN DIE LAUTE*
          TO THE LUTE

                                  29. TO THE LUTE

     Friedrich Rochlitz

Leiser, leiser, kleine Laute,
softer softer little lute

Flüstre, was ich dir   vertraute,
whisper what I   to you entrusted

Dort zu jenem Fenster hin!
there to that window thither

Wie die Wellen sanfter Lüfte,
like the waves of gentle breezes

Mondenglanz und Blumendüfte,
moonlight and flower-scents

Send' es der   Gebieterin!
send it to the mistress

Softer, softer, little lute! Whisper my secret message up there to that window. Send it like a gently billowing breeze; like moonlight and the scent of flowers, to my mistress.

Neidisch sind des   Nachbars Söhne,
jealous are of the neighbour sons

Und im   Fenster jener   Schöne
and in the window of that fair one

Flimmert noch ein einsam   Licht.
glimmers still a   solitary light

Drum   noch leiser, kleine Laute:
therefore still softer little lute

Dich vernehme die Vertraute,
you hear   the entrusted one

Nachbarn aber Nachbarn nicht!
neighbours but neighbours not

The neighbours' sons are jealous – a solitary light glimmers in the window of my fair one. So play still softer, little lute, so my beloved hears you – but not the neighbours, not the neighbours!

30. LOB   DER   TRÄNEN
PRAISE OF THE TEARS

30. IN PRAISE OF TEARS

August Wilhelm von Schlegel

Laue Lüfte,
warm breezes

Blumendüfte,
flower-scents

Alle Lenz-   und Jugendlust;
all spring- and youth-joy

Frischer Lippen
of cool lips

Küsse nippen,
kisses sip

Sanft gewiegt an zarter Brust;
softly rocked on tender breast

Dann der   Trauben
then of the grapes

Nektar rauben;
nectar to steal

Reihentanz und Spiel und Scherz;
dance   and play and jest

Was die Sinnen
what the senses

Nur gewinnen;
only gain

Ach, erfüllt es je   das Herz?
ah   fulfils it ever the heart

Warm breezes, scent of
flowers, all the joys of spring
and youth; cool lips touched by
kisses, softly rocked on tender
breast; stolen nectar of grapes,
dancing and merry-making; all
that the senses enjoy – O can
it ever fulfil the heart?

Wenn die feuchten
when the moist

Augen leuchten
eyes shine

Von der Wehmut   lindem Tau,
of the melancholy gentle dew

Dann entsiegelt,
then unseals

Drin   gespiegelt,
therein mirrored

Sich   dem   Blick die Himmelsau.
(herself) to the glance the Heaven's pasture

Wie erquicklich
how refreshingly

Augenblicklich
in an instant

Löscht es jede wilde Glut!
quenches it each wild passion

Wie vom   Regen
as by the rain

When our moist eyes shine
with the gentle dew of
melancholy, there unveiled and
mirrored is a glimpse of Heaven's
grassy plains. How each flaming
passion is quenched in an
instant! And as flowers are
refreshed by the rain, so the
faint-spirited are revived.

Blumen pflegen,
flowers are used

Hebet sich der matte Mut.
raises itself the faint spirit

Nicht mit süssen
not with sweet

Wasserflüssen
water-rivers

Zwang Prometheus unsern Leim:*
compelled Prometheus our (size)

Nein, mit Tränen;
no with tears

Drum im Sehnen
therefore in the yearning

Und im Schmerz sind wir daheim.
and in the grief are we at home

Bitter schwellen
bitter swell

Diese Quellen
these springs

Für den erdumfangnen Sinn.
for the earth-encircled sense

Doch sie drängen
yet they press

Aus den Engen
from the narrowness

In das Meer der Liebe hin.
into the ocean of the love towards

Not with sweet river water did Prometheus mould our clay, but with tears; thus yearning and grief are natural to our being. These springs rise bitter to our earthly senses, yet from narrow straits they strive towards the ocean of Love.

Ewiges Sehnen
eternal longing

Floss in Tränen
flowed in tears

Und umgab die starre Welt,
and surrounded the benumbed world

Die in Armen
which in arms

Sein Erbarmen
his mercy

Immerdar umflutend hält.
ever washed around holds

Soll dein Wesen
shall your being

Denn genesen
then recover

Von dem Erdenstaube los,
from the earth-dust free

God's eternal longing flowed in tears about an unfeeling world, which, held in His arms, was encompassed like waves by His mercy. If then you would be free of the earth's dust, it is in your weeping you must unite with the heavenly bosom of those eternal waters.

*=*Lehm* (poetic licence)
clay

Musst im   Weinen
must in the weeping

Dich   vereinen
yourself to unite

Jener   Wasser heilgem Schoss.
of those waters to holy (bosom)

31. *DER TOD   UND DAS MÄDCHEN*
THE DEATH AND THE MAIDEN

Matthias Claudius

(Das Mädchen)
the maiden

'Vorüber, ach, vorüber
by   ah   by

Geh, wilder Knochenmann!
pass savage Death (as a skeleton)

Ich bin noch jung, geh, Lieber!
I   am still young go   dear fellow

Und rühre mich nicht an.'
and touch me   not   –

(Der Tod)
the death

'Gib deine Hand, du schön und zart   Gebild,
give your hand you fair and gentle creature

Bin Freund und komme nicht zu strafen.
am friend and come   not   to to punish

Sei gutes   Muts! Ich bin nicht wild,
be of good courage I   am not   savage

Sollst sanft in meinen Armen schlafen.'
shall gently in my   arms to sleep

31. DEATH AND THE MAIDEN

(The maiden)

   'Pass by! Oh, pass by, cruel
Death! I am still young – go,
kind Death, and do not touch
me!'

(Death)

   'Give me your hand, O fair
and gentle creature. I am your
friend, and do not come to
judge you harshly. Be of good
courage! I am not cruel – you
will sleep gently in my arms.'

32. *GANYMED*
GANYMED

32. GANYMEDE

Johann Wolfgang von Goethe
(also set by Wolf)

Wie im   Morgenglanze
how in the morning-splendour

Du rings mich anglühst,
you around me   glow at

Frühling, Geliebter!
spring   beloved

Mit tausendfacher Liebeswonne
with thousandfold love's-ecstasy

Sich   an mein Herz drängt
herself on my   heart presses

Deiner ewigen Wärme
your   eternal warmth

Heilig Gefühl,
divine sensation

Unendliche Schöne!
infinite   beauty

How you glow around me in
your morning splendour, Spring,
beloved! In a thousandfold
ecstasy of love, the divine
sensation of your eternal warmth
presses against my heart,
infinite beauty!

Dass ich dich fassen möcht
that I   you to hold might

In diesen Arm!
in these arm(s)

Could I but hold you in my
arms!

Ach, an deinem Busen
ah on your   bosom

Lieg ich und schmachte,
lie I   and languish

Und deine Blumen, dein Gras
and your flowers your grass

Drängen sich   an   mein Herz.
press (themselves) against my   heart

Du kühlst den brennenden
you cool   the burning

Durst meines Busens,
thirst of my bosom

Lieblicher Morgenwind,
delightful morning-breeze!

Ruft drein die Nachtigall
calls thereto the nightingale

Liebend nach mir aus dem Nebeltal.
lovingly to   me from the misty-valley

Ah, I lie languishing at
your breast, and your flowers
and your grasses press against
my heart. You cool the burning
thirst within my breast,
delightful morning breeze! The
nightingale calls lovingly to
me from the misty valley.

Ich komm,   ich komme!
I am coming I am coming

Wohin? Ach wohin?
whither oh whither

I am coming, I am coming!
Whither, O whither?

Hinauf! Hinauf strebt's.
upwards upwards strives it

Es   schweben die Wolken
(it) float   the clouds

Abwärts, die Wolken
downwards the clouds

Neigen sich   der   sehnenden Liebe.
bow down (themselves) to the yearning love

Mir! Mir!
to me to me

In eurem Schosse
in your lap

Aufwärts!
upwards

Umfangend umfangen!
embracing embraced

Aufwärts an deinen Busen,
upwards on your   bosom

Alliebender Vater!
all-loving father

Upwards, striving upwards!
The clouds float down, reaching
towards yearning love; to me, to
me! In your lap, now upwards;
embracing, embraced - upwards
to your bosom, all-loving Father!

33. DER JÜNGLING UND DER TOD
   THE YOUTH   AND THE DEATH

33. THE YOUTH AND DEATH

Josef von Spaun

(Der Jüngling)
the youth

(The youth)

Die Sonne sinkt,
the sun   is sinking

The sun is sinking - 0, if I
could but flee away for ever with
her last ray, and leave these
nameless torments to go into a
fairer world!

O könnt' ich mit ihr scheiden
O could I   with her to depart

Mit ihrem letzten Strahl entfliehn!
with her last   ray   to flee away

Ach diese namenlosen Qualen   meiden
ah these nameless   torments to avoid

Und weit in schön're Welten zieh'n!
and far in fairer   world to go

O komme, Tod!
O come   death

Come, O Death, and loosen
these bonds! I smile at you,
Death. 0 lead me gently away
into the land of which I dream.
Come, lay your hands on me! 0
come!

Und löse diese Bande!
and loosen these bonds

Ich lächle dir,   o Knochenmann,
I   smile to you O skeleton

Entführe mich leicht in geträumte Lande!
lead away me   lightly into dreamed of land

O komm und rühre mich doch :an,
O come and touch me   indeed –

O komm!
O come

    (Der Tod)   (Death)
    the death

Es ruht sich   kühl   und sanft in meinen Armen,   You may rest gently in my
it rests itself coolly and gently in my   arms   cool arms. You call! I will

Du rufst, ich will mich   deiner Qual   have mercy on you in your
you call I   will (myself) of your torment   torment.
  erbarmen.
  to have mercy

    34. AN DIE MUSIK   34. TO MUSIC
       TO THE MUSIC

    Franz von Schober

Du holde   Kunst, in wieviel grauen Stunden,   O gracious art, how often in
you gracious art   in how many grey   hours   dark hours, when caught in life's

Wo   mich des   Lebens wilder   Kreis umstrickt   tumultuous round, you have
when me of the life   turbulent circle ensnared   kindled warm love in my heart,

Hast du mein Herz zu warmer Lieb entzunden,   and carried me into a better
have you my   heart to warm   love kindled   world!

Hast mich in   eine bessre Welt entrückt!
have me   into a   better world carried off

Oft   hat ein Seufzer, deiner   Harf entflossen,   How often a sigh, flowing
often has a   sigh   (of) your harp flowed from   from your harp, a sweet, divine

Ein süsser, heiliger Akkord von dir   chord, has unlocked for me a
a sweet   divine   chord from you   heaven of fairer moments. O

Den Himmel bessrer Zeiten mir   erschlossen,   gracious art, for this I thank
the heaven of better times to me unlocked   you!

Du holde   Kunst, ich danke dir dafür!
you gracious art   I   thank you for it

35. DIE FORELLE
   THE TROUT

Christian Friedrich Daniel Schubart

In einem Bächlein   helle,
in a   little brook bright

Da   schoss in froher Eil
there darted in gay   haste

Die launische   Forelle
the moody (playful) trout

Vorüber wie ein Pfeil.
past   like an arrow

Ich stand an dem Gestade
I   stood on the bank

Und sah   in süsser Ruh
and watched in sweet quiet

Des   muntern Fischleins Bade
of the lively little fish bath

Im   klaren Bächlein   zu.
in the clear   little brook -

In a sparkling little brook,
a playful trout darted gaily
past with the speed of an arrow.
I stood on the bank in quiet
content, watching the lively
little fish bathing in the
clear brook.

Ein Fischer mit der Rute
an angler with the rod

Wohl   an dem Ufer stand,
indeed on the bank stood

Und sah's mit kaltem Blute,
and saw it with cold   blood

Wie sich   das Fischlein   wand.
how (itself) the little fish turned about

So lang' dem   Wasser Helle,
so long to the water transparency

So dacht   ich, nicht gebricht,
so thought I   not   is wanting

So fängt   er die Forelle
so catches he the trout

Mit seiner Angel   nicht.
with his   fishing-rod not

An angler, standing with his
rod on the bank, watched with a
cold eye how the little fish
turned itself about. So long as
the water remains clear, I
thought, he will not catch the
trout with his line.

Doch   endlich ward dem   Diebe,
however at last was to the thief

Die Zeit zu lang. Er macht'
the time too long he made

Das Bächlein   tückisch trübe,
the little brook artfully muddy

Und eh   ich es gedacht,
and before I   it thought

So zuckte seine Rute,
so jerked his   rod

Das Fischlein zappelt dran,
the little fish writhed on it

But at last the thief was
tired of waiting. Cunningly he
muddied the little brook, and
before I had time to think, he
jerked his rod - the little fish
was writhing on it, and I, my
blood stirred, gazed at the
cheated trout.

SCHUBERT

Und ich mit regem Blute
and I with excited blood

Sah die Betrogne an.
looked the cheated one at

36. *GRUPPE AUS DEM TARTARUS*
GROUP OUT OF THE TARTARUS

36. GROUP IN TARTARUS

Friedrich von Schiller

Horch - wie Murmeln des empörten Meeres,
listen like murmur of the enraged sea

Wie durch hohler Felsen Becken weint ein Bach,
as through of hollow rocks vortex weeps a brook

Stöhnt dort dumpfigtief ein schweres, leeres
groans there dankly-deep a heavy empty

Qualerpresstes Ach!
torment-extorted ah

Schmerz verzerret
grief distorts

Ihr Gesicht! Verzweiflung sperret
their face despair opens wide

Ihren Rachen fluchend auf.
their throats cursing -

Hohl sind ihre Augen, ihre Blicke
hollow are their eyes their glances

Spähen bang nach des Cocytus Brücke,
peer anxiously towards of the Cocytus bridge

Folgen tränend seinem Trauerlauf.
follow weeping his mourning-course

Fragen sich einander ängstlich leise,
ask (themselves) one another anxiously quiet

Ob noch nicht Vollendung sei?
if yet not completion be

Ewigkeit schwingt über ihnen Kreise,
eternity swings over them circles

Bricht die Sense des Saturns entzwei.
breaks the scythe of the Saturn in two

Listen - like the murmuring of an angry sea, or a brook weeping amongst dank hollow rocks - listen to the deep groans wrung forth, a heavy empty wail of torment!

Grief distorts their faces, despair twists open their mouths with cursing. Their hollow eyes peer anxiously towards the bridge over the Cocytus, and tearfully follow the way of mourning.

With low uneasy voices they ask each other if the end has not yet come! Eternity circles over them, breaking Saturn's scythe in two.

37. LITANEI (AUF DAS FEST 'ALLER SEELEN')
    LITANY   ON   THE FEAST OF ALL SOULS

37. LITANY (FOR THE FEAST OF
    ALL SOULS)

Johann Georg Jacobi

Ruhn in Frieden alle Seelen,
rest in peace   all souls

Die vollbracht ein banges Quälen,
who achieved   an anxious tormenting

Die vollendet süssen Traum,
who achieved sweet   dream

Lebenssatt,   geboren kaum,
life-satiated born   scarcely

Aus   der Welt hinüberschieden:
out of the world over there departed

Alle Seelen ruhn in Frieden!
all souls rest in peace

Rest in peace, all souls;
those who suffered anxious
torment, those who enjoyed
sweet dreams; those tired of
life, and those scarcely born;
all who have departed this
world, all souls rest in peace!

Liebevoller Mädchen Seelen,
of loving   maidens souls

Deren Tränen nicht zu zählen,
whose tears not   to to count

Die ein falscher Freund verliess
who a false   friend left

Und die blinde Welt verstiess:
and the blind world rejected

Alle, die von hinnen schieden,
all who from here   departed

Alle Seelen ruhn in Frieden!
all souls rest in peace

The loving souls of maidens,
whose tears were without number,
deserted by faithless lovers and
rejected by a blind world – all
who have departed this life, all
souls rest in peace!

Und die   nie   der   Sonne lachten,
and those never of the sun   laughed

Unterm   Mond auf Dornen wachten,
under the moon on thorns watched

Gott, im   reinen Himmelslicht,
God in the pure   heaven's-light

Einst zu sehn von Angesicht:
one day to to see by face

Alle, die von hinnen schieden,
all who from hence departed

Alle Seelen ruhn in Frieden!
all souls rest in peace

And those on whom the sun
never smiled, who lay on thorns
beneath the moon, to see one day
the face of God in the pure
light of Heaven; all who have
departed this life, all souls
rest in peace!

38. *Fragment aus dem Gedichte:*
Fragment from the poem

DIE GÖTTER GRIECHENLANDS
THE GODS   OF GREECE

Friedrich Schiller

Schöne Welt, wo   bist du? Kehre   wieder,
lovely world where are you come back again

Holdes   Blütenalter   der   Natur!
gracious blossom-epoch of the nature

Ach, nur in dem Feenland der   Lieder
alas only in the fairyland of the songs

Lebt noch deine fabelhafte Spur.
lives still your mythical   vestige

Ausgestorben trauert das Gefilde,
died out   mourns the countryside

Keine Gottheit zeigt   sich   meinem Blick.
no   deity   appears (herself) to my glance

Ach von jenem lebenwarmen Bilde
ah from that life-warm   image

Blieb der Schatten nur zurück.
stayed the shadow   only back.

38. THE GODS OF GREECE

    O lovely world, where are
you? Come back, you gracious
age when Nature bloomed! Alas,
only in the make-believe of song
does any vestige of your myths
live on. The countryside is
dead and mourning, no deities
appear. Ah, from that warm and
living image, only a shadow
remains.

39. *DIE VÖGEL*
THE BIRDS

Friedrich von Schlegel

Wie lieblich und fröhlich,
how lovely   and gay

Zu schweben, zu singen,
to to hover to to sing

Von glänzender Höhe
from shining   heights

Zur   Erde zu blicken!
to the earth to to look

Die Menschen sind töricht,
the men   are stupid

Sie können nicht fliegen.
they can   not   to fly

Sie jammern in Nöten,
they complain in troubles

Wir flattern gen   Himmel.
we flutter towards heaven

39. THE BIRDS

    How sweet and joyful it is
to hover and sing, and look down
on the earth from our shining
heights!

    Men are foolish - they
cannot fly! In their troubles
they complain, while we fly up
to heaven.

Der Jäger will töten,
the hunter wants to kill

Dem   Früchte wir pickten;
to him fruit   we pecked

Wir müssen ihn höhnen,
we must   him to jeer at

Und Beute gewinnen.
and booty to gain

The hunter whose fruit we
pecked, he wants to kill us,
and so we mock him, and carry
off our prize.

40. *FRÜHLINGSGLAUBE*
    SPRING-FAITH

40. SPRING'S PROMISE

Ludwig Uhland

Die linden Lüfte   sind erwacht,
the soft   breezes are   awakened

Sie säuseln und wehen Tag und Nacht,
they whisper and blow day and night

Sie schaffen an allen Enden.
they work   in all   ends

O frischer Duft, o neuer Klang!
O fresh   scent O new   sound

Nun, armes Herze, sei nicht bang!
now poor heart be not   anxious

Nun muss sich   alles,   alles   wenden.
now must (itself) everything everything to change

Soft breezes awaken; day and
night they whisper and stir,
busy everywhere. O fresh scents,
new sounds! Be anxious no more,
poor heart – everything,
everything now must change!

Die Welt wird   schöner mit jedem Tag,
the world becomes lovelier with each day

Man weisst nicht, was noch werden   mag,
one knows not   what yet to come to be may

Das Blühen   will nicht enden;
the blossoming wants not   to end

Es   blüht   das fernste, tiefste Tal:
(it) blossoms the furthest deepest valley

Nun, armes Herz, vergiss der Qual!
now poor heart forget the torment

Nun muss sich   alles,   alles   wenden.
now must (itself) everything everything to change

The world is lovelier each
day; we do not know what is yet
to come, for the blossoming is
never-ending – even the
furthest, deepest valley flowers.
Now, poor heart, forget your
torment! Everything, everything
now must change!

41. GEHEIMES
   SECRET

41. THE SECRET

Johann Wolfgang von Goethe

Über meines Liebchens   Äugeln
over my   sweetheart's ogling

Stehn verwundert alle Leute;
stand astonished all   people

Ich, der Wissende,   dagegen,
I   the one who knows on the other hand

Weiss recht gut, was das bedeute.
know very well what that may mean

Denn es heisst: 'Ich liebe diesen,
for it says   I   love this one

Und nicht etwa   den und jenen.'
and not   perhaps him or that one

Lasset   nur, ihr guten Leute,
leave off only you good people

Euer Wundern, eurer Sehnen!
your wondering your   longing

Ja, mit ungeheuren Mächten
yes with enormous   powers

Blicket sie wohl   in die Runde;
glances she indeed (in the) round

Doch, sie sucht nur zu verkünden
yet   she seeks only to to make known

Ihm   die nächste süsse Stunde.
to him the next   sweet hour

Everyone wonders at my sweetheart's roving eye. But I who understand it, know full well what it means.

It means: 'I love this one, and indeed, not that one, or the other.' You good people, you can stop your wondering, your desiring!

So compelling are her glances as she looks all about her – yet she only seeks to tell him of the next sweet hour to come.

42. SULEIKA I
   SULEIKA

42. SULEIKA I

Johann Wolfgang von Goethe*
(from the *West-östlichen Divan*)
          west-east   collection of poems

Was   bedeutet die Bewegung?
what means   the agitation

Bringt der Ost   mir frohe Kunde?
brings the east (wind) to me glad tidings

Seiner Schwingen frische Regung
of his wings   fresh   stirring

Kühlt des   Herzens tiefe Wunde.
cools of the heart   deep wound

What is astir in the air? Is the east wind bringing me glad tidings? The cool rushing of its wings soothes the deep wounds in my heart.

*Suleika I and II are in fact by Marianne
 von Willemer, although included under Goethe's name.

Kosend   spielt er mit dem Staube,
caressing plays he with the dust

Jagt   ihn auf in leichten Wölkchen,
raises him up in light   little clouds

Treibt zur   sichern Rebenlaube
drives to the safe   vine-leaves

Der   Insekten frohes Völkchen.
of the insects happy little folk

It plays with the dust caressingly, raising it in light little clouds. It chases the joyous insect-folk into the safety of the vine leaves.

Lindert sanft der   Sonne Glühen,
tempers gently of the sun   glowing

Kühlt auch mir die heissen Wangen,
cools also to me the burning cheeks

Küsst die Reben noch im   Fliehen,
kisses the grapes still in the fleeing

Die   auf Feld und Hügel prangen.
which on field and hill   shine

Gently it tempers the glow of the sun, and cools my burning cheeks. As it hastens away, it kisses the grapes gleaming in the fields and on the hills.

Und mir   bringt sein leises Flüstern
and to me brings his quiet whispering

Von dem Freunde tausend Grüsse;
from the friend thousand greetings

Eh'   noch diese Hügel düstern,
before yet these hills to grow dusk

Grüssen mich wohl   tausend Küsse.
greet   me   perhaps thousand kisses

And its quiet whispering brings a thousand greetings from my beloved — before dusk falls on these hills, a thousand kisses will greet me!

Und so kannst du weiterziehen!
and so can   you on to go

Diene Freunden und Betrübten,
serve friends and those distressed

Dort, dort, wo   hohe Mauern glühen,
there there where high walls glow

Dort find' ich bald den Vielgeliebten.
there find I   soon the much-loved one

And now you can go your way, serving friends and those cast down. There, where the high walls are gleaming, there will I soon find my dearest love!

Ach, die wahre Herzenskunde,
ah   the true heart's-tidings

Liebeshauch, erfrischtes Leben,
love's-breath refreshed   life

Wird mir   nur aus   seinem Munde,
will to me only out of his   mouth

Kann mir nur sein Atem geben.
can to me only his breath to give

Oh, the message of a true heart, a whisper of love, life renewed, can only come from his lips, be given by his breath alone.

43. *SULEIKA II*
SULEIKA

43. SULEIKA II

Johann Wolfgang von Goethe*
(from the *West-östlichen Divan*)
            west-east   collection of poems

Ach, um deine feuchten Schwingen,
ah (for) your moist   wings

West,   wie sehr ich dich beneide;
west (wind) how much I   you envy

How I envy you your wings,
O moist west wind! For you can
tell him how I suffer in our
separation.

Denn du kannst ihm   Kunde bringen,
for you can   to him news to bring

Was ich in der Trennung   leide!
what I   in the separation suffer

Die Bewegung deiner Flügel
the movement of your wings

Weckt   im   Busen stilles Sehnen;
awakens in the bosom silent longing

The stirring of your wings
awakens a silent longing in my
breast; flowers and meadows,
woods and hills, are bathed in
tears by your breath.

Blumen, Auen,   Wald und Hügel
flowers meadows wood and hill

Steh'n bei deinem Hauch in Tränen.
are   by your   breath in tears

Doch dein mildes, sanftes Wehen,
yet your soft   gentle blowing

Kühlt die wunden Augenlider;
cools the sore   eye-lids

Yet your soft and gentle
fluttering cools the lids of my
sore eyes. Oh, I would pine away
in grief, did I not hope to see
him again!

Ach, für Leid müsst'ich vergehen,
ah   for grief must I   to pine

Hofft' ich nicht zu seh'n ihn wieder.
hoped I   not   to to see him again

Eile   denn zu meinem Lieben,
hasten then to my   loved one

Spreche sanft zu seinem Herzen;
speak   gently to his   heart

Hasten then to my beloved,
speak tenderly, and touch his
heart. But see you do not grieve
him – do not tell him of my
sorrow!

Doch vermeid' ihn zu betrüben
but avoid   him to to grieve

Und verbirg ihm   meine Schmerzen.
and hide   to him my   sorrows

Sag' ihm, aber sag's bescheiden:
say to him but say it discreetly

Seine Liebe sei mein Leben;
his   love be my   life

Tell him, but tell him
gently, his love is my whole
life; and if we both can feel
one joy, this will bring him
near to me.

Freudiges Gefühl von beiden
joyful   feeling of both

Wird mir   seine Nähe   geben.
will to me his   nearness to give

*Suleika I and II are in fact by Marianne
von Willemer, although included under Goethe's name.

44. *DER JÜNGLING AN DER QUELLE*
    THE YOUTH   AT THE SPRING

                                   44. THE YOUTH AT THE SPRING

Johann Gaudenz von Salis

Leise rieselnder Quell!
gently rippling   spring

Ihr wallenden flispernden Pappeln!
you fluttering lisping   poplars

Euer Schlummergeräusch
your slumber-sound

Wecket die Liebe auf.
wakes the love up

Linderung sucht' ich bei euch,
comfort   sought I with you

Und sie zu vergessen die Spröde,
and her to to forget the coy one

Ach, und Blätter und Bach
oh   and leaves and stream

Seufzen, Louise, dir nach.
sigh   Louisa you for

    You gently rippling stream, you fluttering, lisping poplars, your lullaby awakens my love. I sought your comfort to forget her, the coquette. Oh, the leaves and the stream sigh for you, Louisa!

45. *SEI MIR   GEGRÜSST!*
    BE TO ME GREETED

                                   45. I GREET YOU!

Friedrich Rückert

O du Entrissne   mir   und meinem Kusse,
O you torn away one to me and my   kiss

Sei mir gegrüsst! Sei mir geküsst!
be to me greeted be to me kissed

Erreichbar nur meinem Sehnsuchtsgrusse,
within reach only to my longing's-greeting

Sei mir gegrüsst! Sei mir geküsst!
be to me greeted be to me kissed

Du von der Hand der Liebe diesem Herzen
you from the hand of the love to this heart

Gegebne, du von dieser
given one you from this

Brust Genomme mir! Mit diesem Tränengusse
breast taken one to me with this   tears'-gushing

Sei mir gegrüsst! Sei mir geküsst!
be to me greeted be to me kissed

Zum   Trotz   der   Ferne, die sich
to the defiance of the distance that herself
  feindlich trennend,
  hostilely dividing

    O you, who were torn from me and my kisses, I greet you! I kiss you! You, whom only my longing can reach - I greet you! I kiss you!

    You, given to my heart by the very hand of love; you, who were taken from my breast! With the flowing of my tears, I greet you! I kiss you!

    To defy the distance that divides us so cruelly; to vex the envious powers of Fate - I greet you! I kiss you!

Hat zwischen mich und dich gestellt;
has between me   and you put

Dem   Neid der   Schicksalsmächte zum   Verdrusse
to the envy of the Fate's-powers   to the vexation

Sei mir   gegrüsst! Sei mir   geküsst!
be to me greeted   be to me kissed

Wie du mir   je   im   schönsten Lenz   der
as you to me ever in the fairest   spring of the
  Liebe
  love

As once you came to me in
the fairest spring-time of love,
with greetings and kisses – with
the radiant outpouring of my
soul, I greet you! I kiss you!

Mit Gruss   und Kuss entgegenkamst,
with greeting and kiss came towards

Mit meiner Seele glühendsten Ergusse
with of my soul most glowing effusion

Sei mir   gegrüsst! Sei mir   geküsst!
be to me greeted   be to me kissed

Ein Hauch der   Liebe tilget   Räum'
a breath of the love blots out spaces
  und Zeiten,
  and times

A breath of love can erase
both space and time; I am with
you, and you are with me. I hold
you close in my arms, and I
greet you! I kiss you!

Ich bin bei dir, du bist bei mir,
I   am with you you are with me

Ich halte dich in dieses Arms Umschlusse,
I hold you in of this arm embracings

Sei mir   gegrüsst! Sei mir   geküsst!
be to me greeted   be to me kissed

46. *DER WACHTELSCHLAG*
THE QUAIL-SONG

46. SONG OF THE QUAIL

Samuel Friedrich Sauter

Horch, wie schallt's dorten so lieblich   hervor:
listen how sounds it yonder so delightfully forth

Fürchte Gott! fürchte Gott! ruft mir   die
fear   God fear   God   calls to me the
  Wachtel ins   Ohr.
  quail   into the ear

Sitzend im   Grünen, von Halmen umhüllt,
sitting in the green by stalks covered

Mahnt sie den Horcher im   Saaten-gefild:
exhorts she the listener in the corn-fields

Liebe Gott! liebe Gott! er ist so gütig, so mild.
love God love God he is so good so gentle

Wieder bedeutet ihr hüpfender Schlag:
again means   her skipping song

Lobe   Gott! lobe   Gott! der dich zu lohnen   vermag.
praise God praise God who you to to reward are able

Siehst du die herrlichen Früchte im   Feld?
see   you the glorious   fruits in the field

Nimm es du Herzen, Bewohner der   Welt:
take it to heart dweller of the world

Listen how sweetly it
sounds forth – 'Fear the Lord!
Fear the Lord!', the quail calls
to me. Half-hidden in the green
stalks, she exhorts the listener
in the corn-field, 'Worship the
Lord! He is so gentle and good.'
Again her jerky song tells us,
'Praise the Lord! Praise the
Lord! He'll reward you. Do you
see the glorious fruits of the
field? Take it to heart, you
that dwell on the earth. Thank
the Lord! Thank the Lord, who
feeds and keeps you. If the Lord
of nature startles you with his
storms, beseech the Lord,
beseech the Lord!' she calls,
'for He protects the field. If
the perils of the battle alarm
you, trust the Lord, trust the
Lord! See, not for long will
He delay!'

Danke Gott! danke Gott! der dich ernährt   und
thank God   thank God   who you nourishes and
   erhält
   preserves

Schreckt dich im   Wetter   der Herr der   Natur:
startles you in the weather the Lord of the nature

Bitte Gott! bitte Gott! ruft sie, er schonet
ask   God   ask   God   calls she he cares for
   die Flur!
   the field

Machen Gefahren der Krieger dir   bang';
make   perils   the warrior to you anxious

Traue Gott! traue Gott! sieh', er verziehet
trust God   trust God   see   he withdraws
   nicht lang.
   not   long

47. *NACHTVIOLEN*
   DAME'S VIOLETS

47. NIGHT VIOLETS

   Johann Mayrhofer

Nachtviolen,   dunkle Augen, seelenvolle,
dame's-violets dark   eyes   soulful

O violets of the night,
dark, soulful eyes - how
blissful it is to lose oneself
in your velvety blue.

Selig   ist es,
blissful is it

Sich   versenken
oneself to sink

In dem samtnen Blau.
in the velvety blue

Grüne Blätter streben freudig euch zu helfen
green leaves   strive joyfully you to to help

Green leaves joyfully strive
to help adorn you; yet solemn
and silent you gaze into the
mild spring air.

Euch zu schmücken;
you to to adorn

Doch ihr blicket ernst   und schweigend in
yet you look   seriously and silently   into
   die laue Frühlingsluft.
   the mild spring-air

Mit erhabnen Wehmutsstrahlen trafet ihr
with sublime melancholy-rays touched you
   mein treues   Herz,
   my   faithful heart

Gleaming with sublime
melancholy you touched my
faithful heart, and now on
silent nights, the sacred union
blossoms.

Und nun blüht
and now blossoms

In stummen Nächten
in silent nights

Fort die heilige Verbindung.
on   the sacred union

48. DIE LIEBE HAT GELOGEN
THE LOVE HAS DECEIVED

48. LOVE HAS DECEIVED ME

August von Platen

Die Liebe hat gelogen,
the love has deceived

Die Sorge lastet schwer,
the grief burdens heavily

Betrogen, ach, betrogen,
deceived ah deceived

Hat alles   mich umher!
has everything me   about

Es   fliessen heisse Tropfen
(it) flow   hot   drops

Die Wange stets herab,
the cheek always down

Lass ab, mein Herz, zu klopfen,
leave off my   heart to to throb

Du armes Herz, lass ab!
you poor heart leave off

Love has deceived me, the
burden of my grief is heavy;
deceived, alas, deceived by
everyone around me! Hot tears
flow down my cheeks. Cease your
throbbing, O my heart; poor
heart, cease your throbbing!

49. AN DIE LEIER
TO THE LYRE

49. TO THE LYRE

Franz von Bruchmann
(after Anacreon)

Ich will von Atreus' Söhnen,
I   want of Atreus' sons

Von Kadmus will ich singen!
of Cadmus want I   to sing

Doch meine Saiten tönen
but my   strings sound

Nur Liebe im   Erklingen.
only love in the sounding

Ich tauschte um die Saiten,
I exchanged   the strings

Die Leier möcht'ich   tauschen,
the lyre would like I to exchange

Alcidens Siegensschreiten
Alcidens victory-conquest

Sollt' ihrer   Macht entrauschen!
should of their might to thunder out

I would sing of the sons
of Atreus and of Cadmus - but
my strings only send forth the
strains of love.

I have changed the strings,
and would change my lyre, for
they should resound with the
might of Alciden's conquests -

Doch auch die Saiten tönen
but   also the strings sound

Nur Liebe im   Erklingen.
only love   in the sounding

So lebt denn wohl, Heroen,
so fare - then—well heroes

Denn meine Saiten tönen
for my   strings sound

Statt   Heldensang   zu drohen,
instead of heroes' song to to threaten

Nur Liebe im   Erklingen.
only love   in the sounding

and my strings only send
forth the strains of love. So
farewell, heroes, for my strings,
instead of striking up a song
of valiant warriors, only send
forth the strains of love.

50. *DER MUSENSOHN*
   THE MUSES'-SON

50. SON OF THE MUSES

Johann Wolfgang von Goethe

Durch Feld und Wald zu schweifen,
through field and wood to to roam

Mein Liedchen   wegzupfeifen,
my   little song to away to pipe

So geht's von Ort   zu Ort!
so goes it from place to place

Und nach dem   Takte reget
and in   (the) time moves

Und nach dem Mass   beweget
and in   the measure moves

Sich   alles   an mir fort.
(itself) everything with me on

Roaming through field and
forest, piping my little song, I
go from place to place; and
everything stirs to my beat,
everything moves on with me to
my rhythm.

Ich kann sie kaum   erwarten,
I   can her hardly to await

Die erste Blum im   Garten,
the first flower in the garden

Die erste Blüt   am   Baum.
the first blossom on the tree

Sie grüssen meine Lieder,
they greet   my   songs

Und kommt der Winter wieder,
and comes the winter again

Sing ich noch jenen Traum.
sing I   still that dream

I can hardly wait for the
first flower in the garden, and
the first blossom on the tree.
They greet my songs, and when
winter returns I still sing of
this dream.

Ich sing ihn in der Weite,
I   sing him in the wide expanse

Auf Eises Läng   und Breite
on ice's length and breadth

Da   blüht   der Winter schön!
then blossoms the winter fair

I sing of it far and wide,
and all the length and breadth
of the ice, winter blossoms
fair! This vanishes in its turn,
and there on the ploughed slopes
are new delights.

Auch diese Blüte   schwindet,
also this   blossom vanishes

Und neue Freude   findet
and new   delight finds

Sich   auf bebauten   Höhn.
(itself) on   cultivated slopes

Denn wie   ich bei der Linde
for   when I   by   the linden-tree

Das junge Völkchen   finde,
the young (little) folk find

Sogleich erreg ich sie,
at once   excite I   them

Der stumpfe Bursche bläht   sich,
the dull   lad   puffs up himself

Das steife Mädchen dreht   sich
the stiff   girl   turns round herself

Nach meiner Melodie.
to   my   melody

For when I find the young folk by the linden tree, at once I rouse them; dull lads strut about, and awkward girls twirl around to my melody.

Ihr gebt den   Sohlen Flügel,
you give to the soles   wings

Und treibt durch   Tal   und Hügel
and drive   through   valley and hill

Den Liebling weit von Haus.
the darling   far   from home

Ihr lieben, holden Musen,
you dear   kind   Muses

Wann ruh ich ihr   am   Busen
when rest I   to her on the bosom

Auch endlich wieder aus?
ever at last again   -

You Muses, give wings to my feet, and send your favourite son over hill and dale, far from home. Dear, sweet Muses, when shall I find rest again on my beloved's breast?

51. *WANDERERS   NACHTLIED*
     WANDERER'S NIGHT-SONG

51. NIGHT SONG OF THE WANDERER

Johann Wolfgang von Goethe

Über allen Gipfeln
over all   (mountain-) tops

Ist Ruh,
is   peace

In allen Wipfeln
in all   tree-tops

Spürest du
feel   you

Kaum   einen Hauch;
hardly a   breath

Die Vögelein   schweigen im   Walde.
the (little) birds are silent in the wood

Over all the mountain tops is peace. In all the tree-tops you hardly feel the slightest breath; the birds are hushed in the wood. Only wait - soon you too will rest.

Warte nur! Balde
wait   only soon

Ruhest du auch.
rest   you too

52. *AUF DEM WASSER ZU SINGEN*   52. TO BE SUNG ON THE WATER
    ON THE WATER TO TO SING

Friedrich Leopold Graf von Stolberg

Mitten   im   Schimmer der   spiegelnden   Mid the shimmer and sparkle
in the midst in the shimmer of the sparkling   of rippling waves, the boat rocks
    Wellen   gently like a swan; on softly
    waves   shimmering waves of joy, the
                                                            soul glides along like the boat,
Gleitet, wie Schwäne, der wankende Kahn;   and around it the glow of the
glides   like swans   the swaying boat   sunset sky dances on the
                                                            rippling waves.
Ach, auf der   Freude sanftschimmernden Wellen
ah on of the joy   softly-shimmering waves

Gleitet die Seele dahin wie der Kahn;
glides the soul along like the small boat

Denn von dem Himmel herab auf die Wellen
for from the sky   down on the waves

Tanzet das Abendrot   rund um   den Kahn.
dances the sunset glow round about the boat

Über den Wipfeln   des   westlichen Haines   Over the tree-tops in the
over the tree-tops of the westerly   wood   westerly wood, the reddening
                                                        glow gives a cheerful greeting.
Winket uns   freundlich der rötliche Schein;   Beneath the boughs in the
signals to us cheerfully the reddish light   easterly wood, the reeds gently
                                                        rustle in the soft red glow. My
Unter den Zweigen des   östlichen Haines   soul drinks in the radiance of
under the boughs of the easterly wood   the sky, and the peace of the
                                                        woods in the reddening glow.
Säuselt der Kalmus im   rötlichen Schein;
murmurs the calamus in the reddish   light

Freude des   Himmels und Ruhe des   Haines
joy   of the sky   and peace of the wood

Atmet   die Seel im   errötenden Schein.
breathes the soul in the reddening glow

Ach, es entschwindet mit tauigem Flügel   Ah, time slips by on dewy
ah it vanishes   with dewy   wing   wings, as I am gently rocked on
                                                       the waves. Let tomorrow fly
Mir   auf den wiegenden Wellen die Zeit.   shimmering away and vanish like
to me on the rocking   waves   the time   yesterday and today, until I
                                                       myself, on loftier gleaming
Morgen   entschwinde mit schimmerndem Flügel   wings, slip away from the
tomorrow let vanish   with shimmering   wing   changes of Time.

Wieder wie gestern   und heute die Zeit,
again like yesterday and today the time

Bis   ich auf höherem strahlenden Flügel
until I   on loftier shining   wing

Selber entschwinde der   wechselnden Zeit.
myself vanish   to the changing   time

53. *DIE SCHÖNE MÜLLERIN*
    THE FAIR   MILLERESS

53. THE MILLER'S FAIR DAUGHTER

Wilhelm Müller

i.   Das Wandern
    the wandering

i. Roving.

Das Wandern   ist des   Müllers Lust,
the wandering is of the miller delight

Das Wandern!
the wandering

Das muss ein schlechter Müller sein,
that must a bad   miller to be

Dem   niemals fiel das Wandern ein,
to whom never occurs the wandering –

Das Wandern.
the wandering

Roving is a miller's delight,
roving! He'd be a bad miller,
who never thought of roving,
roving!

Vom   Wasser haben wir's gelernt,
from the water have we it learnt

Vom   Wasser!
from the water

Das hat nicht Rast bei Tag und Nacht,
that has not   rest by day and night

Ist stets auf Wanderschaft bedacht,
is always on wandering   intent

Das Wasser!
the water

We learn it from the water,
the water! It never rests by
day or night, is always rushing
on its way, the water!

Das sehn wir auch den Rädern ab,
that learn we also the wheels from

Den Rädern!
the wheels

Die gar   nicht gerne stille stehn,
they at all not like still to stand

Die sich   mein Tag nicht müde drehn,
they themselves (all) my day not tired to turn

Die Räder.
the wheels

We learn it from the mill-
wheels, the mill-wheels! They
never can be still; all day they
never tire of turning, the mill-
wheels!

Die Steine selbst,   so schwer sie sind,
the stones themselves so heavy they are

Die Steine!
the stones

Sie tanzen mit den muntern Reihn
they dance with the merry   dances

Und wollen gar noch schneller sein,
and want   even still faster   to be

Die Steine.
the stones

The very mill-stones, heavy
as they are, the mill-stones –
they join in the merry dance and
would go still faster, the mill-
stones!

O Wandern, Wandern, meine Lust,
O wandering wandering my   delight

O Wandern!
O wandering

Herr Meister und Frau Meisterin
Mr. master and Mrs. mistress

Lasst mich in Frieden weiterziehn
let   me   in peace   further to go

Und wandern.
and to wander

O roving, roving, my delight,
roving – O master and mistress
mine, just let me go my way,
roving!

　　　ii. Wohin?
　　　whither

ii. Whither?

Ich hört' ein Bächlein   rauschen
I   heard a   little brook to rush

Wohl   aus   dem Felsenquell.
probably out of the rocks–spring

Hinab zum   Tale   rauschen
down to the valley to rush

So frisch und wunderhell.
so cool   and wonderfully clear

I heard a little brook
rushing from out a rocky spring,
rushing down into the valley,
cool and wondrously clear.

Ich weiss nicht, wie mir   wurde,
I   know not   how to me became

Nicht, wer den Rat   mir   gab,
not   who the advice to me gave

Ich musste auch hinunter
I   had to too (go) down

Mit meinem Wanderstab.
with my   staff

I do not know what
compelled me, who put it into
my head; I had to go down there
too, with my staff in my hand.

Hinunter und immer weiter,
down   and always further

Und immer dem Bache nach,
and always the brook along

Und immer frischer rauschte
and always cooler   rushed

Und immer heller der Bach.
and always clearer the brook

Down and ever further, ever
following the brook; and ever
cooler and clearer the brook
rushed on.

Ist das denn meine Strasse?
is that then my   way

O Bächlein,   sprich, wohin?
O little brook say   whither

Du hast mit deinem Rauschen
you have with your   rushing

Mir ganz berauscht   den Sinn.
me quite intoxicated the mind

Is this then my path? O
little brook – tell me, where
does it lead? You have quite
bewitched my senses with your
babbling.

Was sag ich denn vom   Rauschen?
what say I   then of the rushing

Das kann kein Rauschen sein:
that can no   rushing to be

Why do I speak of babbling?
That it cannot be; it must be
the water–nymphs singing down
there in the deeps.

Es   singen wohl   die Nixen
(it) sing   probably the water-nymphs

Dort unten ihren Reihn.
there below their dance (-tunes)

Lass singen, Gesell, lass rauschen,
let to sing comrade let to rush

Und wandre fröhlich nach!
and wander merrily after

Es   gehn ja   Mühlenräder
(it) go   indeed mill-wheels

In jedem klaren Bach.
in every clear brook

Let them sing, let them
babble, and follow merrily, my
friend – mill-wheels turn in
every clear brook!

---

    iii. Halt!
       halt

iii. Halt!

Eine Mühle seh ich blinken
a   mill see I   to gleam

Aus den Erlen heraus,
from the alders forth

Durch Rauschen und Singen
through rushing and singing

Bricht Rädergebraus.
breaks wheels-roaring

I see a mill gleaming
through the elders; the roaring
of mill-wheels breaks through
the babbling and singing.

Ei willkommen, ei willkommen,
hey welcome   hey welcome

Süsser Mühlengesang!
sweet mill-song

Und das Haus, wie so traulich!
and the house how so cosy

Und die Fenster, wie blank!
and the windows how shining

Oh welcome, welcome, sweet
song of the mill! How friendly
the house looks! How sparkling
the windows!

Und die Sonne, wie helle
and the sun   how brightly

Vom   Himmel sie scheint!
from the sky   she shines

Ei, Bächlein,   liebes Bächlein,
why little brook dear   little brook

War es also gemeint?
was it thus meant

And how brightly the sun
shines in the sky! Why, little
brook, dear little brook – is
this what was meant?

---

    iv. Danksagung   an den Bach
       giving thanks to the brook

iv. Thanks to the brook

War es also gemeint,
was it thus meant

Mein rauschender Freund?
my   rushing   friend

Dein Singen, dein Klingen,
your singing your sounding

War es also gemeint?
was it thus meant

Is this what was meant, my
rushing friend? Is this what
your singing and babbling
meant?

Zur   Müllerin   hin!
to the miller's daughter thither

So lautet der Sinn.
so ran   the sense

Gelt,   hab' ich's verstanden?
is it not so have I it   understood

Zur   Müllerin   hin!
to the miller's daughter thither

Hat sie dich geschickt?
has she you   sent

Oder hast mich berückt?
or   have me   charmed

Das möcht   ich noch wissen,
that should like I   still to know

Ob sie dich geschickt.
if she you   sent

Nun, wie 's auch mag sein,
well how-it -ever may to be

Ich gebe   mich   drein;
I   submit myself to it

Was ich such, ist gefunden
what I   seek is found

Wie's   immer mag sein.
how-it -ever may to be

Nach Arbeit ich frug.
for work   I   asked

Nun hab ich genug;
now have I   enough

Für die Hände, fürs   Herze
for the hands for the heart

Vollauf   genug!
abundantly enough

            v. Am   Feierabend
               in the evening rest-hour

Hätt ich tausend Arme zu rühren!
had I   thousand arms to to move

Könnt ich brausend die Räder führen!
could I   furiously the wheels to drive

Könnt ich wehen   durch   alle Haine!
could I   to blow through all woods

Könnt ich drehen alle Steine!
could I   to turn all stones

Dass die schöne Müllerin
that the lovely miller's daughter

Merkte   meinen treuen Sinn!
perceived my   true   nature

Go to the miller's
daughter! That was the message.
Is that it? Have I grasped it
aright? Go to the miller's
daughter!

Did she send you? Or did
you bewitch me? I should so
like to know if she sent you.

Well, whatever it was I'll
accept it; I've found what I
was looking for, whatever it was.

I asked for work, now I've
enough for my hands, and my
heart - more than enough!

v. Evening rest

If I had but a thousand arms
to use! If I could furiously
drive the mill-wheels! If I
could blow like the wind through
all the woods! If I could turn
all the mill-stones! If only
the lovely miller's daughter
could know my true heart!

Ach, wie ist mein Arm so schwach!
alas how is my   arm so weak

Was ich hebe, was ich trage,
what I   lift what I   carry

Was ich schneide, was ich schlage,
what I   chop   what I   fell

Jeder Knappe   tut mir's   nach.
every miller's boy does to me it after

Und da   sitz ich in der grossen Runde,
and there sit I   in the great   circle

In der stillen kühlen Feierstunde,
in the still   cool rest-hour

Und der Meister spricht zu allen:
and the master says   to all

Euer Werk hat mir gefallen;
your work has me pleased

Und das liebe Mädchen sagt
and the dear maiden says

Allen   eine gute Nacht.
to everyone a   good night

        vi. Der Neugierige
          the curious one

Ich frage keine Blume,
I   ask   no   flower

Ich frage keiner Stern;
I   ask   no   star

Sie können mir alle nicht sagen,
they can   me all not   to say

Was ich erführ   so gern.
what I   would learn so gladly

Ich bin ja   auch   kein Gärtner,
I   am indeed really no   gardener

Die Sterne stehn zu hoch;
the stars are   too high

Mein Bächlein   will ich fragen,
my   little brook will I   to ask

Ob mich mein Herz belog.
if me   my   heart deceived

O Bächlein   meiner Liebe,
O little brook of my love

Wie bist du heut so stumm!
how are you today so silent

Will ja nur eines   wissen,
will truly only one thing to know

Ein Wörtchen   um   und um
a   little word round and round

Alas, my arm is so weak!
What I can lift, and carry, and
chop, and fell, so can every
other miller's boy.

There I sit in the big
family circle, in the still,
cool hour when work is done. And
the master says to us all, 'Your
work has pleased me', and the
sweet maid bids us all good-
night.

vi. Curiosity

I do not ask the flowers, I
do not ask the stars; none of
them can tell me what I so long
to know.

I am indeed no gardener, and
the stars are too high; I will
ask my little brook if my heart
deceives me.

O little brook of my love,
how silent you are today! I only
want to hear one thing, one
little word again and again.

Ja heisst   das eine Wörtchen,
yes is called that one little word

Das andre heisset   nein,
the other is called no

Die beiden Wörtchen   schliessen
the both   little words enclose

Die ganze Welt mir   ein.
the whole world to me –

O Bächlein   meiner Liebe,
O little brook of my love

Was bist du wunderlich!
what are you strange

Will's ja   nicht weiter sagen,
will it truly not   further to say

Sag, Bächlein,   liebt sie mich?
say little brook loves she me

That one word is 'yes' –
the other is 'no'. These two
words enclose my whole world.

O little brook of my love,
how strange you are! I will tell
no one else – but, little brook,
does she love me?

vii. Ungeduld
impatience

vii. Impatience

Ich schnitt'   es gern in alle Rinden ein,
I   would carve it gladly in all barks into

Ich grüb   es gern in jeden Kieselstein,
I   would engrave it gladly in every pebble

Ich möcht   es sä'n auf jedes frische Beet
I   would like it to sow on every fresh   flower-bed

Mit Kressensamen, der es schnell verrät,
with cress-seeds   which it quickly reveals

Auf jeden weissen Zettel   möcht   ich's
on every white   scrap of paper would like I it
  schreiben:
  to write

Dein ist mein Herz, und soll es ewig   bleiben.
yours is my   heart and shall it for ever to remain

I'd like to carve it on the
bark of every tree! I'd like to
engrave it on every pebble! I'd
like to sow it in every flower-
bed with cress-seeds that would
soon reveal it. On every blank
scrap of paper I'd like to
write, 'My heart is yours, and
will be so for evermore!'

Ich möcht   mir   ziehen einen jungen Star,
I   would like to me to train a   young starling

Bis dass er spräch   die Worte rein und klar,
until that he would say the words pure and clear

Bis er sie spräch   mit meines Mundes Klang,
until he them would say with of my mouth   sound

Mit meines Herzens vollem, heissem Drang;
with of my heart   full   hot   urgency

Dann säng   er hell   durch ihre
then would sing he clearly through her
  Fensterscheiben:
  window-panes

Dein ist mein Herz, und soll es ewig   bleiben.
yours is my   heart and shall it for ever to remain

I'd like to train a young
starling to say the words pure
and clear; say them with the
sound of my voice, with all the
burning desire of my heart. Then
at her window it would brightly
sing, 'My heart is yours, and
will be so for evermore!'

Den Morgenwinden möcht   ich's hauchen   ein,
the morning-winds would like I it to breathe into

Ich möcht   es säuseln   durch   den regen Hain;
I would like it to murmur through the lively wood

O leuchtet' es aus jedem Blumenstern!
O shone   it from every flower-star

Trüg   es der Duft   zu ihr von nah und fern!
carried it the fragrance to her from near and far

Ihr Wogen, könnt ihr nichts als Räder treiben?
you waves could you nothing but wheels to drive

Dein ist mein Herz, und soll es ewig   bleiben.
yours is my heart and shall it for ever to remain

Ich meint, es müsst in meinen Augen stehn,
I thought it must in my   eyes to be

Auf meinen Wangen müsst man's brennen sehn,
on my   cheeks must one it to burn to see

Zu lesen wär's   auf meinem stummen Mund,
to read would be it on my   silent mouth

Ein jeder Atemzug gäb's   laut ihr
an each breath would proclaim it loudly to her
  kund,
  -

Und sie merkt nichts von all dem bangen
and she notices nothing of all the anxious
  Treiben:
  doings

Dein ist mein Herz, und soll es ewig   bleiben!
yours is my heart and shall it for ever to remain

I'd like to whisper it into the morning breeze, I'd like to murmur it in every stirring wood. O if it but shone from every starry flower, whose fragrance could bear it to her from near and far! You ripples there, can you move nothing but mill-wheels? 'My heart is yours, and will be so for evermore!'

I thought it must be shining in my eyes, be seen on my burning cheeks. I thought it must be read on my silent lips, that each breath must betray it. Yet she saw nothing of all this fearful longing, 'My heart is yours, and will be so for evermore!'

    viii. Morgengruss
        morning-greeting

viii. Morning greeting

Guten Morgen, schöne   Müllerin!
good morning beautiful miller's-daughter

Wo   steckst du gleich das Köpfchen   hin,
where put   you at once the little head there

Als wär   dir   was   geschehen?
as would be to you something happened

Verdriesst dich denn mein Gruss so schwer?
vexes   you then my greeting so gravely

Verstört dich denn mein Blick so sehr?
troubles you then my glance so much

So muss ich wieder gehen.
so must I again to go

Good morning, lovely miller's daughter! Why do you hide your face as if something troubled you? Does my greeting so displease you? Does my glance so trouble you? Then I must go away.

O lass mich nur von ferne stehn,
O let me only from afar to stand

Nach deinem lieben Fenster sehn,
at   your dear window to look

Von ferne, ganz von ferne!
from afar   quite from afar

Du blondes Köpfchen, komm hervor!
you fair   little head come forth

O let me but stand at a distance, gazing from afar at your dear window, just from afar! Little fair head, come forth! Little blue morning stars, come forth from your rounded gateway!

Hervor aus eurem runden Tor,
forth from your round gateway

Ihr blauen Morgensterne!
you blue   morning-stars

Ihr schlummertrunknen Äugelein,
you slumber-intoxicated (little) eyes

Ihr taubetrübten Blümelein,
you dew-troubled little flowers

Was scheuet   ihr die Sonne?
what shrink from you the sun

Hat es die Nacht so gut gemeint,
has it the night so well meant

Dass ihr euch   schliesst und bückt und weint
that you yourselves close   and bow   and weep

Nach ihrer stillen Wonne?
for her   silent ecstasy

Little slumber-filled eyes,
little flowers weighed down with
dew, why do you shrink from the
sunlight? Was the night so good
that you close, bow down, and
weep for her silent ecstasy?

Nun schüttelt ab der   Träume Flor,
now shake   off of the dreams veil

Und hebt euch   frisch und frei empor
and lift yourselves freshly and freely upwards

In   Gottes hellen Morgen!
into God's bright morning

Die Lerche wirbelt in der Luft;
the lark   trills in the air

Und aus dem tiefen Herzen ruft
and from the deep   heart calls

Die Liebe Leid und Sorgen.
the love pain and grief

Shake off the veil of dreams,
and fresh and free, raise your
heads into God's bright
morning! A lark trills high in
the air, and from the depths of
my heart, love declares its pain
and grief.

   ix. Des   Müllers Blumen
      of the miller flowers

ix. The miller's flowers

Am   Bach viel kleine Blumen stehn,
by the brook many little flowers are

Aus hellen blauen Augen sehn;
from clear blue   eyes look

Der Bach, der ist der Müllers Freund,
the brook he is the miller's friend

Und hellblau Liebchens   Auge scheint,
and light-blue sweetheart's eye shines

Drum   sind es   meine Blumen.
therefore are they my   flowers

Many little flowers grow
by the brook, gaze up with
clear blue eyes. The brook is
the miller's friend, and my
sweetheart's bright eyes are
blue, so they are my flowers.

Dicht unter ihrem Fensterlein,
close under her   little window

Da   will ich pflanzen die Blumen ein;
there will I   to plant the flowers -

Da   ruft ihr zu, wenn alles   schweigt,
there call her to when everything is silent

Wenn sich ihr Haupt zum   Schlummer neigt,
when itself her head to the slumber   bows

Ihr wisst ja,   was ich meine.
you know certainly what I   mean

Close beneath her little
window I will plant the flowers.
Call to her there, little
flowers, when all is still and
she lays down her head for
slumber - you know what I
would say.

Und wenn sie tät   die Äuglein   zu
and when she would close the little eyes -

Und schläft in süsser, süsser Ruh,
and sleeps in sweet   sweet sleep

Dann lispelt als ein Traumgesicht
then whisper as a   vision

Ihr zu: Vergiss, vergiss mein nicht!
her to forget   forget of me not

Das ist es, was ich meine.
that is it what I   mean

And when she closes her eyes and sleeps in sweet repose, then whisper to her in her dreams: 'Forget, forget me not!' That is what I would say.

Und schliesst sie früh die Laden   auf,
and opens   she early the shutters -

Dann schaut mit Liebesblick   hinauf;
then look   with loving-glance up

Der Tau in euren Äugelein,
the dew in your   (little) eyes

Das sollen meine Tränen sein,
that shall   my   tears to be

Die will ich auf euch weinen.
that will I   on   you to weep

And early when she opens the shutters, gaze up at her lovingly; the dew in your eyes will be the tears that I will weep upon you.

      x. Tränenregen
        tears-rain

    x. Rain of tears

Wir sassen so traulich beisammen
we   sat   so cosily   together

Im   kühlen Erlendach,
in the cool   alder-roof

Wir schauten so traulich zusammen
we   looked at so cosily   together

Hinab den rieselnden Bach.
down the rippling   brook

We sat so close under the cool roof of the alders; and together we gazed at the rippling brook.

Der Mond war auch gekommen,
the moon was also come

Die Sternlein   hinterdrein,
the little stars afterwards

Und schauten so traulich zusammen
and looked   so cosily   together

In   den silbernen Spiegel hinein.
into the silvery   mirror into

The moon appeared, and then the little stars, and they too gazed into the silvery mirror.

Ich sah   nach keinem Monde,
I   looked at   no   moon

Nach keinem Sternenschein,
at   no   star-light

Ich schaute nach ihrem Bilde,
I   looked at her   image

Nach ihren Augen allein.
at   her   eyes alone

I did not look at the moon, nor at the shining stars. I gazed at her image, at her eyes alone.

Und sahe sie nicken und blicken
and saw them to nod and to glance

Herauf aus dem seligen Bach,
up   from the happy   brook

Die Blümlein   am   Ufer, die blauen,
the little flowers on the bank the blue ones

Sie nickten und blickten ihr nach.
they nodded and glanced   her at

I saw them twinkling as they
glanced up from the joyful
brook. The little blue flowers
on the bank nodded as they
looked up at her.

Und in den Bach versunken
and in the brook sunk

Der ganze Himmel schien,
the whole sky   appeared

Und wollte mich mit   hinunter
and wanted me   with (him) downwards

In seine Tiefe ziehn.
into his   depths to draw

The whole sky appeared deep
in the brook, and seemed to draw
me down into its depths.

Und über den Wolken und Sternen,
and above the clouds and stars

Da   rieselte munter der Bach
there rippled merrily the brook

Und rief mit Singen und Klingen:
and called with singing and sounding

Geselle, Geselle, mir nach!
brother brother me after

And above the clouds and
stars the brook rippled merrily,
calling in its singing and
gurgling, 'Brother, brother,
follow me!'

Da   gingen die Augen mir   über,
then went   the eyes to me over

Da   ward es im   Spiegel so kraus;
there was it in the mirror so ruffled

Sie sprach: Es kommt ein Regen,
she said   it comes a   rain

Ade!   ich geh   nach Haus!
farewell I   am going - home -

Then the tears in my eyes
overflowed, and the smooth
mirror was blurred. She said,
'It's beginning to rain.
Goodbye, I'm going home!'

    xi. Mein!
       mine

xi. Mine!

Bächlein,   lass dein Rauschen sein!
little brook let your rushing to be

Räder, stellt eur Brausen ein!
wheels cease your roaring -

All ihr muntern Waldvögelein,
all you merry   little woodland-birds

Gross und klein, endet eure Melodein!
large and small end   your melodies

Little brook, stop your
rushing! Mill-wheels, cease your
roaring! All you merry birds in
the wood, great and small, hush
your melodies!

Durch   den Hain aus und ein
through the wood out and in

Schalle heut ein Reim allein:
sound   today one rhyme alone

Die geliebte Müllerin   ist mein!
the beloved miller's daughter is mine

Today in the wood, let one
refrain alone sound far and
wide: the beloved miller's
daughter is mine!

Frühling, sind das alle dein Blümelein?
spring   are that all   your little flowers

Sonne, hast du keine hellern Schein?
sun   have you no   brighter light

Ach, so muss ich ganz allein,
alas so must I   quite alone

Mit dem seligen Worte mein,
with the blessed word   mine

Unverstanden in der weiten Schöpfung sein!
not understood in the wide   creation to be

Spring, have you no more little flowers? Sun, have you no brighter rays? Alas, in the blindness of creation, I alone must proclaim this precious word, 'mine'.

xii. Pause
pause

xii. Pause.

Meine Laute hab ich gehängt an die Wand,
my   lute have I   hung   on the wall

Hab sie umschlungen mit einem grünen Band –
have her wound round with a   green ribbon

Ich kann nicht mehr singen, mein Herz ist zu voll.
I   can not   more to sing my   heart is too full

Weiss nicht, wie ich's im Reime zwingen soll.
know not   how I it   in the rhyme to force shall

I have hung my lute on the wall, and twined a green ribbon round it – I can no longer sing, my heart is too full. I no longer know how to make it rhyme.

Meiner Sehnsucht allerheissesten Schmerz
of my longing   most-burning   pain

Durft ich aushauchen in Liederscherz,
needed I   to breathe out in song-jest

Und wie ich klagte so süss und fein,
and as I   lamented so sweet and fine

Glaubt ich doch, mein Leiden wär nicht klein.
believed I yet   my   suffering were not   small

I wanted to ease the burning pain of my longing in light-hearted song, yet in my sweet and gentle lament, I felt my suffering far from small.

Ei, wie gross ist wohl meines Glückes Last,
oh how great is indeed of my happiness burden

Dass kein Klang auf Erden es in sich fasst?
that no   sound on earth it in himself contains

Nun, liebe Laute, ruh an dem Nagel hier!
now dear lute   rest on the nail   here

Und weht ein Lüftchen über die Saiten dir,
and blows a   little breeze over the strings to you

Und streift eine Biene mit ihren Flügeln dich,
and brushes a   bee   with her   wings   you

Da wird mir so bange und es
then becomes to me so uneasy and it
  durchschauert mich!
  chills all through me

Oh, how great is the burden of my joy, that no sound on earth can contain it? Now, dear lute, rest here on this nail! But when a gentle breeze flutters over you, or a bee brushes you with its wings, I am uneasy, and a shiver runs through me.

Warum liess ich das Band auch hängen so lang?
why let I   the ribbon ever to hang so long

Oft fliegt's um die Saiten mit seufzendem
often flies it about the strings with sighing
  Klang.
  sound

Why did I let the ribbon hang so long? Often it touches the strings with a sighing sound. Is it the echo of love's pain? Can it be the prelude to new songs?

Ist es der Nachklang meiner Liebespein?
is it the echo   of my loves-pain

Soll es das Vorspiel neuer Lieder sein?
shall it the prelude of new songs to be

      xiii. Mit dem grünen Lautenbande
            with the green lute's-ribbon

'*Schad um   das schöne grüne Band,*
 pity about the lovely green ribbon

Das es verbleicht hier an der Wand,
that it fades   here on the wall

Ich hab das grün so gern!'
I   (am) the green so (fond of*)

So sprachst du, Liebchen, heut zur   mir;
so said   you sweetheart today to the me

Gleich knüpf ich's ab und send es dir:
at once unbind I it   - and send es to you

Nun hab das Grüne gern!
now (be) the green (fond of)

Ist auch dein ganzer Liebster weiss,
is even your whole dearest white

Soll Grün doch haben   seinen Preis,
shall green still to have its   price

Und ich auch hab es gern.
and I   also (am) it (fond of)

Weil   unsre Lieb ist immer grün,
because our   love is ever green

Weil Grün der Hoffnung Fernen   blühn,
because green of the hope   distances to blossom

Drum   haben wir es gern.
therefore (are) we it (fond of)

Nun schlinge in die Locken dein
now twine   in the locks your

Das grüne Band   gefällig ein,
the green ribbon kindly   -

Du hast ja's   Grün so gern.
you (are) indeed it green so (fond of)

Dann weiss ich, wo   die Hoffnung wohnt,
then know I   where the hope   dwells

Dann weiss ich, wo   die Liebe thront,
then know I   where the love reigns

Dann hab ich's Grün erst   gern.
then (am) I it   green more than ever (fond of)

xiii. The lute's green ribbon

   'A pity about the fine green
ribbon, fading here on the wall.
I'm so fond of green!' That is
what you said to me today,
sweetheart. At once I unbound
it, and sent it to you – now
enjoy the green!

   Even if your dearest one is
white and pale, green still has
its price, and I'm fond of it
too. Our love is ever green, and
distance enhances the green of
hope – that's why we're fond of
it.

   Now twine the green ribbon
in your locks, you're so fond
of green. Then shall I know
where hope dwells, then shall I
know where love is enthroned –
only then shall I really love
green.

gern haben - to be fond of

xiv. Der Jäger
   the huntsman

                                       xiv. The huntsman

Was   sucht denn der Jäger   am   Mühlbach
what seeks then the huntsman by the mill-stream
  hier?
  here

Bleib, trotziger Jäger,   in deinem Revier!
stay   obstinate huntsman in your   preserve

Hier gibt es   kein Wild zu jagen   für dich,
here (is there) no   game to to hunt for you

Hier wohnt nur ein Rehlein,   ein zahmes,   für mich.
here lives only a   little doe a   tame (one) for me

Und willst du   das zärtliche Rehlein   sehn,
and want   you the tender   little doe to see

So lass deine Büchsen im   Walde stehn,
so leave your   rifle   in the forest to stand

Und lass deine kläffenden Hunde zu Haus,
and leave your   yelping   dogs   at home

Und lass   auf dem Horne den Saus und Braus,
and leave alone on the horn the rush and roar

Und schere vom   Kinne das struppige Haar;
and shave from the chin the bristly   hair

Sonst   scheut   sich   im   Garten das
otherwise is afraid (itself) in the garden the
  Rehlein   fürwahr.
  little doe truly

Doch besser, du bliebest im   Walde dazu
still better you stayed   in the wood therefore

Und liessest die Mühlen und Müller in Ruh.
and left   the mills and millers in peace

Was taugen   die Fischlein   im
what are of use the (little) fishes in the
  grünen Gezweig?
  green branches

Was will denn das Eichhorn im   bläulichen Teich?
what wants then the squirrel in the bluish   pool

Drum   bleibe, du trotziger Jäger,   im   Hain,
therefore stay   you obstinate huntsman in the wood

Und lass mich mit meinen drei Rädern allein;
and leave me   with my   three wheels alone

Und willst meinem Schätzchen   dich   machen
and want   to my little treasure yourself to make
  beliebt,
  beloved

So wisse, mein Freund, was ihr Herzchen   betrübt:
so know   my   friend what her little heart troubles

Die Eber,   die kommen zu Nacht aus   dem Hain
the wild boars that come   at night out of the wood

Und brechen in   ihren Kohlgarten   ein,
and break   into her   cabbage-garden (in)

What does the huntsman seek here by the mill-stream? Bold huntsman, stay in your own preserve! There's no game here for you to hunt; only a little doe lives here, a tame one, that's mine. If you want to see this gentle doe, then leave your gun in the forest, and leave your yelping hounds at home, and stop all that noise on your horn, and shave off that bristly hair from your chin — or my little doe in her garden will take fright.

Better still, just stay in the woods, and leave mills and millers alone. What would fishes do in green branches? What would a squirrel want in a blue pool? So, bold huntsman, just stay in the woods, and leave me alone with my three mill-wheels. If you want to win favour with my sweetheart, then you should know, my friend, what troubles her little heart: wild boars come out of the wood at night, break into her cabbage patch, trample and root up her field — shoot those boars, you hunting hero!

Und treten und wühlen herum in dem Feld;
and trample and root about in the field

Die Eber, die schiesse, du Jägerheld!
the wild boars them shoot you huntsman-hero

xv. *Eifersucht und Stolz*
jealousy and pride

xv. Jealousy and pride

Wohin so schnell, so kraus und wild, mein
whither so fast so ruffled and wild my
lieber Bach?
dear brook

Eilst du voll Zorn dem frechen Bruder Jäger
hurry you full anger the impudent brother huntsman
nach?
after

Kehr um, und schilt erst deine Müllerin
turn back and scold first your miller's daughter

Für ihren leichten, losen, kleinen Flattersinn.
for her light wanton petty fickleness

Kehr um!
turn back

Whither so fast, so ruffled and wild, dear little brook? Are you hurrying so angrily after our impudent brother huntsman? Turn back, and first scold your miller's daughter for her light, wanton, petty fickleness.

Sahst du sie gestern Abend nicht am
saw you her yesterday evening not at the
Tore stehn,
gate to stand

Mit langem Halse nach der grossen Strasse sehn?
with long neck towards the great road to look

Wenn von dem Fang der Jäger lustig zieht
when from the capture the huntsman gaily goes
nach Haus,
homewards

Da steckt kein sittsam Kind den Kopf zum
then puts no modest child the head to the
Fenster 'naus.
window out

Did you see her last night standing at the gate, craning her neck to see down the road? When the huntsman goes gaily homewards after the kill, no modest girl sticks her head out of the window!

Geh, Bächlein, hin und sag ihr das; doch
go little brook thither and say to her that but
sag ihr nicht,
say to her not

Hörst du, kein Wort von meinem traurigen Gesicht;
hear you no word of my melancholy face

Sag ihr: Er schnitzt' bei mir sich eine Pfeif
say to her he cut by me himself a pipe
aus Rohr
out of reed

Und bläst den Kindern schöne Tänz und
and blows to the children pretty dances and
Lieder vor.
songs (to).

Go, little brook, and tell her this; but not one word, do you hear, of my melancholy face! Tell her, he cut himself a reed-pipe, and plays pretty dances and songs to the children.

xvi. Die liebe   Farbe
   the beloved colour

xvi. The beloved colour

In Grün will ich mich   kleiden,
in green will I   myself to dress

I will dress in green, in
green weeping-willow; my love
is so fond of green. I will seek
a cypress grove, a heath full of
rosemary; my love is so fond of
green.

In grüne Tränenweiden:
in green weeping-willow

Mein Schatz   hat's   Grün   so gern
my   treasure (is) the green so (fond of*)

Will suchen   einen Zypressenhain,
will to seek a   cypress-grove

Eine Heide von grünen Rosmarein:
a   heath of   green rosemary

Mein Schatz   hat's   Grün   so gern.
my   treasure (is) the green so (fond of)

Wohlauf zum   fröhlichen Jagen!
away   to the merry   hunting

Away to the merry hunt, away
through heath and meadow! My
love is so fond of a hunt. The
game I hunt is death, the heath
I call 'love's-grief'; my love
is so fond of a hunt.

Wohlauf durch   Heid und Hagen!
away   through heath and meadows

Mein Schatz   hat's   Jagen   so gern.
my   treasure (is) the hunting so (fond of)

Das Wild, das ich jage, das ist der Tod;
the game that I   hunt that is the death

Die Heide, die heiss ich die Liebesnot:
the heath that call I   the love's-misery

Mein Schatz   hat's   Jagen   so gern.
my   treasure (is) the hunting so (fond of)

Grabt mir ein Grab im   Wasen,
dig   me a   grave in the grass

Dig me a grave in the sward,
and cover me with green turf; my
love is so fond of green. No
black cross, no gay flowers –
let all around be green, green.
My love is so fond of green.

Deckt mich mit grünen Rasen:
cover me   with green turf

Mein Schatz   hat's   Grün   so gern.
my   treasure (is) the green so (fond of)

Kein Kreuzlein   schwarz, kein Blümlein
no   (little) cross black   no   (little) flower
  bunt,
  gay-coloured

Grün, alles   grün so rings und rund:
green everything green so round and round about

Mein Schatz   hat's   Grün   so gern.
my   treasure (is) the green so (fond of)

xvii. Die böse Farbe
    the bad   colour

xvii. The hateful colour

Ich möchte   ziehn in   die Welt hinaus,
I   would like to go into the world forth

I'd like to go out into the
world, out into the wide world.
If only it were not so green, so
green out there in forest and
field!

Hinaus in   die weite Welt;
forth into the wide   world

*gern haben – to be fond of

Wenn's nur so grün, so grün nicht wär,
if it only so green so green not were

Da draussen in Wald und Feld!
there outside in forest and field

Ich möchte die grünen Blätter all
I would like the green leaves all

I'd like to pluck all the
green leaves from every bough;
I'd like to weep on all the
green grass, till it was pale
as death.

Pflücken von jedem Zweig,
to pluck from every twig

Ich möchte die grünen Gräser all
I would like the green grasses all

Weinen ganz totenbleich.
to weep quite deathly-pale

Ach Grün, du böse Farbe du,
ah green you bad colour you

Ah, green, you hateful
colour! Why do you always look
at me, so proud, so impudent, so
gloating - at me, a poor, pale
man?

Was siehst mich immer an
what look me always at

So stolz, so keck, so schadenfroh,
so proud so impudent so gloating

Mich armen weissen Mann?
me poor white man

Ich möchte liegen vor ihrer Tür,
I would like to lie before her door

I'd like to lie at her door
in storm, and rain, and snow,
and sing so softly, day and
night, the one little word,
'farewell!'

In Sturm und Regen und Schnee,
in storm and rain and snow

Und singen ganz leise bei Tag und Nacht
and to sing quite softly by day and night

Das eine Wörtchen ade!
the one little word farewell

Horch, wenn im Wald ein Jagdhorn schallt,
hark when in the forest a hunting-horn sounds

Hark, when a hunting-horn
sounds in the forest, you can
hear her little window! And
though she doesn't look out for
me, I can look in at her.

So klingt ihr Fensterlein,
so sounds her little window

Und schaut sie auch nach mir nicht aus,
and looks she even for me not out

Darf ich doch schauen hinein.
may I yet to look in

O binde von der Stirn dir ab
O unbind from the brow to you -

O unwind that green, green
ribbon from your brow.
Farewell, farewell! And as I
part, give me your hand.

Das grüne, grüne Band;
the green green ribbon

Ade, ade! und reiche mir
farewell farewell and give to me

Zum Abschied deine Hand!
to the parting your hand

xviii. Trockne Blumen
     dry   flowers

xviii. Withered flowers

Ihr Blümlein   alle, die sie mir   gab,
you little flowers all   that she to me gave

Euch soll man legen mit mir ins   Grab.
you   shall one to lay with me   in the grave

Wie seht ihr alle mich an so weh,
how look you all   me   at so sadly

Als ob ihr wüsstet, wie mir   gescheh?
as   if you knew   how to me (would) happen

Ihr Blümlein   alle, wie welk,   wie blass?
you little flowers all   how withered how pale

Ihr Blumlein   alle, wovon   so nass?
you little flowers all   what of so wet

All you little flowers that she gave me shall be laid with me in my grave. How sadly you look at me - do you know what has happened? All you little flowers, why are you so withered, so pale, and why so wet?

Ach, Tränen machen nicht maiengrün,
alas tears make   not   May-green

Machen tote Liebe nicht wieder blühn.
make   dead love not   again to blossom

Und Lenz   wird kommen, und Winter wird gehn,
and spring will to come and winter will to go

Und Blümlein   werden im   Grase stehn.
and little flowers will   in the grass to stand

Und Blümlein   liegen in meinem Grab,
and little flowers lie   in my   grave

Die Blümlein   alle, die   sie mir   gab.
the little flowers all   which she to me gave

Tears, alas, cannot bring the green of May, nor make dead love blossom again. Spring will come, winter will go, and flowers will grow in the grass; little flowers will lie in my grave, all those that she gave me.

Und wenn sie wandelt am   Hügel vorbei
and when she wanders on the hill   by

Und denkt im   Herzen: der meint' es treu!
and thinks in the heart   he meant   it truly

Dann Blümlein   alle, heraus, heraus!
then little flowers all   out   out

Der Mai ist kommen, der Winter ist aus.
the May is   come   the winter has ended

And when she wanders by on the hill, and thinks in her heart, 'His love was true', then, all you flowers, come forth, come forth! Spring has come, winter is ended!

xix. Der Müller und der Bach
     the miller and the brook

xix. The miller and the brook

(Der Müller)
  the miller

(The miller)

Wo   ein treues Herze in Liebe vergeht,
when a   true   heart in love   perishes

Da   welken die Lilien auf jedem Beet;
then fade   the lilies in   every bed

Da   muss in die Wolken der Vollmond gehn,
then must in the clouds the full moon to go

Damit   seine Tränen die Menschen nicht sehn;
so that his   tears the people   not   see

When a faithful heart dies of love, in every flower-bed the lilies fade; the full moon goes behind the clouds, that men should not see her tears; angels cover their eyes, and sobbing, sing the soul to rest.

Da   halten   die Engelein   die Augen
then keep shut the (little) angels the eyes
  sich   zu
  (themselves) -

Und schluchzen und singen die Seele zur   Ruh.
and sob   and sing   the soul to the rest

(Der Bach)
  the brook

Und wenn sich   die Liebe dem   Schmerz entringt,
and when (herself) the love to the sorrow breaks away

Ein Sternlein, ein neues, am   Himmel erblinkt;
a little star a new one in the sky   twinkles

Da   springen drei Rosen, halb rot und halb weiss,
then spring   three roses half red and half white

Die welken nicht wieder, aus Dornenreis.
that wither not   again   from thorn-twig

Und die Engelein   schneiden die Flügel
and the (little) angels clip   the wings
  sich   ab
  themselves off

Und gehn alle Morgen   zur   Erde herab.
and go   all mornings to the earth down

(Der Müller)
  the miller

Ach Bächlein,   liebes Bächlein,   du meinst
ah little brook dear   little brook you mean
  es so gut;
  it so well

Ach Bächlein,   aber weisst du, wie Liebe tut?
ah little brook but know   you how love does

Ach unten, da   unten die kühle Ruh!
ah below there below the cool peace

Ach Bächlein,   liebes Bächlein,   so singe
ah little brook dear   little brook so sing
  nur zu.
  only on

        xx. Des   Baches Wiegenlied
          of the brook cradle-song

Gute Ruh, gute Ruh! tu   die Augen zu!
good sleep good sleep close the eyes -

Wandrer, du müder,   · du bist zu Haus.
wanderer you tired (one) you are at home

Die Treu   ist hier, sollst liegen bei mir,
the fidelity is here shall to lie with me

Bis das Meer will trinken die Bächlein
until the ocean will to drink the little brooks
  aus.
  empty

(The brook)

   And when love struggles free
from sorrow, a new little star
shines in the sky; three roses,
half red and half white, spring
from a thorny twig, never to
wither. And angels clip their
wings, and come down each day
to earth.

(The miller)

   Ah, little brook, dear
little brook, you mean so well -
but do you know what love does?
Ah, there below, is cool peace!
So, little brook, dear little
brook, sing on!

xx. The brook's cradle-song

   Sleep well, sleep well,
close you eyes! Tired
wanderer, you are home; here
you can find fidelity. You shall
rest with me until the little
brook is swallowed by the sea.

Will betten   dich kühl auf weichem Pfühl
will to bed down you cool on soft   pillow

In dem blauen kristallenen Kämmerlein.
in the blue   crystal   little bedroom

Heran, heran, was wiegen kann,
on   on   what to rock can

Woget und wieget   den Knaben mir   ein!
billow and rock   asleep the boy   to me -

For your bed I will make you a cool, soft pillow in my blue crystal chamber. Ever on, ever on, let my son be rocked and lulled to sleep!

Wenn ein Jagdhorn   schallt aus dem
when a   hunting-horn resounds from the
   grünen Wald,
   green wood

Will ich sausen   und brausen wohl   um
will I   to bluster and to rage indeed round
   dich her.
   you about

Blickt nicht herein, blaue Blümelein!
look   not   in here blue   little flowers

Ihr macht meinem Schläfer die Träume so schwer.
you make to my   sleeper   the dreams so heavy

When a hunting-horn sounds forth from the green forest, I will rush and roar all around you. Do not peep in, little blue flowers, for you trouble the dreams of my sleeper.

Hinweg, hinweg, von dem Mühlensteg,
away   away   from the mill-path

Hinweg, hinweg, böses Mägdelein,
away   away   bad   girl

Dass ihn dein Schatten dein Schatten nicht
that him your shadow   your shadow   not
   weckt!
   wakes

Wirf mir   herein dein Tüchlein   fein,
throw to me in here your little kerchief fine

Dass ich die Augen ihm   halte bedeckt.
that I   the eyes to him hold covered

Away, bad girl, away from the mill-path, lest your shadow wake him! Throw in your fine kerchief, so I may cover his eyes.

Gute Nacht, gute Nacht! Bis alles   wacht,
good night good night until everything wakes

Schlaf aus deine Freude, schlaf aus dein Leid!
sleep out your joy   sleep out your sorrow

Der Vollmond steigt, der Nebel weicht,
the full moon rises   the mist gives way

Und der Himmel da   oben, wie ist er so weit!
and the sky   there above how is he so wide

Good-night, good-night! Till everything wakens, sleep away your joy, sleep away your grief! The full moon rises, the mist clears; the sky above is so vast.

54. *DU BIST DIE RUH*
   YOU ARE THE TRANQUILLITY

54. YOU ARE TRANQUILLITY

Friedrich Rückert

Du bist die Ruh,
you are the tranquillity

Der Friede mild,
the peace gentle

Die Sehnsucht du,
the longing   you

Und was sie stillt.
and what she assuages

You are tranquillity,
gentle peace; you are longing,
and its assuaging.

Ich weihe   dir
I   consecrate to you

Voll Lust und Schmerz
full joy and pain

Zur   Wohnung hier
to the dwelling here

Mein Aug und Herz.
my   eye and heart

Full of joy and grief, I
consecrate to you my eyes and
heart for your dwelling.

Kehr ein bei mir,
come in to me

Und schliesse du
and close   you

Still   hinter dir
quietly behind you

Die Pforte zu.
the door   —

Enter this house, and
quietly close the door behind
you.

Treib andern Schmerz
drive other grief

Aus dieser Brust!
from this   breast

Voll sei dies Herz
full be this heart

Von deiner Lust.
of your   joy

Drive other griefs from my
breast! May my heart be full of
your joy!

Dies Augenzelt,
this eyes'-tent

Von deinem Glanz
from your   brightness

Allein erhellt,
alone lit up

O füll es ganz!
O fill it wholly

Your brightness alone lights
the dwelling of my eyes — O fill
it wholly!

55. *LACHEN   UND WEINEN*
     LAUGHING AND WEEPING

55. LAUGHING AND WEEPING

Friedrich Rückert

Lachen   und Weinen   zu jeglicher Stunde
laughing and weeping at each   hour

Ruht bei der Lieb auf so mancherlei Gründe,
rests with the love on so various   reasons

Morgens   lacht'   ich vor Lust,
in the morning was laughing I   for joy

Und warum ich nun weine
and why   I   now weep

Bei des   Abendes Scheine,
in of the evening light

Ist mir   selb' nicht bewusst.
is to me myself not   known

Laughing and weeping at any
hour, with love comes from so
many things – this morning I
was laughing for joy, but why I
weep now in the evening light,
I do not know myself.

Weinen und Lachen   zu jeglicher Stunde
weeping and laughing at each   hour

Ruht bei der Lieb' auf so mancherlei Grunde.
rests with the love on so various   reasons

Abends   weint' ich vor Schmerz;
in the evening wept   I   for grief

Und warum du erwachen
and why   you to waken

Kannst am   Morgen mit Lachen,
can   in the morning with laughing

Muss ich dich fragen, o Herz.
must I   you to ask O heart

Weeping and laughing at any
hour, with love comes from so
many things. In the evening I
can weep for grief – but why I
awaken in the morning filled
with laughter, can I only ask
you, O heart!

56. *AUFLÖSUNG*
     REDEMPTION

56. REDEMPTION

Johann Mayrhofer

Verbirg dich,   Sonne,
hide   yourself sun

Denn die Gluten der   Wonne
for the fires of the ecstasy

Versengen mein Gebein;
scorch   my   bones

Verstummet,   ihr Töne,
become silent you sounds

Frühlingsschöne flüchte dich
spring's-beauty flee   (yourself)

Und lass mich allein!
and leave me   alone

Hide, O sun, for the fires
of ecstasy are scorching me!
Hush, sweet sounds! Flee away,
and leave me in peace, O
beauteous spring!

Quillen doch aus allen Falten
flow   but from all   folds

Meiner Seele liebliche Gewalten,
of my soul sweet   powers

Die mich umschlingen,
that me   embrace

Himmlisch singen;
divinely sing

Geh' unter, Welt, und störe
sink -   world and disturb

Nimmer, die süssen, ätherischen Chöre!
never   the sweet   ethereal   choruses

From every corner of my soul, sublime power flows forth, and envelopes me in divine song. Perish, world, and never more disturb this sweet ethereal harmony!

57. ROMANZE
   ROMANCE

57. ROMANCE

Helmina von Chézy
(from the play *Rosamunde*)

Der Vollmond strahlt auf Bergeshöhn,
the full-moon shines on mountain-tops

Wie hab' ich dich vermisst!
how have I   you missed

Du süsses Herz! es ist so schön
you sweet heart it is so beautiful

Wenn treu die Treue   küsst.
when truly the true one kisses

The full moon shines on the mountain-tops – O how I have missed you! Dear heart, how beautiful it is when true love truly kisses.

Was frommt des   Maien holde Zier?
what avails of the May   lovely adornment

Du warst mein Frühlingsstrahl!
you were my   spring's-ray

Licht meiner Nacht, o lächle mir
light of my night O smile to me

Im   Tode noch einmal!
in the death still once

What avails the lovely blossoming of May? You were my radiant spring! Light of my darkness, O smile at me once more from the grave!

Sie trat hinein beim   Vollmondschein,
she went in   by the full-moon

Sie blickte himmelwärts:
she looked heavenwards

"Im   Leben fern,   im   Tode dein!"
 in the life far off in the death yours

Und sanft brach Herz an Herz.
and softly broke heart on heart

In the light of the full moon she appeared, and looked towards Heaven. "In life apart, yours in death!" and softly our two hearts were broken.

58. *IM   ABENDROT*
    IN THE SUNSET

58. IN THE SUNSET

Carl Lappe

O, wie schön ist deine Welt, Vater,
O how lovely is   your   world Father

Wenn sie golden strahlet!
when she golden shines

Wenn dein Glanz   hernieder fällt
when your brightness down   falls

Und den Staub mit Schimmer malet;
and the dust with lustre   paints

Wenn das Rot, das in der Wolke blinkt,
when the red that in the cloud gleams

In   mein stilles Fenster sinkt!
into my   quiet   window sinks

Könnt' ich klagen? Könnt' ich zagen?
could I   to lament could I   to be afraid

Irre   sein an   dir und mir?
in error to be towards you and me

Nein, ich will im   Busen tragen
no   I   will in the bosom to carry

Deinen Himmel schon   allhier,
your   heaven already here indeed

Und dies Herz, eh'   es zusammenbricht,
and this heart before it breaks

Trinkt noch Glut und schlürft noch Licht.
drinks still glow and sips   still light

How lovely is Your world, O
Father, when it shines golden,
and Your brightness comes down
to paint the earth with its
lustre; when the redness
glowing in the clouds sinks in
through my quiet window. How
can I lament? How can I be
afraid? How can I doubt You?
No, I will carry Your Heaven
here in my breast, that my
heart, before it breaks, may
drink in the glow and the
light.

59. *DER EINSAME*
    THE SOLITARY ONE

59. IN SOLITUDE

Carl Lappe

Wenn meine Grillen schwirren,
when my   crickets whirr

Bei Nacht, am   spät erwärmten Herd,
by night by the late warmed   hearth

Dann sitz' ich, mit vergnügtem Sinn,
then sit I   with contented mind

Vertraulich zu der Flamme hin,
intimately to the flame there

So leicht, so unbeschwert
so light so unburdened

When at night the crickets
chirp, I sit contented by my
warm hearth, and cosily gaze at
the flames, light of heart and
free from care.

Ein trautes stilles Stündchen
a   cosy   quiet   (little) hour

Bleibt man noch gern   am   Feuer wach,
stays one still with pleasure by the fire awake

Man schürt, wenn sich   die Lohe senkt,
one stirs when (herself) the blaze sinks

Die Funken auf, und sinnt   und denkt:
the sparks up and reflects and thinks

Nun abermal ein Tag!
now once more a   day

At this sweet tranquil hour, we love to gaze at the fire; stirring up sparks when the blaze dies down; thinking and reflecting – yet another day.

Was   Liebes   oder Leides
(what) pleasing (thing) or   harmful (thing)

Sein Lauf   für uns daher gebracht,
his course for us here brought

Es geht noch einmal durch den Sinn;
it goes still once   through the mind

Allein das Böse wirft man hin,
only the bad throws one away

Es störe   nicht die Nacht.
it troubles not   the night

All joys and sorrows we encountered in its course, pass once more through the mind; only the bad is cast away, that it may not trouble the night.

Zu einem frohen Traume
to a   happy dream

Bereitet man gemach   sich   zu,
prepares one comfortably himself –

Wann sorgelos ein holdes   Bild
when carefree a   pleasing image

Mit sanfter Lust   die Seele füllt,
with gentle pleasure the soul fills

Ergibt man sich   der   Ruh'.
yields one himself to the sleep

We comfortably prepare ourselves for pleasant dreams, and when some fair image lightens the heart, and longing fills the soul with gentle pleasure, we yield to sleep.

O wie ich mir   gefalle
O how I   to me please

In meiner stillen Ländlichkeit!
in my   quiet   rusticity

Was in dem Schwarm der   lauten Welt
what in the crowd of the noisy world

Das irre   Herz gefesselt hält,
the bewildered heart fettered holds

Gibt nicht Zufriedenheit.
gives not   contentment

O how contented I am in my quiet rustic way! That which enchains the wandering heart in the crowded noisy world brings no happiness.

Zirpt immer, liebe Heimchen,
chirp always dear crickets

In meiner Klause,   eng   und klein,
in my   hermitage narrow and small

Ich duld' euch gern: ihr stört
I suffer you willingly you disturb
 mich nicht,
 me   not

Wenn euer Lied das Schweigen bricht,
when your song the silence   breaks

Bin ich nicht ganz   allein.
am I not   quite alone

Chirp on, dear crickets, I welcome you in my small hermitage. You do not disturb me; when your song breaks the silence, I am no longer alone.

60. *DIE JUNGE NONNE*   60. THE YOUNG NUN
    THE YOUNG NUN

Johann Nickolaus Craigher de Jachelutta

Wie braust durch die Wipfel   der heulende   How the raging storm howls
how rages through the (tree-)tops the howling   in the tree-tops! How the
Sturm!   rafters groan, the house
storm   shudders! How the thunder
                                                       rumbles, and the lightning
Es klirren die Balken, es   zittert   das Haus!   flashes, and the night is dark
(it) clatter the rafters (it) shudders the house   as the grave!

Es rollet der Donner, es leuchtet der Blitz,
(it) rumbles the thunder (it) blazes the lightning

Und finster die Nacht, wie das Grab!
and dark   the night as the grave

Immerhin, so tobt' es auch jüngst   noch in mir!   Yet of late such storms
yet   so raged it also recently still in me   raged in me! My life blustered
                                                       as now the gale; my limbs
Es brauste das Leben, wie jetzo der Sturm,   trembled as the house; my love
(it) blustered the life   as now   the storm   flared as the lightning, and my
                                                       heart was dark as the grave.
Es bebten die Glieder, wie jetzo das Haus,
(it) quivered the limbs   as now   the house

Es flammte die Liebe, wie jetzo der Blitz,
(it) flared the love   as now   the lightning

Und finster die Brust, wie das Grab.
and dark   the breast as the grave

Nun tobe, du wilder gewaltger Sturm,   Now rage, you wild and
now rage you wild mighty   storm   mighty storm! In my heart,is
                                                       peace, in my heart tranquillity.
Im   Herzen ist Friede, im   Herzen ist Ruh!   The loving bride awaits the
in the heart is peace in the heart is tranquillity   Bridegroom, purified in a
                                                       testing fire, wedded to Eternal
Des   Bräutigams harret die liebende Braut,   Love.
(of) the bridegroom awaits the loving bride

Gereinigt in prüfender Glut,
cleansed in testing   fire

Der   ewigen Liebe getraut.
to the eternal love wedded

Ich harre, mein Heiland! mit sehnendem Blick!   I await my Saviour, longing
I await my Saviour with longing   look   in my eyes! Come, heavenly
                                                       Bridegroom, take your bride –
Komm, himmlischer Bräutigam, hole die Braut,   set free my soul from its
come heavenly   bridegroom take the bride   earthly prison.

Erlöse die Seele von irdischer Haft!
set free the soul from earthly imprisonment

Horch, friedlich ertönet das Glöcklein vom   Listen, how peacefully the
listen peacefully sounds the little bell from the   little bell sounds in the
Turm!   steeple! Its sweet tones are
steeple   calling me all-powerfully to the
                                                       eternal heights! Hallelujah!
Es lockt   mich das süsse Getön
(it) is calling me   the sweet sound

Allmächtig   zu ewigen Höhn.
all-powerfully to eternal heights

Alleluja!
Hallelujah

61. *NACHT UND TRÄUME*
    NIGHT AND DREAMS

61. NIGHT AND DREAMS

Matthäus von Collin

Heilige Nacht, du sinkest nieder,
sacred night you sink   down

Nieder wallen auch die Träume,
down   float   also the dreams

Wie dein Mondlicht durch   die Räume,
as your moonlight through the rooms

Durch   der   Menschen stille Brust.
through of the men   still breast

Die belauschen sie mit Lust;
they listen to them with joy

Rufen, wenn der Tag erwacht:
call   when the day awakens

Kehre   wieder, holde Nacht!
come back again   lovely night

Holde Träume, kehret   wieder!
lovely dreams   come back again

O sacred night, gently you
fall, and as your moonlight
steals into each room, dreams
float down and enter the still
hearts of men. They receive
these dreams with joy, and when
day breaks, they call, 'Come
back, sweet night! O lovely
dreams, come back!'

62. *AVE MARIA (ELLENS   DRITTER GESANG)*
    HAIL MARY   ELLEN'S THIRD   SONG

62. HYMN TO THE VIRGIN

(from *The Lady of the Lake*)

Sir Walter Scott
(original text)

Ave Maria!   Jungfrau mild,
hail Mary (Latin) maiden   mild

Erhöre einer Jungfrau Flehen,
hear of a maiden   supplication

Aus diesem Felsen starr und wild
from this   rock   rigid and wild

Soll mein Gebet zu dir hin   wehen.
shall my   prayer to you thither to drift

Ave Maria! maiden mild!
Listen to a maiden's prayer!
Thou canst hear though from the
                         wild;
Thou canst save amid despair.

Wir schlafen sicher bis zum   Morgen,
we sleep   safely till to the morning

Ob   Menschen noch so grausam sind.
though men   still so horrible are

O Jungfrau, sieh der   Jungfrau Sorgen,
O maiden   see of the maiden cares

O Mutter, hör ein bittend   Kind!
O mother hear an entreating child

Ave Maria!

Safe may we sleep beneath thy
                        care,
Though banished, outcast, and
                       reviled;
Maiden! Hear a maiden's prayer –
Mother, hear a suppliant child!

Ave Maria! unbefleckt!
hail Mary   undefiled

Wenn wir auf diesen Fels hinsinken
when we on this   rock sink down

Zum   Schlaf, und uns dein Schutz   bedeckt,
to the sleep   and us your protection covers

Wird weich der harte Fels uns   dünken.
will soft the hard rock to us to seem

Du lächelst, Rosendüfte wehen
you smile   rose-scents drift

In dieser dumpfen Felsenkluft.
in this   heavy   rock-cleft

O Mutter, höre Kindes Flehen,
O mother hear child's supplication

O Jungfrau, eine Jungfrau ruft!
O maiden   a   maiden   calls

Ave Maria!

Ave Maria! Reine Magd!
hail Mary   pure maid

Der   Erde und der   Luft Dämonen,
of the earth and of the air demons

Von deines Auges Huld   verjagt,
by of your eye   benevolence driven away

Sie können hier nicht bei uns wohnen.
they can   here not   with us to live

Wir wolln   uns   still   dem
we are willing (ourselves) quietly to the
  Schicksal beugen,
   fate   to bow

Da   uns dein heilger Trost anweht;
because us your holy   solace blows towards

Der   Jungfrau wolle hold   dich   neigen,
to the maiden   be   gracious (yourself) to incline
                                         towards
Dem   Kind, das für den Vater fleht!
to the child,that for the father supplicates

Ave Maria!

Ave Maria! Undefiled!
The flinty couch we now must
                         share
Shall seem with down of eider
                          piled,
If thy protection hover there.

The murky cavern's heavy air
Shall breathe of balm if thou
                    hast smiled.
Then, Maiden! Hear a maiden's
                        prayer,
Mother, list a suppliant child!

Ave Maria! Stainless styled!
Foul demons of the earth and air,
From this their wonted haunt
                        exiled,
Shall flee before thy presence
                          fair.

We bow us to our lot of care,
Beneath thy guidance reconciled.
Hear for a maid a maiden's
                        prayer
And for a father hear a child!

63. *DIE ALLMACHT*   63. OMNIPOTENCE
    THE OMNIPOTENCE

Johann Ladislav Pyrker

Gross ist Jehovah, der Herr, denn Himmel   Great is the Lord Jehovah;
great is Jehovah the Lord for Heaven   Heaven and earth proclaim His
                                                    might. You hear it in the raging
und Erde verkünden seine Macht.   storm, and in the rushing of
and earth proclaim his   might   forest streams. You hear it in
                                                    the rustling of the woods in
Du hörst sie im   brausenden Sturm,   spring; you see it in the waving
you hear her in the raging   storm   golden corn; in the glowing
                                                    splendour of sweet flowers, in
in des Waldstroms   laut aufrauschendem Ruf;   the brightness of a star-strewn
in the forest-streams loud uprushing   call   sky. Dreadfully it sounds in the
                                                    rolling of thunder, and flashes
du hörst sie in des   grünen Waldes Gesäusel,   in the jagged course of
you hear her in of the green woods rustling   lightning. Yet also in the
                                                    beating heart you feel Jehovah's
siehst sie in wogender Saaten Gold,   might, imploring you to lift
see   her in of waving corn   gold   your gaze on high to the Eternal
                                                    God, and ask His grace and
In lieblicher Blumen glühendern Schmelz,   mercy.
in of sweet   flowers glowing   lustre

im   Glanz   des   sternebesäten Himmels.
in the brilliance of the star-strewn sky

Furchtbar tönt   sie im   Donnergeroll
dreadfully sounds she in the thunder-roll

und flammt in des   Blitzes   schnell hinzuckendem
and flames in of the lightning fast   jerking away
   Flug,
   flight

doch kündet   das pochende Herz dir
yet gives warning the beating heart to you
   fühlbarer   noch
   more perceptibly still

Jehovah's Macht, des   ewigen Gottes,
Jehovah's might of the eternal God

blickst du flehend   empor und hoffst auf
look   you imploringly on high and hope   for
   Huld und Erbarmen.
   grace and mercy

64. *LIED DER   MIGNON I*   64. MIGNON'S SONG I
    SONG OF THE MIGNON

Johann Wolfgang von Goethe
(from *Wilhelm Meister;*
also set by Schumann and Wolf)

Heiss mich nicht reden,   heiss mich schweigen!   Do not ask me to speak,
bid me   not to speak bid me to be silent   rather bid me be silent! I am
                                                       bound by my secret; I long to
Denn mein Geheimnis ist mir   Pflicht;   reveal my innermost self, but
for my   secret   is to me duty   fate will not allow it.

Ich möchte   dir   mein ganzes Innre   zeigen,
I   should like to you my   whole inner self to show

Allein das Schicksal will   es nicht.
but   the fate   ordains it not

Zur   rechten Zeit vertreibt   der   Sonne Lauf
to the right   time drives away of the sun   course

Die finstre Nacht, und sie muss sich   erhellen;
the dark   night and she must herself to light up

Der harte Fels schliesst seinen Busen auf,
the hard rock opens   his   bosom -

Missgönnt der   Erde nicht die tiefverborgnen
begrudges to the earth not   the deeply hidden
    Quellen.
    springs

The sun in its due time
drives away the darkness of
night; light must appear. The
impenetrable rock opens itself
up, for the earth does not
begrudge its deeply hidden
springs.

Ein jeder sucht im   Arm des   Freundes Ruh,
everyone seeks in the arm of the friend   rest

Dort kann die Brust in Klagen sich
there can the breast in laments (herself)
    ergiessen;
    to pour forth

Allein ein Schwur drückt mir   die Lippen zu.
but   an oath   shuts to me the lips   -

Und nur ein Gott vermag sie aufzuschliessen.
and only a   god   can   them to to open

Everyone seeks rest on the
arm of a friend; there the heart
can pour forth its lament. But
an oath seals my lips, and only
a god can open them again.

65. LIED DER   MIGNON II
SONG OF THE MIGNON

65. MIGNON'S SONG II

Johann Wolfgang von Goethe
(from *Wilhelm Meister;*
also set by Beethoven, Schumann and Wolf)

Nur wer die Sehnsucht kennt,
only who the longing   knows

Weiss, was ich leide!
knows what I   suffer

Allein und abgetrennt
alone and separated

Von aller Freude,
from all   joy

Seh ich ans   Firmament
look I   at the firmament

Nach   jener Seite.
towards that side

Ach!   der mich liebt und kennt
ah   (he) who me   loves and knows

Ist in der Weite.
is in the distance

Only he who has ever longed
can know how I suffer! Alone,
severed from all joy, I gaze at
the heavens facing that place.
Ah, the one who loves and
understands me is far away. My
head is spinning; my very bowels
are on fire. Only he who has
ever longed can know how I
suffer!

Es schwindelt mir, es brennt
it is giddy   to me it burns

Mein Eingeweide.
my   bowels

Nur wer die Sehnsucht kennt,
only who the longing   knows

Weiss, was ich leide!
knows what I   suffer

66. *LIED DER   MIGNON III*   66. MIGNON'S SONG III
   SONG OF THE MIGNON

Johann Wolfgang von Goethe
(from *Wilhelm Meister;*
also set by Schumann and Wolf)

So lasst mich scheinen, bis   ich werde;   So let me appear, until I am
so let me   to appear until I   become   become thus — leave me in my
                                                 white robe! I am hastening away
Zieht mir   das weisse Kleid nicht aus!   from the beautiful earth down
take to me the white dress not   off   into that unyielding abode.

Ich eile von der schönen   Erde
I   hurry from the beautiful earth

Hinab in   jenes feste Haus.
down into   that firm house

Dort ruh' ich eine kleine Stille,   There I will rest in peace
there rest I a   little still (moment)   a while, until my eyes are
                                                 opened anew; then I will leave
Dann öffnet sich   der frische Blick;   behind the spotless robe, the
then opens (himself) the new   glance   girdle and the garland.

Ich lasse dann die reine Hülle,
I   leave then the pure covering

Den Gürtel und den Kranz   zurück.
the girdle and the garland behind

Und jene   himmlischen Gestalten,   Those heavenly spirits take
and those heavenly   figures   no heed of 'man' and 'woman',
                                                 and no garments, no folds will
Sie fragen nicht nach Mann und Weib,   cover my transfigured body.
they ask   not about man and woman

Und keine Kleider, keine Falten
and no   clothes no   folds

Umgeben den verklärten   Leib.
surround the transfigured body

Zwar   lebt' ich ohne   Sorg und Mühe,   Though I have lived free
though lived I   without care and trouble   from toil and care, yet I have
                                                 felt deep pain enough; grief has
Doch fühlt' ich tiefen Schmerz genung!   aged me before my time — 0 make
yet felt I   deep pain   enough   me for ever young again!

Vor Kummer altert' ich zu frühe,
for grief aged   I   too early

Macht mich auf ewig wieder jung!
make me   for ever again young

67. *FISCHERWEISE*
FISHER-MELODY

Franz Xaver von Schlechta

Den Fischer   fechten Sorgen
the fisherman assail cares

Und Gram und Leid   nicht an;
and grief and sorrow not   -

Er löst   am   frühen Morgen
he unties in the early   morning

Mit   leichtem Sinn den Kahn.
with light   mind the boat

No cares, no grief or sorrow
trouble the fisherman; early in
the morning he casts off his
boat with a light heart.

Da   lagert   rings noch Friede
there lies spread out around still peace

Auf Wald und Flur   und Bach,
on   wood and meadow and brook

Er ruft   mit seinem Liede
he rouses with his   song

Die gold'ne Sonne wach.
the golden sun   awake

All is peace about him in
the woods and meadows and brooks.
He rouses the golden sun with his
song.

Er singt zu seinem Werke
he sings to his   work

Aus voller frischer Brust,
from full   lively   breast

Die Arbeit gibt ihm   Stärke,
the work   gives to him strength

Die Stärke Lebenslust.
the strength life's-joy

He sings as he labours with
a full and lively heart - it
gives him strength, and strength
gives joy in living.

Bald wird ein bunt Gewimmel
soon is   a   gay throng

In allen Tiefen laut,
in all   deeps about

Und plätschert durch den Himmel,
and splashes   through the sky

Der sich   im   Wasser baut.
which himself in the water   rests

Soon a gay and lively throng
is swarming down below,
splashing in the sky that lies
mirrored in the water.

Doch wer   ein Netz will stellen,
but whoever a   net wants to lay

Braucht Augen klar und gut,
needs   eyes clear and good

Muss heiter gleich den Wellen,
must lively like   the waves

Und frei sein wie die Flut.
and free to be as the stream

Anyone who casts a net needs
a good, clear eye; he must be
lively as the waves, and free
as the stream.

Dort angelt auf der Brücke
there angles on the bridge

Die Hirtin,   schlauer Wicht!
the shepherdess sly   creature

There on the bridge the
shepherdess is fishing. You can
stop your tricks, you sly
creature, the fish won't be
deceived!

Gib' auf nur deine Tücke,
give up only your   trick

Den Fisch betrügst du nicht!
the fish deceive you not

68. IM   FRÜHLING
    IN THE SPRING

68. IN THE SPRING

Ernst Schluze

Still sitz' ich an des   Hügels Hang,
still sit   I on of the hill   slope

Der Himmel ist so klar,
the sky   is so clear

Das Lüftchen   spielt im   grünen Tal,
the little breeze plays in the green valley

Wo   ich beim   ersten Frühlingsstrahl
where I   at the first spring's-ray

Einst, ach, so glücklich war;
once   oh so happy   was

I sit quietly on the hill-side, the sky is so clear. A little breeze plays in the green valley, where in the first spring radiance I was once, O so happy!

Wo   ich an ihrer Seite ging,
where I   at her   side walked

So traulich und so nah',
so intimately and so close

Und tief im   dunkeln Felsenquell
and deep in the dark   rock-spring

Den schönen Himmel blau und hell,
the lovely sky   blue and clear

Und sie im   Himmel sah.
and her in the sky   saw

There I walked at her side, so fondly, so close, and deep in the dark rocky spring I saw the lovely sky, clear and blue, and in the sky her image.

Sieh, wie der bunte   Frühling schon
see how the brightly-coloured spring   already

Aus Knosp und Blüte blickt!
from bud   and blossom looks

Nicht alle Blüten   sind mir gleich,
not   all blossoms are to me equal

Am   liebsten   pflückt' ich von dem Zweig
at the most agreeable would pluck I   from the twig

Von welchem sie gepflückt.
from which   she plucked

See, how the spring already gaily peeps from bud and blossom. Not all of these have equal charm for me – I would most like to pluck from the branch from which she plucked.

Denn alles   ist wie damals noch,
for everything is as then   still

Die Blumen, das Gefild;
the flowers the fields

Die Sonne scheint nicht minder hell,
the sun   shines not less brightly

For everything is as it was then; the flowers, the fields, and the sun shines no less brightly, and no less gladdening is the blue image of the sky floating in the spring.

Nicht minder freundlich schwimmt im   Quell
not   less   friendly   floats   in the spring

Das blaue Himmelsbild.
the blue sky's image

Es   wandeln nur sich   Will' und Wahn,
(it) change only themselves wish and fancy

Es   wechseln Lust und Streit;
(it) change   joy and strife

Vorüber flieht der   Liebe Glück,
past   flees of the love joy

Und nur die Liebe bleibt zurück,
and only the love   remains behind

Die Lieb' und ach, das Leid!
the love and ah   the grief

Only desires and fancies
change, only joy and strife; the
joys of love flee away, and love
alone remains - love, and alas,
grief.

O wär' ich doch   ein Vöglein   nur
O were I indeed a   little bird only

Dort an dem Wiesenhang,
there on the meadow-slope

Dann blieb'   ich auf den Zweigen hier,
then would stay I   on the twig   here

Und säng'   ein süsses Lied von ihr
and would sing a   sweet song of her

Den ganzen Sommer lang.
the whole summer long

O if I were but a little
bird, there on the meadow slope,
then I would stay here on this
twig, and sing a sweet song of
her the whole summer long.

69. STÄNDCHEN
    SERENADE

Translated into German by
August Wilhelm von Schlegel

Horch, horch, die Lerche im   Ätherblau!
hark   hark   the lark   in the sky-blue

Und Phöbus, neu   erweckt,
and Phoebus newly awakened

Tränkt seine Rosse mit dem Tau,
waters his   steeds with the dew

Der Blumenkelche   deckt.
that flower-chalice covers

Der   Ringelblume Knospe schleusst
of the marigold   bud   opens

Die goldnen Äuglein   auf;
the golden (little) eyes -

Mit allem,   was da   reizend ist,
with everything what there charming is

Du süsse Maid, steh auf!
you sweet maiden arise -

69. SERENADE

From *Cymbeline* by
William Shakespeare
(original text)

Hark! hark! the lark at
          heaven's gate sings,
And Phoebus 'gins arise,
His steeds to water at those
                    springs
On chalic'd flowers that lies;
And winking Mary-buds begin
To ope their golden eyes:
With everything that pretty is,
My lady sweet, arise:
Arise, arise!

Weil   du doch   gar so reizend bist;
because you indeed very so charming are

Du süsse Maid, steh auf!
you sweet maiden arise –

70. *DER WANDERER AN DEN MOND*
    THE WANDERER TO THE MOON

70. THE WANDERER TO THE MOON

Johann Gabriel Seidl

Ich auf der Erd', am   Himmel du,
I   on the earth in the sky   you

Wir wandern beide rüstig   zu:
we wander both vigorously –

Ich ernst und trüb,   du mild   und rein,
I   grave and melancholy you gentle and pure

Was mag der Unterschied wohl   sein?
what may the difference I wonder to be

Ich wandre fremd   von Land zu Land,
I   wander unknown from land to land

So heimatlos, so unbekannt;
so homeless   so unknown

Berg   auf, Berg   ab, Wald ein, Wald aus,
mountain up   mountain down wood in   wood out

Doch bin ich nirgend, ach! zu Haus.
but am I nowhere alas at home

Du aber wanderst auf und ab
you but wander   up and down

Aus Westerns Wieg' in   Ostens Grab,
from west's   cradle into east's grave

Wallst Länder ein und Länder aus,
travel lands in and lands out

Und bist doch, wo   du bist, zu Haus.
and are yet where you are at home

Der Himmel, endlos   ausgespannt,
the sky   endlessly stretched out

Ist dein geliebtes Heimatland:
is your beloved   homeland

O glücklich, wer, wohin er geht,
O happy   who whither he goes

Doch auf der   Heimat Boden steht!
yet on of the home   ground stands

I on earth, you in the sky, we are both hardy travellers. I am grave and melancholy, you gentle and pure; I wonder, in what are we different? A stranger, I wander from land to land, homeless and unknown; up the mountains and down, in the woods and out, but alas, nowhere am I at home. But you travel far and near, from your cradle in the west to your grave in the east; out of one land, into another, and yet wherever you are, you are at home. The sky, spanning infinity, is your beloved homeland. O happy is he, who wherever he goes is always in his native place!

71. JÄGERS   LIEBESLIED
HUNTER'S LOVE-SONG

71. HUNTER'S LOVE-SONG

Franz Schober

Ich schiess den Hirsch im   grünen Forst
I   shoot   the stag   in the green   forest

Im   stillen Tal   das Reh,
in the quiet   valley the deer

Den Adler auf dem Klippenhorst,
the eagle on the rocky-eyrie

Die Ente auf dem See.
the duck on the lake

Kein Ort, der Schutz gewähren kann,
no   place the refuge to give can

Wenn meine Flinte zielt;
when my   gun   aims

Und dennoch hab ich harter Mann
and yet   have I harsh man

Die Liebe auch gefühlt!
the love also felt

Hab oft   hantiert in rauher Zeit,
have often worked   in harsh time

In Sturm und Winternacht,
in storm and winter-night

Und übereist   und eingeschneit,
and covered with ice and snowed up

Zum   Bett den Stein gemacht.
to the bed the rock made

Auf Dornen schlief ich wie auf Flaum,
on thorns slept I   as on down

Vom   Nordwind ungerührt,
from the north-wind unmoved

Doch hat der   Liebe zarten Traum
yet has of the love gentle dream

Die rauhe Brust gespürt.
the rugged breast felt

I shoot the stags in the green forest, the deer in the quiet valley; the eagles in their craggy eyries, the ducks on the lake. There's no refuge, no place that's safe from the aim of my gun – yet even I, a ruthless man, have felt love!

Often I've plied my skill in harsh weather, on stormy winter nights, and covered with snow and ice, I've made the rocks my bed.

Der wilde Falk war mein Gesell,
the savage hawk was my   companion

Der Wolf mein Kampfgespann;
the wolf my   fighting-team

Mir   fing der Tag mit Hundgebell,
to me began the day with hounds-baying

Die Nacht mit Hussah! an.
the night with halloo -

Ein Tannreis   war die Blumenzier
a   fir-sprig was the flower-decoration

Auf schweissbeflecktem Hut,
on sweat-stained   hat

Und dennoch schlug die Liebe mir
and yet   beat   the love to me

Ins   wilde Jägerblut.
into the wild hunter's-blood

O Schäfer auf dem weichen Moos,
O shepherd on the soft   moss

Der du mit Blumen spielst,
who you with flowers play

Wer weiss, ob du so heiss, so gross,
who knows if you so hotly so greatly

Wie ich, die Liebe fühlst.
as I   the love feels

Allnächtlich übern   schwarzen Wald,
every night over the black   wood

Vom   Mondenschein umstrahlt,
by the moonlight   shone about

Schwebt königshehr   die Lichtgestalt,
hovers royally majestic the light-vision

Wie sie kein Meister malt.
as her no   master paints

Wenn sie dann auf mich niedersieht,
when she then on me   looks down

Wenn mich ihr Blick durchglüht,
when me   her glance inflames

Da   weiss ich, wie dem   Wild geschieht,
then know I   how to the game happens

Das vor   dem Rohre flieht.
that before the barrel flees

Und doch! mit allem Glück   vereint,
and yet   with all   happiness united

Das nur auf Erden ist,
that only on earth is

Als wenn der allerbeste Freund
as if   the best of all friend

Mich in die Arme schliesst!
me   in the arms clasps

The savage hawk was my
companion, for the fight I
harnessed wolves; my day began
with the baying of hounds, the
night with cries of halloo! A
sprig of fir was the flower
adorning my sweat-stained hat -
and yet love came and beat in my
wild hunter's blood.

O shepherd there on the soft
moss, playing with the flowers,
who knows if your passion burns
as fiercely, as mightily as
mine? Each night in the dark
forest, with the moonlight
shining all around, a vision of
brightness that no Master could
paint hovers majestic and
sublime.

And when she looks down at
me, I am inflamed by her glance.
I know then how the hunted feel
as they flee from the gun. And
yet how I feel at one with all
the joys on earth - as if I were
held in a warm embrace by my
dearest friend.

SCHUBERT

72. DIE WINTERREISE
THE WINTER-JOURNEY

Wilhelm Müller

i. Gute Nacht
good night

i. Good-night

Fremd   bin ich eingezogen,
unknown am I   entered

Fremd   zieh ich wieder aus.
unknown set I   again forth

Der Mai war mir   gewogen
the May was to me well-disposed

Mit   manchem Blumenstauss.
with many a nosegay

Das Mädchen sprach von Liebe.
the girl   spoke   of love

Die Mutter gar von Eh'
the mother even of marriage

Nun ist die Welt so trübe,
now is the world so overcast

Der Weg gehüllt in Schnee.
the way covered in snow

A stranger I came here, a
stranger I depart. In May I was
favoured with many a nosegay of
flowers. The girl spoke of love,
her mother even of marriage. Now
the world is overcast; my way
covered in snow.

Ich kann zu meiner Reisen
I can for my   journey

Nicht wählen   mit der Zeit,
not   to choose with the time

Muss selbst den Weg mir   weisen
must myself the way to me to show

In dieser Dunkelheit.
in this   darkness

Es   zieht ein Mondenshatten
(it) goes a moon-shadow

Als mein Gefährte mit,
as my   companion with (me)

Und auf den weissen Matten
and on the white   meadows

Such ich des   Wildes Tritt.
seek I of the deer   footprint

I cannot choose the time for
my journey; I must find my own
way in the darkness. A shadow
cast by the moon is my
companion; in the white fields
I seek the tracks of deer.

Was soll ich länger weilen,
what shall I   longer to stay

Dass man mich trieb hinaus?
that one me   drove out

Lass irre   Hunde heulen
let   wandering dogs to howl

Vor   ihres Herren Haus!
in front of their master's house

Die Liebe liebt das Wandern –
the love loves the wandering

Why should I linger here,
only to be driven away? Let
straying dogs howl in front of
their master's house! Love ever
wanders from one to another –
God has made it so. And now
good-night, my fair sweetheart!

Gott hat sie so gemacht -
God has her so made

Von einem zu dem andern.
from one   to the other

Fein Liebchen, gute Nacht!
fine sweetheart good night

Will dich im   Traum nicht stören,
want you in the dream not   to disturb

I would not disturb your
dreams, what a pity to spoil
your sleep. You shall not hear
my footsteps - softly, softly
close the door! Write in
passing on your gate, 'Good-
night' - so you may see I
thought of you.

Wär schad um deine Ruh.
were pity for your sleep

Sollst meinen Tritt nicht hören -
shall my   step not   to hear

Sacht, sacht die Türe zu!
softly softly the door close

Schreib im   Vorübergehen
write   in the passing by

Ans   Tor dir: gute Nacht,
on the gate to you good night

Damit du mögest sehen,
so that you may   to see

An dich hab ich gedacht.
of you have I   thought

ii. Die Wetterfahne
the weather-vane

ii. The weather-vane

Der Wind spielt mit der Wetterfahne
the wind plays with the weather-vane

The wind plays with the
weather-vane on my fair
sweetheart's house. In my folly,
I thought it was mocking this
poor fugitive.

Auf meines schönen Liebchens   Haus,
on my   fair   sweetheart's house

Da   dacht ich schon in meinem Wahne,
there thought I   already in my   folly

Sie pfiff den armen Flüchtling aus.
she hissed the poor   fugitive   away

Er hätt es eher   bemerken sollen,
he had it sooner   to notice to have to

He should have noticed sooner
the sign up there on the house;
then he would never have sought
a faithful woman there.

Des   Hauses aufgestecktes Schild,
of the house put up   sign

So hätt er nimmer suchen wollen
so had he never   to seek to want

Im   Haus ein treues Frauenbild.
in the house a   true   woman

Der Wind spielt drinnen mit den Herzen
the wind plays within with the hearts

The wind plays with the
hearts within as it plays on
the roof, but not so loud. What
do they care about my grief?
Their child is a wealthy bride.

Wie auf dem Dach, nur nicht so laut.
as on the roof only not   so loudly

Was fragen sie nach meinen Schmerzen?
what ask   they after my   sorrows

Ihr Kind ist eine reiche Braut.
their child is a   rich   bride

iii. Gefrorne Tränen
    frozen   tears

iii. Frozen tears

Gefrorne Tropfen fallen
frozen   drops   fall

Von meinen Wangen ab:
from my   cheeks off

        Ob es mir   denn entgangen,
(I wonder) if it to me then escaped

Dass ich geweinet hab?
that I wept   have

Frozen drops fall from my cheeks. Did I not know that I was weeping?

Ei Tränen, meine Tränen,
Oh tears   my   tears

Und seid ihr gar so lau,
and are you even so tepid

Dass ihr erstarrt zu Eise,
that you freeze to ice

Wie kühler Morgentau?
like cool   morning-dew

O tears, my tears, are you so tepid that you can turn to ice like cool morning dew?

Und dringt doch aus der Quelle
and urge yet from the spring

Der   Brust so glühend heiss,
of the breast so glowing hot

Als wolltet ihr zerschmelzen
as wanted you to melt

Des ganzen Winters Eis!
the whole winter's ice

And yet you spring from my heart so burning hot, as if you would melt the whole of winter's ice!

iv. Erstarrung
    numbness

iv. Numbness

Ich such   im   Schnee vergebens
I   search in the snow   in vain

Nach ihrer Tritte   Spur,
for of her footprints trace

Wo   sie an meinem Arme
where she on my   arm

Durchstrich   die grüne Flur.
roamed through the green meadow

In vain I search in the snow for her footprints, there where we roamed in a green meadow, arm in arm.

Ich will den Boden küssen,
I want the ground to kiss

Durchdringen Eis und Schnee
to pierce   ice and snow

Mit meinen heissen Tränen,
with my   hot   tears

Bis ich die Erde seh.
until I   the earth see

I long to kiss the ground, to pierce snow and ice with my hot tears, until I see the earth beneath.

Wo   find ich eine Blüte,
where find I   a   blossom

Wo   find ich grünes Gras?
where find I   green grass

Where can I find a blossom? Where can I find green grass? The flowers have withered, the grass is colourless.

Die Blumen sind erstorben,
the flowers are faded away

Der Rasen sieht so blass.
the grass looks so pale

Soll denn kein Angedenken
shall then no keepsake

Ich nehmen mit von hier?
I to take with (me) from here

Wenn meine Schmerzen schweigen,
when my sorrows are still

Wer sagt mir dann von ihr?
who speaks to me then of her

Is there no keepsake that I can take from here? When my sorrows are stilled, who will speak to me of her?

Mein Herz ist wie erfroren,
my heart is as frozen

Kalt starrt ihr Bild darin:
cold stares her image therein

Schmilzt je das Herz mir wieder,
melts ever the heart to me again

Fliesst auch ihr Bild dahin.
melts also her image away

My heart is frozen, her image rigid and cold within. If ever my heart should thaw, her image would melt away.

v. Der Lindenbaum
the linden-tree

v. The linden tree

Am Brunnen vor dem Tore
by the fountain before the gate

Da steht ein Lindenbaum;
there stands a linden-tree

Ich träumt' in seinem Schatten
I dreamt in his shade

So manchen süssen Traum.
so many a sweet dream

By the fountain at the gate stands a linden tree; in its shade I have dreamt many a sweet dream.

Ich schnitt in seine Rinde
I cut in his bark

So manches liebe Wort;
so many a dear word

Es zog in Freud und Leide
it drew in joy and sorrow

Zu ihm mich immer fort.
to him me always forth

In its bark I have carved many words of love; I was drawn to it always, in both joy and sorrow.

Ich musst' auch heute wandern
I had to also today to wander

Vorbei in tiefer Nacht,
past in deep night

Da hab ich noch im Dunkel
then have I even in the darkness

Die Augen zugemacht.
the eyes closed

Now I have had to pass it again, at dead of night; even in the darkness I closed my eyes.

Und seine Zweige   rauschten,
and his   branches rustled

Als riefen sie mir   zu:
as called they to me –

'Komm her zu mir, Geselle,
come here to me   brother

Hier findst du   deine Ruh!'
here find   you your rest

Die kalten Winde bliesen
the cold   winds blew

Mir   grad   ins   Angesicht,
to me straight into the face

Der Hut flog mir vom   Kopfe,
the hat flew me from the head

Ich wendete   mich nicht.
I   turned round myself not

Nun bin ich manche Stunde
now am I   many an hour

Entfernt von jenem Ort,
far away from that place

Und immer hör ich's rauschen:
and ever hear I it to rustle

Du fändest   Ruhe dort!
you would find rest there

          vi. Wasserflut
             water-torrent

Manche Trän aus meinen Augen
many a tear from my   eyes

Ist gefallen in den Schnee;
is fallen   in the snow

Seine kalten Flocken saugen
his   cold   flakes suck

Durstig   ein das heisse Weh.
thirstily in the hot   misery

Wenn die Gräser sprossen wollen,
when the grasses to sprout want

Weht daher ein lauer Wind,
blows along a   tepid wind

Und das Eis zerspringt in Schollen
and the ice breaks   in lumps

Und der weiche Schnee zerrinnt.
and the soft   snow   melts

Schnee, du weisst von meinem Sehnen,
snow   you know of my   longing

Sag, wohin doch   geht dein Lauf?
say whither indeed goes your course

Folge nach nur meinen Tränen,
follow after only my   tears

And its branches rustled
as if they were calling me,
'Come here to me, friend,
here you will find rest!'

The cold wind blew
straight into my face; my
hat flew from my head, but
I did not turn back.

Now I am many hours'
journey from that place.
Yet still I hear a rustling,
'Here you would find rest!'

vi. Torrent

My eyes have shed so
many tears into the snow;
the cold flakes thirstily
drink in my burning anguish.

When the grass begins to
shoot, a mild breeze will
blow; the ice will break in
pieces and the soft snow
melt.

Snow, you know of my
longing – tell me, where
will you flow away? If you
follow my tears, the little
stream will engulf you.

Nimmt dich bald das Bächlein   auf.
takes you soon the little stream up

Wirst mit ihm die Stadt durchziehen,
will with it the town to go through

Together you will flow
through the town, in and out of
the gay streets, and when you
feel my tears burning – there
is my beloved's house.

Muntre Strassen ein und aus;
gay   streets in and out

Fühlst du mein Tränen glühen,
feel you my   tears to glow

Da   ist meiner Liebsten Haus.
there is of my beloved house

vii. *Auf dem Flusse*
    on the stream

vii. On the stream

Der du so lustig rauschtest,
who you so gaily rushed

You bright impetuous
stream, that rushed so
gaily along, how silent you
have become – you bid me no
parting word!

Du heller, wilder Fluss,
you bright wild   river

Wie still bist du geworden,
how silent are you become

Gibst keinen Scheidegruss.
give no   farewell-greeting

Mit harter, starrer Rinde
with hard   stiff crust

You have covered yourself
with a hard, stiff crust,
and lie cold and motionless
stretched out in the sand.

Hast du dich   überdeckt,
have you yourself covered over

Liegst kalt und unbeweglich
lie   cold and motionless

Im   Sande ausgestreckt.
in the sand outstretched

In deine Decke grab' ich
in your   cover engrave I

Now on your icy cover
I engrave with a sharp stone
the name of my beloved, the
hour and the day;

Mit einem spitzen Stein
with a   sharp stone

Den Namen meiner Liebsten
the name of my beloved

Und Stund und Tag hinein:
and hour and day into

Den Tag des   ersten Grusses,
the day of the first greeting

the day of our first
meeting, and the day I went
away. A broken ring encircles
name and figures.

Den Tag, an dem ich ging:
the day on which I   went away

Um   Name' und Zahlen windet
round name and figures winds

Sich   ein zerbrochner Ring.
itself a   broken   ring

Mein Herz, in diesem Bache
my   heart in this   brook

O my heart, do you see
your image in this brook?
Under its icy crust, is there
also a raging torrent?

Erkennst du nun dein Bild?
recognise you now your image

Ob's   unter seiner Rinde
whether it under his   crust

Wohl   auch so reissend schwillt?
perhaps also so tearing   heaves

  viii. Rückblick   viii. Backward glance
     backward-glance

Es brennt mir unter beiden Sohlen,   The soles of my feet
it burns me under both   soles   are burning, though I walk
                                             on ice and snow. I want to
Tret ich auch schon auf Eis und Schnee,   draw no further breath till
tread I   even though on ice and snow   I see the towers and steeples
                                             no more.
Ich möcht   nicht wieder Atem   holen,
I   should like not   again breath to draw

Bis   ich nicht mehr die Türme seh.
until I   not   more the towers see

Hab mich   an jedem Stein gestossen,   I bruised myself on
have myself on every stone knocked   every stone in my haste to
                                             leave the town; the crows
So eilt'   ich zu der Stadt hinaus;   flung snow and hailstones
so hastened I   to the town out   on my hat from every
                                             housetop.
Die Krähen warfen Bäll und Schlossen
the crows   threw balls and hailstones

Auf meinen Hut von jedem Haus.
on my   hat from every house

Wie anders   hast du mich empfangen, How differently you
how differently have you me   welcomed   welcomed me, you fickle
                                             town! Larks and nightingales
Du Stadt der   Unbeständigkeit!   vied with one another before
you town of the inconstancy   your bright windows.

An deinen blanken Fenstern sangen
at your   bright windows sang

Die Lerch' und Nachtigall im   Streit.
the larks and nightingale in the contest

Die runden Lindenbäume blühten,   The rounded linden trees
the round linden-trees blossomed   were in flower, the clear
                                             little streams rushed and
Die klaren Rinnen rauschten hell,   sparkled. Oh, and two
the clear rills rushed   clear   maiden's eyes were glowing –
                                             then indeed were you lost,
Und ach, zwei Mädchenaugen glühten!   my friend!
and ah   two maiden's-eyes glowed

Da war's geschehn um dich, Gesell!
then was it happened to you   brother

Kommt mir   der Tag in   die Gedanken,   Whenever that day comes
comes to me the day into the thoughts   into my mind, I long to look
                                             back once more; I long to
Möcht   ich noch einmal rückwärts sehn, stumble back again and
should like I   more once   back   to look silently stand before her
                                             house.
Möcht   ich zurücke wieder wanken,
should like I   back   again to falter

Vor   ihrem Hause stille   stehn.
before her   house silently to stand

ix. *Irrlicht*
will-o'-the-wisp

In die tiefsten Felsengründe
in the deepest rock-ravines

Lockte mich ein Irrlicht   hin:
enticed me   a   will-o'-the-wisp thither

Wie ich einen Ausgang finde,
how I a   way-out find

Liegt nicht schwer mir   in dem Sinn.
lies not   heavily to me on the mind

A will-o'-the-wisp
lured me deep among rocky
ravines. But how I shall
find a way out does not
trouble me.

Bin gewohnt das Irregehen,
am used to the astray-going

's führt ja   jeder Weg zum   Ziel:
it leads truly every way to the goal

Unsre Freuden, unsre Wehen,
our joys   our   sorrows

Alles eines Irrlichts   Spiel!
all of a will-o'-the-wisp play

I am used to losing my
way - every path leads
somewhere; all our joys and
sorrows are a will-o'-the-
wisp's game!

Durch des   Bergstroms   trockne Rinnen
through of the mountain-stream dry   watercourse

Wind' ich ruhig   mich hinab;
wind I   quietly me   downwards

Jeder Strom wird's Meer gewinnen,
each stream will the sea gain

Jedes Leiden auch sein Grab.
each sorrow also its grave

Along the dry bed of a
mountain stream I wind my
quiet way; every stream
reaches the sea, every sorrow
its grave.

x. *Rast*
rest

x. Resting place

Nun merk   ich erst, wie müd   ich bin,
now perceive I   only how tired I   am

Da ich zur   Ruh   mich lege;
as I   to the sleep myself lie down

Das Wandern   hielt mich munter hin
the wandering kept   me   awake -

Auf unwirtbarem Wege.
on inhospitable paths

Only now as I lie down
to sleep, do I see how tired
I am. Wandering along hostile
paths kept me awake.

Die Füsse frugen nicht nach Rast,
the feet asked not   about rest

Es war zu kalt zum   Stehen;
it was too cold to the standing

Der Rücken fühlte keine Last,
the back   felt   no   burden

Der Sturm half fort   mich wehen.
the storm helped onward me   to blow

My feet asked no rest, it
was too cold to stand; my back
felt no burden for the storm
helped to drive me on.

In eines Köhlers   engem Haus
in of a charcoal-burner narrow house

Hab Obdach ich gefunden;
have shelter I   found

Doch meine Glieder ruhn nicht aus:
yet my   limbs rest not -

So brennen ihre Wunden.
so burn   their bruises

In a charcoal-burner's narrow hut I have found shelter. But my limbs with their aching bruises cannot rest.

Auch du, mein Herz, in Kampf   und Sturm
too you my   heart in struggle and storm

So wild und so verwegen,
so wild and so bold

Fühlst in der Still   erst deinen Wurm
feel   in the stillness only your   serpent

Mit heissem Stich sich   regen!
with hot   sting itself to stir

You too, my heart, midst struggle and storm so savage and bold, feel in its stillness the serpent stir with its hot sting!

     xi. Frühlingstraum
          spring's-dream

xi. Dream of spring

Ich träumte von bunten   Blumen,
I   dreamt of gay-coloured flowers

So wie sie wohl   blühen im   Mai;
so as they perhaps blossom in the May

Ich träumte von grünen Wiesen,
I   dreamt of green meadows

Von lustigem Vogelgeschrei.
of merry   bird-clamour

I dreamt of brightly coloured flowers as they blossom in May; I dreamt of green meadows and the merry call of birds.

Und als die Hähne krähten,
and as the cocks crowed

Da   ward mein Auge wach;
then was my   eye awake

Da war es kalt und finster,
then was it cold and dark

Es   schrieen die Raben vom   Dach.
(it) screamed the ravens from the roof

And as the cocks crowed I opened my eyes; it was cold and dark and ravens were croaking on the roof.

Doch an den Fensterscheiben,
but on the window-panes

Wer malte   die Blätter da?
who painted the leaves there

Ihr lacht wohl   über den Träumer,
you laugh perhaps over the dreamer

Der Blumen im   Winter sah?
who flowers in the winter saw

But who painted those leaves on the window-pane? Are you laughing at the dreamer who sees flowers in the winter?

Ich träumte von Lieb um Liebe,
I   dreamt of .love for love

Von einer schönen   Maid,
of one   beautiful girl

Von Herzen und von Küssen,
of hearts and of kisses

I dreamt of love for love, of a beautiful girl; of hearts and kisses, of joy and ecstasy.

Von Wonne und Seligkeit.
of joy   and bliss.

Und als die Hähne krähten,
and as the cocks crowed

And as the cocks crowed
my heart awoke. I sit here
alone and think on my dream.

Da   ward mein Herze wach;
there was my   heart awake

Nun sitz ich hier alleine
now sit I   here alone

Und denkt dem Traume nach.
and think the dream about

Die Augen schliess ich wieder,
the eyes shut   I   again

I close my eyes again,
still my heart is throbbing.
Leaves on the window, when
will you become green? When
shall I hold my sweetheart
in my arms?

Noch schlägt das Herz so warm.
still beats   the heart so warmly

Wann grünt   ihr Blätter am   Fenster?
when become green you leaves on the window

Wann halt ich mein Liebchen   im   Arm?
when hold I   my   sweetheart in the arm

xii. Einsamkeit
solitude

xii. Solitude

Wie eine trübe Wolke
like a   dark cloud

Durch   heitre Lüfte geht,
through clear air(s) goes

Like a dark cloud moving
in the clear air, when a
gentle breeze blows through
the tops of the firs,

Wenn in der   Tanne   Wipfel
when in of the fir   (tree-) top

Ein mattes Lüftchen weht:
a   faint breeze blows

So zieh ich meine Strasse
so go I   my   road

so do I go my way through
bright and joyous life with
dragging steps, solitary and
without greeting.

Dahin   mit trägem Fuss,
thither with sluggish foot

Durch   helles, frohes Leben
through bright joyous life

Einsam und ohne   Gruss.
solitary and without greeting

Ach, dass die Luft so ruhig!
ah   that the air so calm

Ah, the air is so calm,
the world so full of light!
When storms were raging, I
was not so wretched.

Ach, dass die Welt so licht!
ah   that the world so light

Als noch die Stürme tobten,
as still the storms raged

War ich so elend   nicht.
was I   so wretched not

xiii. Die Post
    the post

xiii. The mail-coach

Von der Strasse her   ein Posthorn klingt.
from the highway over there a   posthorn sounds

A posthorn sounds from
the highway. What is it that
makes you leap so suddenly,
my heart?

Was hat es, dass es so hoch aufspringt,
what has it that it so high leaps up

Mein Herz?
my heart

Die Post   bringt keinen Brief für dich.
the mail-coach brings no   letter for you

The coach brings you no
letter. Then why do you throb
so strangely, my heart?

Was drängst du denn so wunderlich,
what urge you then so strangely

Mein Herz?
my heart

Nun ja, die Post   kommt aus der Stadt,
well yes the mail-coach comes from the town

Oh yes, the coach comes
from the town where I once
had a sweet love, my heart!

Wo ich ein liebes Liebchen   hatt,
where I a   dear   sweetheart had

Mein Herz!
my heart

Willst wohl   einmal hinübersehn
will   perhaps once   to look over there

Do you want just once
to look back, to ask how it
is there, my heart?

Und fragen, wie es dort mag gehn,
and to ask how it there may to go

Mein Herz?
my   heart

xiv. Der greise Kopf
     the hoary head

xiv. The hoary head

Der Reif   hat einen weissen Schein
the hoar-frost has a   white   lustre

The hoar-frost has
scattered a shining white
over my hair; I thought I
was already an old man, and
I was overjoyed.

Mir übers   Haar gestreuet;
to me over the hair scattered

Da glaubt' ich schon ein Greis zu sein
then believed I   already an old man to to be

Und hab mich sehr gefreuet.
and have myself much rejoined

Doch bald ist er hinweggetaut,
but soon is he thawed away

But soon it thawed, and
my hair was black again. I
shudder at my youth – how
far off still is the grave!

Hab wieder schwarze Haare,
have again black   hairs

Dass mir's   vor meiner Jugend graut –
that to me it at my   youth shudders

Wie weit noch bis zur   Bahre!
how far still till to the bier

Von Abendrot zum   Morgenlicht
from sunset to the morning-light

Between dusk and dawn
many a head has turned white.
Who could believe that mine
has not on this whole journey?

Ward mancher Kopf zum   Greise.
became many a head to the old man

Wer glaubt's? und meiner ward   es nicht
who believes it and mine   became it not

Auf dieser ganzen Reise.
on this   whole   journey

xv. *Die Krähe*
the crow

Eine Krähe war mit mir
a   crow was with me

Aus der Stadt gezogen,
from the town gone

Ist bis heute für   und für
is till today (ever) and (ever)

Um   mein Haupt geflogen.
about my   head flown

Krähe, wunderliches Tier,
crow   strange   creature

Willst mich nicht verlassen?
will   me   not   to forsake

Meinst wohl   bald als Beute hier
think possibly soon as prey here

Meinen Leib zu fassen?
my   body to to seize

Nun, es wird nicht weit mehr gehn
well it is   not   far more to go

An dem Wanderstabe.
on my   staff

Krähe, lass mich endlich sehn
crow let me   at last to see

Treue   bis zum   Grabe.
constancy till to the grave

xv. The crow

    A crow was with me
as I left the town. It still
flies back and forth above
my head.

    Crow, you strange
creature, will you not
forsake me? Do you think
my body will soon fall prey
to you?

    My staff will not have
much further to carry me.
O crow, at last let me see
constancy right to the grave!

xvi. *Letzte Hoffnung*
last   hope

Hie und da   ist an den Bäumen
here and there is on the trees

Manches bunte   Blatt zu sehn,
some   gay-coloured leaf to to see

Und ich bleibe vor   den Bäumen
and I   remain before the trees

Oftmals in Gedanken stehn.
often   in thoughts to stand

Schaue nach dem einen Blatte,
look   at   the one   leaf

Hänge meine Hoffnung dran;
hang my   hope   on it

Spielt der Wind mit meinem Blatte,
plays the wind with my   leaf

xvi. Last hope

    Here and there on the
trees a gay leaf may still
be seen. I stand beneath the
trees, lost in thought.

    I gaze at a single leaf,
and hang my hope on it. If
the wind plays with my leaf,
I tremble with all my being.

Zittr   ich,   was   ich   zittern   kann.
tremble I   what I   to tremble can

Ach,   und fällt das Blatt zu Boden,
ah   and falls the leaf to ground

Fällt mit   ihm die Hoffnung ab,
falls with him the hope   off

Fall ich selber mit   zu Boden,
fall I   myself with (it) to ground

Wein auf meiner Hoffnung Grab.
weep on of my   hope   grave

　　　Ah, and if the leaf falls
to the ground, my hope falls
with it. I too fall to the
ground, and weep on the grave
of my hope.

xvii. *Im   Dorfe*
　　　in the village

xvii. In the village

Es   bellen die Hunde, es   rasseln die Ketten;
(it) barks the dogs (it) clank the chains

Es   schlafen die Menschen in ihren Betten,.
(it) sleep   the people in their beds

Träumen sie manches,   was sie nicht haben,
dream they many a thing what they not have

Tun sich   im   Guten und Argen erlaben;
do themselves in the good and bad   to refresh

　　　The dogs are barking,
and rattling their chains,
the people are sleeping in
their beds, dreaming of
many things they do not have,
finding pleasure in the good
and the bad.

Und morgen   früh   ist alles zerflossen,
and tomorrow morning is all   melted away

Je   nun, sie haben ihr   Teil genossen,
well now they have their part enjoyed

Und hoffen, was sie noch übrig   liessen,
and hope   what they still remaining left

Doch wieder zu finden   auf ihren Kissen.
yet   again to to find on their pillows

　　　And next day all has
vanished, but they have
enjoyed their share, and
hope to find what may remain
upon their pillows.

Bellt mich nur fort, ihr wachen   Hunde,
bark me   only away you watchful dogs

Lasst mich nicht ruhn   in der Schlummerstunde!
let me   not   to rest in the slumber-hour

Ich bin zu   Ende mit allen Träumen,
I am at (an) end with all   dreams

Was will ich unter den Schläfern säumen?
what want I   among the sleepers to linger

　　　Warn me away with your
barking, you watch-dogs,
give me no rest in the hours
of slumber! I am done with
all dreaming. Why should I
linger amongst those who
sleep?

xviii. *Der stürmische Morgen*
　　　the stormy   morning

xviii. The stormy morning

Wie hat der Sturm zerrissen
how has the storm rent

Des   Himmels graues Kleid!
of the sky's   grey   dress

Die Wolkenfetzen flattern
the cloud-tatters flutter

Umher   in mattem Streit.
all round in feeble conflict

　　　How the storm has rent
the sky's grey robe! Tattered
clouds flutter about in weary
conflict.

Und rote Feuerflammen
and red fire-flames

Ziehn zwischen ihnen hin:
move between them along

Das nenn ich einen Morgen
that call I   a   morning

So recht nach meinem Sinn!
so right after my   taste

A fiery red blazes
between them; this is a
morning after my own heart!

Mein Herz sieht an dem Himmel
my heart sees in the sky

Gemalt sein eignes Bild –
painted its own   image

Es ist nichts als der Winter,
it is nothing but the winter

Der Winter kalt und wild!
the winter cold and savage

My heart sees its own
image painted in the sky.
It is nothing but winter –
winter, cold and savage!

xix. Täuschung
    illusion

xix. Illusion

Ein Licht tanzt freundlich   vor   mir her,
a   light dances in a friendly way before me –

Ich folg ihm nach die Kreuz und Quer;
I   follow it after the cross and criss

Ich folg ihm gern, und seh's   ihm   an,
I   follow him readily and perceive it to him –

Dass es verlockt den Wandersmann.
that it entices the traveller

A friendly light dances
before me, I follow it
hither and thither. I follow
it readily, even knowing that
it lures me from my way.

Ach! wer wie ich so elend   ist,
ah   who like I   so wretched is

Gibt   gern   sich   hin der   bunten
gives in willingly (himself) – to the fine

  List,
  cunning

Die hinter Eis und Nacht und Graus
that behind ice and night and terror

Ihm   weist ein helles, warmes Haus.
to him shows a   bright warm house

Oh, anyone as wretched
as I willingly gives in to
such dazzling guile, that
shows, beyond the ice and
the darkness and terror, a
warm bright house,

Und eine Liebe Seele drin:
and a   dear soul within

Nur Täuschung ist für mich Gewinn!
only illusion is for me   gain

and a dear one within – but
all I gain is illusion.

xx. Der Wegweiser
    the sign-post

xx. The sign-post

Was vermeid ich denn die Wege,
why avoid   I   then the ways

Wo   die andern Wandrer gehn,
where the other travellers go

Suche mir versteckte Stege
seek to me hidden   footpaths

Why do I avoid the ways
that other travellers go,
and seek out hidden paths
on snow-covered rocky
heights?

cont →

Durch   verschneite   Felsenhöhn?
through snow-covered rocky-heights

Habe ja   doch   nichts begangen,
have certainly however nothing done

I have done no wrong,
that I should shun mankind.
What is this foolish desire
that drives me into the
wilderness?

Dass ich Menschen sollte scheun,
that I   people   should to shun

Welch ein törichtes Verlangen
what a   foolish   desire

Treibt mich in   die Wüstenein?
drives me   into the deserts

Weiser   stehen auf den Strassen,
signposts stand in the roads

Signposts stand by the
roadside pointing to the
towns, but senselessly I
wander, unresting, seeking
rest.

Weisen auf die Städte zu,
point at the towns -

Und ich wandre sonder Massen,
and I   wander without measure

Ohne   Ruh, und suche Ruh.
without rest and seek   rest

Einen Weiser   seh ich stehen
a   signpost see I   to stand

I see a signpost before
me, steady before my gaze -
I must travel the road on
which no one ever returned.

Unverrückt vor   meinem Blick;
steady   before my   glance

Eine Strasse muss ich gehen,
a   road   must I   to go

Die   noch keiner ging zurück.
that yet no one went back

xxi. Das Wirtshaus
the inn

xxi. The inn

Auf   einen Totenacker   hat mich mein Weg gebracht,
on to a   burial-ground has me   my   way led

My way led me to a
graveyard. Here, I thought,
I can spend the night. You
green funeral wreaths could
be the inn signs, inviting
weary travellers into the
cool inn.

Allhier will ich einkehren, hab ich bei mir
here   will I   to turn in have I   to myself
  gedacht.
  thought

Ihr grünen Totenkränze   könnt wohl die Zeichen
you green   funeral wreaths could well the signs
  sein,
  to be

Die müde Wandrer   laden ins   kühle Wirtshaus
that weary wanderers invite into the cool   inn
  ein.
  -

Sind denn in diesem Hause die Kammern   all besetzt?
are   then in this   house the chambers all occupied

Are all the rooms in this
house already taken? I could
fall with weariness, and am
grievously bruised. Yet, O
cruel inn, you turn me away?
So now, trusty staff, let us
go on, let us go on!

Bin matt zum   Niedersinken, bin tödlich schwer
am faint to the sinking down   am mortally grievously
  verletzt.
  hurt

O unbarmherzige Schenke, doch weisest du mich ab?
O unmerciful   inn   yet send   you me   away

Nun weiter denn, nur weiter, mein treuer Wanderstab!
now on   then only on   my   true   staff

xxii. Mut
courage

Fliegt der Schnee mir ins   Gesicht,
flies the snow   to me into the face

Schüttl' ich ihn herunter.
shake off I   him down

Wenn mein Herz im   Busen spricht,
when my   heart in the breast speaks

Sing ich hell   und munter;
sing I   brightly and merrily

Höre nicht, was es mir   sagt,
hear not   what it to me says

Habe keine Ohren,
have no   ears

Fühle nicht, was es mir   klagt,
feel not   what it to me laments

Klagen   ist für Toren.
lamenting is for fools

Lustig in   die Welt hinein
gaily into the world (into)

Gegen   Wind und Wetter!
against wind and weather

Will kein Gott auf Erden sein,
will no   god on earth to be

Sind wir selber   Götter!
are we ourselves gods

xxii. Courage

When the snow flies in
my face I shake it off.
When my heart cries out
within my breast, I sing
a bright and merry song.

Close your ears to what
my heart is saying! Have no
feeling for its lament –
only fools lament.

Stride gaily into the
world against wind and
weather! If there is no
God on earth, we ourselves
can be gods!

xxiii. Die Nebensonnen
the mock-suns

Drei Sonnen sah ich am   Himmel stehn,
three suns   saw I in the sky   to stand

Hab lang und fest   sie angesehn;
have long and steadily them looked at

Und sie auch standen da   so stier,
and they also stood   there so fixedly

Als wollten sie nicht weg von mir.
as wanted they not   away from me

Ach meine Sonnen seid ihr nicht!
ah my   suns   are you not

Schaut andern doch ins   Angesicht!
look   others just into the face

Ja, neulich hatt ich auch wohl   drei;
yes recently had I   also indeed three

Nun sind hinab die besten zwei.
now are down the best   two

xxiii. Phantom suns

I saw three suns in
the sky, and stared at them
long and steadily. And they
stayed so still, as though
they would not leave me.

But you are not my suns –
stare into the faces of
others! Not long ago I also
had three; the two best of
them have gone – if only
the third would follow! It
would be better for me in
the dark.

Ging nur die dritt' erst hinterdrein!
went only the third only after

Im   Dunkeln wird mir   wohler sein.
in the dark   will to me better to be

xxiv. *Der Leiermann*
the organ-grinder

xxiv. The organ-grinder

Drüben   hinterm   Dorfe steht ein
over there behind the village stands an
Leiermann,
organ-grinder

Und mit starren Fingern dreht er, was er kann.
and with numb   fingers turns he what he can

Barfuss auf dem Eise wankt   er hin   und her,
barefoot on the ice staggers he this way and that

Und sein kleiner Teller bleibt ihm   immer leer.
and his little plate remains to him always empty

Keiner mag   ihn hören, keiner sieht ihn an,
no one wants him to hear no one looks him at

Und die Hunde knurren um   den alten Mann.
and the dogs snarl   round the old   man

Und er lässt es gehen, alles wie es will,
and he lets it to go all   as it will

Dreht, und seine Leier steht ihm   nimmer still.
turns and his   organ stands to him never   still

Wunderlicher Alter, soll ich mit dir gehn?
strange   old man shall I with you to go

Willst du meinen Liedern deine Leier drehn?
will   you my   songs   your organ to turn

There beyond the
village an organ-grinder
stands, grinding away with
numb fingers, as best he
can. He stumbles barefoot
to and fro on the ice, and
his little plate is always
empty.

No one wants to hear
him, no one looks at him,
and the dogs snarl round the
old man. He takes it all as
it comes; he goes on turning,
and his organ is never still.

Strange old man, shall
I go with you? Will you
grind your organ to my
songs?

73. *DIE STERNE*
THE STARS

73. THE STARS

Karl Gottfried von Leitner

Wie blitzen die Sterne so hell   durch die
how sparkle the stars so brightly through the
Nacht!
night

Bin oft   schon   darüber vom   Schlummer
am often already over it from the slumber
erwacht;
awakened

Doch schelt' ich die lichten Gebilde d'rum nicht,
but reproach I the light forms   for it not

Sie üben   im   Stillen manch' heilsame
they practise in the stillness many a healing
Pflicht.
duty

How brightly the stars
shine in the night! Often
they awaken me from sleep.
But how can I reproach them
for their radiance, for so
often in the stillness they
bring healing.

Sie wallen hoch oben in Engelgestalt,
they float high above in angel-form

Sie leuchten dem Pilger durch Heiden und
they shine to the pilgrim through heaths and
Wald;
wood

Sie schweben als Boten der Liebe umher,
they hover as messenger of the love all around

Und tragen oft Küsse weit über das Meer.
and bring often kisses far over the sea

High above they float
like angels; lighting the
pilgrim over heath and
through wood; they hover
about us, messengers of
love, bearing kisses far
across the sea.

Sie blicken dem Dulder recht mild
they look to the sufferer very mildly
ins Gesicht,
into the face

Und säumen die Tränen mit silbernem Licht,
and edge the tears with silver light

Und weisen von Gräbern gar tröstlich und
and show from graves very comfortingly and
hold,
kindly

Uns hinter das Blaue mit Fingern von Gold.
us behind the blue with fingers of gold

They bathe the face
of the sufferer in a gentle
light, and edge our tears
with silver; comforting and
kind, they point from the
grave up into the dark blue
with fingers of gold.

So sei denn gesegnet, du strahlige Schar!
so be then blessed you gleaming multitude

Und leuchte mir lange noch freundlich und klar,
and light me long still kindly and clearly

Und wenn ich einst liebe, seid hold
and when I one day love be favourable
dem Verein,
to the union

Und euer Geflimmer lasst Segen uns sein.
and your glittering let blessing us to be

I bless your gleaming
multitude — let your clear
and kindly light ever shine
on me! And when one day I
find love, give us both
your benediction; let us
in your radiance be blessed.

SCHWANENGESANG (74-87)   SWANSONG

74. LIEBESBOTSCHAFT   74. LOVE'S MESSAGE
   LOVE'S-MESSAGE

Ludwig Rellstab

Rauschendes Bächlein, so silbern und hell,
rushing little brook so silver and clear

Eilst zur Geliebten so munter und schnell?
hurry (you) to the loved one so merrily and fast

Ach! trautes Bächlein, mein Bote sei du,
ah dear little brook my messenger be you

Bringe die Grüsse des Fernen ihr zu.
bring the greetings of the distant one to her (to)

Little rushing brook,
so silver and clear, is it
to my love that you hurry
so merrily? O dear little
brook, be my messenger —
carry her greetings from
him who is far away!

All' ihre Blumen im   Garten gepflegt,
all   her   flowers in the garden tended

Die   sie so lieblich   am   Busen trägt,
which she so charmingly at the breast carries

Und ihre Rosen in purpurner Glut,
and her   roses in crimson   glow

Bächlein,   erquicke mit   kühlender Flut.
little brook refresh with cooling   waves

All the flowers she tends in her garden, and so charmingly carries at her breast – little brook, refresh her roses of glowing crimson with your cooling ripples.

Wenn sie am   Ufer, in Träume versenkt,
when she on the bank   in dreams absorbed

Meiner gedenkend, das Köpfchen   hängt,
of me   thinking   the little head hangs

Tröste die Süsse   mit freundlichem Blick,
comfort the sweet one with kindly   glance

Denn der Geliebter kehrt bald zurück.
for   the beloved   comes soon back

When on your bank absorbed in dreams, her head droops as she thinks of me – comfort my sweet one with a kindly glance, for her beloved will soon return.

Neigt sich   die Sonne mit   rötlichem Schein,
lowers (herself) the sun   with reddish   shine

Wiege   das Liebchen in   Schlummer ein,
rock asleep the sweetheart into slumber   –

Rausche sie murmelnd in   süsse Ruh,
rustle   her murmuring into sweet sleep

Flüstre ihr   Träume der   Liebe zu.
whisper to her dreams of the love   (to)

As the sun is sinking with a reddening glow, lull my sweetheart till she sleeps. Rustle and murmur her into sweet slumber, whisper her dreams of love.

75. KRIEGERS AHNUNG
WARRIOR'S FOREBODING

75. WARRIOR'S FOREBODING

Ludwig Rellstab

In tiefer Ruh   liegt um   mich her
in deep   sleep lies   round me   about

Der   Waffenbrüder   Kreis;
of the weapon-brothers circle

Mir   ist das Herz so bang   und schwer,
to me is   the heart so uneasy and heavy

Von Sehnsucht mir so heiss.
from longing   to me so burning

In heavy sleep my comrades-in-arms lie round about me. My heart is leaden and uneasy, so burning with longing.

Wie hab ich oft   so süss   geträumt
how have I   often so sweetly dreamt

An ihrem Busen   warm!
on her   breast warm

Wie freundlich schien des   Herdes Glut,
how friendly   seemed of the hearth glow

Lag sie in meinem Arm!
lay she in my   arm

How often have I sweetly dreamt upon her warm breast! How friendly seemed the glow of the hearth as she lay in my arms.

Hier, wo   der   Flammen düstrer Schein
here where of the flames   dark   light

Ach, nur auf Waffen spielt,
ah   only on weapons plays

Hier fühlt die Brust sich   ganz allein,
here feels the breast (herself) quite alone

Der   Wehmut   Träne quillt.
of the melancholy tear   wells up

> Here where the flames
> gleam dismally, and play
> only on weapons, my heart
> feels so alone, and tears
> of melancholy well up.

Herz! dass der Trost   dich nicht verlässt,
heart that the consolation you   not   forsakes

Es   ruft noch manche Schlacht.
(it) calls still some   battle

Bald ruh' ich wohl und schlafe fest
soon rest I   well and sleep   fast

Herzliebste, gute Nacht!
dearest heart good-night

> O heart of mine, may
> consolation not forsake
> you! Battles still are
> calling. Soon will I sleep,
> sleep deeply. Dearest heart,
> good-night!

76. FRÜHLINGSSEHNSUCHT
    SPRING-LONGING

76. SPRING LONGING

Ludwig Rellstab

Säuselnde Lüfte   wehend so mild,
murmuring breezes blowing so softly

Blumiger Düfte atmend   erfüllt!
of flowery scents breathing filled

Wie haucht ihr mich wonnig   begrüssend an!
how breathe you me   delightfully welcoming on

Wie habt ihr dem   pochenden Herzen getan?
how have you to the throbbing heart done

Es möchte   euch folgen   auf luftiger Bahn,
it would like you to follow on airy   course

Wohin? Wohin?
whither whither

> Murmuring breezes, so
> softly blowing, breathing
> your fill of flowery
> scents - how delightful a
> welcome you whisper to me!
> How you have made my heart
> throb, and long to follow
> your airy course. O whither,
> whither?

Bächlein,   so munter rauschend zumal,
little brooks so merrily rushing   specially

Wollen hinunter silbern ins   Tal.
want   down   silvery into the valley

Die schwebende Welle, dort eilt   sie dahin!
the floating   ripple there hurries she thither

Tief   spiegeln sich   Fluren und Himmel darin.
deeply reflect (themselves) meadows and sky   therein

Was ziehst du mich, sehnend verlangender Sinn,
why draw you me   longing desiring   meaning

Hinab? Hinab?
down   down

> Little brooks, you
> eagerly rush your silvery
> ways down into the valley;
> shimmering ripples hasten
> there, reflecting meadow
> and sky in the deeps. O
> yearning desire, why do you
> draw me down, downwards?

Grüssender Sonne spielendes Gold,
of greeting sun   playing   gold

Hoffende Wonne bringest du hold!
expectant joy   bring   you graciously

Wie labt   mich dein selig begrüssendes Bild!
how delights me   your blessed welcoming   image

Es lächelt am   tiefblauen Himmel so mild
it smiles   in the deep-blue sky   so mildly

Und hat mir   das Auge mit Tränen gefüllt!
and has to me the eye with tears   filled

Warum? Warum?
why   why

Grünend   umkränzet Wälder und Höh,
becoming green wreathes woods and heights

Schimmernd erglänzet   Blütenschnee!
lustrous   shines forth blossom-snow

So dränget sich   alles   zum   bräutlichen
so crowds (itself) everything to the bridal
 Licht;
 light

Es   schwellen die Keime, die Knospe bricht;
(it) swell   the seeds the bud   breaks

Sie haben gefunden, was ihnen   gebricht;
they have found   what to them lacks

Und du? Und du?
and you and you

Rastloses Sehnen! wünschendes Herz,
restless yearning desiring   heart

Immer nur Tränen, Klage und Schmerz?
always only tears   lament and grief

Auch ich bin mir   schwellender Triebe   bewusst!
also I   am to me of rising   impulses conscious of

Wer stillet mir   endlich die drängende Lust?
who quenches to me finally the pressing desire

Nur du befreist den Lenz   in der Brust,
only you set free the spring in the breast

Nur du, nur du!
only you only you

Gold of playing sunlight,
you graciously bring a
promise of bliss in your
greeting. How your joyous
welcoming image delights me!
It softly smiles from deep
blue skies, and my eyes are
filled with tears. Why, O
why?

Woods and heights are
crowned with green; lustrous
blossoms shine radiant as
snow. All things crowd
toward the bridal light;
the seeds swell, and the
buds break! They have
found their fulfilment –
and you? and you?

Restless yearning, a
longing heart, nothing but
tears, lamenting and grief?
I, too, can feel upsurging
life – who will ever still
this turbulent desire? Only
you can set free the spring
within my heart – only you,
only you!

---

77. STÄNDCHEN
SERENADE

Ludwig Rellstab

Leise flehen meine Lieder
softly entreat my   songs

Durch   die Nacht zu dir;
through the night to you

77. SERENADE

Softly through the
night my songs entreat
you. Come down to me, my
love, in the still glade.

In den stillen Hain hernieder,
in the still   glade down

Liebchen,   komm zu mir!
sweetheart come to me

Flüsternd schlanke Wipfel   rauschen
whispering slender (tree-) tops rustle

Slender tree-tops
rustle and whisper in the
moonlight. O fair one, have
no fear of those who might
listen and betray!

In des   Mondes Licht;
in of the moon   light

Des   Verräters feindlich Lauschen
of the betrayer hostile   listening

Fürchte, Holde,   nicht.
fear   gracious one not

Hörst die Nachtigallen schlagen?
hear the nightingales to sing

Do you hear the singing
of the nightingales? Ah,
how they too implore you,
with the sound of their
sweet lament.

Ach! sie flehen dich,
ah   they implore you

Mit der   Töne süssen Klagen
with of the notes sweet lament

Flehen sie für mich.
implore they for me

Sie verstehn   des   Busens Sehnen,
they understand of the breast yearning

They know the yearnings
of the soul, the pain of
love, and touch each gentle
heart with their silvery
tones.

Kennen Liebesschmerz,
know   love's-pain

Rühren mit den Silbertönen
touch with the silver tones

Jedes weiche Herz.
every soft   heart

Lass auch dir   die Brust bewegen,
let also to you the breast to stir

Then let your heart be
stirred, my love, O hear
me! Trembling, I await
you – come give me joy!

Liebchen,   höre mich!
sweetheart hear me

Bebend   harr'ich dir entgegen!
trembling await I you (towards)

Komm beglücke   mich!
come make happy me

78. *AUFENTHALT*
SOJOURN

78. SOJOURN

Ludwig Rellstab

Rauschender Strom,   brausender Wald
rushing   (great) river blustering forest

Rushing river,
blustering forest,
starkest crags – my only
abode! My tears flow in
an endless stream, as wave
follows wave unceasingly.

Starrender Fels, mein Aufenthalt.
rigid   rock my   abode

Wie sich   die Welle an Welle reiht,
as (herself) the wave on wave succeeds

Fliessen die Tränen mir   ewig   erneut.
flow   the tears to me eternally renewed

Hoch in den Kronen   wogend sich's   regt,
high in the (tree-) tops heaving (itself) it stirs

Like the restless
stirring high in the trees,
my heart beats incessantly.

So unaufhörlich mein Herze schlägt.
so incessantly my   heart beats

Unchanging as the rock's
ancient ore, eternal is my
·grief.

Und wie des   Felsen uraltes Erz,
and as of the rock   ancient ore

Ewig   derselbe bleibet mein Schmerz.
eternally the same remains my   grief

---

79. *IN DER FERNE*
    IN THE DISTANCE

79. FROM AFAR

Ludwig Rellstab

Wehe dem   Fliehenden, Welt hinaus ziehenden!
woe to the fugitive one world forth going into

Woe to the fugitive,
driven out into the world,
traversing strange places

Fremde   durchmessenden, Heimat   vergessenden,
strange places traversing   homeland forgetting

and forgetting his homeland;
shunning his birthplace and

Mutterhaus   hassenden, Freunde verlassenden
mother-house hating   friends leaving

forsaking his friends - no
blessing will follow the
traveller on such ways!

Folget   kein Segen,   ach! auf ihren Wegen nach!
follows no   blessing alas on their ways after

Herze, das sehnende, Auge, das tränende,
heart the longing .eye   the weeping

Heart with its yearning,
eyes filled with tears,
endless longing that turns

Sehnsucht, nie   endende, heimwärts sich
longing   never ending   homewards herself
  wendende!
  turning

towards home; O restless
heart, O dying lament, O
evening-star gleaming,
hopelessly sinking.

Busen, der wallende, Klage, verhallende,
bosom the agitated lament dying away

Abendstern, blinkender, hoffnunglos sinkender!
evening-star gleaming   hopelessly sinking

Lüfte, ihr säuslnden, Wellen, sanft kräuselnden,
breezes you rustling   ripples softly curling

Rustling breezes, soft
curling ripples, hastening
sunbeams that never tarry;

Sonnenstrahl eilender, nirgend verweilender:
sunbeam   hastening nowhere tarrying

take the one who broke my
true heart - take her

Die mir   mit Schmerze ach! dies treue Herze brach,
who to me with sorrows ah   this true heart broke

greetings from the fugitive
driven out into the world.

Grüsst von dem Fliehenden, Welt hinaus ziehenden.
greets from the fugitive one world forth going into

80. *ABSCHIED*
   FAREWELL

80. FAREWELL

Ludwig Rellstab

Ade!   du muntre, du fröhliche Stadt, ade!
farewell you gay   you joyful   town   farewell

Schon   scharret mein Rösslein   mit lustigem
already paws   my   little horse with gay
   Fuss;
   foot

Jetzt nimm noch den letzten, den scheidenden
now   take still the last   the parting
   Gruss.
   greeting

Du hast mich wohl   niemals noch traurig gesehn,
you have me   indeed never   yet sad   seen

So kann es auch   jetzt nicht beim Abschied
so can it likewise now   not at the farewell
   geschehn.
   to happen

Farewell to the lively,
joyous town, farewell!
Already my little horse
gaily paws the ground, so
take your last, your final
leave! You have never yet
seen me sad, and will not
now as I say goodbye.
Farewell to the lively,
joyous town, farewell!

Ade,   ihr Bäume, ihr Gärten so grün, ade!
farewell you trees   you gardens so green farewell

Nun reit ich am   silbernen Strome entlang,
now ride I by the silver   river   along

Weit   schallend   ertönet mein Abschiedsgesang;
far off ringing out sounds my   farewell-song

Nie   habt ihr ein trauriges Lied gehört,
never have you a   sad   song heard

So wird euch   auch   keines beim Scheiden
so will to you likewise none   by the parting
   beschert.
   be given

Farewell, you trees and
gardens so green, farewell!
As I ride along the silvery
river, my parting song rings
out far and wide. You have
never heard me sing a
melancholy song, and I'll
not sing one as I leave.

Ade,   ihr freundlichen Mägdlein   dort, ade!
farewell you friendly   young maidens there farewell

Was schaut ihr aus   blumenumdufteten Haus
what look   you out of flower-scented   house

Mit schelmischen, lockenden Blicken heraus?
with arch   enticing looks   (out)

Wie sonst, so grüss ich und schaue mich um,
as usual so bow I   and look   me   round

Doch nimmer wend ich mein Rösslein   um.
but never turn I   my   little horse round

Farewell, you friendly
maidens there, farewell!
Why do you look out so
archly, so enticingly from
your flower-scented houses?
As always I hail you, and
look all about me, but never
will I turn my little horse
back!

Ade,   liebe Sonne, so gehst du zur   Ruh, ade!
farewell dear sun   so go   you to the rest farewell

Nun schimmert der   blinkenden Sterne Gold.
now glimmers of the twinkling stars gold

Wie bin ich euch Sternlein   am   Himmel so
how am I   to you little stars in the sky   so
   hold;
   kindly disposed

Farewell, dear sun, now
go to your rest, farewell!
The twinkling stars glimmer
already with gold. You are
so dear to me, little stars
in the sky; however widely
we travel the world, you
follow us faithfully
everywhere.

Durchziehn wir die Welt   auch weit und breit,
traverse   we   the world even far   and wide

Ihr gebt überall   uns   das treue   Geleit.
you give everywhere to us the faithful escort

Ade!   du schimmerndes Fensterlein   hell, ade!
farewell you gleaming   little window bright farewell

Du glänzest so traulich   mit dämmerndem   Schein,
you gleam   so familiarly with growing dusk shine

Und ladest so freundlich ins   Hüttchen
and invite so kindly   into the little cottage
  uns eins.
  us · (in)

Vorüber, ach, ritt ich so manches Mal,
past   oh   rode I   so many a time

Und wär es denn heute zum   letzten Mal?
and were it then today for the last   time

Ade,   ihr Sterne, verhüllet euch   grau!
farewell you stars   veil   yourselves grey
  Ade!
  farewell

Des   Fensterlein   trübes,   verschimmerndes Licht
of the little window melancholy shimmering   light

Ersetzt ihr unzähligen Sterne mir   nicht.
replace you innumerable stars to me not

Darf ich hier nicht weilen,   muss hier vorbei,
may I   here not   to linger must here past

Was hilft es, folgt ihr mir noch so treu!
what helps it follow you me yet so truly

Farewell, little
window shining brightly,
farewell! Your gleam is
so friendly in the growing
dusk, as it invites us into
the familiar little cottage.
Oh, how often I rode there
in times gone by - is it
really the last time today?

Farewell, you stars!
Veil yourselves with grey -
farewell! Your great
multitude cannot make up
for the sad glimmer of
that one little window.
Here I cannot linger, I
must pass on - your
faithful company can
bring me no comfort!

81. DER ATLAS
THE ATLAS

81. ATLAS

Heinrich Heine

Ich unglückseliger Atlas! Eine Welt,
I   miserable   Atlas a   world

Die ganze Welt der   Schmerzen muss ich tragen.
the whole world of the sorrows   must I   to bear

Ich trage Unerträgliches,   und brechen
I   bear (the) intolerable and to break

Will mir   das Herz im   Leibe.
wants to me the heart in the body

Du stolzes Herz, du hast es ja   gewollt!
you arrogant heart you have it indeed wanted

Du wolltest glücklich sein, unendlich glücklich,
you wanted   happy   to be infinitely happy

Oder unendlich elend,   stolzes Herz,
or   infinitely miserable arrogant heart

Und jetzo bist du elend!
and now   are you miserable

I, wretched Atlas,
must bear the world, a
whole world of sorrows.
I bear the intolerable,
and my heart would break
within my body.

O arrogant heart, this
was your desire! You wanted
happiness, infinite
happiness - or infinite
misery; and now, arrogant
heart, you have misery!

82. *IHR BILD*
   HER PICTURE

82. HER PORTRAIT

Heinrich Heine

Ich stand in dunklen Träumen
I stood in dark   dreams

Und starrt' ihr Bildnis an,
and stared her portrait at

Und das geliebte Antlitz
and the loved   face

Heimlich zu leben   begann.
secretly to to live began

In a dark mysterious
dream I stood and gazed
at her portrait, and her
beloved face came
secretly to life.

Um   ihre Lippen zog   sich
about her lips   stretched itself

Ein Lächeln wunderbar,
a   smile   wonderfully

Und wie von Wehmutstränen
and as   from melancholy-tears

Erglänzte ihr Augenpaar.
shone   her eye-pair

A wondrous smile played
about her lips, and her
eyes glistened as if with
tears of melancholy.

Auch meine Tränen flossen
also my   tears flowed

Mir   von den Wangen herab –
to me from the cheeks down

Und ach, ich kann es nicht glauben,
and ah I   can it not   to believe

Dass ich dich verloren hab!
that I you lost   have

And my tears flowed
down my cheeks. Oh, I
cannot believe that I
have lost you!

83. *DAS FISCHERMÄDCHEN*
   THE FISHER-MAIDEN

83. THE FISHER-MAIDEN

Heinrich Heine

Du schönes Fischermädchen,
you beautiful fisher-maiden

Treibe den Kahn ans   Land;
urge   the boat to the land

Komm zu mir und setze dich   nieder,
come to me and sit· (yourself) down

Wir kosen Hand in Hand.
we caress hand in hand

O beautiful fisher-
maiden, bring your little
boat to the shore. Come
and sit here with me,
lovingly hand in hand.

Leg an mein Herz dein Köpfchen
lay on my   heart your little head

Und fürchte   dich   nicht zu sehr;
and be afraid (yourself) not   too much

Lay your little head
upon my breast; and do not
be uneasy, you who so
carefree entrust yourself
each day to the wild ocean!

Vertraust du   dich   doch   sorglos
trust   you (yourself) indeed carefree

Täglich dem   wilden Meer!
daily   to the wild   ocean

Mein Herz gleicht   ganz   dem   Meere,
my   heart resembles wholly to the ocean

Hat Sturm und Ebb und Flut,
has storm and ebb and flow

Und manche schöne   Perle
and many a beautiful pearl

In seiner Tiefe ruht.
in its   deeps rests

My heart is just like
the ocean, with its tides
and its storms – and with
many a beautiful pearl
resting in its deeps.

84. DIE STADT
   THE TOWN

84. THE TOWN

Heinrich Heine

Am   fernen Horizonte
on the far   horizon

Erscheint, wie ein Nebelbild,
appears   like a mist-apparition

Die Stadt mit ihren Türmen,
the town with her   steeples

In Abenddämmrung   gehüllt.
in evening-twilight veiled

On the far horizon,
like a misty vision, the
town appears with its
steeples veiled in the
twilight.

Ein feuchter Windzug   kräuselt
a   damp   current of air ruffles

Die graue Wasserbahn;
the grey water-course

Mit traurigem Takte   rudert
with sad   measure rows

Der Schiffer in meinem Kahn.
the sailor   in my   boat

A damp current of air
ruffles the grey stretch
of water; with dreary
measure the boatman rows
my little boat.

Die Sonne hebt sich   noch einmal
the sun   rises (herself) again once

Leuchtend vom   Boden empor,
shining   from the ground upwards

Und zeigt mir jene Stelle,
and shows to me that place

Wo   ich das Liebste   verlor.
where I   the dearest one lost

From the earth the
gleaming sun rises once
more, and shows me the
place where I lost my
dearest beloved.

85. AM   MEER   85. BY THE SEA
    BY THE SEA

Heinrich Heine

Das Meer erglänzte weit hinaus   The sea was shimmering
the sea sparkled far out   far out in the last
                                              evening light. We sat by
Im   letzten Abendscheine;   the solitary fisherman's
in the last   evening-light   hut, silent and alone.

Wir sassen am   einsamen Fischerhaus,
we sat   by the solitary fisherman's-house

Wir sassen stumm und alleine.
we sat   silent and alone

Der Nebel stieg, das Wasser schwoll,   The mist was rising,
the mist rose   the water swelled   the waters surged; a
                                              sea-gull was flying to and
Die Möwe   flog hin und wieder;   fro. Tears fell from your
the sea-gull flew to and fro   loving eyes.

Aus deinen Augen liebevoll
from your eyes lovingly

Fielen die Tränen nieder.
fell the tears down

Ich sah sie fallen auf deine Hand   I saw them fall on
I   saw them to fall on your hand   your hand, and I sank to
                                              my knees; from your
Und bin aufs   Knie gesunken;   white hand I drank away
and am on to the knee sunk   the tears.

Ich hab von deiner weissen Hand
I   have from your white hand

Die Tränen fortgetrunken.
the tears drunk away

Seit jener Stunde verzehrt sich   mein Leib,   From that hour my
since that hour consumes (himself) my body   body is wasting away, and
                                              my soul dying with longing.
Die Seele stirbt vor Sehnen;   She, the miserable woman,
the soul dies with longing   has poisoned me with her
                                              tears.
Mich hat das unglücksel'ge Weib
me has the miserable woman

Vergiftet mit ihren Tränen.
poisoned with her tears

86. DER DOPPELGÄNGER   86. THE DOUBLE
    THE DOUBLE

Heinrich Heine

Still ist die Nacht, es ruhen die Gassen,   The night is still,
still is the night it sleeps the (narrow) streets the narrow streets
                                              sleeping; in this house
In diesem Hause wohnte mein Schatz;   lived my sweetheart. She
in this house lived my sweetheart   left the town long ago,
                                              but the house still stands
Sie hat schon längst die Stadt verlassen, in the same place.
she has already long ago the town left

Doch steht noch das Haus auf demselben Platz.
yet stands still the house on the same place

Da steht auch ein Mensch und starrt in die
there stands also a man and stares into the
Höhe,
high place

Und ringt die Hände vor Schmerzensgewalt;
and wrings the hands for pain's-violence

Mir graust es, wenn ich sein Antlitz sehe -
to me shudders it when I his face see

Der Mond zeigt mir meine eigne Gestalt.
the moon shows to me my own form

A man is standing there,
staring up at it, wringing
his hands in silent grief;
I shudder as I see his
face - for the moon
reveals my own image.

Du Doppelgänger, du bleicher Geselle!
you double you pallid companion

Was äffst du nach mein Liebesleid,
why mimic you - my love's-suffering

Das mich gequält auf dieser Stelle
that me tormented at this place

So manche Nacht, in alter Zeit?
so many a night in old time

You counterfeit,
pallid companion of mine!
Why do you mimic the
suffering of love which
tormented me here on
many a night, in times
gone by?

87. DIE TAUBENPOST
THE PIGEON-POST

87. PIGEON-POST

Johann Gabriel Seidl

Ich hab' eine Brieftaub' in meinem Sold,
I have a carrier-pigeon in my pay

Die ist gar ergeben und treu;
she is very loyal and true

Sie nimmt mir nie das Ziel zu kurz,
she takes to me never the goal too short

Und fliegt auch nie vorbei.
and flies also never past

I have a carrier-
pigeon to serve me, who
is so loyal and true; she
never fails to reach her
goal, and never flies
too far.

Ich sende sie viel tausendmal
I send her many thousand times

Auf Kundschaft täglich hinaus,
on custom daily out

Vorbei an manchem lieben Ort,
past to many a dear place

Bis zu der Liebsten Haus.
(unto) to of the dearest house

I send her out on
missions a thousand times
a day, past many well-
loved places, right to
my sweetheart's house.

Dort schaut sie zum Fenster heimlich hinei
there looks she at the window secretly in

Belauscht ihren Blick und Schritt,
spies out her glance and step

Gibt meine Grüsse scherzend ab
delivers my greetings chaffing up

There she peeps in at
the window, and notes
each glance and step. She
gaily delivers my greetings
and brings back hers in
return.

Und nimmt die ihren mit.
and takes the hers with (her)

Kein Briefchen brauch'ich zu schreiben mehr,
no note   need I to to write more

Die Träne selbst geb' ich ihr;
the tear itself give I   to her

O sie verträgt sie sicher   nicht,
O she miscarries them certainly not

Gar eifrig   dient sie mir.
very zealously serves she me

I no longer need to write messages, I give her my very tears. She certainly will not lose them, for she serves me with such zeal.

Bei Tag, bei Nacht, im   Wachen, im   Traum,
by day by night in the waking in the dream

Ihr   gilt   das alles gleich:
to her is worth this all   (the) same

Wann sie nur wandern, wandern kann,
when she just to roam to roam can

Dann ist sie überreich!
then is she extremely rich

By day or night, awake or asleep, it is all one to her. If she can only roam, she is quite content.

Sie wird   nicht müd', sie wird   nicht matt,
she becomes not   tired she becomes not   exhausted

Der Weg ist stets ihr   neu;
the way is always to her new

Sie braucht nicht Lockung,   braucht nicht Lohn,
she needs   not   enticement needs   not   reward

Die Taub' ist so mir   treu.
the dove is so to me true

She never tires, is never weary, her way seems always new. She needs no enticement, and no reward, to me she is always true.

Drum   heg' ich sie auch   so treu an
therefore cherish I   her really so truly to
  der Brust,
  the breast

Versichert des   schönsten Gewinns;
assured   of the fairest   gain

Sie heisst: die Sehnsucht - kennt ihr sie?
she is called the longing   know you her

Die Botin   treuen Sinns?
the messenger of true mind

And so, I clasp her lovingly to my heart, assured of the greatest favours. Her name is longing - do you know her? She is the messenger of fidelity.

88. DER HIRT   AUF DEM FELSEN
    THE SHEPHERD ON THE ROCK

88. THE SHEPHERD ON THE
ROCK

Wilhelm Müller

Wenn auf dem höchsten Fels ich steh',
when on the highest rock I   stand

In's   teife Tal   hernniederseh',
into the deep valley look down

Und singe,
and sing

When I stand on the highest rock, and look down into the deep valley, and sing - far away in the deep, dark valley, the echo rises up from the ravine.

Fern   aus dem tiefen, dunkeln Tal
distantly from the deep   dark   valley

Schwingt sich   empor   der Wiederhall
soars   itself upwards the echo

Der   Klüfte.
of the ravine

Je weiter meine Stimme dringt,
the further my   voice penetrates

Je heller sie mir   wiederklingt
the clearer she to me sounds back

Von unten.
from below

Mein Liebchen wohnt so weit von mir,
my   dear one lives so far from me

Drum   sehn' ich mich   so heiss   nach ihr
therefore long I   (myself) so ardently for her

Hinüber.
over there

The further my voice
reaches, the clearer it
echoes back to me from
below. My beloved lives
so far away, and I long
so passionately for her,
there beyond.

In tiefem Gram verzehr' ich mich,
in deep   grief devour I   myself

Mir   ist die Freude hin,
to me is the joy   lost

Auf Erden mir   die Hoffnung wich,
on earth to me the hope   withdrew

Ich hier so einsam bin.
I   here so lonely am

I am torn by deep
sorrow, joy for me has
passed. Hope for me on
earth has faded, I am
so lonely here.

So sehnend klang   im   Wald das Lied,
so longing sounded in the wood the song

So sehnend klang es durch die Nacht,
so longing sounded it through the night

Die Herzen es zum   Himmel zieht
the hearts it to the heaven draws

Mit wunderbarer Macht.
with wonderful   power

Der Frühling will kommen,
the spring   will come

Der Frühling, meine Freud',
the spring   my   delight

Nun mach' ich mich   fertig
now make I   myself ready

Zum   Wandern bereit.
to the wandering ready

In the wood my song
echoed so full of longing,
so full of longing in the
night. It lifts all hearts
to heaven with its strange
power. The spring will
come, the spring, my
delight. I'll make ready
now to be gone!

Robert Schumann
(1810-1856)

1. *LIEDERKREIS, Op.24*
   SONG—CYCLE

1. SONG CYCLE, Op.24

Heinrich Heine

i.

i.

Morgens   steh' ich auf und frage:
each morning get   I   up and ask

Kommt Feinsliebchen heut?
comes sweetheart   today

Abends   sink' ich hin und klage:
each evening sink I   down and lament

Aus blieb sie auch heut'.
away stayed she also today

Each morning I rise and ask: Will my sweet love come today? Each evening I sink into bed downcast: today again she did not come.

In der Nacht mit meinem Kummer
in the night with my   sorrow

Lieg' ich schlaflos, wach;
lie I sleepless   awake

Träumend, wie im   halben Schlummer,
dreaming as in the half slumber

Wandle ich bei Tag.
wander I   by day

All night I lie awake, sleepless with sorrow. All day I wander in a dream, half in sleep.

ii.

ii.

Es treibt mich hin, es treibt mich her!
it drives me there it drives me   here

Noch wenige Stunden, dann soll ich sie schauen,
still a few hours   then shall I her to see

Sie selber, die schönste der   schönen Jungfrauen.
she herself the fairest of the fair   maidens

Du armes Herz, was pochst du schwer?
you poor heart what throb you heavily

I am driven here, driven there - in a few hours I will see her, the fairest of the fair! Poor heart, how violent is your throbbing!

Die Stunden sind aber ein faules Volk!
the hours   are but a lazy folk

Schleppen sich   behaglich träge,
move slowly themselves comfortably idle

The hours are such a lazy crowd; dawdling in their comfortable and idle way, they creep along yawning - hurry yourselves, you laggards!

Schleichen gähnend ihre Wege;
creep   yawning their ways

Tummle dich,   du faules Volk!
hurry yourselves you lazy folk

Tobende Eile mich treibend erfasst!
raging haste me urging on seizes

Aber wohl   niemals liebten die Horen;
but perhaps never loved the hours

Heimlich im   grausamen Bunde verschworen,
secretly in the cruel   band forsworn

Spotten sie   tückisch der   Liebenden Hast.
mock   they spitefully of the loving ones haste

I am seized by raging
impatience - perhaps the Hours
were never in love; in cruel
and secret conspiracy, they
mock spitefully at mens' haste.

iii.

Ich wandelte unter den Bäumen
I wandered under the trees

Mit meinem Gram allein,
with my   grief alone

Da   kam das alte Träumen
when came the old dreams

Und schlich mir in's   Herz hinein.
and stole   to me into the heart (into)

iii.

I was wandering beneath the
trees, alone with my grief,
when my old dreams came back
again, and stole right into
my heart.

Wer hat euch dies Wörtlein   gelehret,
who has you this little word taught

Ihr Vöglein   in luftiger Höh'?
you little birds in airy   height

Schweigt still, wenn mein Herz es höret,
be   silent when my   heart it hears

Dann tut es noch einmal so weh.
then does it more once so hurt

Who taught you that little
word, you birds up high in the
air? Be still, for when I hear
it, it brings my heart such
pain.

"Es kam ein Jungfräulein gegangen,
(it came) a maiden   walked

Die sang es immerfort,
who sang it always on

Da   haben wir Vöglein   . gefangen
then have we little birds caught

Das hübsche, goldene Wort."
the pretty golden word

'A young girl once came
walking here, and sang it
again and again. And we birds
caught it, that pretty, golden
word.'

Das sollt ihr mir nicht erzählen,
that must you to me not   to tell

Ihr Vöglein   wunderschlau,
you (little) birds very crafty

Ihr wollt meinen Kummer mir   stehlen,
you want my   grief to me to steal

Ich aber niemandem trau'.
I but no one   trust

You should not have told
me that, you crafty little
birds. You want to steal away
my grief, but no one do I
trust.

iv.

Lieb' Liebchen, leg's Händchen   aufs
dear sweetheart lay the (little) hand on the
    Herze mein;
    heart mine

Ach, hörst du, wie's pochet im   Kämmerlein?
ah ‧ hear you how it throbs in the little room

Da   hauset ein Zimmermann schlimm und arg,
there dwells a   carpenter bad   and wicked

Der zimmert mir   einen Totensarg.
who makes   to me a   coffin

Es hämmert und klopfet bei Tag und bei Nacht,
it hammers and taps   by day and by night

Es hat mich schon längst um den Schlaf gebracht.
it has me   -long ago- of the sleep deprived

Ach, sputet euch,   Meister Zimmermann,
oh   hurry yourself master carpenter

Damit   ich balde schlafen kann.
so that I   soon to sleep can

Lay your hand on my heart,
dear love - do you hear how it
throbs in its little room?
There dwells a wicked carpenter,
who is making a coffin for me.

There's a hammering and
tapping night and day, and I
can sleep no more. Oh, make
haste, Master Carpenter, that
I soon may sleep!

v.

Schöne Wiege meiner Leiden,
lovely cradle of my sorrows

Schönes Grabmal meiner Ruh,
lovely tomb   of my rest

Schöne Stadt, wir müssen scheiden -
lovely town   we must   to part

Lebe wohl, ruf' ich dir   zu.
fare-well call I to you (to)

Lebe wohl, du heil'ge Schwelle,
fare-well you hallowed threshold

Wo   da   wandelt Liebchen   traut;
where there wanders sweetheart dear

Lebe wohl, du heil'ge Stelle,
fare-well you hallowed place

Wo   ich sie zuerst geschaut.
where I   her first saw

Hätt' ich dich doch nie   geseh'n,
had   I   you indeed never seen

Schöne Herzenskönigin!
fair heart's-queen

Nimmer wär   es dann geschehen,
never would be it then happened

Dass ich jetzt so elend   bin.
that I   now so wretched am

Nie   wollt' ich dein Herze rühren,
never wanted I   your heart to move

Liebe hab' ich nie   erfleht;
love have I   never begged for

Lovely cradle of my sorrows,
lovely tomb of my tranquillity;
lovely city, we must part - I
call to you, farewell!

Farewell, you hallowed
threshold, where my dear
sweetheart passed; farewell,
you hallowed place, where I
first saw her.

Had I but never seen you,
fair queen of my heart, never
would I have been as now, so
wretched.

I never sought to touch
your heart; I never begged for
love. I only desired to live
at peace, breathing the air
you breathe.

Nur ein stilles Leben führen
only a   peaceful life to lead

Wollt' ich, wo   dein Odem   weht.
wanted I   where your breath blows

Doch du drängst mich selbst von hinnen,
but you urge   me   even away from here

Bitt're Worte spricht dein Mund;
bitter words speaks your mouth

Wahnsinn wühlt in meinen Sinnen,
frenzy   stirs up in my   thoughts

Und mein Herz ist krank und wund.
and my heart is sick and sore

But you even drive me away from here, and your lips speak bitter words. My mind is stirred to a frenzy, my heart is sick and sore.

Und die Glieder matt und träge,
and the limbs   feeble and indolent

Schlepp' ich fort am   Wanderstab,
drag   I   onward on the walking stick

Bis mein müdes Haupt ich lege
till my weary head I lay

Ferne   in ein kühles Grab.
far away in a   cool   grave

My limbs are feeble and spent, as I drag myself onward with my staff, till I can lay my weary head in a cool grave far away.

vi.   vi.

Warte, warte, wilder Schiffsmann,
wait   wait   wild boatman

Gleich folg' ich zum   Hafen dir;
soon   follow I to the port you

Von zwei Jungfrau'n nehm' ich Abschied,
from two maidens   bid I   farewell

Von Europa und von ihr.
from Europe and from her

Wait, wait, wild boatman, I'll follow you soon to the harbour; I must say farewell to my two loves, to Europe and to her.

Blutquell, rinn' aus meinen Augen,
blood-spring flow from my   eyes

Blutquell, brich aus meinem Leib,
blood-spring break from my   body

Dass ich mit dem heissen Blute
that I   with the hot   blood

Meine Schmerzen niederschreib:
my   griefs   write down

May a stream of blood flow from my eyes, may a stream of blood pour forth from my body, that in the scalding blood I may write of my griefs.

Ei, mein Lieb, warum just heute
ah, my dear   why   just today

Schaudert dich, mein Blut zu seh'n?
shudder   you   my   blood to to see

Sahst mich bleich und herzeblutend
saw   me   pale   and heart-bleeding

Lange Jahre vor   dir steh'n.
long years before you to stand

Ah, my love, why do you shudder today, at the sight of my blood? You have seen me pale, my heart bleeding, for many a long year.

Kennst du noch das alte Liedchen
know   you still the old (little) song

Von der Schlang' im   Paradies,
of the serpent in the Paradise

Do you remember the old tale of the serpent in Paradise, that with the evil gift of an apple plunged our forefather into misery?

Die durch   schlimme Apfelgabe
that through evil   apple-gift

Unsern Ahn'   ins   Elend stiess?
our   forefather in the misery threw

Alles Unheil   brachten Äpfel,
all   calamity brought apples

Eva bracht' damit   den Tod,
Eva brought therewith the death

Eris brachte Trojas Flammen
Paris brought Troy's flames

Du bracht'st beides, Flamm' und Tod.
you brought   both   flames and death

      Apples have brought all
kinds of evil; with them Eve
brought death, and Paris
brought flames to Troy. Now
you have brought both, flames
and death!

    vii.

    vii.

Berg'   und Burgen   schau'n herunter
mountains and fortresses look   down here

In   den spiegelhellen Rhein,
into the mirror-bright Rhine

Und mein Schiffchen segelt munter,
and my   little boat sails merrily

Rings umglänzt   von Sonnenschein.
around shone about by sunshine

      Mountain and fortress look
down into the mirror-bright
Rhine. My little boat sails
merrily along, sunshine
dancing all around it.

Ruhig   seh' ich zu dem Spiele
quietly look I   at the playing

Gold'ner Wellen, kraus   bewegt,
of golden waves   ruffled moved

Still   erwachen die Gefühle,
softly awaken   the feelings

Die ich tief im   Busen hegt'.
that I   deep in the bosom cherished

      Quietly I watch the playing
of the golden waves, moving in
ripples. Softly the feelings
I once cherished reawaken in
my heart.

Freundlich   grüssend und verheissend
in a friendly way greeting and promising

Lockt hinab des   Stromes Pracht;
tempts down of the river   splendour

Doch ich kenn' ihn; oben gleissend,
but I   know him above glistening

Birgt sein Inn'res   Tod und Nacht.
hides his inner self death and night

      The river in its splendour,
friendly and welcoming, is
tempting in its depths; but I
know, that beneath the gleaming
surface, its soul hides death
and night.

Oben Lust, im   Busen Tücken,
above joy   in the bosom malice

Strom, du bist der   Liebsten Bild!
river you are of the beloved   image

Die kann auch so freundlich   nicken,
she can also so in a friendly way to nod

Lächelt auch so fromm   und mild.
smiles   also so innocently and tenderly

      Joyful without, a treacherous
heart within; river, you are the
very image of my beloved! She,
too, gives a friendly greeting,
a smile, so tender and pure.

viii.

viii.

Anfangs wollt' ich fast verzagen,
at first wanted I almost to despair

  At first I was nearly in
despair, and thought I could
never bear it; and yet I have
endured it – but never ask me
how?

Und ich glaubt', ich trüg' es nie,
and I believed I would bear it never

Und ich hab' es doch getragen –
and I have it yet borne

Aber fragt mich nur nicht: wie?
but ask me only not how

ix.

ix.

Mit Myrten und Rosen, lieblich und hold,
with myrtles and roses lovely and charming

  With myrtles and roses,
charming and fair, with
fragrant cypresses and gold,
I would adorn this book like a
shrine and bury my songs
within.

Mit duft'gen Cypressen und Flittergold
with fragrant cypresses and tinsel

Möcht' ich zieren dies Buch wie 'nen Totenschrein,
would like I to adorn this book like a shrine

Und sargen meine Lieder hinein.
and to put in a coffin my songs inside

O könnt' ich die Liebe sargen hinzu!
O could I the love to put in a coffin beside

  O, if I could but bury my
love there too! On the grave
of love grows the flower of
peace; it blooms there for
someone to pluck, but for me
it will only blossom, when I
too am in my grave.

Auf dem Grabe der Liebe wächst Blümlein der
* Ruh',*
on the grave of the love grows little flower of the
 peace

Da blüht es hervor, da pflückt man es ab,
there blooms it forth there plucks one it off

Doch mir blüht's nur, wenn ich selber im Grab.
but to me blossoms it only when I myself in the grave

Hier sind die Lieder, die einst so wild,
here are the songs that once so furious

  There are the songs that
once poured forth as furious
as the lava from Mount Etna,
hurled from the very depths
of my soul, showering fiery
sparks around.

Wie ein Lavastrom, der dem Ätna entquillt,
as a lava-stream that to the Etna flows forth

Hervorgestürzt aus dem tiefsten Gemüt,
hurls forth out of the deepest soul

Und rings viel blitzende Funken versprüht.
and around many sparkling sparks sprays.

Nun liegen sie stumm und totengleich,
now lie they silent and death-like

  They lie now silent as
death, staring coldly, pale
as the mist; yet the old
fire would quicken, if a
loving spirit hovered near.

Nun starren sie kalt und nebelbleich.
now stare they cold and mist-pale

Doch auf's neu' die alte Glut sie belebt,
yet – anew – the old glow them quickens

Wenn der Liebe Geist einst über sie schwebt.
when of the love spirit once over them hovers

Und es wird mir im Herzen viel Ahnung
* laut,*
and it becomes to me in the heart much presentiment
 known

  And I know well in my
heart that one day a loving
spirit will rekindle them;
for one day this book will
come into your hands, my
sweet love, in that far-off
land.

Der Liebe Geist einst über sie taut;
of the love spirit one day over them thaws

Einst   kommt dies Buch in   deine Hand,
one day comes this book into   your   hand

Du süsses Lieb, im   fernen Land.
you sweet love in the far-off land

Dann löst   sich des   Liedes Zauberbann,
then loosens itself of the song   magic-spell

Die blassen Buchstaben schau'n dich an,
the pale   letters   look   you at

Sie schauen dir   flehend   ins   schöne Aug',
they look   to you imploring in the lovely eye

Und flüstern mit Wehmut   und Liebeshauch.
and whisper with melancholy and love's-breath

Then the spell that
binds my songs will break,
the pale letters will look
up at you - will gaze
imploringly into your lovely
eyes, and whisper with the
melancholy breath of love.

From *MYRTEN*
   MYRTLES

from MYRTLES

2. *WIDMUNG*
   DEDICATION

2. DEDICATION

Friedrich Rückert

Du meine Seele, du mein Herz,
you my   soul   you my   heart

Du meine Wonn', o du mein Schmerz,
you my   joy   O you my   sorrow

Du meine Welt, in der   ich lebe,
you my   world in which I   live

Mein Himmel du, darein ich schwebe,
my   heaven you into it I   soar

O du mein Grab, in das   hinab
O you my   grave in which down

Ich ewig   meinen Kummer gab!
I   for ever my   grief gave

Du bist die Ruh', du bist der Frieden,
you are the rest you are the peace

Du bist vom   Himmel mir   beschieden.
you are from the Heaven to me bestowed

Dass du mich liebst, macht mich mir   wert,
that you me   love   makes me   to me worthy

Dein Blick hat mich vor   mir verklärt,
your glance has me before me transfigured

Du hebst mich liebend über mich,
you raise me lovingly above myself

Mein guter Geist, mein bess'res Ich.
my   good spirit my   better   I

You, my soul, you, my
heart! You, my joy, O you,
my sorrow! You, the world in
which I live! You, the heaven
to which I aspire! O you, the
grave where I for ever laid
my grief - you are rest, you
are peace; you were bestowed
on me by Heaven. Because you
love me, I find my own worth,
I see myself transformed by
your glance. Lovingly you
raise me up - you, my good
spirit, my better self.

3. FREISINN
   SENSE OF FREEDOM

3. FREEDOM

Johann Wolfgang von Goethe
(from the *Westöstlicher Divan*)
            west-east   collection of poems

Lasst mich nur auf meinem Sattel gelten!
let   me   only on my   saddle prove worth

Bleibt in euren Hütten, euren Zelten!
stay   in your huts   your tents

Und ich reite froh   in   alle Ferne,
and I   ride joyfully into all   distance

Über meiner Mütze nur die Sterne.
above my   cap   only the stars

   Let me prove myself in
the saddle! Stay in your huts
and tents! And joyfully I'll
ride far, far away, with only
the stars above my head.

Er hat euch die Gestirne   gesetzt
he has you   the constellations placed

Als Leiter zu Land und See,
as guide to land and sea

Damit   ihr euch   daran   ergötzt,
so that you (yourselves) thereon take delight

Stets   blickend in   die Höh'.
constantly looking   into the high place

   He placed the constellations
to guide you over land and sea;
so you can take delight in a
constant upward gaze.

4. DER NUSSBAUM
   THE NUT-TREE

4. THE NUT-TREE

Julius Mosen

Es   grünet   ein Nussbaum vor   dem Haus,
(it) grows green a   nut-tree in front of the house

Duftig,   luftig breitet er blättrig die Blätter aus.
fragrantly airily spreads he leafily the leaves out

   A nut tree unfolds its
green before the house;
fragrantly, airily, it
spreads its leaves.

Viel liebliche Blüten   stehen d'ran;
many lovely   blossoms stand on it

Linde Winde kommen, sie herzlich   zu umfahn.
soft winds come   them affectionately to to embrace

   It bears many lovely
blossoms; soft breezes
come to caress them.

Es   flüstern je   zwei zu zwei gepaart,
(it) whisper each two to two   paired

Neigend, beugend zierlich zum   Kusse die
bending bowing daintily to the kiss the
   Häuptchen   zart.
   (little) heads delicate

   They whisper together in
their pairs, gracefully nodding
and bowing their delicate
heads to kiss.

Sie flüstern von einem Mägdlein,   das
they whisper of a   young maiden who

Dächte die Nächte und Tage lang, wusste, ach!
thought the nights and days long knew   ah
   selber nicht was.
   herself not   what

   They whisper of a young
girl, who thinks night and
day - ah, she herself knows
not what!

Sie flüstern, wer mag verstehn   so gar
they whisper   who may to understand so very

They whisper - but who
can understand so soft an
air? - whisper of a
bridegroom and next year.

Leise Weis'? - Flüstern von Bräut'gam und
soft air   whisper of bridegroom and

nächstem Jahr.
next   year

Das Mägdlein   horchet, es rauscht im   Baum;
the young maiden listens   it rustles in the tree

The young girl listens,
the tree softly rustles;
yearning, wondering, she
sinks smiling into sleep
and dreams.

Sehnend, wähnend sinkt es lächelnd in   Schlaf
yearning fancying sinks it smiling   into sleep

und Traum.
and dream

---

5. *JEMAND*
   SOMEONE

5. FOR THE SAKE OF SOMEONE

German translation by W. Gerhard
(There are minor discrepancies in
meaning between the two versions)

Robert Burns
(original text)

Mein Herz ist betrübt ich sag' es nicht
my heart is troubled I   tell it not

My heart is sair, I dare na tell,
My heart is sair for somebody;
I could wake a winter night,
For the sake o' somebody!
Oh-hon! for somebody!
Oh-hey! for somebody!
I could range the whole world
                              around,
For the sake o' somebody.

Mein Herz ist betrübt um Jemand;
my   heart is troubled for somebody

Ich könnte wachen   die längste Nacht,
I   could to be awake the longest night

Und immer träumen von Jemand.
and always to dream of   somebody

O Wonne! von Jemand;
O bliss of   somebody

O Himmel! von Jemand;
O heaven of somebody

Durchstreifen könnt' ich die ganze Welt,
roam through could I   the whole world

Aus Liebe zu Jemand.
from love for somebody

Ihr Mächte, die ihr Liebe hold,
you powers who you love sweetly

Ye powers that smile on
                    virtuous love,
O, sweetly smile on somebody!
Fra ilka danger keep him free,
And send me safe my somebody.
Oh-hon! for somebody!
Oh-hey! for somebody!
I wad do - what wad I not?
For the sake o' somebody!

O lächelt freundlich auf Jemand!
O smile kindly   on somebody

Beschirmt ihn, wo   Gefahren droh'n;
protect   him where dangers threaten

Gebt sicher Geleite dem   Jemand!
give safe escort to the somebody

O Wonne! dem   Jemand;
O bliss to the somebody

O Himmel! dem   Jemand!
O heaven to the somebody

Ich wollt' ich wollte was wollt' ich nicht
I   would I   would what would I   not

Für meinen, meinen Jemand!
for my   my   somebody

6. *SITZ' ICH ALLEIN*
    SIT   I   ALONE

Johann Wolfgang von Goethe
(from the *West-östlicher Divan*)
        west-east   collection of poems

Sitz' ich allein,
sit   I   alone

Wo   kann ich besser sein?
where can I   better to be

Meinen Wein
my   wine

Trink' ich allein;
drink I   alone

Niemand setzt mir Schranken,
no one sets me limits

Ich hab' so meine eignen Gedanken.
I   have so my   own   thoughts

6. I SIT ALONE

    I sit alone - can I be
anywhere better? I drink my
wine alone. No one sets limits
about me. I have just my own
thoughts.

7. *TRINKLIED*
    DRINKING-SONG

Johann Wolfgang von Goethe
(from the *West-östlicher Divan*)
        west-east   collection of poems

Setze mir   nicht, du Grobian,
set   to me not   you boor

Mir den Krug   so derb   vor   die Nase!
to me the tankard so roughly in front of the nose

Wer mir   Wein bringt, sehe mich freundlich an,
who to me wine brings look me   affably   at

Sonst   trübt sich   der Eilfer
otherwise clouds himself the (special) wine
  im   Glase!
  in the glass

Du zierlicher Knabe, du, komm' herein,
you pretty   lad   you come in here

Was stehst du denn da   auf der Schwelle,
why stand you then there on the threshold

7. DRINKING-SONG

    Don't set the tankard
so roughly in front of my
nose, you rude fellow!
Whoever brings my wine must
be civil, or the fine grape
will cloud in the glass.

    You pretty lad, come here!
Why do you stand there at the
door? Hereafter you shall be
the one to serve me - every
wine is choice and clear.

Du sollst mir künftig   der Schenke   sein,
you shall to me henceforth the pourer-out to be

Jeder Wein ist schmackhaft und helle.
every wine is tasty   and clear

8. *DIE LOTOSBLUME*
  THE LOTUS-FLOWER
8. THE LOTUS FLOWER

Heinrich Heine

Die Lotosblume   ängstigt
the lotus-flower distresses

Sich   vor   der   Sonne Pracht,
herself before of the sun   splendour

Und mit gesenktem Haupte
and with sunk   head

Erwartet sie träumend die Nacht.
awaits   she dreaming the night

The lotus flower is afraid of the sun's great splendour, and with bowed head she dreamily awaits the coming of the night.

Der Mond, der ist ihr Buhle,
the moon who is her sweetheart

Er weckt sie mit seinem Licht,
he wakes her with his   light

Und ihm   entschleiert sie freundlich
and to him unveils   she amiably

Ihr frommes Blumengesicht.
her innocent flower-face

The moon, who is her loved one, awakens her with his light; smiling, she unveils for him her innocent flower face.

Sie blüht und glüht und leuchtet,
she blooms and glows and glimmers

Und starret stumm   in   die Höh';
and stares silently into the high place

Sie duftet   und weinet und zittert
she sends forth fragrance and weeps and trembles

Vor Liebe und Liebesweh.
with love and love's-pain

She blooms and glows and glimmers, silently gazing upwards; breathes forth her fragrance, and weeps and trembles with love, and the pains of love.

9. *TALISMANE*
  TALISMAN

9. TALISMAN

Johann Wolfgang von Goethe
(from the *West-östlicher Divan*)
        west-east   collection of poems

Gottes ist der Orient!
of God is the Orient

Gottes ist der Occident!
of God is the Occident

The Orient is of God! The Occident is of God! The North and the South rest in the peace of His hands.

Nord- und südliches Gelände
North and South   land

Ruht im   Frieden seiner Hände.
rests in the peace   of His hands

Er der Einzige, Gerechte,
He the only One righteous One

Will   für jedermann das Rechte.
desires for every man the justice

Sei von seinen hundert Namen
be of His   hundred names

Dieser   hochgelobet! Amen.
this one magnified   amen

    He, the only One, the
righteous One, desires
justice for all mankind.
May He of a hundred names
be magnified! Amen.

Gottes ist der Orient!
of God is the Orient

Gottes ist der Occident!
of God is the Occident

    The Orient is of God!
The Occident is of God!

Mich verwirren will das Irren,
me to confuse will the erring

Doch du weisst mich zu entwirren.
but you know me to to extricate

Wenn ich handle, wenn ich dichte,
when I act   when I   write poems

Gib du meinem Weg die Richte!
give you my   way the direction

    My erring sets me in
confusion, but you know how
to free me. Whatever I may
do, whatever I may write,
direct me on my way!

10. LIED DER   SULEIKA
    SONG OF THE SULEIKA

10. SULEIKA'S SONG

    Johann Wolfgang von Goethe
    (from the *West-östlicher Divan*)
         west-east   collection of poems

Wie mit innigstem   Behagen,
how with most fervent enjoyment

Lied, empfind' ich deinen Sinn!
song sense   I   your   meaning

Liebevoll du scheinst zu sagen,
lovingly you seem   to to say

Dass ich ihm   zur   Seite bin.
that I   to him to the side am

    With what deep
contentment, O song, do
I hear your message!
Lovingly you seem to say
that I am at his side;

Dass er ewig   mein gedenket,
that he for ever of me thinks

Seiner Liebe Seligkeit
of his love bliss

Immerdar der   Fernen   schenket,
always   to the distant one bestows

Die ein Leben ihm   geweiht.
who a   life to him dedicated

    that he always thinks of me,
and bestows the rapture of
his love on the one who is
far away, who dedicates her
life to him.

Ja, mein Herz, es ist der Spiegel,
yes my   heart it is the mirror

Freund, worin   du dich   erblickt;
friend wherein you yourself saw

Diese Brust, wo   deine Siegel
this   breast where your   seal

Kuss auf Kuss hereingedrückt.
kiss on kiss pressed in

Süsses Dichten,   lautre   Wahrheit,
sweet writing of poetry undefiled truth

Fesselt   mich in Sympathie!
captivate me   in sympathy

Rein   verkörpert Liebesklarheit.
purely embodied   love's-clarity

Im   Gewand der   Poesie.
in the garment of the poetry

Yes, dear friend, my
heart is the mirror in which
you see yourself; this breast,
the place whereon you pressed
your seal, kiss by kiss.

Sweet poetry, truth
undefiled, your spirit
enthral me! Love's bright
purity, embodied in the
guise of poetry.

11. *DIE HOCHLÄNDER-WITWE*
THE HIGHLAND   WIDOW

11. THE HIGHLAND WIDOW'S
LAMENT

German translation by W. Gerhard
(There are minor discrepancies in
meaning between the two versions)

Robert Burns
(original text)

Ich bin gekommen ins   Niederland
I   am come   into the Lowlands

O weh, O weh, O weh!
O woe O woe O woe

So ausgeplündert haben sie mich,
so plundered   have they me

Dass ich vor Hunger vergeh'!
that I   for hunger perish

So war's in meinem Hochland nicht;
so was it in my   Highlands not

O weh, O weh, O weh!
O woe O woe O woe

Ein hochbeglückter   Weib, als ich,
a   more highly happy woman than I

War nicht auf Tal   und Höh'!
was not   on valley and hill

Denn damals hatt' ich zwanzig Küh';
for then   had   I   twenty cows

O weh, O weh, O weh!
O woe O woe O woe

Die gaben Milch und Butter mir,
they gave milk and butter to me

Und weideten im   Klee.
and grazed   in the clover

Oh! I am come to the low
                       countrie,
Och-on, och-on, och-rie!
Without a penny in my purse,
To buy a meal to me.

It was nae sae in the
                   Highland hills,
Och-on, och-on, och-rie!
Nae woman in the countrie wide,
Sae happy was as me.

For then I had a score o'kye,
Och-on, och-on, och-rie!
Feeding on yon hills so high,
And giving milk to me.

Und sechzig Schafe hatt' ich dort;
and sixty   sheep   had   I   there

O weh, O weh, O weh!
O woe O woe O woe

Die wärmten mich mit weichem Vlies
they warmed me with soft   fleece

Bei Frost und Winterschnee.
by frost and winter-snow

Es konnte kein' im   ganzen Clan
(it) could   no one in the whole clan

Sich   grössern Glückes   freu'n;
(himself) of greater happiness to rejoice

Denn Donald war der schönste Mann,
for Donald was the finest   man

Und Donald, der war mein!
and Donald he was mine

So blieb's,   so blieb's,   bis Charlie Stuart
so remained it so remained it till Charlie Stuart
    kam,
    came

Alt-Schottland zu befrei'n;
old Scotland   to to set free

Da musste Donald seinen Arm
then had to Donald his   arm

Ihm   und dem Lande leih'n.
to him and to the land   to lend

Was sie befiel, wer weiss es nicht?
what them befell who knows it not

Dem Unrecht wich das Recht,
to the wrong yielded the right

Und auf Cullodens blut'gem Feld
and on Culloden's bloody field

Erlagen Herr und Knecht.
slayed master and servant

O! dass ich kam ins   Niederland!
O that I   came into the Lowlands

O weh, O weh, O weh!
O woe O woe O woe

Nun gibt's kein unglücksel'ger Weib
now is there no   more wretched woman

Vom   Hochland bis zur See!
from the Highlands (unto) to the sea

And there I had three score
                    o'yowes,
Och-on, och-on, och-rie!
Skipping on yon bonnie knowes,
And casting woo' to me.

I was the happiest of the clan,
Sair, sair, may I repine.
For Donald was the bravest lad,
And Donald he was mine.

Till Charlie Stuart cam at
                    last,
Sae for to set us free,
My Donald's arm was wanted then
For Scotland and for me.

Their waefu' fate what need I
                    tell?
Richt to the wrong did yield:
My Donald and his country fell
Upon Culloden field.

Oh! I am come to the low
                    countrie,
Och-on, och-on, och-rie!
Nae woman in the world wide
Sae wretched now as me.

12. *LIED DER   BRAUT I*
    SONG OF THE BRIDE

12. SONG OF THE BRIDE

Friedrich Rückert

Mutter, Mutter! glaube nicht,
mother mother believe not

Weil   ich ihm lieb' allsosehr,
because I him love all so much

Dass nun Liebe mir   gebricht,
that now love to me is wanting

Dich zu lieben, wie vorher.
you to to love as before

O, mother, do not think
because I love him so much,
I do not love you as I did
before.

Mutter, Mutter! seit ich ihn
mother mother since I him

Liebe, lieb' ich erst   dich sehr.
love love I more than ever you much

Lass mich an mein Herz dich zieh'n,
let me to my heart you to draw

Und dich küssen wie mich er!
and you to kiss as me he

O, mother, since I have
loved him, my love for you
is greater than ever. Let
me draw you to my heart, and
kiss you, as he kisses me!

Mutter, Mutter! seit ich ihn
mother mother since I him

Liebe, lieb' ich erst   dich ganz,
love love I more than ever you completely

Dass du mir   das Sein verlieh'n
that you to me the being gave

Das mir   ward zu solchem Glanz.
that to me grew to such   splendour

O, mother, since I so
loved him, my love for you
is only now complete — for
you gave me my being, that
has grown to enjoy such
splendour.

13. *LIED DER BRAUT II*
    SONG OF THE BRIDE

13. SONG OF THE BRIDE II

Friedrich Rückert

Lass mich ihm   am   Busen hangen,
let me   to him on the bosom to cling

Mutter, Mutter! lass   das Bangen.
mother mother refrain from the being afraid

Frage nicht: wie soll sich's   wenden?
ask   not   how shall itself it to turn

Frage nicht: wie soll das enden?
ask   not   how shall that to end

Enden? Enden soll sich's   nie;
to end to end shall itself it never

Wenden? noch nicht weiss ich, wie!
to turn yet not   know I   how

Let me cling to his
breast — O mother, cease
your fears! Do not ask:
will it ever change? Do
not ask: how will it end?
End? It must never end!
Change? I cannot yet know
how! Let me cling to his
breast — O let me!

Lass mich ihm   am   Busen hangen,
let me   to him on the bosom to cling

Lass mich!
let me

14. *HOCHLÄNDERS ABSCHIED*   14. MY HEART'S IN THE
     HIGHLANDER'S FAREWELL   HIGHLANDS

German translation by W. Gerhard
(There are minor discrepancies in   Robert Burns
meaning between the two versions)   (original text)

Mein Herz ist im   Hochland, mein Herz ist   My heart's in the Highlands,
my heart is in the highlands my   heart is   my heart is not here;
  nicht hier;   My heart's in the Highlands,
  not   here   a-chasing the deer;
                                                     Chasing the wild deer, and
Mein Herz ist im   Hochland, im   Waldesrevier; following the roe,
my heart is in the Highlands in the forest-reserve My heart's in the Highlands
                                                      wherever I go.
Dort jagt es den Hirsch und verfolget das Reh;   Farewell to the Highlands,
there hunts it the red deer and follows   the roe   farewell to the North,
                                                     The birthplace of valour, the
Mein Herz ist im   Hochland, wohin ich auch geh'! country of worth;
my   heart is in the Highlands where- I -ever go   Wherever I wander, wherever
                                                      I rove,
Leb' wohl, mein Hochland, mein heimischer Ort!   The hills of the Highlands
fare-well my   Highlands my   native   place   for ever I love.
                                                     Farewell to the mountains,
Die Wiege der   Freiheit, des   Mutes ist dort.   high covered with snow;
the cradle of the freedom   of the valour is there Farewell to the straths and
                                                      green valleys below;
Wohin ich auch wandre, wo   immer ich bin: Farewell to the forests and
where- I -ever wander where-ever I   am   wild-hanging woods;
                                                     Farewell to the torrents
Auf die Berg'; auf die Berge, zieht es mich hin.   and loud-pouring floods.
on the hills on the hills draws it me   thither

Lebt wohl ihr Berge,   bedecket mit Schnee!
fare-well you mountains covered with snow

Lebt wohl, ihr Täler   voll Blumen und Klee!
fare-well you valleys full flowers and clover

Lebt wohl, ihr Wälder, bemoostes   Gestein,
fare-well you forests moss-covered rocks

Ihr stürzenden Bächlein   im
you rushing   (little) streams in the
  farbigen Schein!
  coloured light

15. HOCHLÄNDISCHES WIEGENLIED
    HIGHLAND   CRADLE-SONG

German translation by W. Gerhard
(There are minor discrepancies in
meaning between the two versions)

Schlafe, süsser kleiner Donald,
sleep   sweet little Donald

Ebenbild des   grossen Ronald!
image of the great   Ronald

Wer ihm kleinen Dieb gebar,
who him little thief bore

Weiss der edle Clan aufs Haar.
knows the noble clan to the hair

Schelm, hast Äuglein   schwarz wie Kohlen!
rogue hast (little) eyes black as coals

Wenn du gross bist, stiehl ein Fohlen;
when you big are   steal a   foal

Geh' die Eb'ne ab und zu.
go   the plain fro and to

Bringe heim 'ne Carlisle-Kuh!
bring home a Carlisle cow

Darfst in Niederland nicht fehlen;
may in Lowlands   not   to be missing

Dort, mein Bübchen,   magst du   stehlen;
there my   little boy may   you to steal

Stiehl dir   Geld und stiehl dir   Glück,
steal to you money and steal to you fortune

Und ins   Hochland komm zurück!.
and (in)to the Highlands come back

16. AUS DEN HEBRÄISCHEN GESÄNGEN
    FROM THE HEBREW   MELODIES

German translation by Julius Körner
(There are considerable discrepancies
in meaning between the two versions)

Mein Herz ist schwer! Auf! von der Wand
my heart is heavy arise from the wall

Die Laute, nur sie allein mag   ich noch hören;
the lute only her alone desire I   still to hear

Entlocke mit geschickter Hand
draw from with dexterous   hand

Ihr Töne, die das Herz betören!
her strains that the heart infatuate

15. HEE BALOU

Robert Burns
(original text)

Hee balou, my sweet wee Donald,
Picture of the great
           Clanronald;
Brawlie kens our wanton chief
Wha got my young Highland
           thief.

Leeze me on thy bonnie craigie!
An' thou live, thou'll steal
         a naigie;
Travel the country thro'
      and thro',
And bring home a Carlisle cow.

Through the Lowlands o'er the
         border,
Weel, my babie, may thou
         furder:
Herry the louns o' the laigh
         countree,
Syne to the Highlands hame
         to me.

16. MY SOUL IS DARK
    (from 'Hebrew Melodies')

Lord Byron
(original text)

My soul is dark - Oh! quickly
         string
The harp I yet can brook to
         hear;
And let thy gentle fingers
         fling
Its melting murmurs o'er my
         ear.

Kann noch mein Herz ein Hoffen nähren,
can still my heart a hope to nourish

Es zaubern diese Töne her,
it charm these sounds forth

Und birgt mein trock'nes Auge Zähren,
and conceals my dry eye tears

Sie fliessen, und mich brennt's nicht mehr!
they flow and me burns it not more

Nur tief sei, wild der Töne Fluss,
only deep be wild of the strains flow

Und von der Freude weg gekehret!
and from the joy away turned

Ja, Sänger, dass ich weinen muss,
yes singer that I to weep must

Sonst wird das schwere Herz verzehret!
or else is the heavy heart consumed

Denn sieh'! Vom Kummer ward's genähret,
for see from the sorrow was it nursed

Mit stummen Wachen trug es lang,
with silent watchfulness bore it long

Und jetzt, vom Äussersten belehret,
and now by the extremity instructed

Da brech' es oder heil' im Sang.
there break it or heal in the song

If in this heart a hope be
                              dear,
That sound shall charm it
                        forth again:
If in these eyes there lurk
                        a tear,
'Twill flow, and cease to
                        burn my brain.

But bid the strain be wild
                        and deep,
Now let thy notes of joy
                        be first:
I tell thee, minstrel, I
                        must weep,
Or else this heavy heart will
                        burst;

For it hath been in sorrow
                        nurs'd,
And ach'd in sleepless
                        silence long;
And now 'tis doom'd to know,
                        to know the worst,
And break at once - or yield
                        to song.

17. VENETIANISCHES LIED I
VENETIAN   SONG

German translation by Ferdinand Freiligrath
(There are minor discrepancies of
meaning between the two versions)

Leis' rudern hier, mein Gondolier, leis', leis'!
gently row here my gondolier softly softly

Die Flut vom Ruder sprüh't so
the tide from the oar scatters drops so
  leise dass,
  softly that

Dass sie uns nur vernimmt, zu der wir zieh'n!
that she us only hears to whom we go

O, könnte, wie er schauen kann, der Himmel
O could as he to see can the heaven
  reden traun,
  to speak to venture

Er spräche vieles wohl von dem, was nachts
he would say much. indeed of that which at night
  die Sterne schau'n!
  the stars see

Leis', leis', leis', leis'!
softly softly softly softly

17. VENETIAN SONG I

Thomas Moore
(original text)

Now gently here, my gondolier,
  softly, so softly wake the
  tide,
That not an ear on earth may
  hear, but hers to whom we
  glide.
Had heav'n but tongues to
  speak, as well as starry
  eyes to see,
Oh think what tales 'twould
  have to tell of wandering
  youths like me!
Hush, hush, hush, hush!

Nun rasten hier, mein Gondolier, sacht, sacht!
now rest   here my   gondolier gently gently

Ins   Boot die Ruder! sacht, sacht!
into the boat the oars   gently gently

Auf zum   Balkone schwing' ich mich,   doch du
on to the balcony swing   I   myself but you
  hältst unten Wacht.
  keep   below watch

O, wollten halb so eifrig nur dem   Himmel wir
O would   half so eagerly only to the heaven we
  uns   weih'n,
  ourselves to dedicate

Als schöner   Weiber Diensten traun, wir
as to lovely women worship   to trust we
  könnten Engel sein!
  could   angels to be

Sacht, sacht, sacht, sacht!
gently gently gently gently

| |
Now rest thee here, my
   gondolier, rest here! for up
   I go,
Hush, hush,
To climb yon light balcony's
   height, while thou keeps't
   watch below.
Ah! Did we take for heav'n
   above but half the pains
   that we
Take day and night for woman's
   love, what angels we should
   be!
Hush, hush, hush, hush!

---

18. VENETIANISCHES LIED II
   VENETIAN   SONG

18. VENETIAN SONG II

German translation by Ferdinand Freiligrath
(There are· minor discrepancies of
meaning between the two versions)

Thomas Moore
(original text)

Wenn durch die Piazzetta die Abendluft   weht,
when through the Piazzetta the evening-breeze blows

Dann weisst du, Ninetta, wer wartend hier steht.
then know   you Ninetta who waiting here stands

Du weisst, wer trotz   Schleier und Maske dich
you know   who in spite of veil   and mask you
  kennt,
  knows

Wie Amor die Venus am   Nachtfirmament.
as Love the Venus in the night-firmament

When through the Piazz-
etta night breathes the
cool air,
Then dearest Ninetta, I'll
come to thee there.
Beneath thy mask shrouded
I'll know thee afar,
As Love knows, though
clouded, its own Ev'ning
Star.

Ein Schifferkleid trag' ich zur   selbigen Zeit,
a   sailor's-dress wear I   at the same   time

Und zitternd dir   sag' ich: das Boot liegt bereit!
and trembling to you say I   the boat lies ready

O komm, wo   den Mond noch Wolken umzieh'n!
O come where the moon still clouds overcast

Lass durch die Lagunen, mein Leben, uns flieh'n!
let through the lagoons   my life   us   to flee

In garb then resembling
some gay gondolier,
I'll whisper thee, trembling,
'Our bark, love, is near.'
Now, now while there hover
those clouds near the moon,
'Twill waft thee safe over
yon silent lagoon.

19. HAUPTMANNS WEIB
   CAPTAIN'S WIFE

19. THE CAPTAIN'S LADY

German translation by W. Gerhard
(There are some considerable discrepancies
in meaning between the two versions)

Robert Burns
(original text)

Hoch zu Pferd!
high to horse

O mount and go!
Mount and make you ready:

Stahl auf zartem Leibe,
steel on tender body

O mount and go,
And be the Captain's Lady.

Helm   und Schwert
helmet and sword

Ziemen Hauptmanns Weibe.
become captain's wife

Tönet   Trommelschlag
resounds drum-beat

When the drums do beat,
And the cannons rattle,

Unter Pulverdampf,
under powder-smoke

Thou shalt sit in state
And see thy love in battle.

Siehst du blut'gen Tag
see   you bloody   day

Und dein Lieb im   Kampf.
and your love in the battle

Schlagen wir den Feind,
vanquish we the foe

When the vanquished foe
Sues for peace and quiet,

Küssest du den Gatten,
kiss   you the husband

To the shades we'll go,
And in love enjoy it.

Wohnst mit ihm vereint
live   with him united

In des   Friedens Schatten.
in of the peace   shadow

20. DU BIST WIE EINE BLUME
   YOU ARE LIKE A   FLOWER

20. YOU ARE LIKE A FLOWER

Heinrich Heine

Du bist wie eine Blume,
you are like a   flower

You are like a flower,
so sweet and lovely and pure.

So hold und schön und rein;
so sweet and lovely and pure

I look at you, and melancholy
steals into my heart.

Ich schau' dich an, und Wehmut
I   look   you at and melancholy

Schleicht mir ins   Herz hinein.
steals   to me into the heart (into)

Mir   ist, als ob ich die Hände
to me is as if I   the hands

I feel I must lay my
hands upon your head,

Aufs   Haupt dir   legen sollt',
on the head to you to lay should

praying that God may keep
you so pure, and lovely, and
sweet.

Betend, dass Gott dich erhalte
praying that God you may keep

So rein und schön und hold.
so pure and lovely and sweet

21. *AUS DEN 'ÖSTLICHEN ROSEN'*
    FROM THE EASTERN ROSES

21. FROM 'EASTERN ROSES'

Friedrich Rückert

Ich sende einen Gruss   wie Duft der   Rosen,
I send a   greeting like scent of the roses

Ich send' ihn an ein Rosenangesicht,
I send him to a   rose-face

Ich sende einen Gruss   wie Frühlingskosen,
I send a   greeting like spring's-caressing

Ich send' ihn an ein Aug' voll Frühlingslicht.
I send him to an eye full spring's-light

Aus Schmerzensstürmen, die   mein Herz
from grief's-storms   which my   heart
   durchtosen,
   raged through

Send' ich den Hauch, dich unsanft rühr'
send I   the breath you harshly may touch
   er nicht!
   he not

Wenn du gedenkest an den Freudelosen,
when you think   of the joyless one

So wird   der Himmel meiner Nächte licht.
so becomes the sky   of my nights light

I send a greeting like
the scent of roses; I send
it to her whose face is
lovely as a rose. I send a
greeting like the caresses
of spring; I send it to her
whose eyes are filled with
the light of spring.

From the storms of
grief which rage through
my heart, I send a tiny
breeze - may its touch
never be harsh! Should you
think of the one who knows
no joy, then would the sky
of his dark nights be
lightened.

22. *JASMINENSTRAUCH*
    JASMINE-BUSH

22. THE JASMINE BUSH

Friedrich Rückert

Grün ist der Jasminenstrauch
green is the jasmine-bush

Abends   eingeschlafen.
at night fallen asleep

Als ihn mit des   Morgens Hauch
when him with of the morning breeze

Sonnenlichter trafen,
sunbeams   touched

The jasmine bush was
green as it fell asleep
last night. But this
morning, woken by sunlight
and a light breeze,

Ist er schneeweiss aufgewacht:
is he snow-white woken up

"Wie geschah mir   in der Nacht?"
what happened to me in the night

Seht, so geht es Bäumen,
see   so goes it to trees

Die im   Frühling träumen.
that in the spring   dream

it was snowy-white. 'What
happened to me in the night?'
Well, this is what happens
to trees that dream in the
springtime.

23. *VOLKSLIEDCHEN*
    (LITTLE) FOLK-SONG

23. LITTLE FOLK-SONG

Friedrich Rückert

Wenn ich früh in   den Garten geh' in meinem
when I   early into the garden go   in my
  grünen Hut,
  green hat

Ist mein erster Gedanke, was nun mein
is my   first thought what now my
  Liebster tut?
  beloved is doing

Am   Himmel steht kein Stern, den ich dem
in the sky   stands no   star   that I   to the
  Freund nicht gönnte.
  friend not   would not begrudge

Mein Herz gäb'   ich ihm   gern, wenn
my   heart would give I to him gladly if
  ich's heraus tun   könnte.
  I it out   to take could.

    When I go into the
garden early in my little
green hat, my first thought
is of my sweetheart, and
what he might be doing. O,
I would give my darling
every star in the sky - if
I could, I'd gladly give
him my heart!

24. *DER ARME PETER*
    THE POOR PETER

24. POOR PETER

Heinrich Heine

    i.

i.

Der Hans und die Grete tanzen herum,
the Hans and the Grete dance   around

Und jauchzen vor lauter Freude,
and exult   for sheer joy

Der Peter steht so still und stumm,
the Peter stands so still and silent

Und ist so blass wie Kreide.
and is so pale as chalk

    Hans and Greta are
dancing together, and
laughing for sheer joy.
Peter stands silent and
still, his face as white
as chalk.

Der Hans und die Grete sind Bräut'gam und Braut,
the Hans and the Greta are bridegroom and bride

Und blitzen im   Hochzeitsgeschmeide.
and sparkle in the wedding-jewels

Der arme Peter die Nägel kaut,
the poor Peter the nails chews

Und geht im   Werkeltagskleide.
and goes in the workaday clothes.

Hans and Greta are bridegroom and bride sparkling in their wedding jewels. Poor Peter chews his nails as he goes his way in workaday clothes.

Der Peter spricht leise   vor   sich   her,
the Peter talks   quietly in front of himself –

Und schauet betrübet auf beide:
and looks   miserably at both

"Ach! wenn ich nicht gar zu vernünftig wär',
 alas if   I   not   much too sensible were

Ich täte   mir   was   zu Leide."
I   would do to me something (to) injury

Peter mutters to himself, as he miserably watches them both, 'Alas! If I hadn't so much sense, I'd do myself some real harm.'

        ii.

"In meiner Brust, da   sitzt ein Weh,
 in my   breast there sits a   pain

Das will die Brust zersprengen;
that wants the breast to burst

Und wo   ich steh' and wo   ich geh'
and where I   stand and where I   go

Will's mich von hinnen drängen.
wants it me   from here   to urge

Es treibt mich nach der   Liebsten Näh'
it drives me   to (of) the dearest nearness

Als könnt's die Grete heilen;
as could it the Greta to heal

Doch wenn ich der   in's   Auge seh',
but when I to her into the eye look

Muss ich von hinnen eilen.
must I   from here   to hasten

Ich steig' hinauf des   Berges Höh',
I   climb up there of the mountain top

Dort ist man doch   alleine;
there is one indeed alone

Und wenn ich still dort oben steh',
and when I   still there up   stand

Dann steh' ich still   and weine"
then stand I   silently and weep

ii.

'The grief that weighs in my heart will surely burst my breast; wherever I am, and wherever I go, it drives me away from here.

It drives me to my loved one's side, as if Greta could ease my pain. But when I look into her eyes, I have to hasten away.

I climb right to the mountain-top, for there I can be alone. And when I stand up there so still, silently I weep.'

        iii.

Der arme Peter wankt   vorbei.
the poor Peter staggers past

Gar langsam, leichenblass und scheu.
very slowly   corpse-pale and timid

Es bleiben fast, wie sie ihn seh'n,
(it) remain almost as they him see

iii.

Poor Peter falters slowly along, timid and pale as death. In the streets the passers-by almost stop when they see him.

Die Leute auf den Strassen steh'n.
the people on the streets. to stand

Die Mädchen flüstern sich   in's   Ohr:
the girls   whisper (themselves) into the ear

"Der stieg wohl   aus   dem Grab hervor?"
he climbed perhaps out of the grave forth
.

"Ach nein, ihr lieben Jungfräulein,
oh no   you dear   maidens

Der steigt erst in   das Grab hinein.
he climbs just into the grave (into)

Er hat verloren seinen Schatz,
he has lost   his   treasure

Drum   ist das Grab der beste Platz,
therefore is the grave the best place

Wo   er am   besten liegen mag
where he (at) the best   to lie may

Und schlafen bis   zum   Jüngsten Tag."
and to sleep until to the judgement day

Girls whisper to each other: 'Has he just climbed out of his grave?' 'Oh no, my dear young ladies - he's just on his way there!

He's lost his sweetheart, and so the grave's the best place for him to lie and sleep till the day of Judgement.'

25. DIE BEIDEN GRENADIERE
   THE TWO   GRENADIERS

Heinrich Heine

25. THE TWO GRENADIERS

Nach Frankreich zogen zwei Grenadier,
to France   went two grenadiers

Die waren in Russland gefangen.
who were in Russia captured

Und als sie kamen ins   deutsche Quartier,
and as they came into the German quarter

Sie liessen die Köpfe hangen.
they let   the heads to hang

Da   hörten sie beide die traurige Mär':
there heard they both the sorrowful news

Dass Frankreich verloren gegangen,
that France   lost   gone

Besiegt   und geschlagen das tapfere Heer -
vanquished and routed   the brave army

Und der Kaiser, der Kaiser gefangen!
and the emperor the emperor captured

Da   weinten zusammen die Grenadier'
then wept   together the grenadiers

Wohl ob   der kläglichen Kunde.
indeed over the lamentable news

Der eine sprach: "Wie weh   wird mir
the one said   how painful is to me

Two grenadiers, prisoners from Russia, were making their way back to France. And when they came to German soil, they hung their heads in sorrow.

There they heard the tragic news, that France was lost; the brave army vanquished and routed, and the Emperor, their Emperor, a prisoner!

Then the grenadiers both wept at this lamentable news. One said: 'I'm in such pain - my old wound, how it burns!'

Wie brennt meine alte Wunde!"
how burns my   old wound

Der andre sprach: "Das Lied ist aus,
the other said   the song is over

Auch ich möcht'   mit dir sterben,
also I   would like with you to die

Doch hab' ich Weib und Kind zu Haus,
but have I   wife and child at home

Die ohne   mich verderben."
who without me   perish

"Was schert   mich Weib, was schert
what care for (I) me   wife what care for (I)
  mich Kind,
  me   child

Lass sie betteln gehn, wenn sie hungrig sind –
let them to beg to go if   they hungry are

Ich trage weit bessres Verlangen;
I   carry far better desire

Mein Kaiser, mein Kaiser gefangen!
my   Emperor my   Emperor captured

Gewähr' mir, Bruder, eine Bitt':
grant   me brother a   request

Wenn ich jetzt sterben werde,
if   I   now   to die will

So nimm meine Leiche nach Frankreich mit,
so take my   corpse to   France   with (you)

Begrab' mich in Frankreichs Erde."
bury   me   in France's   earth

Das Ehrenkreuz   am   roten Band
the cross of honour on the red   ribbon

Sollst du aufs Herz mir legen;
shall you on the heart to me to lay

Die Flinte gib mir in die Hand,
the musket give me in the hand

Und gürt' mir um   den Degen.
and buckle to me about the sword

So will ich liegen und horchen   still,
so will I   to lie and to listen silently

Wie eine Schildwach, im   Grabe,
as a   sentry   in the grave

Bis   einst ich höre Kanonengebrüll
until one day I   hear cannon-roar

Und wiehernder Rosse   Getrabe.
and of neighing chargers trotting

Dann reitet mein Kaiser wohl   über mein Grab,
then rides my   Emperor perhaps over my   grave

Viel Schwerter klirren und blitzen;
many swords   clash   and flash

Dann steig ich gewaffnet hervor aus   dem Grab –
then rise I   armed   forth out of the grave

Den Kaiser, den Kaiser zu schützen!"
the Emperor the Emperor to to defend

The other said: 'All is lost! And I would die with you, but at home I have a wife and child, and without me they would perish.'

'What do I care for wife and child! Mine is a nobler desire! If they are hungry, let them beg – my Emperor, my Emperor, a prisoner!

Grant me, brother, a last wish: if I should die, take my body to France, and bury me in French soil.'

Lay my Cross of Honour and red ribbon upon my heart; put my musket in my hand, and buckle on my sword.

There will I lie in my grave like a sentry, and listen until one day I hear again the roar of cannons, and the gallop of neighing chargers.

Then will my Emperor ride over my grave, glittering swords will clash; and I will rise up armed from the grave to defend the Emperor, my Emperor!'

26. LIEDERKREIS Op.39   26. SONG-CYCLE Op.39
   SONG-CYCLE

Josef von Eichendorff

i. In der Fremde I   i. In foreign parts I
   in the foreign parts

Aus der Heimat   hinter den Blitzen   rot   From there beyond the
from the homeland behind the lightning red   lightning flashes, clouds
                                                     come from my homeland.
Da   kommen die Wolken her,   Father and mother are long
there come   the clouds here   since dead, and no one
                                                     there knows me any more.
Aber Vater und Mutter sind lange tot,
but father and mother are long dead

Es   kennt mich dort keiner mehr.
(it) knows me   there no one more

Wie bald, ach wie bald kommt die stille Zeit,   How soon, oh, how soon
how soon oh how soon comes the quiet time   will come that quiet time
                                                     when I too shall rest! And
Da   ruhe ich auch, und über mir   over me in lovely solitude,
when rest I   also and over me   the woods will rustle, and
                                                     no one here will know me
Rauscht die schöne Waldeinsamkeit,   any more.
rustles the lovely woods-solitude

Und keiner kennt mich mehr hier.
and no one knows me   more here

ii. Intermezzo   ii. Intermezzo
    intermezzo

Dein Bildnis wunderselig   In wondrous joy I hold
your image   wonderfully-happy   your image deep in my
                                                     heart. It looks at me so
Hab' ich im   Herzensgrund,   brightly, so gaily, every
have I   in the heart's-bottom   hour of the day.

Das sieht so frisch und fröhlich
that looks so lively and gaily

Mich an zu jeder Stund'.
me   at at every hour

Mein Herz still   in sich   singet   Softly my heart sings
my   heart quietly in itself sings   itself an old and lovely
                                                     song, that soars into the
Ein altes, schönes Lied,   air and swiftly flies to
an old   lovely song   you.

Das in die Luft sich   schwinget
that in the air   itself soars

Und zu dir eilig   zieht.
and to you speedily goes

iii. Waldesgespräch
wood-conversation

iii. Dialogue in the woods

"Es ist schon   spät, es ist schon   kalt,
it is already late it is already cold

Was reit'st du einsam durch   den Wald?
why ride   you alone through the wood

Der Wald ist lang, du bist allein,
the wood is long you are alone

Du schöne Braut! ich führ' dich heim!"
you lovely bride I bring you home

'Already it is late, already cold – why do you ride alone through the woods? The way through the woods is long, and you are alone. You lovely bride, I will carry you home!'

"Gross ist der   Männer Trug   und List,
great is of the men   deceit and cunning

Vor Schmerz mein Herz gebrochen ist,
for grief   my heart broken   is

Wohl   irrt   das Waldhorn her   und hin,
indeed strays the horn   this way and that way

O flieh'! Du weisst nicht, wer ich bin."
O flee   you know   not   who I am

'Great is the guile and cunning of men, my heart is broken with grief. The straying horn sounds here and there. O fly! You know not who I am!'

So reich geschmückt ist Ross und Weib,
so richly adorned   is horse and woman

So wunderschön   der junge Leib;
so wondrously beautiful the young body

Jetzt kenn' ich dich – Gott steh' mir bei!
now   know I you   God stand me by

Du bist die Hexe Lorelei."
you are the witch Lorelei

In fine array are horse and bride, her young form of wondrous beauty; I know you now – may God protect me! You are the siren, Lorelei!

"Du kennst mich wohl, von hohem Stein
you know   me   indeed from high rock

Schaut still mein Schloss tief in   den Rhein.
looks still my   castle deep into the Rhine

Es ist schon   spät, es ist schon   kalt,
it is already late it is already cold

Kommst nimmermehr aus   diesem Wald!"
come   nevermore out of this   wood

'You do indeed know me – from a high rock my castle looks still and deep into the Rhine. Already it is late, already cold – nevermore will you leave these woods!'

iv. Die Stille
the tranquillity

iv. Tranquillity

Es   weiss und rät   es doch   keiner,
(it) knows and guesses it indeed no one

Wie mir so wohl ist, so wohl!
how me so happy is   so happy

Ach, wüsst' er nur Einer, nur Einer,
ah   knew   it only one   only one

Kein Mensch es sonst   wissen soll!
no· person it otherwise to know shall

No one knows, no one can guess how happy I am, how happy! Ah, if one alone but knew, just the one – and no one else at all!

So still ist's nicht draussen im   Schnee,
so still is it not   outside in the snow

So stumm und verschwiegen sind
so silent and secret   are

The snow outside is not as still, nor the stars in their heights as silent and secret as my thoughts.

Die Sterne nicht in der Höh',
the stars   not   in the heights

Als meine Gedanken sind.
as my   thoughts are

Ich wünscht', ich wär' ein Vöglein,   I wish I were a little
I would wish I were a   little bird   bird flying across the
                                              sea – over the sea and far
Und zöge über das Meer,   beyond until I were in
and went over the sea   heaven!

Wohl über das Meer und weiter,
indeed over the sea and further

Bis   dass ich im   Himmel wär'!
until that I   in the heaven were

v. Mondnacht
   moon-night   v. Moonlit night

Es war, als hätt' der Himmel   It was as if heaven
it was as had   the sky   had softly kissed the earth,
                                              and earth in blossoming
Die Erde still geküsst,   splendour could only dream
the earth quietly kissed   of heaven.

Dass sie im   Blütenschimmer
that she in the blossom-splendour

Von ihm nur träumen müsst'!
of him only to dream had to

Die Luft ging durch die Felder,   A breeze passing over
the breeze went through the fields   the fields gently swayed
                                              the ears of corn. The woods
Die Ähren   wogten sacht,   rustled softly, and the
the ears (of corn) rocked gently   night was bright with stars.

Es rauschten leis' die Wälder,
(it) rustled softly the woods

So sternklar war die Nacht.
so star-bright was the night

Und meine Seele spannte   And my soul spread
and my   soul spread   wide its wings, and flew
                                              over the silent land, as
Weit ihre Flügel aus,   if it were flying home.
wide her wings out

Flog durch die stillen Lande,
flew through the silent land

Als flöge sie nach Haus.
as flew she homeward

vi. Schöne Fremde
   lovely foreign land   vi. Lovely foreign land

Es rauschen die Wipfel und schauern,   The tree-tops rustle
(it) rustle the tree-tops and shiver   and shiver, as if at this
                                              very hour the ancient gods
Als machten zu dieser Stund'   were making their round of
as made   at this   hour   the half-ruined walls.

Um die halb versunkenen Mauern
about the half sunken   walls

Die alten Götter die Rund'.
the old   gods   the round

Hier hinter den Myrtenbäumen
here behind the myrtle-trees

Im   heimlich dämmernder   Pracht,
in the secretly growing dusk splendour

Was sprichst du wirr,   wie in Träumen,
what say   you confused as in dreams

Zu mir, phantastische Nacht?
to me   fantastic   night

Here behind the
myrtles, in the secret
splendour of dusk - 0
fantastic night, what are
you saying to me, confused,
as in a dream?

Es   funkeln auf mich alle Sterne
(it) twinkle on me   all   stars

Mit glühendem Liebesblick,
with glowing   love's-glance

Es   redet   trunken   die Ferne
(it) speaks intoxicated the distance

Wie von künftigem grossen Glück!
as of coming   great   happiness

All the stars look
down on me, twinkling and
glowing with love, and
speak in ecstasy from afar
of great joy to come!

vii. Auf einer Burg
    in a   castle

vii. In a castle

Eingeschlafen auf der Lauer
fallen asleep on the look-out

Oben   ist der alte Ritter;
on high is the old knight

Drüben   gehen Regenschauer,
over there go   rain-showers

Und der Wald rauscht durch   das Gitter.
and the wood rustles through the lattice

Up there keeping
watch, the old knight has
fallen asleep; rain showers
down, and the woods rustle
through the lattice.

Eingewachsen Bart und Haare,
grown-as-one beard and hair

Und versteinert   Brust und Krause,
and turned to stone breast and ruffle

Sitzt er viele hundert Jahre
sits he many hundred years

Oben   in der stillen Klause.
on high in the silent cell

With his beard and hair
grown together, his breast
and ruffle turned to stone,
he has sat up there in his
silent cell, many hundreds
of years.

Draussen ist es still und friedlich,
outside is it still and peaceful

Alle sind ins   Tal   gezogen,
all are into the valley moved

Waldesvögel   einsam   singen
woodland-birds solitarily sing

In den leeren Fensterbogen.
in the empty window-arches

Outside it is peaceful
and still. Everyone has
gone to the valley;
solitary woodland birds
sing in the empty window
arches.

Eine Hochzeit fährt da   unten
a   wedding sails there below

Auf dem Rhein im   Sonnenscheine,
on the Rhine in the sun-shine

A wedding party sails
by on the sunlit Rhine
below; musicians play
merrily, and the lovely
bride weeps.

Musikanten spielen munter,
musicians play   merrily

Und die schöne Braut, die weinet.
and the lovely bride she weeps

        viii. In der Fremde II   viii. In a foreign land II
             in the foreign land

Ich hör' die Bächlein   rauschen   I hear little streams
I   hear the little brooks to rush   rushing in the woods all
                                             around; in the woods with
Im   Walde her und hin,   the rushing, I hardly know
in the wood here and there   where I am.

Im   Walde, in dem Rauschen
in the wood   in the rushing

Ich weiss nicht, wo   ich bin.
I   know not   where I   am

Die Nachtigallen schlagen   Here in this solitude
the nightingales sing   the nightingales sing, as
                                             if they would tell of
Hier in der Einsamkeit,   lovely times long ago.
here in the solitude

,*Als wollten sie was   sagen*
as wanted they something to say

Von der alten schönen Zeit.
of the old   lovely time(s)

Die Mondeschimmer fliegen,   In the shimmer of
the moon-gleams   fly   moon-beams, it was as if
                                             I saw the castle in the
Als sah ich unter   mir   valley, yet it is far from
as saw I   beneath me   here!

Das Schloss im   Tale   liegen,
the castle in the valley to lie

Und ist doch so weit von hier!
and is yet so far from here

Als müsste in dem Garten   As if in the garden
as had to in the garden   full of white and red
                                             roses, my beloved awaited
Voll Rosen weiss und rot,   me - yet she died long
full roses white and red   ago.

Meine Liebste auf mich warten,
my   dearest for me   to wait

Und ist doch so lange tot.
and is yet so long dead

        ix. Wehmut   ix. Melancholy
             melancholy

Ich kann wohl   manchmal singen,   I can even sing at
I   can perhaps sometimes to sing   times, as if I were happy;
                                             but secretly tears well
Als ob   ich fröhlich sei,   up, and my heart is set
as though I   happy   were   free.

Doch heimlich Tränen dringen,
but secretly tears   throng

Da   wird   das Herz mir   frei.
then becomes the heart to me free

Es   lassen Nachtigallen,
(it) let   nightingales

Spielt draussen Frühlingsluft,
play   outside spring-breeze

Der   Sehnsucht Lied erschallen
of the longing   song to sound

Aus   ihres Kerkers Gruft.
from their prison's grave

When spring breezes
play outside, nightingales
sing a song of longing
from their grave-like
prison.

Da   lauschen alle Herzen,
then listen   all   hearts

Und alles   ist erfreut,
and everything is gladdened

Doch keiner fühlt die Schmerzen,
yet no one feels the griefs

Im   Lied das tiefe Leid.
in the song the deep   suffering

Then all hearts listen
and are made glad, but no
one feels the grief and
deep suffering in the
song.

     x. Zwielicht
       twilight

x. Twilight

Dämm'rung will die Flügel spreiten,
dusk   wants the wings to spread out

Schaurig   rühren sich   die Bäume,
gruesomely stir   themselves the trees

Wolken ziehn wie schwere Träume –
clouds move like heavy   dreams

Was will   dieses Grau'n bedeuten?
what (does) this   dread to signify

Dusk begins to spread
its wings, the trees
shudder and stir; clouds
gather like heavy dreams –
what can these signs of
unease portend?

Hast ein Reh du lieb   vor   andern,
(have) a roe you (dear) above others

Lass es nicht alleine grasen,
let it not   alone   to graze

Jäger   zieh'n im   Wald und blasen,
huntsmen go along in the wood and blow

Stimmen hin und wieder wandern.
voices   to and fro   wander

If you have a
favourite deer, let it
not graze alone! Huntsmen
are blowing their horns
in the woods, here and
there voices call.

Hast du einen Freund hienieden,
have you a   friend here below

Trau' ihm nicht zu dieser Stunde,
trust him not   at this   hour

Freundlich wohl   mit Aug' und Munde,
friendly   perhaps with eye and mouth

Sinnt   er Krieg im   tück'schen Frieden.
schemes he war   in the malicious peace

If you have a friend
on this earth, do not trust
him at this hour! His eyes
and mouth may perhaps
smile, but he schemes
beneath a mask of peace.

Was heut' geht müde   unter,
what today goes wearily down

Hebt sich morgen neugeboren.
rises itself tomorrow new-born

Who today wearily
sinks to rest, will rise
tomorrow reborn. But
many a one is lost in the
night – take care, be
watchful and awake!

Manches   geht in Nacht verloren –
many a thing goes in night lost

Hüte   dich,   sei wach   und munter!
take care yourself be watchful and awake

      xi. Im   Walde
         in the wood

         xi. In the woods

Es   zog eine Hochzeit den Berg   entlang,
(it) went a   wedding the mountain along

Ich hörte die Vögel schlagen,
I   heard the birds to sing

Da   blitzten viel Reiter, das Waldhorn klang,
when flashed many riders the horn   sounded

Das war ein lustiges Jagen!
that was a   merry   hunting

        A wedding party passed
below the mountain slopes,
I heard the birds singing.
Many riders flashed by,
the horn sounded – it was
a merry hunt.

Und eh'   ich's gedacht, war alles   verhallt,
and before I it thought was everything faded away

Die Nacht bedecket die Runde,
the night covers   the company

Nur von den Bergen   noch rauschet der Wald,
only from the mountains still rustles the wood

Und mich schauert's im   Herzensgrunde.
and me   dreads it in the heart's-bottom

        Before I had time to
think, it had all faded
from sight; the company
was enfolded in darkness.
Now only the woods rustle
on the mountains, and my
heart is filled with
foreboding.

      xii. Frühlingsnacht
         spring night

         xii. Spring night

Über'm   Garten durch   die Lüfte
over the garden through the breezes

Hört'ich Wandervögel   zieh'n,
heard I birds of passage to move

Das bedeutet Frühlingsdüfte,
that means   spring-scents

Unten fängt's   schon an zu blüh'n.
below begins it already – to to blossom

        I heard the birds of
passage flying over the
garden on the breeze,
heralds of spring's fragrance;
there below blossoms begin
to appear.

Jauchzen   möcht'   ich, möchte
to shout with joy should like I   should like
  weinen,
  to weep

Ist mir's   doch, als könnt's nicht sein!
is to me it yet   as could it not   to be

Alte Wunder   wieder scheinen
old miracles again appear

Mit dem Mondesglanz   herein.
with the moon's-splendour in here

        I want to shout with
joy, I want to weep – I
can hardly believe it is
true! The old miracles
appear again in the
splendour of the moonlight.

Und der Mond, die Sterne sagen's,
and the moon the stars say it

Und im   Traume rauscht's der Hain,
and in the dream rustles it the wood

        The moon and the stars
all say it, the wood
whispers it in a dream,
the nightingales call it
forth, 'She is yours, she
is yours!'

Und die Nachtigallen schlagen's:
and the nightingales sing it

"Sie ist deine, sie ist dein!"
she is yours she is yours

27. *DICHTERLIEBE*
    POET'S-LOVE

Heinrich Heine

i.

Im   wunderschönen   Monat Mai,
in the wondrously beautiful month May

Als alle Knospen sprangen,
when all buds   were bursting

Da   ist in meinem Herzen
then is in my   heart

Die Liebe aufgegangen.
the love risen

Im   wunderschönen   Monat Mai,
in the wondrously beautiful month May

Als alle Vögel sangen,
when all birds were singing

Da   hab' ich ihr   gestanden
then have I   to her confessed

Mein Sehnen und Verlangen.
my   longing and desire

  ii.

Aus meinen Tränen spriessen
from my   tears sprout

Viel blühende Blumen hervor,
many blossoming flowers forth

Und meine Seufzer werden
and my   sighs   become

Ein Nachtigallenchor.
a   choir of nightingales

Und wenn du mich lieb hast, Kindchen
and if   you me   - love -   (little) child

Schenk' ich dir   die Blumen all',
give   I   to you the flowers all

Und vor   deinem Fenster soll klingen
and before your   window shall to sound

Das Lied der   Nachtigall.
the song of the nightingale

27. POET'S LOVE

i.

    In the wondrous beauty
of May-time, when all the
buds were bursting, love
sprang up in my heart.

    In the wondrous beauty
of May-time, when all the
birds were singing, I told
her of my longing and
desire.

ii.

    From my tears spring
forth many blossoming
flowers, and my sighs
become as a choir of
nightingales.

    And if you love me,
little one, I'll give
you all the flowers, and
at your window shall sound
the song of the nightingale.

iii.

iii.

Die Rose, die Lilie, die Taube, die Sonne,
the rose   the lily   the dove   the sun

The rose, the lily, the dove, the sun; I loved them all in love's delight. I love them no more - I only love the little one, the fine one, the pure one, the only one! She is all of love's delight - the rose, the lily, the dove, the sun.

Die liebt' ich einst alle in Liebeswonne.
them loved I   once all in love's-delight

Ich lieb' sie nicht mehr, ich liebe alleine
I   love them not   more   I   love only

Die Kleine,   die Feine,   die Reine,   die Eine;
the little one the fine one the pure one the only one

Sie selber, aller Liebe Wonne
she herself of all love   delight

Ist Rose und Lilie und Taube und Sonne.
is rose and lily   and dove   and sun

iv.

iv.

Wenn ich in   deine Augen seh',
when I into your eyes   look

When I look into your eyes, my suffering and pain all vanish; but when I kiss your lips, my very being is restored.

So schwindet all mein Leid   und Weh;
so disappears all my   suffering and pain

Doch wenn ich küsse deinen Mund,
but when I kiss your mouth

So werd' ich ganz und gar   gesund.
so become I wholly and completely restored

Wenn ich mich lehn' an deine Brust,
when I   myself recline on your breast

When I lie upon your breast, I am overcome with heaven's delight; yet when you say, 'I love you!' I must weep most bitterly.

Kommt's über mich wie Himmelslust;
comes it over me   like heaven's-delight

Doch wenn du sprichst: ich liebe dich!
but when you say   I   love you

So muss ich weinen bitterlich.
so must I   to weep bitterly

v.

v.

Ich will meine Seele tauchen
I   will my   soul to plunge

I will steep my soul in the cup of the lily; the lily shall breathe a song of my beloved.

In den Kelch der   Lilie hinein;
in the cup of the lily (into)

Die Lilie soll klingend hauchen
the lily shall sounding to breathe

Ein Lied von der Liebsten mein.
a   song of the beloved mine

Das Lied soll schauern und beben,
the song shall to tremble and to quiver

The song will tremble and quiver like the kiss from her lips, the kiss she once gave me in a wonderfully sweet hour.

Wie der Kuss von ihrem Mund,
like the kiss from her mouth

Den sie mir einst gegeben
which she to me once given

In wunderbar süsser Stund'.
in wonderfully sweet hour

vi.

Im   Rhein, im   heiligen Strome,
in the Rhine in the sacred   river

Da   spiegelt sich in den Well'n,
there reflects itself in the ripples

Mit seinem grossen Dome,
with its   great   cathedral

Das grosse heilige Köln.
the great sacred Cologne

Im   Dom   da   steht ein Bildnis,
in the cathedral there stands a   portrait

Auf goldenem Leder   gemalt;
on golden   leather painted

In meines Lebens Wildnis
in of my life   wilderness

Hat's freundlich hineingestrahlt.
has it kindly   into shone

Es   schweben Blumen und Englein
(it) hovers   flowers and (little) angels

Um   unsre liebe Frau;
round Our (dear) Lady

Die Augen, die Lippen, die Wänglein,
the eyes the lips   the (little) cheeks

Die gleichen der   Liebsten genau.
they resemble of the beloved exactly

vii.

Ich grolle   nicht, und wenn das Herz
I hear a grudge not   and if   the heart
  auch bricht,
  even breaks

Ewig   verlor'nes Lieb! ich grolle
for ever lost   love I bear a grudge
  nicht.
  not

Wie du auch strahlst in Diamentenpracht,
how-you -ever shine   in diamond-splendour

Es   fällt kein Strahl in deines Herzens Nacht.
(it) falls no   ray   in of your heart   night

Dass weiss ich längst. Ich sah dich ja
that knew I   long ago I   saw you indeed
  im   Traume,
  in the dream

Und sah die Nacht in deines Herzens Raume,
and saw the night in of your heart   place

Und sah die Schlang', die dir   am
and saw the serpent   which to you at the
  Herzen frisst,
  heart/gnaws

Ich sah, mein Lieb, wie sehr du elend   bist.
I saw my   dear how much you wretched are

vi.

The sacred river
Rhine reflects in its
ripples mighty, sacred
Cologne, with its great
cathedral.

In the cathedral there
is a portrait, painted on
golden leather; it has
cast a kindly gleam into
the wilderness of my life.

Flowers and angels
hover round Our Lady;
her eyes, her lips, her
cheeks are those of my
beloved.

vii.

I am not bitter, even
though my heart is
breaking. Love lost for
ever! I am not bitter.
However much your splendid
diamonds glitter, no ray
pierces the darkness of
your heart.

I knew it long ago. I
saw you in a dream, and
saw the night within your
soul, and saw the serpent
eating at your heart. I
saw, my love, your
wretchedness.

viii.

Und wüssten's die Blumen, die kleinen,
and if knew it the flowers the little ones

Wie tief   verwundet mein Herz,
how deeply wounded   my   heart

Sie würden mit mir weinen,
they would with me to weep

Zu heilen meinen Schmerz.
to to heal my   pain

Und wüssten's die Nachtigallen,
and if knew it the nightingales

Wie ich so traurig und krank,
how I   so sad   and sick

Sie liessen   fröhlich erschallen
they would let gladly   to sound

Erquickenden Gesang.
comforting   song

Und wüssten sie mein Wehe,
and if knew they my   pain

Die goldenen Sternelein,
the gold   little stars

Sie kämen   aus ihrer Höhe,
they would come from their height

Und sprächen   Trost   mir ein.
and would speak comfort to me –

Sie alle können's nicht wissen,
they all can   it not   to know

Nur Eine kennt meinen Schmerz;
only one knows my   sorrow

Sie hat ja   selbst zerrissen,
she had indeed herself broken

Zerrissen mir   das Herz.
broken   to me the heart

viii.

And if the tiny
flowers knew how deeply
wounded my heart is, they
would weep with me to
heal my grief.

And if the nightingales
knew how sad and sick I am,
they would gladly sing a
heartening song.

And if the little
golden stars knew of my
grief, they would come down
from their heights to
comfort me.

None of them can know
my sorrow, it is known
by only one – she who has
broken my heart.

ix.

Das ist ein Flöten   und Geigen,
that is a   playing-of-flutes and fiddling

Trompeten schmettern darein;
trumpets resound   thereto

Da   tanzt wohl   den Hochzeitsreigen
there dances probably the wedding-dance

Die Herzallerliebste mein.
the dearest-heart   mine

Das ist ein Klingen und Dröhnen,
that is a   ringing and droning

Ein Pauken   und ein Schalmei'n;
a .beating-of-drums and a   playing-of-shawms

ix.

There's a playing of
flutes and fiddles, and
resounding trumpets too.
There dancing, perhaps
her wedding round, is my
dearest love.

There's a thudding
and piping on drums and
shawms, and there amongst
them sob and groan sweet
little angels.

Dazwischen   schluchzen und stöhnen
there amongst sob   and groan

Die lieblichen Engelein.
the sweet   little angels

    x.   x.

Hör' ich das Liedchen   klingen,
hear I   the little song sounding

Das einst die Liebste   sang,
that once the dearest one sang

So will mir   die Brust zerspringen
so wants to me the breast to burst

Von wildem Schmerzendrang.
from wild   grief's-violence

    If I should hear the
melody that once my
dearest sang, then would
my heart be torn by the
wild violence of grief.

Es treibt mich ein dunkles Sehnen,
(it) drives me   a   dark   longing

Hinauf   zur   Waldeshöh',
up there to the wooded heights

Dort löst   sich auf in Tränen
there dissolves itself - in tears

Mein übergrosses Weh'.
my   overwhelming sorrow

    A dark longing drives
me to the wooded heights;
there my infinite sorrow
overflows in tears.

    xi.   xi.

Ein Jüngling liebt ein Mädchen,
a   lad   loves a   girl

Die hat einen andern erwählt;
who has -another- chosen

Der andre   liebt eine andre,
the other (lad) loves another (girl)

Und hat sich   mit dieser   vermählt.
and has himself with this (girl) wed

    A lad loves a girl,
who has chosen another;
this other loves another,
and has married her.

Das Mädchen nimmt aus   Ärger
the girl   takes out of anger

Den ersten besten Mann,
the first best   man

Der ihr   in den Weg gelaufen;
who to her in the way run .

Der Jüngling ist übel d'ran.
the lad   is -badly-off -

    The girl, out of
pique, takes the first
man who comes along, and
our lad gets the worst of
it.

Es ist eine alte Geschichte,
it is an   old story

Doch bleibt sie immer neu;
yet remains it always new

Und wem   sie just passieret,
and to whom she just happened

Dem   bricht das Herz entzwei.
to him breaks the heart in two

    It is an old, old
story, but stays for
ever new; and he to whom
it happens - his heart
breaks.

168SCHUMANN

xii.

Am   leuchtenden Sommermorgen
on the bright   summer-morning

Geh' ich im   Garten herum.
walk I   in the garden about

Es   flüstern und sprechen die Blumen,
(it) whisper and speak   the flowers

Ich aber wandle stumm.
I   but wander silently

Es   flüstern und sprechen die Blumen,
(it) whisper and speak   the flowers

Und schau'n mitleidig mich an:
and look   pityingly me   at

"Sei unsrer Schwester nicht böse,
 be to our sister   not   angry

Du   trauriger, blasser Mann."
you sad   pale   man

On a bright summer
morning I wander in the
garden. The flowers speak
in whispers, but I pass
silently by.

The flowers speak in
whispers, and gaze at me
in pity. 'Bear our sister
no malice, you pale and
sorrowful man!'

xiii.

Ich hab' im   Traum geweinet,
I   have in the dream wept

Mir   träumte, du lägest   im   Grab.
to me dreamt   you were lying in the grave

Ich wachte auf, und die Träne
I   woke   up   and the tear

Floss noch von der Wange herab.
flowed still from the cheek down

Ich hab' im   Traum geweinet,
I   have in the dream wept

Mir   träumt', du verliessest   mich.
to me dreamt   you were forsaking me

Ich wachte auf, und ich weinte
I   woke   up   and I   wept

Noch lange bitterlich.
still long bitterly

Ich hab' im   Traum geweinet,
I   have in the dream wept

Mir   träumte, du wär'st mir   noch gut.
to me dreamt   you were   to me still good

Ich wachte auf, und noch   immer
I   woke   up   and - still -

Strömt meine Tränenflut.
streams my   flood of tears

In my dream I was
weeping; I dreamt you
lay in your grave. I
woke, and a tear was
rolling down my cheek.

In my dream I was
weeping; I dreamt you
were forsaking me. I
woke, and wept long and
bitterly.

In my dream I was
weeping; I dreamt you
cared for me still. I
woke, and even now my
streaming tears flood
on.

xiv.

Allnächtlich im   Traume seh' ich dich,
every night in the dream see I   you

Und sehe dich freundlich grüssen,
and see you kindly   to greet

Each night in a dream
I see you, and lovingly
you greet me; sobbing
loudly, I throw myself
at your dear feet.

Und laut   aufweinend   stürz' ich mich
and loudly bursting into tears throw I   myself

Zu deinen süssen Füssen.
to your   dear   feet

Du siehest mich an wehmütiglich
you look   me   at sadly

Und schüttelst das blonde Köpfchen;
and shake   the fair   little head

Aus deinen Augen schleichen sich
from your   eyes   steal   (themselves)

Das Perlentränentröpfchen.
the (little) pearl-drops-of-tears

       You look at me so
sadly, and shake your
small, fair head; from
your eyes steal tears
like pearls.

Du sagst mir   heimlich ein leises Wort
you say to me secretly a   gentle word

Und gibst mir   den Strauss von Zypressen.
and give to me the bunch   of cypresses

Ich wache auf, und der Strauss ist fort,
I   wake up   and the bunch   is gone

Und's   Wort hab' ich vergessen.
and the word have I   forgotten

       You whisper a gentle
word to me, and give me
a wreath of cypress. I
wake – the wreath is
gone, and the word I
have forgotten.

    xv.

Aus alten Märchen   winkt   es
from old   fairy tales beckons it

Hervor mit weisser Hand,
forth with white   hand

Da   singt   es und da   klingt   es
there is singing (it) and there is ringing (it)

Von einem Zauberland;
from a   magic-land

    xv.

       From the old fairy
tales a white hand
beckons; there is a
singing and a ringing
from a magic land.

Wo   bunte Blumen blühen
where gay   flowers bloom

Im   gold'nen Abendlicht,
in the golden   evening light

Und lieblich duftend glühen,
and sweetly scented glow

Mit bräutlichem Gesicht;
with bridal   face

       There gay flowers
bloom in the golden
evening light, and,
sweetly-scented, glow
with bridal faces.

Und grüne Bäume singen
and green trees sing

Uralte Melodei'n,
ancient melodies

Die Lüfte heimlich klingen,
the breezes secretly sound

Und Vögel schmettern drein;
and birds warble   thereto

       And green trees
chant ancient melodies;
and breezes softly murmur
to the warbling of birds.

Und Nebelbilder   steigen
and misty figures rise

Wohl   aus der Erd' hervor,
(indeed) out of the earth (out)

       And misty figures
rise up from the earth –
their strange company
circle in airy dance.

Und tanzen luft'gen Reigen,
and dance airy   dances

Im   wunderlichen Chor;
in the strange   chorus

Und blaue Funken brennen
and blue sparks burn

An jedem Blatt und Reis,
on every leaf   and twig

Und rote Lichter rennen
and red lights run

Im   irren, wirren   Kreis;
in the crazy confused circle

                                   And blue sparks dart
on every leaf and twig,
and red lights flitter
in a frenzy all around.

Und laute Quellen brechen
and loud springs gush

Aus wildem Marmorstein,
from rough marble-rock

Und seltsam   in den Bächen
and strangely in the streams

Strahlt fort der Widerschein.
shines   forth the reflection

                                   And riotous springs
gush forth from craggy
marble rock, and in the
streams shine weird
reflections.

Ach, könnt ich dorthin kommen,
ah   could I   thither to come

Und dort mein Herz erfreu'n,
and there my   heart to gladden

Und aller Qual   entnommen,
and all anguish taken away

Und frei und selig sein!
and free and blissful to be

                                   Oh, if only I
could go there to restore
my heart, and take away
all anguish, and be happy
and free!

Ach! jenes Land der   Wonne,
ah   that land of the delight

Das seh' ich oft   im   Traum,
that see I   often in the dream

Doch kommt die Morgensonne,
but comes the morning sun

Zerfliesst's wie eitel Schaum.
melts it   like mere foam

                                   Ah, what a land of
delight I see in my
dreams! But with the
morning sun it vanishes
like foam.

    xvi.   xvi.

Die alten, bösen Lieder,
the old   bad   songs

                                   The old hurtful songs,
the evil, sad dreams, let

Die Träume bös' und arg,
the dreams bad and mischievous

us bury them now – so
fetch a great coffin!

Die lasst uns jetzt begraben,
them let us now to bury

Holt einen grossen Sarg.
fetch a   great   coffin

Hinein leg' ich gar   manches,
in it lay I   indeed many a thing

Doch sag' ich noch nicht was;
but say I yet not what

Der Sarg muss sein noch grösser
the coffin must to be still larger

Wie's Heidelberger Fass.
than the of Heidelberg tun

Und holt eine Totenbahre,
and fetch a   bier

Und Bretter fest und dick;
and planks firm and thick

Auch   muss sie sein noch länger,
likewise must it to be still longer

Als wie zu Mainz die Brück'.
than as at Mainz the bridge

Und holt mir   auch zwölf Riesen,
and fetch to me also twelve giants

Die müssen noch stärker sein,
they must   still stronger to be

Als wie der starke Christoph,
than as the strong Christopher

Im   Dom   zu Köln am   Rhein.
in the cathedral at Cologne on the Rhine

Die sollen den Sarg   forttragen,
they shall the coffin to carry away

Und senken in's Meer hinab;
and to sink in the ocean down

Denn solchem   grossen Sarge
for to such (a) great   coffin

Gebührt ein grosses Grab.
is due a   great   grave

Wisst ihr, warum der Sarg wohl
know you why   the coffin indeed

So gross und schwer mag sein?
so huge and heavy may to be

Ich senkt' auch meine Liebe
I sank indeed my   love

Und meinen Schmerz hinein.
and my   grief in it

Many things will I
lay within, but what I
will not yet say; the
coffin must be even
larger than the tun of
Heidelberg.

Then fetch a bier
and firm, thick planks,
even longer than the
bridge at Mainz!

And fetch me
twelve giants, even
stronger than the great
St. Christopher in the
cathedral at Cologne on
the Rhine.

They shall carry the
coffin away, to sink
deep in the ocean; for so
mighty a coffin deserves
a mighty grave.

And do you know why
the coffin had to be so
heavy and huge? There I
have sunk all my love,
and all my grief.

28. DEIN ANGESICHT
    YOUR FACE

28. YOUR FACE

Heinrich Heine

Dein Angesicht, so lieb und schön,
your face   so dear and lovely

Das hab' ich jüngst im   Traum geseh'n,
that have I   lately in the dream seen

Es ist so mild und engelgleich,
it is so mild and angelic

Und doch so bleich, so schmerzenreich.
and yet so pale   so sorrowful

Und nur die Lippen, die sind rot;
and only the lips   they are red

Bald aber küsst sie bleich der Tod.
soon but kisses them pale   the death

Erlöschen   wird das Himmelslicht,
to become dim will the heaven's-light

Das aus   den frommen Augen bricht.
that out of the innocent eyes   breaks

    Last night in a
dream I saw your sweet
and lovely face; so
gentle and angelic, and
yet so sorrowful, so pale.

    Only your lips are
rosy still, but soon they
will fade when kissed by
death, and the heavenly
light that shines in your
innocent eyes will be
dimmed.

29. FRAUENLIEBE UND -LEBEN
    WOMEN'S LOVE AND WOMEN'S LIFE

29. WOMAN'S LOVE AND LIFE

Adalbert von Chamisso

i.

i.

Seit ich ihn gesehen,
since I   him seen

Glaub' ich blind zu sein;
believe I blind to to be

Wo   ich hin   nur   blicke,
where- I   towards-soever look

Seh' ich ihn allein;
see I   him only

Wie im   wachen Traume
as in the awake dream

Schwebt sein Bild mir vor,
hovers his image me before

Taucht aus   tiefstem Dunkel,
emerges out of deepest darkness

Heller   nur empor.
brighter only up

    Since first I saw
him I have been as if
blind; I see only him
wherever I look. His
image hovers before me
as in a waking dream,
and rises all the brighter
from deepest darkness.

Sonst ist licht-   und farblos
else is without light and colourless

Alles   um   mich her,
everything round me   about

Nach   der Schwestern Spiele
towards the sisters'   playing

Nicht begehr'   ich mehr,
not   hanker after I   more

Möchte   lieber weinen,
would like rather to weep

Still im   Kämmerlein;
quietly in the little bedroom

Seit ich ihn gesehen,
since I   him seen

Glaub' ich blind zu sein.
believe I   blind to to be

Everything around
me is colourless and
dull; I care no longer
for my sisters' frolics.
I would rather weep alone
in my little room; since
first I saw him I have
been as if blind.

ii.

ii.

Er, der Herrlichste   von allen,
he the most splendid of all

Wie so milde, wie so gut!
how so gentle how so good

Holde   Lippen, klares Auge,
gracious lips   clear eye

Heller Sinn und fester Mut.
clear mind and firm   courage

He, the most
splendid of all, as
gentle as he is good –
with tender lips, bright
eyes, a clear mind and
firm courage.

So wie dort in blauer Tiefe,
so as there in blue   depth

Hell   und herrlich, jener Stern,
bright and glorious that star

Also Er in meinem Himmel,
so he in my   firmament

Hell   und herrlich, hehr   und fern.
bright and glorious exalted and remote

Like a bright and
glorious star in the
lofty blue, bright and
glorious is he in my
firmament, exalted and
remote.

Wandle, wandle, deine Bahnen,
travel travel your paths

Nur betrachten deinen Schein,
just to behold your   shine

Nur in Demut   ihn betrachten,
just in humility it to behold

Selig   nur und traurig sein!
blissful just and sad   to be

Go, go your way;
just let me look upon
your radiance; in
humility let me look,
full of joy and misery.

Höre nicht mein stilles Beten,
hear not   my   silent praying

Deinem Glücke   nur geweiht;
to your happiness only dedicated

Darfst mich nied're Magd nicht kennen,
may   me lowly   maid not to know

Hoher Stern der   Herrlichkeit.
high star of the splendour

You shall not hear
my silent prayer offered
for your joy alone. You,
high star of splendour,
can never know a lowly
maid like me.

Nur die Würdigste von allen,
only the worthiest of all

Darf beglücken deine Wahl,
may to make happy your choice

Und ich will die Hohe segnen,
and I will the sublime one to bless

Viele tausend Mal.
many thousand times(s)

Only she, the most
worthy of all can make
your choice a happy one,
and I will give a thousand
blessings to her in her
sublimity.

Will mich freuen dann und weinen,
will (myself) to rejoice then and to weep

Selig, selig, bin ich dann;
blissful blissful am I then

Sollte mir das Herz auch brechen,
should to me the heart even break

Brich, O Herz, was liegt daran?
break O heart what lies thereon

Then I will rejoice
and weep; blissful,
blissful I will be. Even
though my heart should
break – break, O heart,
what matter?

iii.

Ich kann's nicht fassen, nicht glauben,
I can it not to grasp not to believe

Es hat ein Traum mich berückt;
(it) has a dream me beguiled

Wie hätt' er doch unter allen
how had he really among all

Mich Arme erhöht und beglückt?
me poor one exalted and blessed

iii.

I can't grasp it,
I can't believe it, I've
been beguiled by a dream!
Have I really from among
so many been thus exalted
and blessed?

Mir war's, er habe gesprochen:
to me was it he had spoken

"Ich bin auf ewig dein",
I am for ever yours

Mir war's ich träume noch immer,
to me was it I were dreaming –still–

Es kann ja nimmer so sein.
it can surely never so to be

I thought that he
said, 'I am yours for
ever!' I thought I must
still be dreaming – it
can surely never be true!

O lass im Traume mich sterben,
O let in the dream me to die

Gewieget an seiner Brust,
rocked upon his breast

Den seligen Tod mich schlürfen,
the blessed death me to sip

In Tränen unendlicher Lust.
in tears of infinite joy

O let me die in this
dream, cradled upon his
breast! Let me embrace
a blessed death with
tears of infinite joy!

iv.

Du Ring an meinem Finger,
you ring on my finger

Mein goldenes Ringelein,
my golden little ring

Ich drücke dich fromm an die Lippen,
I press you devoutly to the lips

iv.

O ring upon my
finger, little ring of
gold, I press you with
reverence to my lips, and
to my heart.

Dich fromm   an das Herze mein.
you devoutly to the heart mine

Ich hatt' ihn ausgeträumet,
I   had   it ceased dreaming

Der   Kindheit friedlich schönen   Traum,
of the childhood peacefully beautiful dream

Ich fand allein mich, verloren
I   found alone myself lost

Im   öden,   unendlichen Raum.
in the desolate immense   space

The serene beauty of
my childhood dream was
gone; I found myself
lost and alone in an
immense, desolate world.

Du Ring an meinem Finger,
you ring on my   finger

Da   hast du mich erst   belehrt,
there have you me   for the first time instructed

Hast meinem Blick erschlossen
have to my glance disclosed

Des   Lebens unendlichen, tiefen Wert.
of the life   eternal   deep value

O ring upon my
finger, you taught me,
and opened my eyes for
the first time to the
deep and eternal in life.

Ich will ihm dienen, ihm   leben,
I   want him to serve to him to live

Ihm   angehören   ganz,
to him to belong to wholly

Hin   selber mich geben   und finden
(there) myself me   to surrender and to find

Verklärt   mich in seinem Glanz.
transfigured myself in his   splendour

I want to serve him,
live for him, wholly
belong to him; I want to
surrender myself and be
transfigured by his
splendour.

    v.   v.

Helft mir, ihr Schwestern,
help me   you sisters

Freundlich mich schmücken,
kindly   me   to adorn

Dient der   Glücklichen heute mir,
serve of the happy one   today to me

Windet geschäftig
twine busily

Mir um   die Stirne
to me round the brow

Noch   der   blühenden Myrte Zier.
besides of the blossoming myrtle decoration

Help me, sisters,
lovingly to adorn myself,
help me today in my joy.
Busily twine the
blossoming myrtle about
my brow.

Als ich befriedigt,
when I   satisfied

Freudigen Herzens,
of joyful heart

Sonst   dem   Geliebten im   Arme lag,
formerly to the beloved in the arms lay

Immer noch   rief er,
always (still) called he

Sehnsucht im   Herzen,
longing   in the heart

Whenever my beloved
held me in his arms, my
heart was full of joy,
whilst he always looked
forward with such
longing to this day.

Ungeduldig   den heutigen Tag.
impatiently the today's day

Helft mir, ihr Schwestern,
help me   you sisters

Helft mir verscheuchen
help me to banish

Eine törichte Bangigkeit,
a   foolish anxiety

Dass ich mit klarem
that I   with clear

Aug' ihn empfange,
eye him may receive

Ihn, die Quelle der   Freudigkeit.
him the source of the joyfulness

      Help me, sisters,
help me banish my
foolish anxiety, so that
I may receive him, the
source of my joy, with
eyes unclouded.

Bist, mein Geliebter,
are my beloved

Du mir   erschienen,
you to me appeared

Gibst du mir, Sonne, deinen Schein?
give you to me sun   your   light

Lass mich in Andacht,
let me   in devotion

Lass mich in Demut,
let me in humility

Lass mich verneigen dem   Herren mein.
let me   to bow   to the lord   mine

      When my beloved
comes for me, will you
shine on me, O sun? Let
me in devotion and
humility bow to my lord.

Streuet ihm,   Schwestern,
strew   to him sisters

Streuet ihm   Blumen
strew   to him flowers

Bringet ihm   knospende Rosen dar,
bring   to him budding   roses –

Aber euch, Schwestern,
but you   sisters

Grüss' ich mit Wehmut
greet I   with melancholy

Freudig scheidend aus eurer Schar.
joyfully parting   from your flock

      Strew him with
flowers, dear sisters –
bring him blossoming
roses! Whilst I bid you
a sad farewell, as I
leave you in my joy.

     vi.

     vi.

Süsser Freund, du blickest
sweet friend you look

Mich verwundert an,
me   wonderingly at

Kannst es nicht begreifen,
can   it not   to understand

Wie ich weinen kann;
how I   to weep can

Lass der feuchten Perlen
let the moist   pearls

      Dearest one, you
look at me in wonder; you
cannot understand how I
can weep. But let the
wet pearls' rare adornment
tremble with bright joy
in my eyes.

Ungewohnte   Zier
unaccustomed embellishment

Freudighell   erzittern
joyously bright to tremble

In dem Auge mir.
in the eye to me

Wie so bang   mein Busen,
how so anxious my   bosom

How anxious is my
heart, how full of delight!
If only I could find the
words to say! Come, hide
your face upon my breast,
then I can whisper in
your ear of all my joy.

Wie so wonnevoll!
how so full of delight

Wüsst ich nur mit Worten,
knew I   only with words

Wie ich's sagen soll;
how I it to say shall

Komm und birg   dein Antlitz
come and conceal your face

Hier an meiner Brust,
here on my   breast

Will ins   Ohr dir   flüstern
will into the ear to you to whisper

Alle meine Lust.
all my   joy

Weisst du nun die Tränen,
know   you now the tears

Now you understand
the tears I weep. Should
you not see them, beloved
husband? Stay near my
heart, and feel its beat,
so I may hold you ever
closer.

Die   ich weinen kann,
which I   to weep can

Sollst du nicht sie sehen
should you not   them to see

Du geliebter Mann?
you beloved   husband

Bleib' an   meinen Herzen,
stay   against my   heart

Fühle dessen Schlag,
feel whose beat

Dass ich fest und fester
that I   firm and firmer

Nur dich drücken mag.
only you to press may

Hier an meinem Bette
here by my   bed

Here beside my bed
will be the cradle,
quietly sheltering my
lovely dream. The morning
will come when the dream
awakes, and your image
will smile up at me.

Hat die Wiege Raum,
has the cradle place

Wo   sie still   verberge
where it quietly may hide

Meinen holden Traum;
my   lovely dream

Kommen wird der Morgen,
to come will the morning

Wo   der Traum erwacht,
when the dream awakens

Und daraus   dein Bildnis
and from it your image

Mir   entgegen lacht.
to me towards   laughs

vii.

An meinem Herzen, an meiner Brust,
on my   heart   on my   breast

Du meine Wonne, du meine Lust!
you my   joy   you my   delight

Das Glück   ist die Liebe, die Lieb' ist das
the happiness is   the love   the love is   the
   Glück,
   happiness

Ich hab's   gesagt und nehm's nicht zurück.
I   have it said and take it not   back

Hab' überschwenglich mich   geschätzt
have rapturous   myself considered

Bin überglücklich aber jetzt.
am overjoyed   but now

Nur die   da   säugt, nur die
only the (one) there suckles only the (one)
   da   liebt,
   there loves

Das Kind, dem   sie die Nahrung   gibt;
the child to whom she the nourishment gives

Nur eine Mutter weiss allein
only a   mother knows alone

Was lieben heisst und glücklich sein.
what to love means and happy   to be

O, wie bedaur' ich doch   den Mann,
O how pity   I   indeed the man

Der Mutterglück   nicht fühlen kann!
who mother-happiness not   to feel can

Du lieber, lieber Engel, du,
you dear   dear angel you

Du schauest mich an und lächelst dazu!
you look   me at and smile   besides

viii.

Nun hast du mir   den ersten Schmerz getan,
now have you to me the first pain   done

Der aber   traf.
which however struck (home)

Du schläfst, du harter, unbarmherz'ger Mann,
you sleep   you cruel   merciless   man

Den Todesschlaf.
the death's-sleep

Es   blicket die Verlass'ne   vor   sich
(it) gazes   the abandoned one in front of herself
   hin,
   there

---

vii.

Lying on my heart,
on my breast, you my
delight, my joy! Joy is
love, love is joy – I
will say it, and say it
again! I thought I knew
rapture, but now I have
found perfect bliss.
Only she who has suckled
and cherished the child
she nourishes, only a
mother can know the
meaning of happiness
and love. O how I pity
a man, who cannot know
a mother's joy! My dear
little angel, how you
look at me and smile!

viii.

Now, for the first
time you have caused me
grief, and it has struck
deep. Cruel and merciless,
you sleep the sleep of
death.

Abandoned, I stare
before me; the world is
empty. I have loved and
lived, but now I live no more.

Die Welt ist leer.
the world is empty

Geliebet hab' ich und gelebt, ich bin
loved have I and lived I am

Nicht lebend mehr.
not living more

Ich zieh' mich in mein Inn'res still zurück,
I draw myself into my inner self quietly back

Der Schleier fällt,
the veil falls

Da hab' ich dich und mein verlor'nes Glück,
there have I you and my lost happiness

Du meiner Welt!
you my world

Silently I withdraw
into myself, the veil
falls. There I hold you
and my lost happiness –
you, my whole world.

30. *DIE KARTENLEGERIN*
THE CARD-LAYER

30. THE FORTUNE-TELLER

Adalbert von Chamisso

Schlief die Mutter endlich ein
fell asleep the mother at last –

Über ihrer Hauspostille?
over her book of family devotions

Nadel, liege du nun stille,
needle lie you now still

Nähen, immer nähen, nein!
to sew always to sew no

Legen will ich mir die Karten.
to lay want I to me the cards

Ei, was hab' ich zu erwarten?
ah what have I to to expect

Ei, was wird das Ende sein?
ah what will the end to be

Has mother fallen
asleep at last over her
prayer-book? Now, needle,
you can be still. Sewing,
nothing but sewing – no!
I'll just read the cards.
Well, what does the
future hold for me? Ah,
where's it all leading?

Trüget mich die Ahnung nicht,
deceives me the presentiment not

Zeigt sich Einer, den ich meine,
shows himself one whom I mean

Schön, da kommt er ja, der Eine,
good there comes he indeed the one

Coeur-Bub kannte seine Pflicht.
knave of hearts recognised his obligation

Eine reiche Witwe? Wehe!
a rich widow oh dear

Ja, er freit sie, ich vergehe!
yes he is courting her I am lost

O verruchter Bösewicht!
O wicked villain

If I'm not deceived,
the one and only is
there – *the* one, I mean
Oh good, there he comes,
my own love; the knave
of hearts knew what to
do. A rich widow? Oh
dear! Yes, he's courting
her, I am lost! The
wicked villain!

Herzeleid, und viel Verdruss,
sorrow   and much annoyance

Eine Schul' und enge   Mauern -
a   school and narrow walls

Carreau-König,   der bedauern
king of diamonds who is sorry for (me)

Und zuletzt   mich trösten   muss.
and in the end me   to comfort must

Ein Geschenk auf   art'ge Weise -
a   present in (a) nice   way

Er entführt   mich, eine Reise -
he carries off me   a   journey

Geld und Lust   in Überfluss!
money and pleasure in plenty

Sorrow, and a lot of trouble. A school with high, narrow walls, but the king of diamonds is sorry for me, and in the end he comforts me with a nice present. He takes me off on a journey - wealth and pleasure in plenty!

Dieser Carreau-König   da
this king of diamonds there

Muss ein Fürst sein, oder König,
must a   prince to be or   king

Und es fehlt daran   nur wenig,
and it lacks thereon only little

Bin ich selber Fürstin ja.
am I   myself princess indeed

Hier ein Feind, der mich zu schaden
here an enemy who me   to to harm

Sich   bemüht   bei seiner Gnaden,
himself takes trouble with his   lordship

Und ein Blonder   steht mir nah.
and a   blond person stands me   near

Now, this king of diamonds must be at least a prince, or even a king, and it won't take much to make me a princess! But there's an enemy trying to spoil it all for me with his Lordship. A fair man is close at hand -

Ein Geheimnis kommt zu Tage,
a   secret   comes to day-(light)

Und ich flüchte noch beizeiten -
and I   flee   still in good time

Fahret wohl, ihr Herrlichkeiten,
fare-well   you splendours

O das war ein harter Schlag!
O that was a   hard   blow

Hin ist Einer - eine Menge
gone is one   a   crowd

Bilden um   mich ein Gedränge,
grows round me   a   throng

Dass ich sie kaum   zählen mag.
that I   them hardly to count may

A secret comes to light - and I get away by the skin of my teeth. Goodbye to all these fine things - oh, that was a bad blow! One has gone, now a crowd appears all round me, more than I can possibly count.

Kommt das dumme Frau'ngesicht,
comes the stupid woman's-face

Kommt die Alte ·   da   mit Keuchen,
comes the old (woman) there with wheezing

Lieb' und Lust mir zu verscheuchen,
love and joy me to to drive away

Eh'   die Jugend mir gebricht?
before the youth me is wanting

And here's the face of a silly old woman. Is she coming wheezing along to drive away all the love and happiness of my youth? Oh, it's mother woken up, and getting ready to scold me. Oh no, the cards don't lie!

Ach, die Mutter ist's, die aufwacht,
ah   the mother is it who wakes up

Und den Mund zu schelten aufmacht,
and the mouth to to scold opens

Nein, die Karten lügen nicht!
no   the cards lie   not

31. *SONNTAGS   AM   RHEIN*
    ON SUNDAYS BY THE RHINE

31. SUNDAY BY THE RHINE

Robert Reinick

Des   Sonntags in der Morgenstund'
of the Sunday   in the morning-hour

Wie wandert's sich   so schön
how wanders it (itself) so beautifully

Am   Rhein, wenn rings in weiter Rund'
by the Rhine when around in wider circle

Die Morgenglocken geh'n!
the morning-bells go

How good it is to wander by the Rhine on a Sunday morning, when all around the church bells are ringing for matins.

Ein Schifflein zieht auf blauer Flut,
a   little boat moves on blue   tide

Da   singt's und jubelt's   drein;
there sings it and rejoices it in there

Du Schifflein, gelt,   das fährt sich
you little boat isn't that so that sails (itself)
  gut
  well

In all die Lust   hinein?
in all the pleasure into

A little boat sails by on the blue waters, and there is shouting and singing. Little boat, it's good sailing along in all this gaiety, isn't it?

Vom   Dorfe   hallet Orgelton,
from the village echoes organ-sound

Es   tönt ein frommes Lied,
(it) sounds a   religious song

Andächtig dort die Prozession
devoutly there the procession

Aus der Kapelle zieht.
from the chapel moves

From the village echo the strains of the organ; a hymn can be heard, as a procession moves reverently away from the church.

Und ernst   in all die Herrlichkeit
and solemnly in all the splendour

Die Burg   hernieder schaut
the castle down   looks

Und spricht von alter, guter Zeit,
and speaks of old   good time

Die auf den Fels gebaut.
that on the rock built

And a castle looks solemnly down in all its splendour, telling of the good old days when it was built on its rock.

Das alles   beut   der prächt'ger Rhein
(the) everything offers the glorious   Rhine

An seinem Rebenstrand,
on his   vine-shore

Und spiegelt recht im   hellsten Schein
and reflects truly in the clearest brilliance

Das ganze Vaterland;
the whole fatherland

Das fromme, treue Vaterland
the hallowed true fatherland

In seiner vollen Pracht,
in his   full   splendour

Mit Lust und Liedern allerhand
with joy and songs   of all kinds

Vom   lieben Gott bedacht.
by the dear   God provided for

All this is laid
before us on the vine-
clad shores of the Rhine,
that reflects all the
Fatherland in its clear
brilliance;

our glorious country,
hallowed and true,
blessed by the good Lord
with joy and song.

32. *DER HIDALGO*
    THE (SPANISH) GENTLEMAN

    Emanuel Geibel

Es ist so süss zu scherzen
it is so sweet to to have fun

Mit Liedern und mit Herzen
with songs   and with hearts

Und mit dem ernsten Streit!
and with the serious combat

Erglänzt des   Mondes Schimmer,
shines   of the moon   glimmer

Da   treibt's mich fort vom   Zimmer,
there urges it me   away from the room

Durch   Platz und Gassen weit;
through square and streets far

Da   bin zur   Lieb' ich immer
there am to the love   I   always

Wie zum   Gefecht bereit.
as to the fight   ready

Die Schönen   von Sevilla
the fair ones of Seville

Mit Fächern und Mantilla
with fan   and mantilla

Blicken den Strom entlang;
glance the river along

Sie lauschen mit Gefallen,
they listen   with pleasure

Wenn meine Lieder schallen
when my   songs sound

32. THE SPANISH
    GENTLEMAN

How sweet it is to
enjoy the delights of
songs and hearts, and
fierce combat. When the
moon shines brightly, I
must leave my room to
roam the streets and
squares; there I'm as
ready for love as for
a duel.

The fair ladies of
Seville, with their fans
and mantillas, gaze down
the river, and listen
with delight to the echo
of my songs and
mandoline, and dark roses
fall down to me from
their balconies to show
their favour.

Zum   Mandolinenklang,
to the mandoline-sound

Und dunkle Rosen fallen
and dark   roses fall

Mir   vom   Balkon zum   Dank.
to me from the balcony to the thanks

Ich trage, wenn ich singe,
I   carry when I   sing

Die Zither. und die Klinge,
the zither and the sword

Vom   Toledan'schen Stahl.
of the Toledan   steel

Ich sing' an manchem Gitter
I   sing at many a railing

Und höhne manchem Ritter
and mock many   cavaliers

Mit keckem Lied zumal,
with bold   song above all

Den Damen gilt   die Zither,
the ladies is intended for the zither

Die Klinge dem Rival.
the sword the rival

I carry my zither
when I sing, and my
sword, with its blade
of Toledo steel. I sing
by many a gateway,
mocking all the cavaliers
with the boldness of my
songs. The mandoline is
for the ladies, the
sword for my rivals.

Auf denn zum   Abenteuer,
on then to the adventure

Schon losch   der   Sonne Feuer
already blotted of the sun fire

Jenseits der   Berge   aus.
beyond   of the mountains out

Der   Mondnacht   Dämmrungsstunden,
of the moonlight-night twilight-hours

Sie bringen Liebeskunden,
they bring love's-tidings

Sie bringen blut'gen Strauss,
they bring bloody   combat

Und Blumen oder Wunden
and flowers or   wounds

Trag' morgen ich nach Haus.
carry next day I   - home -

Away then, to
adventure! Already the
fiery sun has gone down
behind the mountains.
The twilight hours of
this moonlit night bring
tidings of love, or
deadly combat. Tomorrow
I'll return home with
flowers - or wounds.

33. *LUST DER   STURMNACHT*
    JOY OF THE STORMY-NIGHT

33. JOY IN A STORMY
    NIGHT

Justinus Kerner

Wenn durch   Berg'   und Tale   draussen
when through mountain and valley outside

Regen schauert, Stürme brausen,
rain pours   storms rage

Schild   und Fenster hell   erklirren,
inn-sign and windows loudly clatter

Und in Nacht die Wandrer   irren,
and in night the travellers lose their way

Ruht es sich   so süss   hier innen,
rests it itself so sweetly here within

Aufgelöst in sel'ges Minnen;
abandoned in blissful loving

All' der gold'ne Himmelsschimmer
all the golden heaven's-shine

Flieht   herein ins   stille Zimmer.
retreats in here into the quiet room

Reiches Leben, hab' Erbarmen!
abundant life   have mercy

Halt' mich fest in linden Armen!
hold me   fast in gentle arms

Lenzesblumen   aufwärts dringen,
spring-flowers upwards press

Wölklein   ziehn und Vöglein   singen.
(little) clouds move and (little) birds sing

Ende nie, du Sturmnacht wilde!
end   never you storm-night wild

Klirrt, ihr Fenster, schwankt, ihr Schilde,
clatter you windows sway   you (inn)-signs

Bäumt   euch,   Wälder, braus', o Welle,
rear up (yourselves) woods roar   O wave

Mich umfängt des   Himmels Helle.
me   embraces of the Heaven brightness

When outside the
rain pours down in the
mountains and valleys,
and storms rage, so that
inn-signs and windows
clatter, and wayfarers
lose their way by night;
how sweet is the still-
ness here within, where
we are lost in love's
delights. All the
shining gold of heaven
retreats into this
quiet room. O abundant
life, have mercy! Hold
me fast in your gentle
arms! Spring flowers are
thrusting upwards, clouds
race and birds sing. May
you never end, you wild
and stormy night! Let
windows clatter and inn-
signs sway! Let the
woods surge, and the
waves roar! I am
embraced in the radiance
of Heaven.

34. *WANDERLIED*   34. SONG OF THE
   WANDERING-SONG   WANDERER

Justinus Kerner

Wohlauf! Noch   getrunken den funkelnden Wein!
come on further drunk   the sparkling wine

Ade   nun, ihr Lieben!   Geschieden muss sein.
farewell now you dear friends parted   must to be

Ade   nun, ihr Berge,   du väterlich Haus!
farewell now you mountains you paternal house

Es treibt in   die Ferne   mich mächtig
it compels into the distant place me   mightily
   hinaus.
   forth

Die Sonne, sie bleibet am   Himmel nicht steh'n
the sun   she remains in the sky   not to stand

Es treibt sie, durch Länder und Meere zu geh'n.
it drives her   through lands and seas to to go

Die Woge nicht haftet am   einsamen Strand,
the wave not   clings on the lonely   shore

Die Stürme, sie brausen mit Macht durch
the storms they bluster with might through
   das Land.
   the land

Mit eilenden Wolken der Vogel dort zieht
with hastening clouds the bird there moves

Und singt in der Ferne   ein heimatlich Lied.
and sings in the distance a   native   song

So treibt es den Burschen durch Wälder und Feld,
so drives it the youth   through woods and field

Zu gleichen der   Mutter, der   wandernden
to to be like (to) the mother (to) the wandering
   Welt.
   world

Da   grüssen ihn Vögel bekannt über'm   Meer,
there greet   him birds familiar over the sea

Sie flogen von Fluren der   Heimat hierher;
they flew   from meadows of the homeland here

Da   duften   die Blumen vertraulich
there are fragrant the flowers familiarly
   um   ihn,
   about him

Sie trieben vom   Lande die Lüfte   dahin.
them drove   from the land the breezes thither

Come, drink one
more glass of sparkling
wine! And now farewell,
dear friends, we must
part. Farewell, you
mountains! Farewell,
my father's house, for
I am mightily stirred
to go forth to distant
lands!

The sun is never
still in the sky; it
hastens on over land
and sea, waves never
cling to lonely shores;
raging storms bluster
over the land.

The bird flies with
the hastening clouds,
and far away it sings
its native song. The
young man is driven
through woods and
fields, to roam like
wandering Mother Nature.

Across the sea
familiar birds greet
him, flown from his
native meadows; the
familiar fragrance of
flowers is borne on
breezes from his own
land.

Die Vögel, die kennen sein väterlich Haus,
the birds they know   his paternal house

Die Blumen, die pflanzt' er der   Liebe
the flowers that planted he to the love
   zum   Strauss,
   to the nosegay

Und Liebe, die folgt   ihm, sie geht ihm   zur
and love   she follows him she goes to him to the
Hand:
hand

So wird   ihm   zur   Heimat das ferneste   Land.
so becomes to him to the home   the most distant land

The birds, they
know his father's house,
the flowers are the ones
he sowed to make
garlands for his
sweetheart, and love
follows him, and is
close at hand — so the
most distant place
becomes his home.

---

35. *ERSTES GRÜN*
    FIRST GREEN

35. FIRST GREEN

Justinus Kerner

Du junges Grün, du frisches Gras!
you young green you fresh   grass

Wie manches Herz durch   dich genas,
how many a heart through you got well

Das von des   Winters Schnee erkrankt,
that from of the winter   snow   fell ill

O wie mein Herz   nach dir verlangt!
O how my   heart for you longs

You green so new,
you grass so fresh,
how many hearts you
have healed, that pined
with winter's snow! O
how my heart longs for
you!

Schon   wächst du aus   der Erde Nacht,
already grow   you out of the earth night

Wie dir mein Aug' entgegenlacht!
how you my   eye laughs towards

Hier in des   Waldes stillem Grund
here in of the wood   quiet   earth

Drück ich dich, Grün, an Herz und Mund.
press I you   green to heart and mouth

Already you grow
from the darkness of
the earth — how my
eyes laugh with joy
when they see you! Here
on the quiet earth of
the woods, I press you,
green, to my heart and
lips.

Wie treibt's mich von den Menschen fort!
how drives it me   from the people   away

Mein Leid das hebt   kein Menschenwort;
my   grief that removes no   people's-word

Nur junges Grün, ans   Herz gelegt,
only young green to the heart laid

Macht, dass mein Herze stiller schlägt.
makes that my   heart quieter beats

I am driven away
from my fellow men; no
words of theirs can
assuage my grief. Only
you, fresh young green,
laid on my heart can
calm its beating.

36. STILLE LIEBE
SILENT LOVE

36. SILENT LOVE

Justinus Kerner

Könnt' ich dich in Liedern preisen,
could I   you in song   to praise

Säng'   ich dir   das längste Lied,
would sing I   to you the longest song

Ja, ich würd' in allen Weisen
yes I   would in all   tunes

Dich zu singen nimmer müd'.
you to to sing never   weary

    If I could but
praise you in my songs,
how endless they would
be, and never would I
weary of singing them
to you.

Doch was   immer mich betrübte,
but what always me   grieved

Ist, dass ich nur immer stumm
is   that I only always silent

Tragen kann dich, Herzgeliebte!
to bear can you   beloved heart

In des   Busens Heiligtum.
on of the bosom shrine

    But it always
grieves me, dear love,
that I can only hold
you silently in the
shrine of my heart.

Dieser Schmerz hat mich bezwungen,
this   grief   has me   overcome

Dass ich sang dies kleine Lied,
that I   sang this little song

Doch   von bitterm Leid durchdrungen,
indeed with bitter grief penetrated

Dass noch keins auf dich geriet.
that yet none to you succeeded

    My grief has
overcome me, so I sing
this little song. I am
filled with bitterness,
for not one that I sang
was ever worthy of you.

37. STILLE TRÄNEN
SILENT TEARS

37. SILENT TEARS

Justinus Kerner

Du bist vom   Schlaf erstanden
you are from the sleep risen

Und wandelst durch   die Au',
and wander   through the meadow

Da   liegt ob   allen Landen,
there lies above all   countryside

Der Himmel wunderblau.
the sky   wonderfully blue

    You rise from sleep
and wander through the
meadow; the heavens in
their wondrous blue
reach over all the land.

So lang du ohne   Sorgen
so long you without cares

Geschlummert schmerzenlos,
slumbered   painlessly

    But whilst you
slumbered so free of
care, these heavens wept
never-ending tears the
whole night through.

Der Himmel bis zum   Morgen
the sky   till to the morning

Viel Tränen niedergoss.
many tears   poured down

In stillen Nächten weinet
in still   nights weeps

Oft   mancher   aus den Schmerz,
often many a man away the grief

Und morgens   dann ihr meinet,
and each morning then you suppose

Stets fröhlich sei sein Herz.
always glad   be his heart

> In such still nights
> many a man weeps away
> his grief. And in the
> morning you would think
> his heart was always
> glad.

38. DIE SOLDATENBRAUT
   THE SOLDIER-BRIDE

38. THE SOLDIER'S BRIDE

Eduard Mörike

Ach, wenn's nur der König auch wüsst',
ah if it only the king also knew

Wie wacker mein Schätzelein   ist!
how brave my   (little) sweetheart is

Für den König, da   liess   er sein Blut,
for the king   there would let run he his blood

Für mich aber ebenso gut.
for me but just as well

> Oh, if the king
> only knew how brave
> my sweetheart is! He
> would lay down his life
> for the king – but he'd
> do the same for me.

Mein Schatz   hat kein Band und kein' Stern,
my sweetheart has no ribbon and no   star

Kein Kreuz, wie die vornehmen Herrn,
no cross like the grand   gentlemen

Mein Schatz   wird   auch kein General:
my sweetheart will be also no   general

Hätt' er nur seinen Abschied einmal!
had he only his   discharge once

> My sweetheart has
> no ribbons or stars, no
> crosses like fine
> gentlemen. My sweetheart
> will never be a general –
> if only he were a soldier
> no more!

Es   scheinen drei Sternen so hell
(it) shine   three stars so brightly

Dort über Marienkapell';
there over Mary's-chapel

Da   knüpft uns ein rosenrot Band,
there unites us a   rose-red ribbon

Und ein Hauskreuz ist auch bei der   Hand.
and a   home-cross is also at (the) hand

> Three stars are
> shining brightly over
> St. Mary's church; to
> unite us there'll be a
> rose-red ribbon – and at
> home he'll also get his
> cross.

39. *ROMANZE*   39. ROMANCE
   ROMANCE

Emanuel Geibel

Flutenreicher   Ebro, blühendes   Ufer,
richly-flooding Ebro of blossoming shore

All' ihr grünen Matten, Schatten des   Waldes,
all you green meadows shadows of the wood

Fraget die Geliebte, die unter euch ruhet,
ask   the beloved   who under you rests

Ob in ihrem Glücke   sie meiner gedenket.
if in her happiness she of me thinks

Und ihr tauigen Perlen, die ihr im   Frührot
and you dewy   pearls that you in the sunrise

Den grünenden   Rasen bunt   mit Farben
the becoming-green grass bright with colours
   schmückt,
   adorn

Fraget die Geliebte, wenn sie Kühling   atmet,
ask   the beloved   when she freshness breathes

Ob in ihrem Glücke   sie meiner gedenket.
if in her happiness she of me thinks

Ihr laubigen Pappeln, schimmernde Pfade,
you leafy   poplars shimmering paths

Wo   leichten Fusses mein Mädchen wandelt,
where light   of foot my girl   wanders

Wenn sie euch begegnet, fragt sie, fragt sie,
when she you meets   ask her ask   her

Ob in ihrem Glücke   sie meiner gedenket.
if in her happiness she of me thinks

Ihr schwärmenden Vögel, die   den Sonnenaufgang
you swarming   birds that the sunrise
   singend
   singing

Ihr begrüsset mit Flötenstimmen,
you greet   with flute-voices

Fraget die Geliebte, dieses Ufers Blume,
ask   the beloved   of this shore flower

Ob in ihrem Glücke   sie meiner gedenket.
if in her happiness she of me thinks

O richly flooding
Ebro, with your
blossoming shores, all
you green meadows, and
woodland shades — ask
my beloved as there she
rests, if in her joy
she thinks of me?

   And you dewy pearls
that at sunrise adorn
the green grass with
bright colours — ask my
beloved, as she breathes
the cool air if in her
joy she thinks of me?

   You leafy poplars,
you shimmering paths,
where light of foot
my sweetheart roams —
ask her when she meets
you, ask her, if in
her joy she thinks of
me?

   You flocks of
birds, that greet the
dawn with your fluting
voices — ask my beloved,
flower of these shores,
if in her joy she
thinks of me?

40. *SONNTAG*
SUNDAY

40. SUNDAY

Hoffmann von Fallersleben

Der Sonntag ist gekommen, ein Sträusschen
the Sunday is come   a   little bunch of flowers
  auf dem Hut;
  on the hat

Sein Aug' ist mild   und heiter, er meint's
his eye is gentle and serene   he means (it)
  mit allen gut.
  with all   well

Er steiget auf die Berge,   er wandelt durch
he climbs on the mountains he wanders through
  das Tal,
  the valley

Er ladet   zum   Gebete die Menschen allzumal.
he summons to the prayer the people   altogether

Und wie in schönen Kleidern nun pranget   jung
and as in lovely   clothes   now look fine young
  und alt,
  and old

Hat er für sie gedschmücket die Flur   und auch
has he for them bedecked   the meadow and also
  den Wald.
  the wood

Und wie er allen   Freude und Frieden bringt
and as he to everyone joy   and peace   brings
  und Ruh',
  and rest

So ruf' auch du nun jedem   "Gott grüss' dich!"
so call also you now to each God greet you
  freundlich   zu.
  in a friendly way (to)

Sunday has come,
with flowers in his hat.
His eyes are gentle and
serene, to all he bears
good-will. He climbs
the mountains, and
wanders through the
valley, summoning
everyone to prayer.

And as young and
old all don their
Sunday best,
for them he bedecks
the meadows and the
woods. He brings joy
and peace to everyone,
so with a friendly
'God be with you!' you
should greet each other.

41. *DER SANDMANN*
THE SANDMAN

41. THE SANDMAN

Gustav Hermann Kletka

Zwei feine Stieflein   hab' ich an,
two fine little boots have I   on

Mit wunderweichen Söhlchen   dran;
with very soft   (little) soles on them

Ein Säcklein   hab' ich hintern auf,
a   (little) sack have I   behind on

Husch! tripp' ich rasch   die Trepp' hinauf,
quick trip I   quickly the stairs up

Und wenn ich in   die Stube tret',
and when I   into the room go

Die Kinder .   beten   ihr Gebet;
the children are praying their prayer

I wear two fine
little boots, with the
softest of little soles;
with a little sack on my
back, in a twinkling, I
trip up the stairs. As
I go into the bedroom,
the children are
saying their prayers.
I drop two little grains
of sand into their eyes,
and then they will
sleep the whole night
through, watched over
by God and his angels.

Von meinem Sand zwei Körnerlein
from my   sand two (little) grains

Streu' ich auf ihre Äugelein,
strew I   on their (little) eyes

Da   schlafen sie die ganze Nacht
then sleep   they the whole night

In Gottes und der Englein   Wacht.
in God's and the (little) angels watch

Von meinem Sand zwei Körnerlein
from my   sand two (little) grains

Streut' ich auf ihre Äugelein:
strewed I   on their (little) eyes

Den   frommen Kindern soll gar schön
to the good   children shall very beautifully

Ein froher Traum vorübergehn.
a   happy dream go past

Nun risch und rasch mit Sack und Stab
now 'snip' and 'snap' with sack and staff

Nur wieder jetzt die Trepp' hinab,
only again now   the stairs down

Ich kann nicht länger müssig stehn,
I can not   longer idle   to be

Muss heut' noch zu gar Vielen gehn –
must today still to very many   to go

Da   nickt ihr schon und lacht im   Traum,
there nod   you already and laugh in the dream

Und öffnete mein Säcklein   kaum.
and opened my   (little) sack hardly

I dropped two
little grains of sand
in their eyes, for good
children should have
sweet dreams. Now, snip
snap, with my sack and
stick, I trip downstairs
again. I cannot be idle
any longer, for I have
many to go and see
tonight. Already you
are nodding and smiling
in your dreams – and I
hardly opened my sack
at all!

42. *MARIENWÜRMCHEN*
    LADYBIRD

42. LADYBIRD

(From *Des   Knaben Wunderhorn,*
     of the boy   magic-horn
folk poems published by
Achim von Arnim and Clemens Brentano)

Marienwürmchen, setze dich
ladybird   seat yourself

Auf meine Hand, auf meine Hand,
on my   hand on my   hand

Ich tu' dir   nichts zu Leide,
I do to you nothing to harm

Es soll dir   nichts zu Leid' gescheh'n
it shall to you nothing to harm to happen

Will nur deine bunten Flügel seh'n
want only your bright wings to see

Bunte Flügel, meine Freude!
bright wings my   joy

O ladybird, come,
sit on my hand! I'll
do you no harm;

no harm will come to
you. I want to see your
bright wings – I love
bright wings!

Marienwürmchen, fliege weg,
ladybird   fly   away

Dein Häuschen   brennt, die Kinder   schrei'n
your little house burns   the children cry

So sehre, wie so sehre.
so much   how so much

O ladybird, fly away - your house is on fire, and your children cry with all their might.

Die böse Spinne spinnt sie   ein,
the bad   spider spins   them in

Marienwürmchen, flieg' hinein,
ladybird   fly   in there

Deine Kinder   schreien sehre.
your   children cry   much

A wicked spider spins a web all round them. Ladybird, fly home - your children are crying with all their might.

Marienwürmchen, fliege hin
ladybird   fly   there

Zu Nachbars   Kind', zu Nachbars   Kind',
to neighbour's children to neighbour's children

Sie tun dir   nichts zu Leide,
they do   to you nothing to harm

O ladybird, fly away to the children next-door, they'll do you no harm;

Es soll dir   da   kein Leid gescheh'n,
it shall to you there no   harm to happen

Sie wollen deine bunten Flügel seh'n,
they want   your bright wings to see

Und grüss' sie alle   beide.
and greet   them (both of them)

no harm will come to you. They want to see your bright wings - just go and say hallo.

43. *DIE WANDELNDE GLOCKE*
      THE WALKING   BELL

43. THE WALKING BELL

Johann Wolfgang von Goethe

Es   war ein Kind, das   wollte nie
there was a   child that would never

Zur   Kirche sich   bequemen,
to the church (itself) to condescend (to go)

Und sonntags   fand es stets ein Wie,
and on Sundays found it always a   how

Den Weg in's   Feld zu nehmen.
the way into the field to to take

There was once a child who would never go to church. And on Sundays he always found his way off into the fields.

Die Mutter sprach: "Die Glocke tönt,
the mother said   the bell   is ringing

Und so ist dir's   befohlen,
and so is to you it ordered

Und hast du dich   nicht hingewöhnt
and have you yourself not   got used to (going) there

Sie kommt und wird dich holen."
she comes and will you   to fetch

His Mother said, 'The bell is ringing telling you to come, and if you don't obey, it'll come and fetch you.'

Das Kind, es denkt: "Die Glocke hängt
the child it thinks   the bell   hangs

Da   droben   auf dem Stuhle,"
there up above on the belfry

Schon hat's den Weg in's   Feld gelenkt,
already has it the way into the field wended

Als   lief' es aus   der Schule.
as (if) ran   it out of the school

The child thinks, 'The bell hangs up there in the belfry!' And already he's on his way to the fields, as if he were playing truant from school.

Die Glocke, Glocke, tönt nicht mehr,
the bell   bell   rings not   more

Die Mutter hat gefackelt.
the mother has fibbed

Doch welch' ein Schrecken hinterher!
but what   a   fright   afterwards

Die Glocke kommt gewackelt.
the bell   comes wobbling

The bell stops ringing, Mother was making it up. But oh, what a fright! there's the bell, wobbling along!

Sie wackelt schnell, man glaubt   es kaum;
she wobbles fast   one believes it hardly

Das arme Kind im   Schrecken,
the poor child in the fright

Es läuft, es rennt als wie im   Traum;
it runs   it runs as if in the dream

Die Glocke wird es decken.
the bell   will it to cover

It wobbles along fast, it's hard to believe. The poor child in his fright runs and runs as in a bad dream - the bell will come and cover him up!

Doch nimmt es richtig seinen Husch, -
but takes it properly its   rush

Und mit gewandter Schnelle,
and with nimble   speed

Es eilt   durch Anger,   Feld und Busch
it hurries through village green field and bush

Zur   Kirche, zur   Kapelle,
to the church to the chapel

But he goes like the wind, and nimbly speeds through the fields and woods, rushes across the village green to the church, to the chapel.

Und jeden Sonn- und Feiertag
and every Sun- and Feast-day

Gedenkt   es an den Schaden,
remembers it of the mischief

Lässt durch   den ersten Glockenschlag
lets through the first bell-stroke

Nicht in Person sich   laden.
not   in person itself be summoned.

Now on Sundays and Feastdays he remembers his fright; at the first stroke of the bell he's off - he doesn't wait for anyone to fetch him!

44. MEIN SCHÖNER STERN
    MY   LOVELY STAR

44. MY LOVELY STAR

Friedrich Rückert

Mein schöner Stern! ich bitte dich,
my lovely star I beg you

O lasse du dein heitres Licht
O let   you your serene light

Nicht trüben   durch   den Dampf in mir,
not   to darken through the cloud in me

Vielmehr den Dampf in mir zu Licht,
rather the mist in me to light

Mein schöner Stern, verklären   hilf!
my lovely star to transfigure help

Mein schöner Stern! ich bitte dich,
my lovely star I beg you

Nicht senk' herab zur   Erde dich,
not   sink down to the earth yourself

Weil   du mich noch hier unten siehst,
because you me   still here below see

Heb' auf vielmehr zum   Himmel mich,
raise up rather   to the Heaven me

Mein schöner Stern, wo   du schon   bist!
my lovely star where you already are

O lovely star! I beg
you not to let your
serene light be dimmed by
the darkness within me;
rather let my darkness be
transfigured by your
light, O lovely star!

O lovely star! I beg
you not to come down to
the earth because you see
me here below; but rather
raise me up to Heaven,
where you, O lovely star,
already are!

45. AUFTRÄGE
    MESSAGES

45. MESSAGES

Christian L'Egru

Nicht so schnelle, nicht so schnelle!
not   so fast   not   so fast

Wart' ein wenig, kleine Welle!
wait a   little little wave

Will dir einen Auftrag geben
want you a   message to give

An die Liebste mein.
to the beloved mine

Wirst du ihr   vorüberschweben,
will you to her past to float

Grüsse sie mir   fein!
greet her to me fine

Sag' ich wäre   mitgekommen,
say I   would be come along with

Auf dir selbst   herabgeschwommen:
on you yourself down swum

Für den Gruss   einen Kuss
for the greeting a   kiss

Not so fast, not so
fast - wait a moment,
little wave! I've a
message for you to give
my sweetheart. As you
flow past her, give her
my dear love!

Tell her I would have
come too, swimming along
with you, boldly to beg a
kiss in return for my
greeting. But the time
was too pressing, and
wouldn't have allowed it.

Kühn mir   zu erbitten,
boldly to me to to beg for

Doch der   Zeit Dringlichkeit
but of the time urgency

Hätt'   es nicht gelitten.
would have it not   allowed

Nicht so eilig! halt! erlaube,
not   so hurried stop allow (me)

Not so fast – stop,
please, light–winged
little dove! I've a
message for you to give
my sweetheart. Give her a
thousand greetings, and
then a hundred more!

Kleine, leicht beschwingte Taube!
little light– winged   dove

Habe dir   was   aufzutragen
have to you something to to charge with

An die Liebste mein!
to the beloved mine

Sollst ihr tausend Grüsse   sagen,
shall her thousand greetings to say

Hundert obendrein.
hundred over and above

Sag' ich wär   mit dir geflogen,
say I would be with you flown

Tell her I would
have flown with you over
mountain and river,
boldly to beg a kiss in
return for my greeting.
But the time was too
pressing, and wouldn't
have allowed it.

Über Berg'   und Strom gezogen:
over mountain and river gone

Für den Gruss   einen Kuss
for the greeting a   kiss

Kühn mir   zu erbitten,
boldly to me to to beg for

Doch der   Zeit Dringlichkeit
but of the time urgency

Hätt'   es nicht gelitten.
would have it not   allowed

Warte nicht, dass ich dich treibe,
wait not   that I   you urge on

O you lazy moon,
don't wait for me to urge
you on – you know what I
asked you to do for my
sweetheart; peep through
her window, and give her
my dear love!

O du   träge Mondesscheibe!
O you lazy moon's-disc

Weisst's ja,   was ich dir befohlen
know it indeed what I   you bidden

Für die Liebste mein:
for the beloved mine

Durch das Fensterchen   verstohlen
through the little window secretly

Grüsse sie mir   fein!
greet her to me fine

Sag', ich wär'   auf dich gestiegen,
say I would be on you climbed

Tell her I would have
climbed on your back and
flown myself to her,
boldly to beg a kiss in
return for my greeting.
It's your fault – I was
far too impatient!

Selber zu ihr hinzufliegen:
myself to her to to fly

Für den Gruss   einen Kuss
for the greeting a   kiss

Kühn mir   zu erbitten,
boldly to me to to beg for

Du seist Schuld,   Ungeduld
you be   (at) fault impatience

Hätt'   mich nicht gelitten.
would have me   not   allowed

46. *RÖSELEIN,   RÖSELEIN!*   46. LITTLE ROSE
    LITTLE ROSE, LITTLE ROSE

Wilfried von der Neun

Röselein,   Röselein
little rose little rose

Müssen denn Dornen sein?
must   then thorns to be

Schlief   am   schatt'gen Bächelein
went to sleep by the shady   little brook

Einst zu süssem Träumen ein,
once to sweet dreaming -

Sah in goldner Sonne Schein
saw in golden sun   -shine

Dornenlos ein Röselein,
thornless a   little rose

Pflückt' es auch und küsst' es fein:
plucked it also and kissed it delicately

"Dornenloses Röselein!"
thornless   little roses

Ich erwacht' und schaute drein:
I   awoke   and looked towards it

"Hätt ich's doch! Wo   mag es sein?"
had   I it indeed where may it to be

Rings im   weiten   Sonnenschein
around in the spacious sunshine

Standen nur Dornröselein!
stood   only thorn-(little)roses

Und das Bächlein   lachte mein:
and the little brook laughed of me

"Lass du nur ein Träumen sein!
let   you only a   dreaming to be

Merk dir's   fein:
mark to you it well

Dornröslein   müssen sein!"
thorn-(little) roses must   to be

Little rose, little rose, must you have thorns? Once I fell asleep by a shady little brook, and dreamed so sweetly; I saw in the golden sunlight a little rose without thorns. I plucked it, and kissed it gently. 'O little rose without thorns!'

I awoke and looked about me: 'If only I had it! I wonder where it is?' All around in the sunlight grew only roses with thorns. And the little brook laughed at me! 'You were only dreaming! Mark my words - roses must have thorns!'

47. MEINE ROSE
   MY   ROSE

47. MY ROSE

Nikolaus Lenau

Dem   holden Lenzgeschmeide,
to the lovely spring-jewels

Der   Rose, meiner Freude,
to the rose to my joy

Die schon gebeugt und blasser
that already bowed   and paler

Vom   heissen Strahl der   Sonnen,
from the hot   ray   of the sun

Reich' ich den Becher Wasser
hold out I   the cup   water

Aus dunklem, tiefem Bronnen.
from dark   deep   spring

Du Rose meines Herzens!
you rose of my heart

Vom   stillen Strahl des Schmerzens
from the silent ray of the grief

Bist du gebeugt und blasser;
are you bowed   and paler

Ich möchte   dir   zu   Füssen,
I   would like to you to (your) feet

Wie dieser Blume Wasser,
as   to this flower water

Still   meine Seele giessen!
silently my   soul to pour

Könnt' ich dann auch nicht sehen
could I   then also not   to see

Dich freudig auferstehen.
you joyously rise up

To this lovely jewel of Spring, to the rose, my joy, already pale and bowed by the scorching rays of the sun: I hold out this cup of water from the dark, deep spring.

O rose of my heart! You are pale and bowed by the silent pangs of grief; I would silently pour out my soul at your feet, as I pour water on this flower. May I not then see you joyously revive again?

48. REQUIEM
REQUIEM

48. REQUIEM

Catholic poem

Ruh' von schmerzensreichen Mühen
rest from deeply- afflicted troubles

Aus und heissem Liebesglühen;
- and ardent love's-glowing

Der nach seligem Verein
he after blissful union

Trug Verlangen,
bore yearning

Rest in peace, after the deep suffering of fervent love; he who so long did yearn for blissful union has entered the dwelling of his Saviour.

Ist gegangen
is gone

Zu des   Heilands Wohnung ein.
to of the Saviour's dwelling in

Dem   Gerechten leuchten helle   Bright stars shine
to the righteous shine   bright   on the tomb of the
                                                              righteous one, who
Sterne in des   Grabes Zelle,   himself will appear as a
stars in of the grave's cell   star, when he beholds the
                                                              Lord in the glory of
Ihm,   der selbst als Stern der   Nacht   Heaven.
to him who himself as star of the night

Wird erscheinen,
will to appear

Wenn er seinen
when he his

Herrn erschaut in Himmelspracht.
Lord beholds in Heavens's-glory

Seid Fürsprecher, heil'ge Seelen,   Intercede for him,
be   intercessors holy   souls   you holy souls, let your
                                                              comfort not fail him,
Heil'ger Geist, lass Trost   nicht fehlen.   Holy Spirit. Hark,
Holy   Spirit let comfort not   be lacking   triumphant psalms
                                                              resound in solemn tones,
Hörst du? Jubelsang   erklingt,   and the singing of the
hear you jubilation-song resounds   angels' harp:

Feiertöne,
solemn tones

Darein die schöne
thereto the lovely

Engelsharfe singt:
angel's-harp sings

Ruh' von schmerzensreichen Mühen...   Rest in peace, after
rest from deeply-afflicted   troubles   the deep suffering...

Richard Wagner
(1813-1883)

1. *FÜNF GEDICHTE FÜR EINE FRAUENSTIMME*
FIVE POEMS   FOR A   WOMAN'S-VOICE

Mathilde Wesendonck

    i. *Der Engel*
      the angel

In der   Kindheit frühen Tagen
in of the childhood early days

Hört ich oft   von Engeln sagen,
heard I   often of angels to tell

Die des   Himmels hehre   Wonne
who of the heaven sublime joy

Tauschen mit der Erdensonne,
exchange with the earth's-sun

Dass,   wo   bang   ein Herz in Sorgen
so that where anxiously a   heart in griefs

Schmachtet vor   der Welt verborgen,
pines   before the world hidden

Dass wo   still   es will verbluten,
so that where silently it will to shed blood

Und vergehn   in Tränenfluten,
and to waste away in tears-floods

Dass, wo   brünstig sein Gebet
that where ardently its prayer

Einzig um Erlösung   fleht,
only for deliverance implores

Da   der Engel niederschwebt,
then the angel floats down

Und es sanft   gen Himmel   hebt.
and it tenderly -heavenwards- raises

Ja, es stieg auch mir   ein Engel nieder,
yes it came also to me an angel down

Und auf leuchtendem Gefieder
and on gleaming   plumage

Führt er, ferne jedem   Schmerz,
bears he far   to every grief

Meinen Geist nun himmelwärts!
my   spirit now heavenwards

1. FIVE SONGS

i. The angel

    When I was very
young, I often heard
tell of angels, who
left the sublime joys
of heaven for the sunny
earth,

where hidden from the
world a heart was pining
in anxious grief. It
would silently bleed and
waste away mid floods of
tears,

its prayer ardently
begging only for
deliverance. Then an
angel would descend
and bear it tenderly
to Heaven.

    Yes, an angel came
down to me too, and
bore my spirit on
gleaming wings far from
all grief to Heaven!

ii. Stehe still!
stand still

ii. Be still!

Sausendes, brausendes Rad der Zeit,
blustering raging   wheel of the time

Messer du der Ewigkeit;
measurer you of the eternity

Leuchtende Sphären im weiten All,
gleaming   spheres in the wide universe

Die ihr umringt den Weltenball;
who you encircle the world-globe

Urewige Schöpfung, halte doch ein,
ancient-eternal creation   halt indeed –

Genug des Werdens, lass mich sein!
enough of the evolution leave me to be

Blustering, raging wheel of time, you who measure eternity; gleaming spheres in the wide universe encircling the globe; O halt, primeval creation – enough of evolution, let me alone!

Halte an dich, zeugende Kraft,
hold to yourself procreating power

Urgedanke, der ewig schafft!
ancient-thought which eternally creates

Hemmet den Atem, stillet den Drang,
curb   the breath stay   the impulse

Schweigend nur eine Sekunde lang!
being silent only one second long

Schwellende Pulse, fesselt den Schlag;
rising   pulses fetter the beat

Ende, des Wollens ewiger Tag!
end   of the desiring eternal day

Hold back, creative power – ancient of thoughts eternally creating! Curb your breath, stay your impulse, be still one second long! Throbbing pulses, restrain your beat. End, eternal day of desiring,

Dass in selig süssem Vergessen
that in blessed sweet oblivion

Ich mög alle Wonnen ermessen!
I   may all raptures consider

Wenn Aug in Auge wonnig trinken,
when eye in eye blissfully drink

Seele ganz in Seele versinken;
soul wholly in soul submerges

Wesen in Wesen sich wiederfindet,
being in being itself again finds

Und alles Hoffens Ende sich kündet,
and all   of hope end itself announces

Die Lippe verstummt in staunendem Schweigen,
the lip   grows dumb in astonished silence

Keinen Wunsch mehr will das Innre zeugen:
no   desire more wants the inner self to show

Erkennt der Mensch Ewgen Spur,
perceives the man Eternal trace

Und löst dein Rätsel, heilge Natur!
and solves your enigma sacred nature

that in blessed sweet oblivion, I may consider all joys on earth! When eyes in eyes are blissfully absorbed, and soul submerged in soul; being rediscovers being, and the end of all hoping is revealed; lips grow dumb in astonished silence, and no further desire betrays the heart – then man perceives the mark of the Eternal, and penetrates your mystery, sacred Nature.

iii. Im   Treibhaus
        in the greenhouse

iii. In the greenhouse

Hochgewölbte Blätterkronen,
high-arched leaves' crowns

Baldachine von Smaragd,
canopies   of emerald

Kinder   ihr aus fernen Zonen,
children you from far off zones

Saget mir, warum ihr klagt?
tell   me   why   you lament

High-arching leafy
crowns, canopies of
emerald - you children
from far off lands, tell
me, why do you lament?

Schweigend neiget ihr die Zweige,
silently bow   you the branches

Malet Zeichen in   die Luft,
paint signs   into the air

Und der   Leiden   stummer Zeuge
and of the suffering silent witness

Steiget aufwärts, süsser Duft.
rises   upwards   sweet fragrance

Silently you bow
down your branches,
making signs in the air,
and in silent witness of
suffering, your sweet
fragrance rises upwards.

Weit in sehnendem Verlangen
wide in yearning   desire

Breitet ihr die Arme aus,
stretch you the arms out

Und umschlinget wahnbefangen
and embrace   delusion-caught

Öder   Leere nichtgen Graus.
of desolate void empty   horror

You stretch your
arms wide in yearning
desire, and in your
deluding prison, cling
to the empty horror of
a desolate void.

Wohl, ich weiss es, arme Pflanze;
indeed I   know it poor plant

Ein Geschicke teilen wir,
a   fate   share we

Ob   umstrahlt von Licht und Glanze,
whether shone about by light and splendour

Unsre Heimat   ist nicht hier!
our   homeland is not   here

Yes I know, poor
plant, we share one fate;
though light and
splendour surround us,
this is not our homeland!

Und wie froh   die Sonne scheidet
and as gladly the sun   parts

Von des   Tages leerem Schein,
from of the day   empty shine

Hüllet der, der wahrhaft leidet,
wraps he   who truly   suffers

Sich   in Schweigens Dunkel   ein.
himself in silence's darkness -

And as the sun is
glad to leave the
empty light of day, so
those who suffer deeply
seek to enfold
themselves in silent
darkness.

Stille wird's,   ein säuselnd Weben
still becomes it a   murmuring weaving

Füllet bang   den dunklen Raum:
fills uneasily the dark   place

Schwere Tropfen seh ich schweben
heavy   drops   see I   to hover

An der   Blätter grünem Saum.
on of the leaves green edge

It grows still, a
weaving and murmuring
uneasily fill the dark
place. I see heavy
drops hovering on the
edge of the green
leaves.

iv. *Schmerzen*
  sorrows

iv. Sorrows

Sonne, weinest jeden Abend
sun   weep   each evening

Dir   die schönen Augen rot,
to you the lovely eyes red

Wenn im   Meeresspiegel badend
when in the ocean's-mirror bathing

Dich erreicht der frühe Tod!
you reaches the early death

    O sun, you weep
each evening till your
lovely eyes are red;
and floating on the
ocean's mirror, are
overtaken by an early
death.

Doch erstehst in alter Pracht,
yet rise   in old splendour

Glorie der   düstren Welt,
glory of the dark   world

Du am   Morgen neu   erwacht,
you in the morning newly awaken

Wie ein stolzer Siegesheld!
like a   proud   victory-hero

    Yet, newly
awakened in the
morning, you rise like
a proud, triumphant
hero in all your former
splendour – the glory
of a dark world.

Ach, wie sollte ich da   klagen,
ah how should I   then to lament

Wie, mein Herz, so schwer dich sehn,
how my   heart so heavily you to see

Muss die Sonne selbst verzagen,
must the sun herself to despair

Muss die Sonne untergehn?
must the sun   to go down

    Ah, how can I then
lament, and see my
heart bowed down with
sorrow! Must the sun
herself despair, must
even she go down?

Und gebieret   Tod   nur Leben,
and brings forth death only life

Geben Schmerzen Wonnen   nur:
give griefs   raptures only

O wie dank ich, dass gegeben
O how thank I   that given

Solche Schmerzen mir   Natur!
such   sorrows   to me nature

    And if death brings
forth only life, and
grief only rapture, O
what thanks I give
that nature bestowed on
me such sorrows!

v. *Träume*
  dreams

v. Dreams

Sag, welch wunderbare Träume
say what wonderful dreams

Halten meinen Sinn umfangen,
hold   my   mind embraced

Dass sie nicht wie leere Schäume
that they not like empty bubbles

Sind in ödes Nichts   vergangen?
are in bleak nothingness lost

    Tell me, what
wonderful dreams are
these that envelop my
mind, and do not like
empty bubbles vanish
into mere nothing?

Träume, die in jeder Stunde,
dreams that in each hour

Jedem Tage Schöner blühn,
to each day more fair blossom

Und mit ihrer Himmelskunde
and with their heaven's-tidings

Selig durchs Gemüte ziehn!
blissfully through the soul move

Träume, die wie hehre Strahlen
dreams that like sacred rays

In die Seele sich versenken,
into the soul (themselves) sink

Dort ein ewig Bild zu malen:
there an eternal image to to paint

Allvergessen, Eingedenken!
allforgetfulness remembrance

Träume, wie wenn Frühlingssonne
dreams as when spring's-sun

Aus dem Schnee die Blüten küsst
out of the snow the blossoms kisses

Dass zu nie geahnter Wonne
that to never suspected rapture

Sie der neue Tag begrüsst,
them the new day greets

Dass sie wachsen, dass sie blühen,
that they grow that they blossom

Träumend spenden ihren Duft,
dreaming bestow their fragrance

Sanft an deiner Brust verglühen,
gently on your breast cease glowing

Und dann sinken in die Gruft.
and then sink into the grave

Dreams, that each
hour, each day,
blossom more fair, and
move with their
heavenly message
blissfully through my
soul!

Dreams, that like
sacred rays penetrate
my soul and paint an
everlasting image there;
oblivion, deep
remembrance.

Dreams, that like
the sun in spring kiss
the blossoms in the
snow, and greet the
new day with unsuspected
rapture;

to grow and flower, and
dreaming spread their
fragrance, then
gradually fade at your
breast, and sink into
the grave.

Johannes Brahms
(1833-1897)

1. LIEBESTREU
  LOVE'S-FIDELITY

1. FIDELITY

Robert Reinick

"O versenk', o versenk' dein Leid, mein Kind,
  O sink   O sink   your grief my   child

In   die See, in   die tiefe See!"
into the ocean into the deep ocean

Ein Stein wohl   bleibt auf des   Meeres Grund,
a   stone perhaps stays on of the ocean bottom

Mein Leid kommt stets in die Höh'.
my   grief comes always - upward -

"Und die Lieb', die du im   Herzen trägst,
 and the love   that you in the heart bear

Brich sie ab, brich sie ab, mein Kind!"
break her off break her off my   child

Ob die Blum' auch stirbt, wenn man sie bricht,
if the flower even dies   when one it   plucks

Treue Lieb' nicht so geschwind.
true love not   so fast

"Und die Treu',   und die Treu',   's war nur ein
 and the fidelity and the fidelity it was only a
  Wort,
  word

In   den Wind damit   hinaus."
into the wind with it out

O Mutter, und splittert der Fels auch im   Wind,
O mother and shatters the rock even in the wind

Meine Treue,   die hält   ihn aus.
my   fidelity it   endures him -

'Sink, O sink
your grief, my child,
in the ocean, the deep
ocean!' A stone will
stay at the bottom of
the sea, but my grief
always rises again.

'And the love
that you bear in your
heart - tear it out,
tear it out, my
child!' A flower may
die when it is plucked,
but not so soon true
love.

'True love, true
love, are only words -
throw them to the
winds!' O mother, a
rock may shatter in
the storm, my true love
will endure.

2. *TREUE LIEBE*
   TRUE LOVE

2. TRUE LOVE

Eduard Ferrand

Ein Mägdlein   sass am   Meeresstrand
a   young maiden sat on the sea-shore

Und blickte voll Sehnsucht in's   Weite:
and looked full longing   into the distance

"Wo   bleibst du, mein Liebster, wo   weilst du
where stay   you my   dearest   where linger you
so lang?
   so long

Nicht ruhen   lässt mich des   Herzens Drang.
not   to rest leaves me   of the heart   craving

Ach kämst   du, mein Liebster, doch heute!"
ah would come you my   dearest   still today

Der Abend   nahte,   die Sonne sank
the evening drew near the sun   sank

Am   Saum des   Himmels darnieder.
on the edge of the sky   down

"So trägt   dich die Welle mir   nimmer zurück?
 so carries you the wave to me never   back

Vergebens späht in   die Ferne   mein Blick.
in vain   peers into the distance my   glance

Wo   find' ich, mein Liebster, dich wieder?"
where find I   my   dearest   you again

Die Wasser umspielten   ihr   schmeichelnd den Fuss,
the waters played round to her caressingly the foot

Wie   Träume von seligen Stunden,
like dreams of blissful hours

Es zog sie zur   Tiefe mit   stiller Gewalt;
it drew her to the deep with silent power

Nie   stand mehr am   Ufer die holde Gestalt,
never stood more on the shore the lovely figure

Sie hat den Geliebten gefunden!
she has the loved one found

A maiden sat on
the sea-shore - with
longing she gazed far
out to sea. 'Where do
you linger so long,
my dearest? The yearning
of my heart gives me no
rest. If only, my
dearest, you would come
this day!'

Evening drew on
and the sun went down
on the edge of the sky.
'Will the waves never
bring you back to me?
In vain I search far
over the sea - O
where can I find you
again, my love?'

The caressing waves
lapped around her feet;
she dreamed of
blissful hours. Its
silent power drew her
into the deeps. The
lovely figure stood
never more on the
strand - at last she had
found her beloved!

3. *DER SCHMIED*
   THE (BLACK)SMITH

3. THE BLACKSMITH

Ludwig Uhland

Ich hör' meinen Schatz,
I   hear my   sweetheart

Den Hammer er schwinget,
the hammer he swings

Das rauschet, das klinget,
that thunders that resounds

I hear the sound of
my sweetheart's hammer;
it clangs as he swings
it, and like a peal of
bells, it echoes away
in the alleys and
square.

Das dringt   in   die Weite
that penetrates into the distance

Wie Glockengeläute
like bells-pealing

Durch   Gassen und Platz.
through alleys and square

Am   schwarzen Kamin
by the black   chimney

Da   sitzet mein Lieber,
there sits   my   dear one

Doch geh' ich vorüber,
but go   I   past

Die Bälge   dann sausen,
the bellows then rush

Die Flammen aufbrausen,
the flames roar

Und lodern um   ihn.
and glow   round him

There sits my
love by his black
chimney. As I pass by,
the bellows roar, and
flames flare up and
glow all around him.

4. AN EINE ÄOLSHARFE
   TO AN   AEOLIAN-HARP

Eduard Mörike
(also set by Wolf)

4. TO AN AEOLIAN HARP

Angelehnt an die Efeuwand
leaning   on the ivy-(clad) wall

Dieser alten Terrasse,
of this old   terrace

Du, einer luftgebor'nen Muse
you of a born-of-air   Muse

Geheimnisvolles Saitenspiel,
mysterious   strings-playing

Fang' an,
- begin -

Fange wieder an
begin again -

Deine melodische Klage.
your melodious lament

Leaning against
the ivy-clad wall of
this old terrace, let
your mysterious strings
begin to play, O Muse,
born of the air!
Begin, then begin again
your tuneful lament.

Ihr kommet, Winde, fern   herüber,
you come   winds   far away over here

Ach, von des   Knaben,
oh   from of the boy

Der mir so lieb war,
who to me so dear was

Frischgrünendem   Hügel.
freshly-becoming green hillock

Und Frühlingsblüten unterwegs   streifend,
and spring-blossoms on the way brushing

Übersättigt mit Wohlgerüchen,
satiated   with perfumes

Wie süss   bedrängt ihr dies Herz!
how sweetly oppress you this heart

Und säuselt her in   die Saiten,
and whisper here into the strings

Angezogen von wohllautender Wehmut,
drawn   by euphonious   melancholy

Wachsend im   Zug meiner Sehnsucht
growing in the wake of my yearning

Und hinsterbend wieder.
and dying away again

You come, winds,
from far away, from the
fresh green grave of
the boy who was so dear
to me, lightly
touching on your way
spring blossoms, heavy
with fragrance. How
sweetly you oppress my
heart! You whisper
here in the strings,
drawn by the melancholy
harmony that grows in
the wake of my
yearning, and dies away
again.

Aber auf   einmal,
but (all) at once

Wie der Wind heftiger herstösst,
as the wind violently buffets

Ein holder Schrei der   Harfe
a   lovely cry   of the harp

Wiederholt mir zu süssem Erschrecken,
repeats   to me to sweet alarm

Meiner Seele plötzliche Regung;
of my soul sudden   motion

Und hier die volle Rose streut geschüttelt
and here the full rose strews shaken

All' ihre Blätter vor   meine Füsse!
all her petals before my   feet

But all at once
with a sudden gust of
wind a lovely cry comes
from the harp, and in
sweet alarm echoes to
me the sudden stirring
in my heart; and here
the full-blown rose
strews all her petals
at my feet.

5. *WIE BIST DU, MEINE KÖNIGIN*
   HOW ARE YOU MY   QUEEN

5. HOW DELIGHTFUL YOU
   ARE, MY QUEEN

Georg Friedrich Daumer

Wie bist du, mein Königin,
how are you my   queen

Durch sanfte Güte   wonnevoll!
through gentle goodness delightful

Du lächle nur, Lenzdüfte   weh'n
you smile only spring-scents drift

How delightful you
are, my queen, in your
gentle goodness! If
you but smile, the scents
of spring drift through
my soul, so sweetly.

Durch   mein Gemüte, wonnevoll!
through my   soul   delightfully

Frish aufgeblühter   Rosen Glanz,
fresh of come into bloom roses splendour

Vergleich' ich ihn dem   deinigen?
compare   I   him to the yours

Ach, über alles,   was da   blüht,
ah   above everything that there blossoms

Ist deine Blüte wonnevoll!
is   your   flower delightful

    Can the radiance of
freshly blooming roses
be compared with yours?
Ah, your blossoming is
more entrancing than
that of any flower!

Durch   tote Wüsten wandle hin,
through dead deserts wander along

Und grüne Schatten breiten   sich,
and green shadows spread out (themselves)

Ob   fürchterliche Schwüle   dort
though frightful   sultriness there

Ohn   Ende brüte, wonnevoll!
without end brooded delightfully

    Even if you
wandered through
desert wastes, where
a sultry heat endlessly
brooded, green shadows
would spread
enchantingly around
you!

Lass mich vergehn   in deinem Arm!
let me   waste away in your   arm

Es ist in ihm ja   selbst der Tod,
it is in him indeed even   the death

Ob   auch die herbste   Todesqual
though even the most bitter death's-torment

Die Brust durchwüte   wonnevoll!
the breast rages-through delightful

    Let me fade away
in your arms! There,
however sharp the pangs
of death might be within
my breast, tormenting
me, death itself
would be ecstasy.

6. SO WILLST DU DES   ARMEN
   SO WILL   YOU OF THE POOR ONE

6. WILL YOU SHOW MERCY

Ludwig Tieck
(from the cycle *Die schöne Magelone*)
        the fair   Magelone

So willst du des   Armen
so will   you of the poor one

Dich   gnädig   erbarmen?
yourself graciously to show mercy

So ist es kein Traum?
so is it no   dream

Wie rieseln die Quellen,
how ripple the springs

Wie tönen   die Wellen,
how resound the waves

Wie rauschet der Baum!
how rustles the tree

Tief lag ich in bangen
deep lay I   in anxious

    Will you show
gracious mercy to this
poor soul? Is this no
dream? How the springs
murmur, and the waves
crash, and the trees
rustle! I lay an uneasy
captive within dark
walls - now I am
greeted by the light.
How the sun-beams play
around me, dazzling and
bringing colour to my
timid face!

Gemäuern gefangen,
walls   caught

Nun grüsst mich das Licht;
now greets me   the light

Wie spielen die Strahlen!
how play   the beams

Sie blenden und malen
they dazzle and paint

Mein schüchtern Gesicht.
my timid   face

Und soll ich es glauben?
and should I it to believe

Wird keiner mir rauben
will no one to me to rob

Den köstlichen Wahn?
the precious   fancy

Doch Träume entschweben,
but dreams soar away

Nur lieben heisst leben;
only to love means to live

Willkommene Bahn!
welcome   path

Wie frei und wie heiter!
how free and how happy

Nicht eile nun weiter,
not   hasten now on

Den Pilgerstab   fort!
the pilgrim - staff away

Du hast überwunden,
you have conquered

Du hast ihn gefunden,
you have him found

Den seligsten   Ort!
the most blessed place

Can I then believe
it? Will no one rob me
of this precious fancy?
But dreams do fly away,
and only in love do we
live. O welcome path!
How happy and free I
am! Not to be hurried
with my pilgrim's staff!
To have conquered and
found it, this blessed
place!

7. *RUHE SÜSSLIEBCHEN*
   SLEEP SWEET-DARLING

7. SLEEP, MY DARLING

Ludwig Tieck
(from the cycle *Die schöne Magelone*)
             the fair   Magelone

Ruhe, Süssliebchen, im   Schatten
sleep sweet-darling in the shadow

Der   grünen, dämmernden Nacht;
of the green   growing dusk night

Es säuselt das Gras auf den Matten,
(it) rustles the grass in the meadows

Es fächelt und kühlt dich der Schatten
(it) fans   and cools you the shadow

Sleep, my darling,
in the shadow of green
twilight; the grass
rustles in the meadows,
shadows fan and cool
you, while true love
keeps watch. Sleep, go
to sleep! The wood
whispers softly, 'I am
yours for ever!'

Und treue Liebe wacht.
and true love watches

Schlafe, schlaf   ein,
sleep   go to sleep -

Leiser rauscht der Hain,
softer rustles the wood

Ewig   bin ich dein.
for ever am I   yours

Schweigt, ihr versteckten Gesänge,
be silent you hidden   songs

Und stört   nicht die süsseste Ruh'!
and disturb not   the sweetest rest

Es   lauscht der   Vögel Gedränge,
(it) listen of the birds throng

Es   ruhen die lauten Gesänge,
(it) rest the loud   songs

Schliess, Liebchen, dein Auge zu.
close   darling   your eye -

Schlafe, schlaf   ein,
sleep   go to sleep -

Im   dämmernden Schein,
in the growing dusk light

Ich will dein Wächter sein.
I   will your watcher to be

Murmelt fort, ihr Melodien,
murmur on   you melodies

Rausche nur, du   stiller Bach.
rush   only you quiet   brook

Schöne   Liebesphantasien
beautiful love's-fantasies

Sprechen in den Melodien,
speak   in the melodies

Zarte   Träume schwimmen nach,
tender dreams float   after (them)

Durch   den flüsternden Hain
through the whispering wood

Schwärmen goldene Bienelein
swarm   golden (little) bees

Und summen zum   Schlummer dich ein.
and hum   to the slumber   you (into)

Hush, all you
hidden singers, do not
disturb her sweet rest!
Throngs of birds listen,
their twittering
chorus stilled. Close
your eyes, my darling.
Sleep, go to sleep -
in the light of the
gathering dusk, I will
watch over you.

Murmur on your
melodies; babble on,
quiet little brook!
Sweet fantasies of love
speak in your melodies,
and tender dreams float
with them. In the
whispering wood golden
bees fly around, and
hum you to sleep.

8. *VON EWIGER LIEBE*
   OF ETERNAL LOVE

8. ETERNAL LOVE

Josef Wenzig

Dunkel, wie dunkel in Wald   und in Feld!
dark   how dark   in forest and in field

Abend   schon   ist es, nun schweiget die Welt.
evening already is it   now is silent the world

Nirgend noch Licht und nirgend noch Rauch,
nowhere still light and nowhere still smoke

Ja, und die Lerche sie schweiget nun auch.
yes and the lark   she is silent now too

How dark it is in
forest and field! It is
evening, all the earth
is still. No light, no
smoke are to be seen,
and even the lark is
silent.

Kommt aus   dem Dorfe   der Bursche heraus,
comes out of the village the youth   forth

Gibt das Geleit der   Geliebten   nach   Haus,
gives the escort to the sweetheart towards home

Führt sie am   Weidengebüsche vorbei,
leads her by the willow-bushes past

Redet so viel und so mancherlei:
talks so much and so many things

A youth leaves the
village, taking his
sweetheart home on the
path by the willows.
He has many things to
say:

"Leidest du Schmach   und betrübest du dich,
 suffer you humiliation and distress you yourself

Leidest du Schmach   von andern um   mich,
suffer   you humiliation from others about me

Werde die Liebe getrennt so geschwind,
let be the love   separated as quickly

Schnell wie wir früher vereiniget sind.
quickly as we earlier united   are

Scheide   mit Regen und scheide   mit Wind,
let separate with rain and let separate with wind

Schnell wie wir früher   vereiniget sind."
quickly as we formerly united   are

'If they taunt you
because of me, and
cause you pain, then
let us separate in
our love – let us part
in the wind and the
rain as quickly as we
once united.'

Spricht das Mägdelein, Mägdelein spricht:
says   the maiden   maiden   says

"Unsere Liebe sie trennet sich   nicht!
 our   love she separates herself not

Fest ist der Stahl, und das Eisen gar sehr,
firm is the steel and the iron very very much

Unsere Liebe ist fester noch mehr.
our   love is firmer still more

The girl replies,
'Our love cannot
divide us! Iron is
strong and steel still
stronger, but our
love is strongest of
all!

"Eisen und Stahl, man schmiedet sie um,
 iron and steel one recasts   them –

Unsere Liebe, wer wandelt sie um?
our   love who changes her –

Eisen und Stahl, sie können zergehn,
iron and stell they can   to melt

Unsere Liebe muss ewig   bestehn!"
our   love must for ever endure

'Iron and steel
can be recast, but
who can change our
love? Iron and steel
can be melted down –
our love will endure
for ever!'

9. *DIE MAINACHT*
   THE MAY NIGHT

9. MAY NIGHT

Ludwig Hölty

Wann der silberne Mond durch   die Gesträuche blinkt,
when the silver   moon through the bushes   gleams

Und sein schlummerndes Licht über den Rasen streut,
and his slumbering   light over the sward spreads

Und die Nachtigall   flötet,
and the nightingale sings

Wandl' ich traurig von Busch zu Busch.
wander I   sadly   from bush to bush

When the silvery moon gleams through the branches, and spreads its slumbering light over the sward, and the nightingale sings, I wander sadly among the trees.

Überhüllet vom   Laub   girret ein Taubenpaar
enveloped by the foliage coos   a   dove-pair

Sein Entzücken mir vor; aber ich wende   mich,
its delight   me before but I turn away (myself)

Suche dunklere Schatten,
seek darker   shadows

Und die einsame Träne rinnt.
and the solitary tear   runs

Two doves hidden by the leaves are cooing to me enraptured, but I turn away seeking darker shadows, and a lone tear falls.

Wann, o lächelndes Bild, welches wie Morgenrot
when O smiling   image which   like dawn

Durch   die Seele mir   strahlt, find ich auf Erden dich?
through the soul to me shines   find I   on   earth you

Und die einsame Träne
and the solitary tear

Bebt   mir heisser   die Wang' herab!
trembles to me more hotly the cheek down

O smiling image, lighting my soul like the red of dawn, when shall I find you on this earth? And the lone tear trembles hotly on my cheek!

10. *AN DIE NACHTIGALL*
    TO THE NIGHTINGALE

10. TO THE
    NIGHTINGALE

Ludwig Hölty
(also set by Schubert)

Geuss nicht so laut der   liebentflammten Lieder
pour not   so loud of the love-kindled   songs

Tonreichen Schall
tone-rich sound

Vom   Blütenast   des   Apfelbaums hernieder,
from the blossoming-bough of the apple-tree down

O Nachtigall!
O nightingale

Du tönest mir   mit deiner süssen Kehle
you sound to me with your   sweet throat

Die Liebe wach;
the love awake

O nightingale, can you not hush your love-songs, pouring forth with their voluptuous melody from the blossoming boughs of the apple tree! The notes from your sweet throat awake in me feelings of love; already your melting sighs thrill me in the depths of my soul.

Denn schon   durchbebt   die Tiefen meiner Seele
for   already thrills through the depths of my   soul

Dein schmelzend "Ach."
your melting   ah

Dann flieht der Schlaf von neuem dieses Lager,
then flees the sleep - anew - of this bed

Ich starre dann,
I   gaze   then

Mit nassem Blick und totenbleich und hager
with moist   glance and deathly-pale and haggard

Den Himmel an.
the heaven at

Fleuch, Nachtigall, in   grüne Finsternisse,
flee   nightingale into green glooms

Ins   Haingesträuch,
into the glade-thicket

Und spend' im   Nest der   treuen Gattin Küsse,
and bestow in the nest to the true   spouse kisses

Entfleuch, entfleuch!
flee away flee away

Once again you
chase sleep from my
bed, and I stare before
me, pale and drawn,
with tears in my eyes.
Flee away, nightingale,
into the green gloom
of the forest glade!
And there in your nest
bestow your kisses on
your true love. Flee
away, flee away!

11. BOTSCHAFT
MESSAGE

11. MESSAGE

Georg Friedrich Daumer

Wehe, Lüftchen,   lind   und lieblich
blow (little) breeze softly and sweetly

Um   die Wange der   Geliebten,
about the cheek of the loved one

Spiele zart   in ihrer Locke,
play   tenderly in her   lock

Eile   nicht hinwegzuflieh'n!
hasten not   to away to flee

Blow sweetly,
gentle breeze, about
my beloved's cheek;
play tenderly in her
locks and do not hasten
away!

Tut   sie dann vielleicht die Frage,
does (ask) she then perhaps   the question

Wie es um   mich Armen   stehe;
how it about me   poor wretch might stand

Spricht: "Unendlich war sein Wehe,
say   endless   was his   misery

Höchst   bedenklich seine Lage;
most highly critical   his   condition

If she should ask
how I, poor wretch,
am faring, then say:
'His misery is endless,
his plight highly
critical.

Aber jetzo kann er hoffen
but now   can he to hope

Wieder herrlich   aufzuleben,
again gloriously to to return to life

Denn du, Holde,   denkst an ihn."
for you gracious one think of him

But now he can
hope joyously to live
again, for you, 0
gracious one, are
thinking of him!'

12. *SONNTAG*
SUNDAY

12. SUNDAY

Deutsches Volkslied
German   folksong

So hab' ich doch   die ganze Woche
so have I   indeed the whole week

Mein feines Liebchen   nicht geseh'n
my   fine   sweetheart not   seen

Ich sah es an einem Sonntag
I   saw it on a   Sunday

Wohl   vor   der Türe steh'n:
indeed in front of the door to stand

Das tausendschöne   Jungfräulein,
the thousandfold fair young maiden

Das tausendschöne   Herzelein,
the thousandfold fair little heart

Wollte   Gott, ich wär' heute bei   ihr!
would (to) God   I   were today with her

So will mir   doch   die ganze Woche
so wants to me indeed the whole week

Das Lachen   nicht vergeh'n,
the laughter not   to cease

Ich sah es an einem Sonntag
I   saw it on a   Sunday

Wohl   in   die Kirche geh'n:
indeed into the church to go

Das tausendschöne... etc.
the thousandfold fair

I haven't seen
my fine sweetheart
for a whole week. I
saw her on Sunday
standing at her door,
so young and fair, the
dear heart. Would to
Heaven I were with
her!

I haven't been
able to stop smiling
the whole week, since
I saw her on Sunday
going to church, so
young and fair... etc.

13. *O LIEBLICHE WANGEN*
O LOVELY   CHEEKS

13. O LOVELY CHEEKS

Paul Flemming

O liebliche Wangen, ihr macht mir   Verlangen,
O lovely   cheeks you make to me longing

Dies Rote,   dies Weisse,   zu schauen   mit Fleisse.
this redness this whiteness to gaze upon with diligence

Und dies nur   alleine ist's nicht, was   ich meine;
and this only alone   is it not   what I   mean

Zu schauen,   zu grüssen, zu rühren, zu küssen!
to to gaze upon to to greet to to touch to to kiss

O lovely cheeks,
you fill me with
longing, when I gaze
upon your red and your
white! And not only
this - to gaze, to
greet, to touch, to
kiss!

O *Sonne der   Wonne! O Wonne   der   Sonne!*
O sun   of the rapture O rapture of the sun

O *Augen, so saugen das Licht meiner Augen.*
O eyes   so absorb the light of my eyes

O *englische Sinnen! O himmlisch Beginnen!*
O angelic   thoughts O heavenly actions

O *Himmel auf Erden, magst du mir   nicht werden.*
O heaven on earth   may   you to me not   to become

O *Schönste der   Schönen! Benimm   mir   dies Sehnen.*
O fairest of the   fair   take away from me this longing

Komm, eile, komm, komme, du Süsse,   du Fromme;
come hasten come come   you sweet one you innocent one

Ach, Schwester, ich sterbe, ich sterb', ich verderbe,
oh sister   I   am dying I   am dying I   am perishing

Komm komme, komm eile, benimm   mir   dies Sehnen,
come come   come hasten take away to me this longing

O *Schönste der   Schönen!*
O fairest of the   fair

O sun of rapture,
O rapture of sun! O
eyes, drink in the
light of my eyes! O
angelic thoughts, O
heavenly deeds! O
Paradise on earth, can
you not be mine?

O fairest of the
fair, take away my
longing! Come, hasten!
Come, you sweet
innocent one! Ah
sister, I die – I die,
I perish! Come hasten
and take away my
longing, O fairest of
the fair!

14. *DER GANG ZUM   LIEBCHEN*
    THE WAY TO THE SWEETHEART

14. THE WAY TO MY
    SWEETHEART

Bohemian folksong

Es   glänzt der Mond nieder,
(it) shines the moon down

Ich sollte doch   wieder
I   should really again

Zu meinem Liebchen,
to my   sweetheart

Wie mag es ihr   geh'n?
how may it to her to go

Ach weh! sie verzaget
oh dear she despairs

Und klaget,   und klaget,
and complains and complains

Dass sie mich nimmer
that she me   never

Im   Leben wird seh'n!
in the life will to see

Es   ging der Mond unter,
(it) went the moon down

Ich eilte   doch munter,
I   hurried quite merrily

Und eilte, dass keiner
and hurried that no one

Mein Liebchen   entführt.
my   sweetheart carries off

The moon is
shining – I must go
and see my sweetheart
again. I wonder how
she is?

Oh dear she
despairs, and
complains that she'll
never see me again in
all her life!

The moon was
sinking, and I
hurried quite
merrily – I hurried
so no one would
carry my sweetheart
away!

Ihr Täubchen,   o girret,
you little doves O coo

Ihr Lüftchen,   o schwirret,
you little breezes O hum

Dass keiner mein Liebchen,
that no one my   sweetheart

Mein Liebchen   entführt!
my   sweetheart carries off

O coo, little
doves! O murmur
little breezes! – so
no one carries my
sweetheart away!

15. AM   SONNTAG MORGEN
ON THE SUNDAY MORNING

15. ON SUNDAY MORNING

(from *Italienisches Liederbuch*)
     Italian   song-book
translated into German by Paul Heyse

Am   Sonntag morgen zierlich angetan,
on (the) Sunday morning finely   clad

Wohl weiss ich, wo   du da   bist hingegangen,
well know I   where you then are   gone

Und manche Leute waren, die dich sah'n
and some   people were   who you saw

Und kamen dann zu mir, dich zu verklagen.
and came   then to me   you to to accuse

Als sie mir's   sagten, hab' ich laut   gelacht,
as   they to me it said   have I   loudly laughed

Und in der Kammer dann geweint zur   Nacht.
and in the bedroom then wept   at(the) night

Als sie mir's   sagten, fing ich an zu singen,
as   they to me it said   began I   - to to sing

Um   einsam dann die Hände wund zu ringen.
so as alone   then the hands sore to wring

On Sunday morning
I know quite well
where you were going
so finely clad.
Several people saw
you, and came to tell
me their suspicions.
As they spoke I
laughed aloud, but in
my room I wept the
whole night through.
As they spoke I began
to sing, but once I
was alone, I wrung my
hands quite sore.

16. *AN EIN VEILCHEN*
TO A VIOLET

16. TO A VIOLET

Ludwig Hölty

Birg,   o Veilchen, in deinem blauen Kelche,
conceal O violet   in your   blue   cup

Birg   die Tränen der   Wehmut,   bis   mein Liebchen
conceal the tears of the melancholy until my   sweetheart

Diese Quelle besucht! Entpflückt sie lächelnd
this spring visits   plucks away she smiling

Dich dem   Rasen, die Brust mit dir zu schmücken,
you to the grass the breast with you to to adorn

O, dann schmiege   dich   ihr   an's Herz, und sag'
O then press close yourself to her on the heart and say
ihr,
 to her

Dass die Tropfen in deinem blauen Kelche
that the drops in your   blue   cup

Aus der Seele des   treu'sten Jünglings flossen,
from the soul of the truest   youth   flowed

Der sein Leben verweinet und den Tod   wünscht.
who his life weeps away and the death wishes

> Hide, O violet,
> hide my melancholy
> tears in your blue
> petals, till my
> sweetheart comes
> down to the stream!
> If she smiling plucks
> you from the grass to
> adorn her breast, then,
> O then press close to
> her heart! Tell her
> that the drops in
> your blue petals
> flowed from a youth's
> true heart. He wept
> away his life and
> only wished for death!

17. *WIEGENLIED*
CRADLE-SONG

17. CRADLE SONG

Deutsches Volkslied
German   folksong

Guten Abend, gute Nacht,
good evening good night

Mit Rosen bedacht.
with roses roofed over

Mit Näg'lein   besteckt,
with (little) pinks stuck over with

Schlupf' unter die Deck':
slip   under the coverlet

Morgen   früh,   wenn Gott will,
tomorrow (morning) if   God wills

Wirst du wieder geweckt.
will be you again awakened

Guten Abend, gute Nacht,
good evening good night

Von Eng'lein   bewacht,
by (little) angels watched over

Die zeigen im   Traum
who show   in the dream

Dir   Christkindleins Baum:
to you Christ-child's tree

> Good-night,
> good-night, under an
> archway of roses and
> sweet pinks; slip
> under the cover.
> And tomorrow, God
> willing, you will
> wake again.

> Good-night,
> good-night, watched
> over by angels. In
> your dreams they'll
> show you the Christ
> Child's tree. Sleep,
> sleep, serene and
> sweet; in your dreams
> you'll see Paradise.

Schlaf' nur selig   und süss,
sleep   only blissfully and sweetly

Schau' im   Traum's   Paradies.
see   in the dream the Paradise

18. *AUF DEM SEE*
    ON THE LAKE

18. ON THE LAKE

Karl Simrock

Blauer Himmel, blaue Wogen,
blue   sky   blue waves

Rebenhügel um   den See,
vine-hills around the lake

Drüber blauer Berge   Bogen
above of blue mountains curve

Schimmernd weiss im   reinen Schnee.
shimmering white in the pure   snow

Wie der Kahn uns hebt und wieget,
as the boat us lifts and rocks

Leichter Nebel steigt und fällt,
light   mist rises and falls

Süsser Himmelsfriede lieget
sweet Heaven's-peace lies

Über der beglänzten Welt.
over the illuminated world

Stürmend Herz, tu auf die Augen,
raging   heart open - the eyes

Sieh umher und werde mild:
look around and become gentle

Glück   und Frieden magst du saugen
happiness and peace   may you to imbibe

Aus des   Doppelhimmels Bild.
from of the two-fold-Heaven image

Spiegelnd sieh die Flut erwidern
reflecting see the water to return

Turm   und Hügel, Busch und Stadt,
steeple and hill   bush and town

Also spiegle du in Liedern,
thus reflect you in songs

Was die Erde Schönstes   hat.
what the earth most lovely has

Blue sky, blue
ripples, vine-clad
hills all around the
lake; beyond, the
blue curve of
mountains shimmering
with the pure white
of snow.

The little boat
rocks and sways, and
a light mist rises
and falls. A sweet
and heavenly peace
lies over the
radiant world.

O raging heart,
open your eyes, look
around you and be
still - drink in the
joy and peace of
this two-fold image
of Heaven!

See how the
water mirrors hill
and steeple, village
and wood, and let all
that is fair on earth
be reflected in your
songs.

19. *REGENLIED*
    RAIN-SONG

19. SONG OF THE RAIN

Klaus Groth

Walle, Regen, walle nieder,
flow   rain   flow down

Fall, rain, fall,
and bring back those
dreams I dreamed in
my childhood, when
the water foamed in
the sand.

Wecke mir   die Träume wieder,
wake to me the dreams again

Die ich in der Kindheit träumte,
that I   in the childhood dreamed

Wenn das Nass   im   Sande schäumte!
when the wetness in the sand   foamed

Wenn die matte   Sommerschwüle
when the languid summer-sultriness

When the languid
sultriness of summer
lazily wrangled with
the cool freshness,
and the shining leaves
were covered with
drops, and the fields
were a darker blue.

Lässig stritt   mit frischer Kühle,
lazily wrangled with fresh   coolness

Und die blanken Blätter tauten,
and the shining leaves were covered with dew

Und die Saaten   dunkler   blauten,
and the (green)crops more darkly were blue

Welche Wonne, in dem Fliessen,
what   bliss in the trickling down

What bliss to
stand in the
downpour, to ramble
with bare feet in the
grass, to grasp at the
shower with
outstretched hands,

Dann zu stehn   mit nackten Füssen,
then to to stand with bare   feet

An dem Grase hin   zu streifen,
on the grass along to to ramble

Und den Schaum mit Händen greifen.
and the foam   with hands to grasp

Oder mit den heissen Wangen
or   with the hot   cheeks

or to let the cool
drops fall against
hot cheeks, and
freshly awakened
scents fill youthful
lungs.

Kalte Tropfen aufzufangen,
cold drops   to catch up

Und den neuerwachten Düften
and the newly-awakened scents

Seine Kinderbrust   zu lüften.
his   child's-breast to to air

Wie die Kelche,   die da   troffen,
like the flower-cups that there dripped

Like the cup of a
flower the soul stood
open and breathing in,
like a scent-
intoxicated blossom
wrapped in the dews
of Heaven.

Stand die Seele atmend   offen,
stood the soul breathing open

Wie die Blumen, düftetrunken,
like the flowers scents-intoxicated

In den Himmelstau   versunken.
in the Heaven's-dew sunk

Schauernd kühlte jeder Tropfen
shivering cooled each   drop

Tief bis   an des   Herzens Klopfen
deep (unto) to of the heart   beating

Und der   Schöpfung heilig Weben
and of the creation divine activity

Drang   bis   ins   verborgne Leben.
penetrated (unto) into the secret   life

> Each drop fell
> cool and shivering
> against a beating
> heart, and the divine
> stirrings of creation
> reached the very
> secret of life.

Walle, Regen, walle nieder,
flow   rain   flow down

Wecke meine alten Lieder,
awaken my   old   songs

Die wir in der Türe sangen,
that we in the door sang

Wenn die Tropfen draussen klangen!
when the drops   outside sounded

> Fall, rain, fall,
> and awaken those old
> songs we sang in the
> doorways to the sound
> of the raindrops
> outside.

Möchte   ihnen   wieder lauschen,
would like to them again to listen to

Ihrem   süssen, feuchten Rauschen,
to their sweet   damp   rushing

Meine Seele sanft betauen
my   soul softly to bedew

Mit dem frommen Kindergrauen.
with the innocent children-dread

> How I would love
> to hear again their
> sweet, wet pattering,
> and let my soul be
> gently revived with
> the innocent thrill
> of a child.

---

20. *DEIN BLAUES AUGE*
    YOUR BLUE   EYE

Klaus Groth

Dein blaues Auge hält so still,
your blue eye keeps so still

Ich blicke bis   zum   Grund.
I   look (unto) to the bottom

Du fragst mich, was ich sehen will?
you ask   me   what I to see want

Ich sehe mich   gesund.
I   see myself restored

> 20. YOUR BLUE EYES

> Your blue eyes
> are so still, I can
> look into their very
> depths. You ask me
> what I would see in
> them – to see myself
> restored.

Es   brannte mich ein glühend Paar,
(it) burned me   a glowing pair

Noch schmerzt das Nachgefühl:
still hurts   the after-feeling

Das deine ist wie See so klar,
the yours is as lake so clear

Und wie ein See so kühl.
and as a   lake so cool

> Two glowing eyes
> once burned me, the
> pain is with me still;
> your eyes are as clear
> as a lake, and as
> cool.

21. *MEINE LIEBE IST GRÜN*
    MY   LOVE IS GREEN

Felix Schumann

Meine Liebe ist grün wie der Fliederbusch,
my   love is green as the lilac-bush

Und mein Lieb ist schön   wie die Sonne;
and my   love is beautiful as the sun

Die glänzt wohl   herab auf den Fliederbusch
she shines indeed down upon the lilac-bush

Und füllt ihn mit Duft und mit Wonne.
and fills him with scent and with rapture

Meine Seele hat Schwingen der   Nachtigall
my   soul has soaring   of the nightingale

Und wiegt sich   in blühendem Flieder,
and rocks herself in blossoming lilac

Und jauchzet und singet vom   Duft berauscht
and exults   and sings by the scent intoxicated

Viel liebestrunkene Lieder.
many love-drunk   songs

My love is green
as the lilac tree,
and my love is
beautiful as the
sun that shines on
it, filling it with
fragrance, and with
rapture.

My soul soars
like the nightingale,
and, rocked in the
blossoming lilac and
bewitched by its
fragrance, it exults
and sings its
love-intoxicated
songs.

22. *O WÜSST ICH DOCH DEN WEG ZURÜCK*
    O KNEW I ONLY THE WAY BACK

Klaus Groth

O wüsst ich doch den Weg zurück,
O knew I   only the way back

Den lieben Weg zum   Kinderland!
the dear   way to the children's-land

O warum sucht' ich nach dem Glück
O why sought I   after the happiness

Und liess der   Mutter Hand?
and left of the mother hand

O wie mich   sehnet auszuruh'n,
O how myself longs to to rest

Von keinem Streben aufgeweckt,
by no   striving roused

Die müden Augen zuzutun,
the tired eyes to to close

Von Liebe sanft bedeckt!
by love gently sheltered

Und nichts zu forschen, nichts zu späh'n,
and nothing to to seek   nothing to to watch for

Und nur zu träumen leicht und lind;
and only to to dream lightly and softly

Der   Zeiten Wandel nicht zu seh'n,
of the times change not to to see

If I but knew the
way back, the sweet
way to the land of
childhood! O why did
I seek after
happiness and leave my
mother's hand?

How I long to
rest, roused by no
striving – oh, to
close my tired eyes,
gently sheltered by
love!

No restless
seeking, no anxious
watching, just lightly
and softly dreaming,
not seeing time's
changes – once again
a child!

Zum   zweiten Mal ein Kind!
for the second time a   child

O zeig mir   doch den Weg zurück,
O show to me only the way back

Den lieben Weg zum   Kinderland!
the dear   way to the children's-land

Vergebens such' ich nach dem Glück,
in vain   seek I   after the happiness

Ringsum   ist öder   Strand!
round about is desolate shore

    O show me the
way back, the sweet
way to the land of
childhood! In vain
do I seek after
happiness; around
me is but a desolate
shore.

23. *AN DEN MOND*
    TO THE MOON

23. TO THE MOON

Karl Simrock

Silbermond, mit bleichen Strahlen
silver-moon with pale   rays

Pflegst   du Wald und Feld zu malen,
are accustomed you wood and field to to paint

Gibst den   Bergen, gibst den   Talen
give to the mountains give to the valleys

Der   Empfindung Seufzer ein.
of the feeling   sighs   −

    O silvery moon,
you paint field and
woodland with your
pale rays; you give
to hill and valley a
sighing air.

Sei Vertrauter meiner Schmerzen,
be   confidant of my sorrows

Segler in der   Lüfte   See:
sailer in of the breezes sea

Sag' ihr,   die ich trag' im   Herzen,
say to her who I   carry in the heart

Wie mich tötet Liebesweh.
how me   kills love's-grief

    You who sail in
the ocean of the
firmament, I confide
in you my sorrows.
Tell the one who is
always in my heart I
am dying of love and
grief.

Sag' ihr   über tausend Meilen
say to her over thousand miles

Sehne sich   mein Herz nach ihr.
longs (itself) my   heart for her

"Keine Ferne   kann es heilen,
 no   distance can it to heal

Nur ein holder Blick von dir."
only a   gracious glance from you

    Tell her my
heart longs for her
from a thousand miles
away. 'Distance can
never restore me −
only a single loving
glance from you.'

Sag' ihr,   dass zu Tod   getroffen
say to her that by death struck

Diese Hülle bald zerfällt;
this veil soon falls apart

Nur ein schmeichlerisches Hoffen
only a caressing   hope

Sei's, das sie zusammenhält.
be it that it holds together

    Tell her that
soon in death this
earthly veil will fall
away; for only in
loving hope can it
be sustained.

24. *GEHEIMNIS*
   SECRET

24. SECRECY

Karl Candidus

O Frühlingsabenddämmerung!
O spring-twilight

O laues, lindes Weh'n!
O mild   gentle fluttering

Ihr Blütenbäume,   sprecht, was tut
you blossoming-trees say   why do

Ihr so zusammensteh'n?
you so to stand together

Vertraut ihr das Geheimnis euch
confide you the secret   (yourselves)

Von uns'rer Liebe süss?
of our   love sweet

Was flüstert ihr einander   zu
what whisper you one another to

Von uns'rer Liebe süss?
of our   love sweet

    O spring twilight!
O mild and gentle
breeze! You blossoming
trees, tell me - why
do you stand so
close?

    Do you share
together the secret
of our sweet love?
What do you whisper
to one another of
our sweet love?

25. *MINNELIED*
   LOVE-SONG

25. LOVE-SONG

Ludwig Hölty
(also set by Schubert
and Mendelssohn)

Holder   klingt der Vogelsang,
lovelier sounds the bird-song

Wenn die Engelreine,
when the angle-pure one

Die mein Jünglingsherz bezwang,
who my   youth's-heart conquered

Wandelt durch   die Haine.
wanders through the woods

Röter blühen Tal   und Au,
redder blossom valley and pasture

Grüner wird   der Rasen,
greener becomes the grass

Wo   die Finger meiner Frau
where the fingers of my woman

Maienblumen lasen.
May-flowers gathered

    Lovelier is the
song of the birds
when the pure angel,
who conquered my
young heart, passes
through the wood.

    Brighter are the
flowers in field and
valley, brighter the
green of the grass,
where my love's
fingers gathered
the wild lilies of
May.

Ohne   sie ist alles   tot,
without her is everything dead

Welk sind Blüt'   und Kräuter;
faded are blossoms and plants

Und kein Frühlingsabendrot.
and no   spring's-sunset

Dünkt mir   schön und heiter.
seems to me lovely and serene

Traute, minnigliche Frau,
dear   lovely   woman

Wollest nimmer fliehen,
may you never to flee

Dass mein Herz, gleich dieser Au,
that my   heart like   this   pasture

Mög' in Wonne   blühen!
may in ecstasy to bloom

O my dear
beloved, never leave
my side; so my heart,
like this meadow may
bloom in ecstasy!

Without her
everything is dead;
flowers and leaves
all fade, and no
spring sunset seems
serene and lovely
any more.

26. DER KRANZ
   THE GARLAND

26. THE GARLAND

Hans Schmidt

Mutter, hilf mir armen Tochter,
mother help me poor daughter

Sieh' nur, was ein Knabe tat:
see   just what a . boy   did

Einen Kranz   von Rosen flocht er,
a   garland of roses twined he

Den er mich zu tragen bat!
that he me   to to wear begged

"Ei, sei deshalb   unerschrocken,
 oh be because of that undismayed

Helfen lässt sich   dir   gewiss!
to help lets (itself) to you surely

Nimm den Kranz   nur aus den Locken,
take the garland just from the locks

Und den Knaben, den vergiss."
and the boy   him forget

Dornen hat der Kranz, o Mutter,
thorns has the garland O mother

Und die halten fest das Haar!
and they hold   fast the hair

Worte sprach der Knabe, Mutter,
words spoke the boy   mother

An die denk' ich immerdar!
of them think I   for evermore

O mother, help
your poor daughter!
See what that boy
has done - he made
a garland of roses,
and begged me to wear
it!

'Oh, don't let that
dismay you - I'm
sure there's
something you can
do. Take the
garland from your
hair, and just
forget the boy.'

But the garland
has thorns, mother,
that catch in my
hair! And the words
he spoke to me,
mother, I'll
remember them for
ever!

27. *VERGEBLICHES STÄNDCHEN*
   VAIN   SERENADE

27. VAIN SERENADE

Folksong (from the lower Rhine)

(Er)
 he

(He)

Guten Abend, mein Schatz,   guten Abend, mein Kind!
good evening my   sweetheart good   evening my   child

Ich komm' aus   Lieb' zu dir,
I   come   out of love to you

Ach, mach mir   auf die Tür,
oh   open to me - the door

Mach mir   auf die Tür!
open to me -   the door

'Good evening,
my sweetheart, good
evening, my dear! I
come for love of
you – so please
open the door for
me, please open the
door!'

(Sie)
 she

(She)

Mein' Tür ist verschlossen, ich lass' dich nicht ein;
my   door is closed   I   let   you not in

Mutter, die rät   mir klug,
mother she advises me wisely

Wärst   du herein mit Fug,
Would be you in here with right

Wär's   mit mir vorbei!
would be it with me over

'My door is
closed, and I
won't let you in!
Mother was wise
when she said that
if I asked you in,
it would be all up
with me!'

(Er)
 he

(He)

So kalt ist die Nacht, so eisig der Wind,
so cold is the night so icy   the wind

Dass mir   das Herz erfriert,
that to me the heart is freezing

Mein Lieb' erlöschen   wird.
my   love to be extinguished will

Öffne mir, mein Kind!
open to me my   child

'The night's so
cold, and the wind
so icy – my heart is
freezing and my love
will perish – do let
me in, my love!'

(Sie)
 she

(She)

Löschet   dein' Lieb', lass sie
let be extinguished your love   let her
  löschen   nur!
  to be extinguished only

Löschet   sie immerzu,
let be extinguished her all the time

'Let your love
perish then, let it
perish! Go home to
bed, and go to
sleep – good night,
my lad, good night!'

Geh' heim zu Bett, zur Ruh'
go   home to bed   to the sleep

Gute Nacht, mein Knab'!
good night my   boy

28. *IN WALDESEINSAMKEIT*
IN WOOD-SOLITUDE

28. IN THE SOLITUDE
OF THE WOODS

Karl von Lemcke

Ich sass zu deinen Füssen
I   sat at your   feet

In Waldeseinsamkeit;
in wood-solitude

Windesatmen, Sehnen
wind-breathing yearning

Ging durch die Wipfel   breit.
went through the (tree)-tops wide

I sat at your feet in the lonely wood; the sighing of the wind, a yearning, went through the tree-tops.

In stummen Ringen   senkt' ich
in silent struggling sank I

Das Haupt in   deinen Schoss,
the head into your   lap

Und meine bebenden Hände
and my   trembling hands

Um deine   Knie ich schloss.
around your knees I   clasped

In silent care, I laid my head in your lap, and my trembling hands clasped you to me.

Die Sonne ging hinunter,
the sun   went down

Der Tag verglühte   all,
the day ceased to glow wholly

Ferne, ferne, ferne,
far off far off far off

Sang eine Nachtigall.
sang a   nightingale

The sun went down, all the day-light faded; Far, far off a nightingale was singing.

29. *THERESE*
TERESA

29. TERESA

Gottfried Keller

Du milchjunger Knabe,
you milk-young boy

Wie schaust   du mich an?
how are looking you me   at

Was haben deine Augen
what have   your eyes

Why do you look at me like that, you half-weaned boy? What a question there is in your eyes!

Für eine Frage   getan!
for a   question put

Alle Ratsherrn in der Stadt
all   aldermen in the town

Und alle Weisen der   Welt
and all sages of the world

Bleiben stumm auf die Frage,
remain silent on the question

Die   deine Augen gestellt!
which your eyes put

                                                All the elders
                                              of the town, and
all the sages in
the world keep
silent on the
question your eyes
are asking!

Eine Meermuschel liegt
a   sea-shell lies

Auf dem Schrank meiner Bas':
on the cupboard of my   cousin

Da   halte dein Ohr d'ran,
there hold your ear on it

Dann hörst du etwas!
then hear you something

                                              A sea-shell lies
on my cousin's
cupboard; hold it to
your ear now - then
you'll hear
something!

30. *FELDEINSAMKEIT*
FIELD-SOLITUDE

                                              30. SOLITUDE IN THE
FIELDS

Hermann Almers

Ich ruhe still im   hohen grünen Gras
I   rest still in the tall green grass

Und sende lange meinen Blick nach oben,
and send long my   glance - upwards -

Von Grillen rings umschwirrt ohn'Unterlass,
from crickets around whirred about - unceasingly -

Von Himmelsbläue wundersam   umwoben.
from sky's-blue   wonderfully woven about

                                              Motionless I lie
in the tall green
grass, gazing upward,
surrounded by the
ceaseless chirp of
crickets, and over
me the wondrous
tapestry of the blue
sky.

Die schönen   weissen Wolken zieh'n dahin
the beautiful white   clouds move   along

Durchs   tiefe Blau, wie schöne stille Träume;
through the deep blue like lovely calm   dreams

Mir ist, als ob ich längst   gestorben bin
to me is as if I long since died   am

Und ziehe   selig   mit   durch ew'ge
and moved along blissfully with (them) through endless
   Räume.
   spaces

                                              Beautiful white
clouds float through
the deep blue, like
calm and lovely
dreams; it is as if
I had long since
died, and moved
blissfully with them
in endless space.

31. *NACHTWANDLER*
NIGHT-WANDERER

Max Kalbeck

Störe   nicht den leisen Schlummer
trouble not   the gentle slumber

Dess,   den lind   ein Traum umfangen!
of whom him softly a   dream embraces

Lass ihm seinen süssen Kummer!
leave him his   sweet sorrow

Ihm sein schmerzliches Verlangen!
him his sorrowful   yearning

Sorgen und Gefahren drohen,
cares and dangers   threaten

Aber keine wird ihm schrecken,
but no one will him to frighten

Kommst du nicht, den Schlafesfrohen
come   you not   the sleep-glad one

Durch ein hartes Wort zu wecken.
through a   harsh word to to wake

Still   in seinen Traum versunken
tranquilly in his   dream sunk

Geht er über Abgrundtiefen
walks he over abyss-deeps

Wie vom   Licht des   Vollmonds trunken,
as from the light of the full-moon drunk

Weh' den   Lippen, die ihm riefen!
woe to the lips   that him called

Do not trouble
the gentle slumber
that softly enfolds
him in dreams.
Leave him to his
sweet sorrow, to his
yearning grief!

Cares and dangers
are close at hand,
but none will
trouble him, if you
do not wake the
glad sleeper with
harsh words.

Deep in his
tranquil dreams, he
steps across deep
chasms, drunk with
the light of the
full moon. Woe to
the one whose lips
should call him!

32. *SAPPHISCHE ODE*
SAPPHIC   ODE

Hans Schmidt

Rosen brach ich nachts mir am   dunklen Hage;
roses broke I   at night to me on the dark   hedge

Süsser   hauchten Duft   sie, als je   am Tage;
sweeter exhaled fragrance they than ever by day

Doch verstreuten reich   die bewegten Äste
but scattered   abundantly the moving   boughs

Tau, der mich nässte.
dew that me   moistened

I plucked roses
at night from the
dark hedgerow, and
their fragrance was
sweeter than ever
by day; but the
shaken boughs
scattered the wet
dew abundantly upon
me.

Auch der   Küsse Duft   mich wie nie berückte,
also of the kisses fragrance me   as never beguiled

Die ich nachts   vom   Strauch deiner Lippen
that I   at night from the bush   of your lips

    pflückte:
    plucked

Doch auch dir, bewegt im   Gemüt gleich jenen,
but also to you stirred in the soul like   those

Tauten   die Tränen.
fell as dew the tears

      And the fragrance
    of kisses beguiled
    me as never before,
    as I plucked them
    like roses at night
    from your lips; but
    like the rose, your
    soul was stirred,
    and you shed dewy
    tears.

33. BEI DIR SIND MEINE GEDANKEN
WITH YOU ARE MY   THOUGHTS

33. MY THOUGHTS ARE
WITH YOU

Friedrich Ruperti

Bei dir sind meine Gedanken
with you are my   thoughts

Und flattern um   dich her;
and float   around you (here)

Sie sagen, sie hätten   Heimweh,
they say   they would have nostalgia

Hier litt'   es sie nicht mehr.
here suffered it they not   more

Bei dir sind meine Gedanken
with you are my   thoughts

Und wollen von dir nicht fort;
and want   from you not   away

Sie sagen, das wär'   auf Erden
they say   that would be on earth

Der allerschönste   Ort.
the loveliest of all places

Sie sagen, unlösbar hielte
they say   insolubly held

Dein Zauber sie festgebannt;
your magic them spell-bound

Sie hätten   an deinen Blicken
they would have at your   glances

Die Flügel sich   verbrannt.
the wings themselves scorched

      All my thoughts
    are with you,
    floating around you.
    They say they are
    full of longing, and
    they can stay no
    longer here.

      My thoughts are
    with you, and are
    loth to leave you.
    They say they are in
    the loveliest place
    on earth.

      They say your
    magic holds them in
    a spell - but your
    glances could
    scorch their wings.

34. *DER JÄGER*
   THE HUNTER

34. THE HUNTER

Friedrich Halm

Mein Lieb ist ein Jäger,
my   love is a   hunter

Und grün ist sein Kleid,
and green is his dress

Und blau ist sein Auge,
and blue is his eye

Nur sein Herz ist zu weit.
only his heart is too wide

> My love is a hunter, and his garb is green. His eyes are blue – but his heart is too large!

Mein Lieb ist ein Jäger,
my   love is a   hunter

Trifft immer ins   Ziel,
hits   always into the target

Und Mädchen berückt er,
and girls   ensnares he

So viel er nur will.
as many he only wants

> My love is a hunter, and he always hits the mark. He ensnares the girls – as many as he chooses.

Mein Lieb ist ein Jäger,
my   love is a   hunter

Kennt Wege und Spur,
knows ways and track

Zu mir aber kommt er
to me but comes he

Durch die Kirchtüre nur.
through the church-door only

> My love is a hunter, and he knows tracks and trails. But his only way to me is through the church door!

35. *MÄDCHENLIED*
   MAIDEN-SONG

35. MAIDEN'S SONG

Paul Heyse

Am   jüngsten Tag ich aufersteh'
on(the) Judgement Day I   rise from the dead

Und gleich nach meinem Liebsten seh'.
and at once for my   beloved look

Und wenn ich ihn nicht finden kann,
and if   I   him not to find can

Leg'   wieder mich   zum Schlafen dann.
lie down again (myself) to the sleeping then

> On Judgement Day I'll rise from the grave, and look at once for my beloved. And if I cannot find him, then I'll lie down and go to sleep again.

O Herzeleid, die Ewigkeit!
O grief   the eternity

Selbander nur ist Seligkeit!
we two   only is bliss

Und kommt mein Liebster nicht hinein,
and comes my   beloved   not   into there

Mag nicht im   Paradiese sein!
like not   in the Paradise to be

O grief –
eternity! Only with
each other could it
be bliss. And if my
beloved doesn't come,
I don't want to be
in Paradise!

36. DER TOD, DAS IST DIE KÜHLE NACHT
THE DEATH THAT IS   THE COOL   NIGHT

36. DEATH IS COOL
NIGHT

Heinrich Heine

Der Tod, das ist die kühle Nacht,
the death that is the cool night

Das Leben ist der schwüle Tag.
the life is the sultry day

Es dunkelt   schon, mich schläfert,
it grows dark already me   am sleepy

Der Tag hat mich müd' gemacht.
the day has me   weary made

Death is cool
night – life is
sultry day. It grows
dark already; I am
drowsy, for the day
has wearied me.

Über mein Bett erhebt   sich   ein Baum,
over my   bed springs up (himself) a   tree

D'rin singt die junge Nachtigall;
in it sings the young nightingale

Sie singt von lauter Liebe,
she sings of sheer   love

Ich hör' es sogar im   Traum.
I   hear it even in the dream

High grows the
tree above my bed,
and there a young
nightingale sings
of pure love; I
hear it even in my
dreams.

37. WIR WANDELTEN
    WE WANDERED

Georg Friedrich Daumer

Wir wandelten, wir zwei zusammen,
we wandered   we two together

Ich war so still, und du so stille;
I was so silènt and you so silent

Ich gäbe   viel, um zu erfahren,
I would give much so as to to find out

Was du gedacht, in jenem Fall.
what you thought in that case

Was ich gedacht, unausgesprochen
what I   thought unspoken

Verbleibe das! Nur Eines   sag ich:
let rest that only one thing say I

So schön war alles,   was ich dachte,
so lovely was everything what I   thought

So himmlisch heiter war es all!
so beautifully serene was it all

In meinem Haupte die Gedanken
in my   head   the thoughts

Sie läuteten wie gold'ne Glöckchen;
they rang   like golden (little) bells

So wundersüss,   so wunderlieblich
so wondrously sweet so wondrously lovely

Ist in der Welt kein and'rer Hall.
is in the world no   other   sound

We wandered
together, we two;
I was quite silent,
and so were you. I
would have given much
to know what you
were thinking at
that moment. What I
was thinking, let it
remain unspoken.
Only one thing will
I say: it was all so
lovely, all so
wonderfully serene!
In my head the
thoughts rang like
golden bells; so
wondrously sweet and
lovely is no other
sound in the whole
world!

38. NACHTIGALL
    NIGHTINGALE

C. Reinhold

O Nachtigall,
O nightingale

Dein süsser Schall,
your sweet sound

Er dringet   mir durch Mark und Bein.
he penetrates me through marrow and bone

Nein, trauter Vogel, nein!
no   beloved bird, no

Was in mir schafft so   süsse Pein,
what in me brings such sweet pain

Das ist nicht dein,
that is not   of you

O nightingale,
your sweet song
penetrates my very
soul. But no,
beloved bird, no!
What brings me such
sweet sorrow is not
your melody, but
others of heavenly
beauty, for me long
since faded away –
in your song but a
gentle echo!

Das ist von andern, himmelschönen,
that is of others heavenly beautiful

Nun längst für mich verklungenen Tönen,
now long ago for me died away notes

In deinem Lied ein leiser Widerhall!
In your song a gentle echo

39. KOMM BALD
  COME SOON

39. COME SOON

Klaus Groth

Warum denn warten
why then wait

Von Tag zu Tag?
from day to day

Es blüht im Garten
it flowers in the garden

Was blühen mag.
what flower may

Why do I wait
from day to day?
In the garden every
flower is in bloom,

Wer kommt und zählt es,
who comes and counts it

Was blüht so schön?
what blossoms so beautifully

An Augen fehlt es,
in eyes lacks it

Es anzuseh'n.
it to to look at

but who comes to
enjoy this fair
blossoming? No eyes
are there to see it.

Die meinen wandern
the mine wander

Von Strauch zum Baum;
from bush to the tree

Mir scheint auch andern
to me seems also to others

Wär's wie ein Traum.
were it like a dream

My gaze wanders
over bush and tree;
to anyone it must
seem a glorious
vision.

Und von den Lieben,
and of the loved ones

Die mir getreu,
who to me true

Und mir geblieben,
and to me stayed

Wär'st du dabei!
were you thereby

And of those I
loved, who remained
true to me, how I
wish that you were
one!

40. *TRENNUNG*   40. PARTING
    PARTING

Swabian folksong
(in dialect)

Da   unten im   Tale   Down there in
there below in the valley   the valley the
                                              waters are
Läuft's Wasser so trüb,   troubled, and I
runs the water   so troubled   can't tell you how
                                              much I love you.
Und i kann dir's   nit sagen,
and I can to you it not to tell

I hab' di so lieb.
I have you so dear

Sprichst allweil von Liebe;   You always talk
talk   always of love   of love; and of
                                              being true to me,
Sprichst allweil von Treu',   but I think you're
talk   always of fidelity   a little bit false
                                              as well.
Und a bissele   Falschheit
and a little bit falsehood

Is au   wohl   dabei.
is also perhaps thereby

Und wenn i dir's   zehnmal   sag',   If I tell you
and when I to you it ten times tell   ten times over that
                                              I love you and want
Dass i di lieb' und mag,   you, and you still
that I you love and want   won't understand,
                                              then I'll have to
Und du willst nit verstehn,   go away.
and you will   not to understand

Muss i halt weiter gehn.
must I just further to go

Für die Zeit, wo   du g'liebt mi hast,   For the time
for the time   when you loved   me have   when you loved me,
                                              I thank you from
Da   dank i dir schön.   my heart, and I
there thank I you beautifully   hope it'll go
                                              better for you
Und i wünsch', dass dir's anderswo   elsewhere.
and I wish   that you it elsewhere

Besser mag gehn.
better may to go

41. ZIGEUNERLIEDER
GIPSY-SONGS

41. GIPSY SONGS

German translation from the
original Hungarian attributed
to Hugo Conrad

i.

He, Zigeuner, greife in   die Saiten ein!
hey gipsy   strike into the strings –

Spiel das Lied vom   ungetreuen Mägdelein!
play the song of the untrue   maiden

Lass die Saiten weinen, klagen,   traurig bange,
let the strings to weep to lament sadly   uneasily

Bis   die heisse Träne netzet   diese Wange!
until the hot   tear moistens this cheek

i.

Hey, gipsy, strike
up on your strings!
Play the song of the
girl who was untrue!
Let your sad uneasy
strings weep and lament,
until the hot tears
flow down my cheeks!

ii.

Hochgetürmte Rimaflut, wie bist du so trüb';
high-risen Rima-flood how are you so troubled

An dem Ufer klag' ich laut   nach dir, mein Lieb!
on the bank lament I loudly for you my love

Wellen fliehen, Wellen strömen, rauschen an dem Strand
waves flee away waves gush   rush   to the beach

heran zu mir.
hither to me

An dem Rimaufer lasst mich ewig   weinen nach ihr!
on the Rima-bank let me for ever to weep for her

ii.

How troubled are
your high flooding
waters, O river
Rima! On these banks
I lament aloud for you,
my love! The waves rush
and surge towards me
on the shore. Here on
the banks of the Rima,
O let me weep for her
for ever!

iii.

Wisst ihr, wann mein Kindchen   am   allerschönsten ist?
know you when my little one at the fairest of all is

Wenn ihr süsses Mündchen   scherzt und lacht
when her sweet (little) mouth jests   and laughs

und küsst.
and kisses

Mägdelein, du bist mein, inniglich küss' ich dich,
maiden   you are mine fervently kiss I you

Dich erschuf der liebe Himmel einzig nur für mich!
you created the good heaven purely only for me

Wisst ihr, wann mein Liebster am   besten mir gefällt?
know you when my beloved (at) the best me pleases

Wenn in seinen Armen er mich umschlungen hält.
when in his   arms he me   clasped   holds

Schätzelein,   du bist mein, inniglich küss ich dich,
(little) treasure you are mine fervently kiss I you

Dich erschuf der liebe Himmel einzig nur für mich!
you created the good heaven purely just for me

iii.

Do you know when my
sweetheart is most fair?
When her sweet lips jest,
and laugh and kiss. You
are mine, sweet maid! I
kiss you with all my
heart – heaven made you
for me alone!

Do you know when my
beloved best pleases me?
When he holds me clasped
in his arms! You are mine,
my treasure! I kiss you
with all my heart –
heaven made you for me
alone!

iv.

Lieber Gott, du weisst, wie oft   bereut ich hab',
dear   God   you know   how often rued I have

Dass ich meinem Liebsten einst ein Küsschen   gab.
that I   my   beloved once a   (little) kiss gave

Herz gebot, dass ich ihn küssen muss,
heart bade that I him to kiss must

Denk', so lang ich leb', an diesen ersten Kuss.
think so long I live on this first kiss

Lieber Gott, du weisst, wie oft in stiller Nacht
dear   God you know how often in still night

Ich in Lust und Leid an meinem Schatz   gedacht.
I in joy and pain of my   sweetheart thought

Lieb' ist süss, wenn bitter auch die Reu',
love is sweet if bitter also the regret

Armes Herze bleibt ihm   ewig,   ewig   treu.
poor heart stays to him for ever for ever true

v.

Brauner Bursche führt zum   Tanze sein blauäugig schönes
brown lad   leads to the dance his blue-eyed fair
Kind,
child

Schlägt die Sporen keck   zusammen, Csardasmelodie
beats the spurs boldly together Czardas-melody
beginnt,
begins

Küsst und herzt   sein süsses Täubchen,
kisses and embraces his sweet little dove

Dreht sie, führt sie, jauchzt   und springt;
turns her leads her shouts for joy and leaps

Wirft drei blanke Silbergulden
throws three shining silver-guilders

Auf das Zimbal, dass er klingt.
on the zimbalon that he sounds

vi.

Röslein   dreie in der Reihe blühn so rot,
(little) roses three in the row blossom so red

Dass der Bursch zum   Mädel gehe, ist kein
that the lad   to the girl may go is no
Verbot!
forbidden thing

Lieber Gott, wenn das verboten wär'.
dear   God when that forbidden were

Ständ' die schöne weite Welt schon   längst
would be the lovely wide world already long since
nicht mehr;
not more

Ledig bleiben Sünde wär'!
single to stay sin would be

---

iv.

Dear God, you know how often I've rued the day I gave my love a sweet kiss — it was my heart that bade me. As long as I live I'll remember that first kiss!

Dear God, you know how often in the still of night, I've thought with joy and pain of my sweetheart. To love is sweet, to rue is bitter — my poor heart will be true to him for ever!

v.

The swarthy lad leads his fair and blue-eyed love to the dance; he clashes his spurs boldly together as the tune of the Czardas begins. He hugs and kisses his sweet little dove, twirls and leads her, leaps and shouts for joy. He throws three shining silver guilders on the zimbalon, so it rings.

vi.

Three little red roses bloom in a row — no one keeps a lad from his lass. Dear God, if they could, the lovely wide world would be no more. It would be a sin to be single!

Schönstes Städtchen   in Alföld ist Ketschkemet,
fairest   little town in Alföld is Kecskemet,

Dort gibt es   gar viele Mädchen schmuck und nett!
there (are there) very many girls   pretty and neat

Freunde, sucht euch dort ein Bräutchen   aus,
friends seek you there a   (little) bride out

Freit um ihre Hand und gründet euer Haus,
woo for her hand and found your house

Freudenbecher leeret aus!
cups of joy   empty out

In Alföld the
fairest little town is
Kecskemet, and it's full
of sweet pretty girls.
My friend, go there and
choose a bride; woo her,
and found your family –
drink the cup of joy!

vii.

Kommt dir   manchmal in den Sinn, mein süsses Lieb,
comes to you sometimes in the mind my   sweet love

Was du einst mit heil'gem Eide mir   gelobt?
what you once with sacred oath to me vowed

Täusch' mich nicht, verlass mich nicht,
deceive me   not   leave   me not

Du weisst nicht, wie lieb ich dich hab'.
you know   not   how dear I you have

Lieb' du mich, wie ich dich,
love you me   as I you

Dann strömt Gottes Huld auf dich herab!
then flows God's grace on you down

vii.

Do you ever remember,
sweet love, what once you
vowed with a sacred oath?
Don't deceive me, don't
forsake me – you can't
know how much I love you!
If you love me, as I
love you, God's grace
will flow down upon you!

viii.

Rote Abendwolken   zieh'n am   Firmament,
red evening-clouds drift in the firmament

Sehnsuchtsvoll nach dir,
full of longing for you

Mein Lieb, das Herze brennt,
my   love the heart is burning

Himmel strahlt in glüh'nder Pracht,
sky   shines in glowing splendour

Und ich träum' bei Tag und Nacht
and I dream by day and night

Nur allein von dem süssen Liebchen mein.
only alone of the sweet sweetheart my

viii.

The red clouds of
evening drift across
the sky, filled with my
longing for you. Dear
love, my heart is
burning; the heavens
shine in their flaming
glory, and day and
night I dream only of
my sweet love.

42. *WIE MELODIEN ZIEHT ES*
    LIKE MELODIES GOES IT

42. LIKE A MELODY

Klaus Groth

Wie Melodien zieht es
like melodies goes it

Mir   leise durch   den Sinn,
to me gently through the sense

Wie Frühlingsblumen blüht   es
like spring-flowers blossoms it

Und schwebt wie Duft   dahin.
and floats like fragrance away

       Like a quiet
melody it pervades
my senses. Like
spring flowers it
blossoms and its
fragrance drifts
away.

Doch kommt das Wort und fasst es
but comes the word and grasps it

Und führt es vor   das Aug',
and leads it before the eye

Wie Nebelgrau erblasst es
like misty-grey fades   it

Und schwindet wie ein Hauch.
and vanishes like a   breath

       But if the
word comes, and
grasps it, then
leads it before the
eyes, it fades as a
grey mist, and
vanishes as a
breath.

Und dennoch ruht   im   Reime
and yet   reposes in the rhyme

Verborgen wohl   ein Duft,
hidden   perhaps a   fragrance

Den mild   aus stillem Keime
that gently from tranquil germ

Ein feuchtes Auge ruft.
a   moist   eye summons

       And yet in the
rhyme a secret
fragrance is
hidden, that gently
from its tranquil
source brings tears
to the eyes.

43. *IMMER LEISER WIRD   MEIN SCHLUMMER*
    EVER QUIETER BECOMES MY   SLUMBER

43. EVER QUIETER IS
    MY SLUMBER

Hermann Lingg

Immer leiser wird   mein Schlummer,
ever quieter becomes my   slumber

Nur wie Schleier liegt mein Kummer
only as veil   lies my   grief

Zitternd über mir.
trembling over me

Oft   im   Traume hör' ich dich
often in the dream hear I   you

Rufen   drauss vor   meiner Tür,
to call outside before my   door

Niemand wacht   und öffnet dir,
no one is awake and opens to you

       My slumber grows
gentle and still;
like a mere veil
my grief trembles
over me. Often in a
dream I hear you
calling before my
door. No one wakes
and lets you in. I
awake, and weep
bitterly.

Ich erwach' und weine bitterlich.
I   awake   and weep bitterly

Ja, ich werde sterben müssen,
yes I   shall to die   to have to

Eine andre wirst du küssen,
- another - will   you to kiss

Wenn ich bleich und kalt.
when I   pale   and cold

Eh' die Maienlüfte weh'n,   .
before the May-breezes blow

Eh' die Drossel singt im   Wald:
before the thrush sings in the wood

Willst du mich noch einmal seh'n,
want   you me   still once   to see

Komm', o komme bald!
come   O come soon

I know that I
must die, that you
will embrace another
when I lie pale and
cold. Before the May
breezes blow, and
the thrush sings in
the wood, if you
would see me once
again - come, O come
soon!

44. AUF DEM KIRCHHOFE
   IN   THE CHURCHYARD

44. IN A CHURCHYARD

Detlev von Liliencron

Der Tag ging regenschwer und sturmbewegt,
the day went rain-heavy   and storm-stirred

Ich war an manch' vergess'nem Grab gewesen,
I   was by many a forgotten   grave been

Verwittert Stein und Kreuz, die Kränze alt,
weathered   stone and cross   the wreaths old

Die Namen überwachsen, kaum   zu lesen.
the names overgrown   hardly to to read

Der Tag ging sturmbewegt   und regenschwer,
the day went storm-stirred and rain-heavy

Auf allen Gräbern fror   das Wort: gewesen.
on   all   graves froze the word been

Wie sturmestot die Särge   schlummerten,
how storm-dead the coffins slumbered

Auf allen Gräbern taute still: Genesen.
on   all   graves thawed softly made well

The day was
heavy with rain and
swept with storms, I
wandered by some
forgotten graves;
weathered stone and
cross, old wreaths,
the names   all
overgrown, and hard
to read.

The day was
swept by storms and
heavy with rain. On
all the graves the
word froze: ended.
The storm was
silent, the coffins
slumbered. On all
the graves it thawed
- and new life
began.

45. STÄNDCHEN
SERENADE

45. SERENADE

Paul Kugler

Der Mond steht über dem Berge,
the moon is   over the mountain

So recht für verliebte Leut';
so right for in love   people

Im   Garten rieselt ein Brunnen,
in the garden trickles a   fountain

Sonst   Stille   weit und breit.
otherwise stillness far   and wide

Neben der   Mauer im   Schatten,
near to the wall in the shadow

Da   stehn der   Studenten drei,
there stand of the students three

Mit Flöt' und Geig' und Zither,
with flute and fiddle and zither

Und singen und spielen dabei.
and sing   and play   thereby

Die Klänge schleichen der   Schönsten
the sounds steal   to the most beautiful one

Sacht in   den Traum hinein,
softly into the dream (into)

Sie schaut den blonden Geliebten
she sees   the fair   lover

Und lispelt: "Vergiss nicht mein!"
and murmurs softly forget   not   of me

The moon shines
above the mountains,
just right for those
in love; a fountain
gently plays in the
garden – all around
it is still.

In the shadows
under the wall stand
three students,
singing and playing
away on flute,
fiddle and zither.

The sounds steal
softly into the
dreams of the
beautiful beloved,
who gazes upon her
fair lover, and
murmurs, 'Forget me
not!'

46. SALAMANDER

46. SALAMANDER

Karl Lemcke

Es   sass ein Salamander
(it) sat a   salamander

Auf einem kühlen Stein,
on a   cool   stone

Da warf ein böses Mädchen
when threw a wicked girl

Ins   Feuer ihn hinein.
Into the fire him thither

A salamander was
sitting on a cold
stone, when a
wicked girl threw
him into the fire.

Sie meint', er soll   verbrennen,
she thought he should to burn

Ihm   ward erst wohl zu   Mut,
to him was   only – in good spirit –

Wohl wie mir   kühlem Teufel
good as to me cool   devil

Die heisse Liebe tut.
the hot   love   does

She thought he
would burn, but he
felt quite at home,
just as I, cool
devil that I am,
flourish in the
passions of love.

47. DAS MÄDCHEN SPRICHT
   THE MAIDEN SPEAKS

47. THE MAIDEN SPEAKS

Otto Friedrich Gruppe

Schwalbe, sag' mir an,
swallow   tell me (to)

Ist's dein alter Mann,
Is it your old   husband

Mit dem du's   Nest gebaut,
with whom you the nest built

Oder hast du   jüngst
Or   have you lately

Erst dich   ihm   vertraut?
just yourself to him entrusted

Swallow, tell
me, is that your
old husband with
whom you first
built your nest?
Or have you just
lately got married?

Sag' was   zwitschert ihr,
say what twitter   you

Sag' was   flüstert ihr
say what whisper you

Des   Morgens so vertraut?
of the morning so intimately

Gelt,   du bist wohl   auch
isn't it so you are   perhaps even

Noch nicht lange Braut?
yet   not   long bride

Tell me, what
are you twittering
about? What do you
whisper each
morning so secretly?
Perhaps you've not
long been a bride?

48. MÄDCHENLIED
    MAIDEN-SONG

48. MAIDEN'S SONG

Paul Heyse

Auf die Nacht in der Spinnstub'n,
at   the night in the spinning-room

Da   singen die Mädchen,
there sing   the maidens

Da   lachen die Dorfbub'n,
there laugh   the village-lads

At night in the
spinning-room the
maidens are singing,
and the village lads
are laughing. How
nimbly the little
wheels whirr!

Wie flink   geh'n die Rädchen!
how nimbly go   the little wheels

Spinnt Jedes   am   Brautschatz,
spins each one at the trousseau

Dass der Liebste sich   freut.
that the beloved himself rejoices

Nicht lange, so gibt es
not   long   so (is there)

Ein Hochzeitsgeläut.
a   wedding-peal

Kein Mensch, der mir   gut   ist,
no   person who to me good is

Will nach mir fragen;
will after me to ask

Wie bang   mir   zu Mut   ist,
how anxious to me - in spirit - is

Wem   soll ich's klagen?
to whom shall I it   to lament

Die Tränen rinnen mir
the tears   run   to me

  übers   Gesicht –
  over the face

Wofür   soll ich spinnen?
for what shall I   to spin

Ich weiss es nicht!
I   know it not

Each is spinning
her trousseau to
please her beloved;
before long wedding
bells will ring.

But no one cares
for me, no one asks
for me; my heart is
so heavy, but who is
there to hear my
lament?

Tears run down
my face – for what
am I spinning? I
do not know.

49. VIER ERNSTE GESÄNGE
FOUR SERIOUS SONGS

49. FOUR SERIOUS
   SONGS

Martin Luther (translated from the Bible)

(Authorised Version)

i.

i. (Eccl. III 19-22)

Denn es gehet dem   Menschen wie dem   Vieh; wie
for it is   to the man   as to the beast as

dies   stirbt, so stirbt er auch; und haben alle
this one dies   so dies he also and have all

einerlei   Odem; und der Mensch hat nichts
one and the same breath and the man   has nothing

mehr denn das Vieh; denn ist alles eitel.
more than the beast for is all   vain

Es fährt alles   an einen Ort; es ist alles
it goes everything to one   place it is all

von Staub gemacht und wird   wieder zu Staub.
of dust made   and becomes again to dust

For that which
befalleth the sons of
men befalleth beasts;
as the one dieth, so
dieth the other; yea,
they have all one
breath; so that a man
hath no preeminence
above a beast: for all
is vanity.

All go unto one
place; all are of the
dust, and all turn to
dust again.

Wer weiss, ob der Geist des   Menschen aufwärts
who knows if the spirit of the man   upwards

fahre,   und der Odem des   Viehes unterwärts
would go and the breath of the beast downwards

unter die Erde fahre?
under the earth would go

Darum   sahe ich, dass nichts Bessers ist, denn
therefore saw I   that nothing better is   than

dass der Mensch fröhlich sei in seiner Arbeit, denn
that the man   joyful   be in his   work   for

das ist sein Teil. Denn wer will ihn dahin bringen,
that is his   part for who will him there to bring

dass er sehe   was nach ihm geschehen wird?
that he might see what after him to happen will

Who knoweth the
spirit of man that
goeth upward, and the
spirit of the beast
that goeth downward to
the earth?

Wherefore I
perceive that there is
nothing better, than
that a man should
rejoice in his own
works; for that is his
portion: for who shall
bring him to see what
shall be after him?

ii.

Ich wandte   mich   und sahe   an alle, die
I   turned round myself and looked at all   who

Unrecht   leiden unter der Sonne; und siehe, da
injustice suffer under the sun   and see   there

waren Tränen, derer,   die Unrecht   litten, und
were tears   of those who injustice suffered and

hatten keinen Tröster,   und die ihnen   Unrecht
had   no   comforter and who to them injustice

täten,   waren zu mächtig, dass sie keinen
would do were too powerful that they no

Tröster   haben   konnten.
comforter to have were able to

Da lobte   ich die Toten, die schon   gestorben
then praised I   the dead   who already dead

waren, mehr als die Lebendigen, die noch das Leben
were   more than the living   who still the life
  hatten;
  had

Und der   noch nicht ist, ist besser, als alle
and (he) who yet not   is   is better   than (all)

beide, und des   Bösen nicht inne wird,   das
both   and of the evil not   aware becomes that

unter der Sonne geschieht.
under the sun   is done

ii. (Eccl. IV 1-3)

So I returned, and
considered all those
oppressions that are
done under the sun:
and behold the tears
of such as were
oppressed, and they
had no comforter; and
on the side of their
oppressors there was
power; but they had no
comforter.

Wherefore I
praised the dead
which are already
dead more than the
living which are yet
alive.

Yea, better is he
than both they, which
hath not yet been, who
hath not seen the evil
work that is done under
the sun.

iii.

O Tod, wie bitter bist du, wenn an dich gedenket
O death how bitter are you when of you remembers

ein Mensch, der gute Tage und genug hat und ohne
a man who good days and enough has and without

Sorge lebet; und dem es wohl geht in allen
care lives and to whom it well goes in all

Dingen und noch wohl essen mag! O Tod, wie wohl
things and still well to eat may O death how good

tust du dem Dürftigen, der da schwach
to you to the needy who there weak

und alt ist, der in allen Sorgen steckt, und
and old is who in all troubles is fixed and

nichts Bessers zu hoffen noch zu erwarten hat!
nothing better to to hope nor to to expect has

iv.

Wenn ich mit Menschen- und mit Engelszungen
if I with men's and with angels' tongues

redete, und hätte der Liebe nicht, so wär
spoke and had of the charity not so should be

ich ein tönend Erz oder eine klingende Schelle.
I a sounding brass or a tinkling cymbal

Und wenn ich weissagen könnte, und wüsste
and if I to prophesy could and understood

alle Geheimnisse und alle Erkenntnis: und
all mysteries and all knowledge and

hätte allen Glauben, also, dass ich Berge
had all faith so that I mountains

versetzte; und hätte der Liebe nicht, so
removed and had of the love not so

wäre ich nichts.
should be I nothing

Und wenn ich alle meine Habe den Armen gäbe,
and if I all my goods to the poor gave

und liesse meinen Leib brennen und hätte der
and let my body to burn and had of the

Liebe nicht, so wäre mir's nichts nütze.
charity not so would be to me it nothing of use

Wir sehen jetzt durch einen Spiegel in einem
we see now through a glass in a

dunkeln Worte; dann aber von Angesicht zu
dark word then but from face to

Angesicht. Jetzt erkenne ich's stückweise; dann
face now know I it piecemeal then

---

iii. (Ecclesiasticus XLI 1-2, from the Apocrypha)
O death, how bitter is the remembrance of thee to a man that liveth at rest in his possessions, unto the man that hath nothing to vex him, and that hath prosperity in all things: yea, unto him that is yet able to receive meat! O death, acceptable is thy sentence unto the needy, and unto him whose strength faileth, that is now in the last age, and is vexed with all things, and to him that despaireth, and hath lost patience!

iv. (I Cor. XIII 1-3, 12-13)
Though I speak with the tongues of men and of angels, and have not charity, I am become as sounding brass, or a tinkling cymbal.

And though I have the gift of prophecy, and understand all mysteries, and all knowledge; and though I have all faith, so that I could remove mountains, and have not charity, I am nothing.

And though I bestow all my goods to feed the poor, and though I give my body to be burned, and have not charity, it profiteth me nothing.

For now we see through a glass, darkly; but then face to face: now I know in part; but then shall I know even as also I am known.

aber werd ich's erkennen, gleichwie ich erkennet bin.
but   shall I it to know   even as   I   known   am

Nun aber bleibet Glaube, Hoffnung, Liebe   diese
now but remains faith   hope   charity these

       And now abideth
faith, hope, charity,
these three; but the
greatest of these is
charity.

drei, aber die Liebe   ist die grösseste unter
three but the charity is the greatest   amongst

ihnen.
them

Hugo Wolf
(1860-1903)

1. ÜBER NACHT
OVER NIGHT

1. AT NIGHT

Julius Sturm

Über Nacht, über Nacht kommt still   das Leid,
over night over night comes silently the grief

Und bist du   erwacht, o traurige Zeit,
and are   you awakened O sad   time

Du grüssest den dämmernden Morgen
you greet   the dawning   morning

Mit Weinen und mit Sorgen.
with weeping and with cares

At night, at
night, grief steals
in silently, and if
you wake, O my
sorrow, you will
greet the dawn with
weeping and care.

Über Nacht, über Nacht kommt still   das Glück,
over night over night comes silently the happiness

Und bist du   erwacht, o selig Geschick,
and are   you awakened O blessed destiny

Der düstre   Traum ist zerronnen,
the melancholy dream is melted

Und Freude ist gewonnen.
and joy   is won

At night, at
night joy steals in
silently, and if
you wake, O my
blessed destiny,
melancholy dreams
are banished and
joy triumphs.

Über Nacht, über Nacht kommt Freud und Leid,
over night over night comes joy   and sorrow

Und eh   du's gedacht, verlassen dich beid
and before you it thought leave   you both

Und gehen dem   Herrn zu sagen,
and go   to the Lord to to say

Wie du sie getragen.
how you them bore

At night, at
night joy and
sorrow both steal
in, and in no time
at all, they leave
you, go to the
Lord and tell Him
how you have borne
them.

2. *BESCHEIDENE LIEBE*
   MODEST   LOVE

2. UNDEMANDING LOVE

Poet unknown

Ich bin wie andre Mädchen nicht,
I   am like other girls   not

Die wenn sie lieben, schweigen
who when they love   are silent

Und ihr   Geheimnis hütend stumm,
and their secret   keeping dumb

Das kranke Köpfchen   neigen.
the sick   little head to bow

Ja, meine Liebe ist nicht stumm,
yes my   love is not   silent

Mein Plaudern   geb ich nicht darum;
my   chattering give I   not   for it

Ich liebe doch ganz eigen.
I   love but quite individually

I'm not like other girls, who when in love say nothing, and keep their secret in their love-sick little heads. No, my love's not silent – it could never make me give up chattering. I have to love in my own way.

Ich bin wie andre Mädchen nicht,
I   am as other girls   not

Die, wenn sie lieben, hoffen,
who when they love   hope

Ich trage meine Lieb zur   Schau
I   bear my   love for the show

Vor   aller Welt ganz offen.
before all   world quite open

Oft   hat mich schon   lieb Mütterlein
often has me   already dear (little)mother

Mit dem Herzallerliebsten   mein
with the dearest-of-my-heart my

Beim Kosen   angetroffen.
by the caressing come across

I'm not like other girls in love, full of expectations. Everyone can see my love, it's there for all the world. Often my dear mother catches me kissing my sweetheart.

Ich bin wie andre Mädchen nicht,
I   am as other girls   not

Doch glücklich, wie ich glaube,
but lucky   as I   believe

Denn meine Liebe richtet sich
for my   love directs (herself)

Auf Trauring   nicht und Haube.
on wedding-ring not and (marriage)head-dress

Er bleibt mein trauter Bräutigam,
he remains my   dear   bridegroom

Er girrt so süss, er ist so zahm,
he coos so sweetly he is so tame

Mein Lieb ist meine Taube.
my   love is my   dove

I'm not like other girls, I know how lucky I am. My love's not intent on a wedding ring and getting married. He's a true bridegroom; he's so tame, and coos so sweetly – my sweetheart is my dove.

3. *MORGENTAU*   3. MORNING-DEW
   MORNING-DEW

Aus   einem alten Liederbuch
from an   old   song-book

Der Frühhauch   hat gefächelt   An early breeze
the early-breeze has fanned   has fanned away the
Hinweg die schwüle Nacht,   sultry night; the
away   the sultry night   meadow smiles, so
Die Flur   holdselig   lächelt   charming in her
the meadow most charmingly smiles   spring splendour.
In ihrer Lenzespracht;
in her   spring-splendour

Mild   singt vom   dunklen Baume   From the dark
softly sings from the dark   tree   tree a little bird
Ein Vöglein   in der Früh,   softly sings its
a   little bird in the early morning   early morning
Es singt noch halb im   Traume   song; half in
it sings still half in the dream   dream, it sings so
Gar   süsse Melodie.   sweet a melody.
very sweet melody

Die Rosenknospe hebet   The rose-bud
the rose-bud   raises   timidly raises on
Empor ihr Köpfchen   bang,   high her little
up   her little head timidly   head, as the sweet,
Denn wundersam   durchbebet   exquisite song
for   exquisitely thrilled through   thrills within her.
Hat sie der süsse Sang;
has her the sweet song

Und mehr und mehr enthüllet   Gradually her
and more and more discloses   petals unclose in
Sich   ihrer Blätter Füll,   their glory, and a
itself of her petals profusion   tear wells up,
Und eine Träne quillet   silently, secretly.
and a   tear springs
Hervor so heimlich still.
forth so secretly silent

4. WIEGENLIED (IM SOMMER)
CRADLE-SONG IN THE SUMMER

4. SUMMER
CRADLE-SONG

Robert Reinick

Vom Berg hinabgestiegen
from the mountain descended

Ist nun des Tages Rest;
is now of the day rest

Mein Kind liegt in der Wiegen,
my child lies in the cradle

Die Vögel all im Nest.
the birds all in the nest

Nur ein ganz klein Singvögelein,
only one quite small little song-bird

Ruft weit daher im Dämmerschein:
calls far away in the twilight

"Gut' Nacht! Gut' Nacht!
good night good night

Lieb' Kindlein, gute Nacht!"
dear little child good night

Die Wiege geht im Gleise,
the cradle goes in the rail

Die Uhr tickt hin und her,
the clock ticks to and fro

Die Fliegen nur ganz leise
the flies only quite softly

Sie summen noch daher.
they hum still away

Ihr Fliegen, lasste mein Kind in Ruh!
you flies leave my child in peace

Was summt ihr ihm so heimlich zu?
what hum you to it so secretly (to)

"Gut' Nacht! Gut' Nacht!
good night good night

Lieb' Kindlein, gute Nacht!"
dear little child good night

Der Vogel und die Sterne
the bird and the stars

Und alle rings umher,
and all round about

Sie haben mein Kind so gerne,
they - my child so (love*)

Die Engel noch viel mehr.
the angels still much more

Sie decken's mit den Flügeln zu
they cover it with the wings -

The last light of day has sunk behind the mountain. My child lies in the cradle, all the birds in their nests. Just one tiny song-bird calls from afar in the twilight, 'Good-night! Good-night, dear little one, good-night!'

The cradle rocks, the clock ticks to and fro, and insects still softly hum. Little creatures, leave my child in peace! What do you hum so secretly to him? 'Good-night! Good-night, dear little one, good-night!'

The bird and the stars, and all things around love my child, and the angels still more. They cover him with their wings and quietly sing, 'Sleep peacefully, good-night! Good-night dear little one, good-night!'

(*gerne haben - to love)

Und singen leise: "Schlaf in Ruh!
and sing   quietly   sleep   in peace

Gut' Nacht! Gut' Nacht!
good night   good night

Lieb Kindlein,   gute Nacht!"
dear little child good night

<table>
<tr><td>5. MAUSFALLEN-SPRÜCHLEIN
   MOUSE-TRAP LITTLE SAYING</td><td>5. MAGIC CHANT TO
   CATCH A MOUSE</td></tr>
</table>

Eduard Mörike

(Das Kind   geht dreimal   um   die Falle
  the child goes three times round the trap
  und spricht:)
  and says

Kleine Gäste, kleines Haus,
little guests little   house

Liebe Mäusin,   oder Maus,
dear (female) mouse or   (male) mouse

Stelle dich   nur kecklich ein
present yourself only boldly   –

Heute Nacht bei Mondenschein,
today night by moonlight

Mach aber die Tür fein   hinter dir zu
shut but the door nicely behind you –

Hörst du?
hear you

Dabei   hüte dein Schwänzchen!
at the same time watch your little tail

Nach Tische singen wir,
after table sing   we

Und machen ein Tänzchen!
and do   a   little dance

Witt! Witt!
Psst! Psst!

Meine alte Katze tanzt wahrscheinlich mit.
my   old cat   dances probably   with (us)

(The child walks
three times round
the trap saying:)

Tiny guests,
tiny house; dear
Mr. Mouse or Mrs.
Mouse, just come
boldly along
tonight, by
moonlight! But shut
the door nicely
behind you, do you
hear? And mind your
little tail! After
supper we will sing
and skip, and do a
little dance. Psst!
Psst! My old cat
will probably join
in!

6. *ZUR   RUH, ZUR   RUH*
   TO THE REST TO THE REST

6. GO TO YOUR REST

Justinus Kerner

Zur   Ruh, zur   Ruh, ihr müden Glieder!
to the rest to the rest you weary limbs

Schliesst fest euch   zu, ihr Augenlider!
shut   tight (yourselves) up you eyelids

Ich bin allein, fort ist die Erde;
I am alone   away is   the earth

Nacht muss es sein, dass Licht mir   werde,
night must it to be that light to me may grow

O führt mich ganz,   ihr innern Mächte!
O lead me   wholly you inner   powers

Hin   zu dem Glanz   der   tiefsten Nächte.
thither to the splendour of the deepest nights

Fort aus dem Raum der   Erdenschmerzen
away from the place of the earth-sorrows

Durch   Nacht und Traum zum   Mutterherzen!
through night and dream to the mother-heart

Go to your
rest, weary limbs;
and eyelids, close!
I am alone, the
world left behind;
night must come,
that I may be
enlightened. O
lead me, inner
powers, to the
splendours of
deepest night. Take
me far from earth's
sorrows, through
night and dreams
home to the mother
heart!

7. *DER GENESENE   AN DIE HOFFNUNG*
   THE CONVALESCENT TO THE HOPE

7. TO HOPE
   (from one who is
    recovering)

Eduard Mörike

Tödlich graute mir   der Morgen:
deadly dawned to me the morning

Doch schon   lag mein Haupt, wie süss!
but already lay my   head   how sweetly

Hoffnung, dir   im   Schoss verborgen,
hope   to you in the lap   concealed

Bis   der Sieg   gewonnen hiess.
till the victory won   was called

Opfer   bracht' ich allen Göttern,
sacrifice brought I   to all gods

Doch vergessen warest du;
but forgotten were   you

Seitwärts von den ew'gen Rettern
sideways   from the eternal saviours

Sahest du dem   Feste   zu.
watched you to the festival -

Deathly grey
dawned the
morning, but
already my head lay
at your breast, O
hope, sweetly
sheltering until
the victory was won.
I had sacrificed to
all the gods, but
had forgotten you.
As you watched the
rites, you stood
apart from those
other eternal
saviours.

O vergib, du Vielgetreue!
O forgive you very faithful one

Tritt aus deinem Dämmerlicht,
step from your twilight

Dass ich dir ins ewig neue,
that I to you into the eternally new

Mondenhelle Angesicht
moon-bright face

Einmal schaue, recht von Herzen,
once see right from heart

Wie ein Kind und sonder Harm;
as a child and without affliction

Ach, nur einmal ohne Schmerzen
oh only once without pains

Schliesse mich in deinen Arm!
enfold me in your arm

O forgive me,
you who were ever
faithful! Leave
your twilight, that
I may gaze into
your face as clear
and ageless as the
moon; that my very
soul may see you, as
a child sees,
without affliction.
And just once free
from pain, enfold
me in your arms!

8. DER TAMBOUR
THE DRUMMER

Eduard Mörike

8. THE DRUMMER-BOY

Wenn meine Mutter hexen könnt',
if my mother to practise sorcery could

Da müsst' sie mit dem Regiment
then would have to she with the regiment

Nach Frankreich, überall mit hin,
to France everywhere with thither

Und wär' die Marketenderin.
and would be the woman seeing to the food

Im Lager, wohl um Mitternacht,
in the camp perhaps at midnight

Wenn niemand auf ist als die Wacht,
when no one up is but the watch

Und alles schnarchet, Ross und Mann,
and everybody snores horse and man

Vor meiner Trommel säss' ich dann:
in front of my drum would sit I then

Die Trommel müsst' eine Schüssel sein,
the drum would have to a bowl to be

Ein warmes Sauerkraut darein,
a warm pickled cabbage in it

Die Schlegel Messer und Gabel,
the drum-sticks knife and fork

Ein' lange Wurst mein Sabel;
a long sausage my sabre

Mein Tschako wär' ein Humpen gut,
my shako would be a tankard good

If only my mother
were a witch, then she
could go everywhere
in France with my
regiment, and look
after the food. In the
camp at midnight, when
no one but the watch
was about, and all the
horses and men were
snoring, I'd sit in
front of my drum, as if
it were a bowl full of
hot pickled cabbage.
I'd use my drum sticks
as knife and fork, and
my sabre could be a
long sausage. My cap
would make a fine
tankard that I'd fill
with blood-red Burgundy.
And as there'd be no
light, the moon would
shine into my tent in
French style, and I'd
think of my sweetheart.
Oh dear, now the fun is
over! If only my
mother were a witch!

Den füll'   ich mit Burgunderblut.
that would fill I   with Burgundy-blood

Und weil   es mir   an Lichte fehlt,
and because it to me of light   lacks

Da   scheint der Mond in   mein Gezelt;
there shines the moon into my   tent

Scheint er auch auf franzö'sch herein,
shines he also in French   into

Mir   fällt   doch meine Liebste ein:
to me comes to mind   my   beloved –

Ach weh! Jetzt hat der Spass ein End!
oh dear now   has the fun   an end

– Wenn nur meine Mutter hexen   könnt!
  if   only my   mother to practice sorcery could

9. *ER IST'S*   9. IT'S HERE!
   HE IS IT

   Eduard Mörike
   (also set by Schumann)

Frühling lässt sein blaues Band   Spring once
spring lets his blue   ribbon   again floats her
                                           blue ribbons on the
Wieder flattern   durch   die Lüfte;   breezes; sweet
again to flutter through the breezes   familiar scents
                                           drift through the
Süsse, wohlbekannte Düfte   countryside, full
sweet familiar   scents   of promise. Already
                                           violets are
Streifen ahnungsvoll   das Land.   dreaming; soon they
rove   full of expectation the countryside will appear. Listen,
                                           a harp sounds
Veilchen träumen schon,   softly from afar!
violets dream   already   Spring, it is
                                           you indeed – it is
Wollen balde kommen.   you I have heard!
want   soon to come

Horch, von fern ein leiser Harfenton!
listen from afar a   quiet harp-note

Frühling, ja   du bist's!
spring   indeed you are it

Dich hab ich vernommen!
you have I   heard

10. *DAS VERLASSENE MÄGDLEIN*
    THE FORSAKEN   GIRL

10. THE FORSAKEN
    GIRL

Eduard Mörike
(also set by Schumann)

Früh, wann die Hähne krähn,
early when the cocks crow

Eh'   die Sternlein   schwinden,
before the little stars vanish

Muss ich am   Herde   stehn,
must I   at the kitchen range to stand

Muss Feuer zünden.
must fire to kindle

Early at cock
crow, before the
little stars fade,
I must stand at
the hearth and
kindle the fire.

Schön   ist der   Flammen Schein,
beautiful is of the flames shine

Es   springen die Funken;
(it) leap   the sparks

Ich schaue so darein,
I   look   so into it

In Leid versunken.
in grief sunk

The glow of the
flames is beautiful,
sparks spring up. I
gaze at them sunk in
grief.

Plötzlich, da   kommt es mir,
suddenly   there comes it to me

Treuloser Knabe,
unfaithful youth

Dass ich die Nacht von dir
that I   the night of you

Geträumet habe.
dreamt   have

Suddenly it
comes to me, that
last night I dreamt
of you, my
unfaithful love.

Träne auf Träne dann
tear on tear then

Stürzet hernieder;
gushes down

So kommt der Tag heran –
so comes the day near

O ging'   er wieder!
O would go he again

Tear after tear
runs down my face.
Another day begins
– would it were
ended!

11. *BEGEGNUNG*
   ENCOUNTER

11. ENCOUNTER

Eduard Mörike

Was   doch   heut Nacht   ein Sturm gewesen,
what indeed - tonight - a   storm been

Bis   erst   der Morgen sich   geregt!
until (just) the morning itself stirred

Wie hat der ungebetne Besen
how has the unbidden broom

Kamin   und Gassen ausgefegt!
chimney and alleys swept out

Da   kommt ein Mädchen schon   die Strassen,
there comes a   girl   already the streets

Das halb verschüchtert um   sich   sieht;
that half scared   about herself looks

Wie Rosen, die der Wind zerblasen,
like roses that the wind blew apart

So unstet   ihr Gesichtchen glüht.
so unsteadily her little face glows

Ein schöner Bursch tritt ihr entgegen,
a   handsome lad   comes her towards

Er will voll   Entzücken nahn:
he wants full (of) delight   to approach

Wie sehn sich   freudig und verlegen
how look (themselves) joyfully and confused

Die ungewohnten Schelme an!
the unaccustomed rogues at

Er scheint zu fragen, ob das Liebchen
he seems to to ask if the sweetheart

Die Zöpfe schon   zurecht   gemacht,
the plaits already to rights put

Die heute Nacht im   offnen Stübchen
that - tonight - in the open   little room

Ein Sturm in Unordnung gebracht.
a   storm in disorder brought

Der Bursche träumt noch von den Küssen,
the youth   dreams still of the kisses

Die ihm   das süsse Kind getauscht,
that to him the sweet child exchanged

Er steht, von Anmut hingerissen,
he stands by charm overcome

Derweil sie um   die Ecke   rauscht.
whilst   she round the corner rustles

What a storm
there was last
night, right until
the break of day!
Look how the
unbidden broom
swept the chimneys
and alleyways!

A girl is
coming along the
street, looking
timidly about her;
her little face is
blushing like a
windblown rose.

A handsome lad
goes eagerly to
meet her. How
joyfully, how
awkwardly they look
at one another,
these unaccustomed
rogues!

He seems to be
asking if his
sweetheart has yet
found time to
rebraid her hair,
that last night
in the open room
the 'storm'
disarranged.

The youth still
dreams of the kisses
he exchanged with
the sweet girl. He
stands there
overcome by her
charm, whilst with
a rustle, she slips
round the corner.

12. *NIMMERSATTE LIEBE*
    INSATIABLE LOVE

12. LOVE NEVER
    SATISFIED

Eduard Mörike

So   ist die Lieb'! So   ist die Lieb'!
thus is the love   thus is the love

Mit Küssen nicht zu stillen.
with kisses not   to to satisfy

Wer ist der Tor und will ein Sieb
who is the fool and wants a   sieve

Mit eitel Wasser füllen?
with mere water to fill

Und schöpfst du an   die tausend Jahr',
and draw   you about the thousand years

Und küssest ewig,   ewig   gar,
and kiss   for ever for ever even

Du tust ihr   nie   zu   Willen.
you do   to her never to(her) will

Thus is love,
thus is love –
not satisfied with
kisses. What fool
would try to fill
a sieve with
water? And if you
drew water for a
thousand years, or
kissed for ever and
ever, you would
never please her.

Die Lieb', die Lieb' hat alle Stund'
the love   the love has every hour

Neu wunderlich Gelüsten;
new strange   desires

Wir bissen uns   die Lippen wund,
we bit   (ourselves) the lips   sore

Da wir uns   heute küssten.
as we (ourselves) today kissed

Das Mädchen hielt in guter Ruh'
the girl   kept in good   stillness

Wie's Lämmlein   unterm   Messer;
like the (little) lamb under the knife

Ihr Auge bat: "Nur immer zu,
her eye   asked only always on

Je weher desto besser!"
the sorer the   better

Each hour of
the day love has
new and strange
desires. We made
each other's lips
quite sore today
as we kissed. My
love kept still as
a lamb under the
knife, and her
eyes said, 'Go on,
go on – the more
it hurts the
better!'

So   ist die Lieb' und war auch so,
thus is the love and was also thus

Wie lang es   Liebe gibt,
as long (there) love (is)

Und anders   war Herr Salomo,
and otherwise was Lord Solomon

Der Weise, nicht verliebt.
the sage   not   in love

Love is thus,
and was ever thus
as long as love was
there. And no
different was
Solomon, the sage,
when he was in
love.

13. *FUSSREISE*
    FOOT-JOURNEY

13. JOURNEY ON FOOT

Eduard Mörike

Am   frischgeschnittnen Wanderstab,
with the freshly-cut   walking-staff

Wenn ich in der Frühe
when I   in the early morning

So durch Wälder ziehe,
so through woods go

Hügel auf und ab:
hill up and down

Dann, wie's Vöglein   im   Laube
then as the little bird in the foliage

Singet und sich rührt,
sings and itself stirs

Oder wie die gold'ne Traube
or   like the golden grape

Wonnegeister   spürt
spirits of ecstasy feels

In der ersten Morgensonne:
in the first morning-sunshine

So fühlt auch mein alter, lieber
so feels also my   old   dear

Adam Herbst- und Frühlingsfieber,
Adam autumn and spring-fever

Gottbeherzte,
divinely emboldened

Nie   verscherzte
never trifled away

Erstlings-Paradieseswonne.
first-born Paradise delight

Also bist du nicht so schlimm, o alter
so are you not so bad   O old

Adam, wie die strengen Lehrer sagen;
Adam as the stern   sages say

Liebst und lobst du immer doch,
love   and praise you still indeed

Singst und preisest immer noch,
sing and glorify always still

Wie an ewig   neuen Schöpfungstagen,
as on eternally new creation's-days

Deinen lieben Schöpfer und Erhalter.
your   dear Creator and Saviour

Möcht's es dieser geben,
might it this   to give

Und mein ganzes Leben
and my whole life

Wär' im   leichten Wanderschweisse
would be in the easy   walking-sweat

Eine solche Morgenreise!
a   such morning's journey

Early in the morning, a fresh-cut sapling in my hand, I stride through the woods, up hill and down. For like a little bird fluttering and chirruping in the leaves - or the golden grape delighting in the first morning sunshine - so is the dear old Adam in me seized by an autumn and spring fever; a godlike courage, a new-born delight in Paradise, never to be trifled away.

You are not after all so bad, old Adam, as the stern sages say; you can still love and give praise, still glorify and sing to your beloved Creator and Saviour, as at an ever-new Creation. If this is so, then my whole life can become as the eager toil of such a morning's journey!

14. *VERBORGENHEIT*
SECLUSION

Eduard Mörike

Lass, o Welt, o lass mich sein!
leave O world O leave me   to be (alone)

Locket nicht mit Liebesgaben,
tempt not   with love's-gifts

Lass dies Herz alleine haben
leave this heart alone   to have

Seine Wonne, seine Pein!
its   rapture its   pain

Was ich traure, weiss ich nicht,
what I   mourn   know I   not

Es ist unbekanntes Wehe;
it is   unknown   misery

Immerdar durch Tränen sehe
always   through tears   see

Ich der Sonne liebes Licht.
I   of the sun   dear   light

Oft bin ich mir kaum bewusst,
often am I   to me hardly conscious

Und die helle Freude zücket
and the clear joy   quivers

Durch die Schwere, so mich drücket,
through the heaviness so me   weighs down

Wonniglich in meiner Brust.
delightfully in my   breast

Lass, o Welt, etc.

14. WORLD WITHIN

Leave me in peace, O world – tempt me not with bribes of love! Leave my heart alone with its rapture and its torment!

I know not why I grieve. It is a strange new misery; only through tears do I see the sweet light of the sun.

Often I am in a daze, and then through the weight of my despair, pure joy sends a quiver of ecstasy within my breast.

15. *IM FRÜHLING*
IN THE SPRING

Eduard Mörike

Hier lieg' ich auf dem Frühlingshügel:
here lie I   on the spring's-hill

Die Wolke wird mein Flügel,
the cloud becomes my   wing

Ein Vogel fliegt mir voraus.
a   bird flies me before

Ach, sag' mir, alleinzige Liebe,
alas tell me   unique   love

Wo du bleibst, dass ich bei dir bliebe!
where you stay   that I   with you may stay

Doch du und die Lüfte, ihr habt kein Haus.
but you and the breezes you have no   house

15. IN SPRING

I lie here on this hill in springtime; clouds are my wings, a bird flies on before me. O tell me, my one and only love, where you are, that I might be with you! But you, like the breezes, have no home.

Der   Sonnenblume gleich steht   mein Gemüte offen,
to the sunflower   like   stands my   heart open

Sehnend,
yearning

Sich   dehnend
itself stretching

In Lieben und Hoffen.
in love   and hope

Frühling,   was bist du gewillt?
spring   (to)what are you disposed

Wann werd'   ich gestillt?
when will be I   stilled

Die Wolke seh' ich wandeln   und den Fluss,
the cloud see I   to wander and the river

Es   dringt   der   Sonne gold'ner Kuss
(it) penetrates of the sun   golden   kiss

Mir   tief bis   ins   Geblüt hinein;
to me deep (unto) into the blood   into

Die Augen, wunderbar   berauschet,
the eyes   wonderfully enchanted

Tun, als schliefen   sie ein,
do   as went to sleep they –

Nur noch das Ohr dem   Ton   der   Biene lauschet.
only still the ear to the sound of the bee   hearkens

Ich denke dies und denke das,
I   think this and think that

Ich sehne mich,   und weiss nicht recht   nach was:
I   long (myself) and know not   rightly for what

Halb ist es Lust, halb ist es Klage;
half is it joy   half is it lament

Mein Herz, o sage,
my   heart O say

Was webst du für Erinnerung
what weave you for memory

In golden grüner   Zweige Dämmerung?
in golden of green twigs twilight

– Alte unnennbare Tage!
  old ineffable days

My heart is
open like a
sunflower,
yearning,
stretching out in
love and hope. O
Spring, what is it
you desire? When
will my longing be
stilled?

I see the
drifting clouds,
and the river; the
golden kiss of the
sun penetrates
deep into my blood.
My eyes, wondrously
enchanted, feign
sleep, and only my
ear hearkens to the
sound of the bees.

I think of this
and think of that,
and am filled with
longing, I hardly
know for what;
half is joy, and
half lament. O my
heart, tell me
what memories you
weave in the
twilight of green
branches?
Ineffable days of
old!

16. *AUF EINER WANDERUNG*   16. ON A WALKING-TRIP
    ON A   WALKING-TRIP

Eduard Mörike

In ein freundliches Städtchen   tret ich ein,   I came into a
in a   friendly   little town enter I   (in)   friendly little
                                                     town; the streets
In den Strassen liegt roter Abendschein,   were filled with
in the streets lies red   evening-light   the red evening
                                                     light. From an
Aus einem offnen Fenster eben,   open window full of
from an   open   window just   flowers, I heard a
                                                     sound floating
Über den reichsten Blumenflor   away like golden
over the richest   show of flowers   bells. The voice
                                                     was like a choir
Hinweg, hört man Goldglockentöne   schweben,   of nightingales,
away   hears one golden-bells'-notes to float   and it made the
                                                     blossoms tremble,
Und eine Stimme scheint ein Nachtigallenchor,   the breezes stir,
and a   voice seems a   nightingale-choir   and the roses glow
                                                     more brightly.
Dass die Blüten   beben,
that the blossoms tremble

Dass die Lüfte   leben,
that the breezes live

Dass in höherem Rot die Rosen leuchten vor.
that in higher red the roses glow   (out)

Lang hielt   ich staunend, lustbeklommen.   For a long time
long stopped I   astonished delight-seized   I stood there
                                                     entranced. How I
Wie ich hinaus vors   Tor   gekommen,   found my way
how I   outside in front of the gateway come   through the
                                                     gateway I truly
Ich weiss es wahrlich selber nicht.   cannot say. Ah,
I   know it truly   myself not   here lies the world
                                                     so bright and
Ach hier, wie liegt die Welt so licht!   clear; the skies
ah here how lies the world so bright   bathed in a tumult
                                                     of crimson, and
Der Himmel wogt   in purpurnem Gewühle,   behind me the town
the sky   rocked in crimson   tumult   in a golden haze.
                                                     How the stream
Rückwärts die Stadt in goldnem Rauch,   rushes past the
backwards the town in golden haze   alders by the mill!
                                                     I am confused,
Wie rauscht der Erlenbach,   wie rauscht im   Grund   intoxicated. O
how rushes the alders-brook how rushes in the ground Muse, you have
  die Mühle,   touched my heart
  the mill   with a breath of
                                                     love!
Ich bin wie trunken,   irrgeführt –
I   am as intoxicated confused

O Muse, du hast mein Herz berührt
O Muse you have my   heart touched

Mit einem Liebeshauch!
with a   love's-breath

17. *ELFENLIED*   17. SONG OF THE ELF
ELF-SONG

Eduard Mörike

Bei Nacht im   Dorf   der Wächter rief:
at night in the village the watchman called
  "Elfe":
  eleven (=elf)

Ein ganz kleines Elfchen   im   Walde schlief -
a   quite small   little elf in the wood was sleeping
wohl um die Elfe! -
indeed at the eleven

Und meint, es rief   ihm aus dem Tal
and thinks it called him from the valley

Bei seinem Namen die Nachtigall,
by his   name   the nightingale

Oder Silpelit hätt ihm gerufen.
or   Silpelit had him called

Reibt sich   der Elf die Augen aus,
rubs (himself) the elf the eyes (out)

Begibt sich   vor   sein Schneckenhaus
proceeds (himself) in front of his snail-shell

Und ist als wie ein trunken Mann,
and is as if a   drunken man

Sein Schläflein   war nicht voll getan,
his (little)sleep was not   fully done

Und humpelt also,   tippe, tapp,
and hobbles therefore tip   tap

Durchs   Haselholz ins   Tal   hinab,
through the hazel-wood into the valley down

Schlupft an der Mauer hin   so dicht,
slips   to the wall   there so close

Da   sitzt der   Glühwurm Licht an Licht.
there sits of the glow-worm light to light

"Was sind das helle Fensterlein?
 what are the bright little window(s)

Da   drin   wird eine Hochzeit sein:
there in there will a   wedding to be

Die Kleinen   sitzen beim   Mahle,
the little ones sit   at the banquet

Und treiben's   in dem Saale:
and carry on it in the hall

Da   guck ich wohl   ein wenig 'nein!"
there peep I   perhaps a   little in there

- Pfui, stösst den Kopf an harten Stein!
 ouch hits   the head on hard   stone

Elfe, gelt,   du hast genug?
elf   isn't it you have enough

Gukuk! Gukuk!
cuckoo cuckoo

One night in
the village the
nightwatchman
called, 'Eleven!'
A little elf is
sleeping in the
wood just at
eleven, and he
thinks a
nightingale in the
valley has called
him, or Silpelit
perhaps? The elf
rubs his eyes, and
stumbles out of
his snail-shell
house like a
drunken man. Half
asleep, he
staggers,
tip-a-tap, through
the hazel wood
down into the
valley. He creeps
close to the wall
that is shining
with the light of
many glow-worms.
'What are those
bright little
windows? There
must be a wedding
in there! They'll
all be sitting at
the feast, and
making merry in the
hall. I'll just
peep in.' Ouch!
He hits his head on
the hard stone!
Little elf, you've
had enough,
haven't you?
Cuckoo! Cuckoo!

18. *DER GÄRTNER*   18. THE GARDENER
    THE GARDENER

Eduard Mörike
(also set by Schumann)

Auf ihrem Leibrösslein,   On her
on her   favourite little horse   favourite little
                                              horse, as white as
So weiss wie der Schnee,   snow, the most
as white as the snow   beautiful princess
                                              is riding down
Die schönste   Prinzessin,   the avenue.
the most beautiful princess

Reit't durch   die Allee.
rides   through the avenue

Der Weg, den   das Rösslein   On the path
the road which the little horse   where her little
                                              horse prances so
Hintanzet   so hold,   gracefully, the
dances along so gracefully   sand I strewed
                                              sparkles like
Der Sand, den   ich streute,   gold.
the sand which I   strewed

Er blinket wie Gold!
it sparkles like gold

Du rosenfarb's   Hütlein   Little rose-
you rose-coloured little hat   coloured hat,
                                              bobbing up and
Wohl   auf und wohl   ab,   down, O secretly
(whether) up and (whether) down   throw me a feather!

O wirf eine Feder,
O throw a   feather

Verstohlen herab!
secretly   down

Und willst du dagegen   And if in
and want   you in exchange   exchange you'd
                                              like a flower,
Eine Blüte von mir,   take a thousand
a   bloom from me   for your one –
                                              take them all!
Nimm tausend für eine,
take thousand for one

Nimm alle dafür!
take all for it

19.· *UM MITTERNACHT*
   AT MIDNIGHT

19. AT MIDNIGHT

Eduard Mörike

Gelassen stieg   die Nacht ans   Land,
calmly   climbed the night on the land

Lehnt träumend an der   Berge   Wand,
leans dreaming on of the mountain wall

Ihr Auge sieht die goldne Waage nun
her eye sees the golden scales now

Der   Zeit in gleichen Schalen stille ruhn;
of the time in equal   scales quietly to rest

Und kecker rauschen die Quellen hervor,
and bolder rush   the springs forth

Sie singen der   Mutter, der   Nacht, ins   Ohr
they sing   of the mother of the night into the ear

Vom   Tage,
of the day

Vom   heute gewesenen Tage.
of the today been   day

Das uralt   alte Schlummerlied,
the age-old old slumber-song

Sie achtet's   nicht, sie ist es müd;
she pays heed it not   she is it weary

Ihr   klingt des   Himmels Bläue süsser noch,
to her sounds of the sky   azure sweeter still

Der   flücht'gen Stunden gleichgeschwung'nes Joch.
of the fleeting hours   equally-swung   yoke

Doch immer behalten die Quellen das Wort,
but always keep   the springs the word

Es   singen die Wasser im   Schlafe noch fort
(it) sing the waters in the sleep   still on

Vom   Tage,
of the day

Vom   heute gewesenen Tage.
of the today been   day

The night rose
calmly over the
land, and now
leans dreaming
on the
mountain-side. She
sees the golden
scales of Time
quietly at rest
in equal measure.
And the springs
gush boldly forth,
and sing to the
night, their
mother, of the day,
the day that is
gone.

She pays no
heed to the
age-old lullaby;
she is weary of it.
To her the dark
blue of the sky,
and the balanced
yoke of the
fleeting hours
hold greater
charms. But the
springs murmur on,
singing in their
sleep of the day,
the day that is
gone.

20. *SEUFZER*
    SIGH

Eduard Mörike

Dein Liebesfeuer,
Thy love's-fire

Ach Herr! Wie teuer
oh Lord   how dearly

Wollt' ich es hegen,
desired I   it to cherish

Wollt' ich es pflegen!
desired I   it to tend

Hab's   nicht geheget
have it not   cherished

Und nicht gepfleget,
and not   tended

Bin tot im   Herzen,
am dead in the heart

O Höllenschmerzen!
O hell's-pains

The fire of
Thy love, O Lord —
how dearly I
wanted to tend it,
how dearly I
desired to
cherish it! I have
failed to tend it,
I have failed to
cherish it; my
heart is dead, and
I feel the torments
of Hell!

21. *AUF EIN ALTES BILD*
    ON   AN   OLD   PICTURE

Eduard Mörike

In grüner   Landschaft Sommerflor,
in of green landscape   summer-blossoming

Bei kühlem Wasser, Schilf, und Rohr,
by cool   water   rush   and reed

Schau, wie das Knäblein   sündelos
look   how the little boy sinless

Frei   spielet auf der   Jungfrau Schoss!
freely plays   on of the Virgin   lap

Und dort im   Walde wonnesam,
and there in the wood   delightfully

Ach, grünet   schon   des   Kreuzes Stamm!
ah   turns green already of the cross   trunk

Summer
blossoms in a
green landscape,
by cool water,
rush and reed;
see how the little
boy in happy
innocence is
playing on the
Virgin's lap! And
in the wood, ah,
there already a
radiant green
unfolds on the
trunk marked for
the cross.

22. *IN DER FRÜHE*
    IN THE EARLY MORNING

22. IN THE EARLY
    MORNING

Eduard Mörike

Kein Schlaf noch kühlt das Auge mir,
no   sleep yet cools the eye to me

Dort gehet schon   der Tag herfür
there goes already the day forth

An meinem Kammerfenster.
at my   bedroom-window

Es wühlet   mein verstörter Sinn
it stirs up my   troubled   mind

Noch zwischen Zweifeln her und hin
still between doubts   to and fro

Und schaffet Nachtgespenster.
and creates night-phantoms

Ängst'ge,   quäle
make anxious torment

Dich   nicht länger, meine Seele!
yourself not   longer   my   soul

Freu   dich!   Schon sind da   und dorten
rejoice (yourself) already are here and there

Morgenglocken wach geworden.
morning-bells awake become.

My eyes are
not yet cooled by
sleep; already day
is breaking at my
window. My
troubled mind is
stirred by doubts,
and conjures up
dark phantoms. Be
anxious no more,
torment yourself
no longer! O my
soul, rejoice!
Already all around
the morning bells
are waking.

23. *SCHLAFENDES JESUSKIND*
    SLEEPING   JESUS-CHILD

23. SLEEPING
    CHRIST CHILD

Eduard Mörike

Sohn der   Jungfrau, Himmelskind! am   Boden
son of the Virgin   Heaven's-Child on the ground

Auf dem Holz der   Schmerzen eingeschlafen,
on the wood of the griefs   gone to sleep

Das der fromme Meister sinnvoll   spielend
that the devout master significantly playing

Deinen leichten Träumen unterlegte;
your   gentle dreams put underneath

Blume du, noch in der Knospe dämmernd
flower you still in the bud   dawning

Eingehüllt die Herrlichkeit des   Vaters!
wrapped in the glory   of the Father

O wer sehen könnte, welche Bilder
O who to see could which images

Hinter dieser Stirne, dieser schwarzen
behind this brow   these black

Wimpern, sich   in sanftem Wechsel   malen!
eyelashes (themselves) in gentle succession reflect

Son of the
Virgin, Child of
Heaven, sleeping
on the bare
boards of grief,
that the devout
Master lightly
places, so full
of meaning,
beneath you as
you gently dream –
O you flower,
even in this bud
wrapped in a
half-light, you
are the very
glory of the
Father! If we
could but see the
gentle succession
of images
flickering below
that brow, and
those dark lashes!

24. *GEBET*
    PRAYER

24. PRAYER

Eduard Mörike

Herr! schicke was du   willt,
Lord send   what Thou wilt

Ein Liebes oder Leides;
a   joy   or   sorrow

Ich bin vergnügt, dass beides
I   am content   that both

Aus deinen Händen quillt.
from Thy   hands   flow

Wollest   mit Freuden
may (Thou) with joy

Und wollest   mit Leiden
and may (Thou) with sorrow

Mich nicht überschütten!
me   not   to overwhelm

Doch   in der Mitten
indeed in the middle

Liegt holdes Bescheiden.
lies pure   humility

Lord, send
what Thou wilt,
joy or sorrow;
I am content, for
both flow from
Thee.

But may Thou
not pour too
great a sorrow or
joy upon me — for
it is between
these that lies
pure humility.

25. *LEBE WOHL*
    FARE-WELL

25. FAREWELL

Eduard Mörike

"Lebe wohl": - Du fühlest   nicht,
 fare-well   you are aware not

Was es heisst, dies Wort der   Schmerzen;
what it means   this word of the sorrows

Mit getrostem Angesicht
with confident face

Sagtest du's und   leichtem Herzen.
said you it and(with) light   heart

"Lebe wohl!" - Ach tausendmal
 fare-well   ah thousand-times

Hab' ich mir   es vorgesprochen,
have I   to me it said aloud

Und in nimmersatter Qual
and in insatiable   torment

Mir   das Herz damit   gebrochen!
to me the heart with that broken

'Farewell!'
You do not know
what it means,
this word of
sorrow. You say
it with a
cheerful face and
a light heart.

'Farewell!'
Oh, I have said it
aloud a thousand
times, and its
never-ending
torment has
broken my heart!

26. HOMESICKNESS

26. *HEIMWEH*
   HOMESICKNESS

Eduard Mörike

Anders   wird   die Welt mit jedem Schritt,
different becomes the world with every step

The world
changes with every
step I take away
from my beloved;
my heart would go
no further. Here
the sun shines
coldly on the
earth; here all
seems strange to
me, even the
flowers by the
stream. Everything
has an unfamiliar
air, so false a
face. The little
stream murmurs and
seems to say
'Come here to me,
poor boy, for here
too you will find
forget-me-nots.'
Oh yes, they are
beautiful
everywhere — but
not so lovely as
there. Oh, let me
go on — my eyes
are brimming with
tears.

Den ich weiter von   der Liebsten mache;
that I   further from the beloved   make

Mein Herz, das will nicht weiter mit,
my   heart that wants not   further with (me)

Hier scheint die Sonne kalt ins   Land,
here shines the sun   coldly into the land

Hier deucht mir   alles   unbekannt,
here seems to me everything unknown

Sogar die Blumen am   Bache!
even the flowers by the stream

Hat jede Sache
has each thing

So fremd   eine Miene, so falsch ein Gesicht.
so strange an   air   so false a   face

Das Bächlein   murmelt wohl   und spricht:
the little stream murmurs perhaps and says

"Armer Knabe, komm bei mir vorüber,
  poor boy   come near me past

Siehst auch hier Vergissmeinnicht!"
see   also here forget-me-nots

Ja, die sind schön an jedem Ort,
yes they are lovely in every place

Aber nicht wie dort.
but not   as there

Fort, nur fort!
on   only on

Die Augen gehn mir   über!
the eyes   go   to me over

27. *DENK   ES, O SEELE.*
    REFLECT IT O SOUL

27. CONSIDER, O
    MY SOUL

Eduard Mörike

Ein Tännlein   grünet   wo,   wer weiss, im
a   little fir-tree becomes green where who knows in the
Walde,
wood

Ein Rosenstrauch, wer sagt, in welchem Garten?
a   rose-bush   who says in which   garden

Sie sind erlesen schon, denk es, o Seele,
they are   chosen already think it O soul

Auf deinem Grab zu wurzeln   und zu wachsen.
on   your   grave to to take root and to to grow

Zwei schwarze Rösslein   weiden auf der Wiese,
two black   little horses graze in the meadow

Sie kehren heim zur   Stadt in muntern Sprüngen.
they return home to the   town in gay   leaps

Sie werden schrittweis gehn mit deiner Leiche;
they will   step by step to go with your   dead body

Vielleicht, vielleicht noch eh   an ihren Hufen
perhaps   perhaps   still before on their hooves

Das Eisen   los wird, das ich blitzen sehe!
the iron horseshoe loose becomes that I   to flash see

A little fir
tree grows green
in a wood – who
knows where? A
rose bush in a
garden – who can
say which?
Consider, O my
soul, they are
already chosen to
take root, and
grow on your grave.

Two little
black horses·
graze in the´
meadow, then come
trotting gaily
home to the town.
One day, step by
step, they will
draw your coffin –
perhaps even
before they cast
from their hooves
those shoes that
I now see flashing.

28. *LIED EINES VERLIEBTEN*
    SONG OF AN IN–LOVE–ONE

28. LOVER'S SONG

Eduard Mörike

In aller Früh,   ach, lang vor   Tag,
in all   earliness oh   long before day

Weckt mich mein Herz, an dich zu denken,
wakes me   my   heart of you to to think

Da   doch   gesunde Jugend schlafen mag.
where indeed healthy youth to sleep may

Hell   ist mein Aug' um Mitternacht.
bright is my   eye at midnight

Heller als frühe Morgenglocken:
brighter than early morning-bells

Wann hätt'st du je am   Tage mein gedacht?
when had   you ever in the day of me thought

In the early hours,
long before dawn, my
heart awakens me to
think of you, when
healthy youth should
sleep.

My eyes are bright
at midnight, brighter
than the early morning
bells – but when did
you ever think of me,
even by day?

Wär' ich ein Fischer, stünd' ich auf,
were I a fisherman would get I up

Trüge   mein Netz hinab zum   Flusse,
would carry my net down to the river

Trüg'   herzlich froh die Fische zum   Verkauf.
would carry heartily glad the fish to the selling

In der Mühle, bei Licht,   der Müllerknecht
in the mill by illumination the miller's-boy

Tummelt   sich,   alle Gänge   klappern;
bustles about (himself) all workings clatter

So rüstig   Treiben wär'   mir   eben recht!
so vigorous activity would be to me just right

Weh, aber ich! o armer Tropf!
alas but I   0 poor wretch

Muss auf dem Lager mich   müssig grämen,
must on the bed   myself idly   to grieve

Ein ungebärdig Mutterkind   im   Kopf.
an unruly   mother's-child in the head

If I were a
fisherman, I would
rise and carry my nets
down to the river, and
light of heart I
would take my fish to
the market.

By the light of a
lamp the miller's boy
is already at work, and
all around it clatters
in the mill – oh, such
hard toil would
suit me well!

But alas, I, poor
wretch, lie idly,
grieving in my bed,
with nothing in my
head but a mother's
unruly daughter.

29. GESANG WEYLAS
    SONG WEYLA'S

29. WEYLA'S SONG

Eduard Mörike

Du bist Orplid, mein Land!
you are Orplid my   land

Das ferne   leuchtet;
that far away gleams

Vom   Meere dampfet   dein besonnter Strand
from the sea evaporates your sunlit   shore

Den Nebel, so der   Götter Wange feuchtet.
the mist so of the gods   cheek moistens

Uralte Wasser steigen
ancient waters rise

Verjüngt   um   deine Hüften, Kind!
rejuvenated about your hips   child

Vor   deiner Gottheit beugen
before your   divinity bow

Sich   Könige, die deine Wärter   sind.
(themselves) kings who your attendants are

You are my
land, Orplid,
gleaming far
away; sea mists
rise from your
sunlit shores,
as if to moisten
the cheeks of the
gods.

Ancient waters
rise renewed about
your hips, my
child! Before your
divinity, kings
bow down as your
servants.

30. *STORCHENBOTSCHAFT*
    STORK'S MESSAGE

Eduard Mörike

Des   Schäfers sein Haus und das steht auf
of the shepherd his house and that stands on
    zwei Rad,
    two wheel(s)

Steht hoch auf der Heiden, so frühe wie spat;
stands high on the heath   so early as late

Und wenn nur ein mancher so'n Nacht-quartier hätt'!
and if   only a   someone such a night-quarters had

Ein Schäfer tauscht nicht mit dem König sein Bett.
a   shepherd exchanges not   with the king his bed

Und käm'   ihm   zur   Nacht auch was
and happened to him to the night even something
    Seltsames vor,
    strange   –

Er betet sein Sprüchel   und legt sich   aufs
he prays his little text and lays himself on the
    Ohr;
    ear

Ein Geistlein,   ein Hexlein,   so luftige
a   (little) ghost a (little) witch so airy
    Wicht'
    wights

Sie klopfen ihm   wohl, doch er antwortet nicht.
they knock   to him perhaps but he answers   not

Einmal doch,   da ward es ihm   wirklich zu
once   however then was it to him really   too
    bunt:
    vivid (i.e. much)

Es knopert am   Laden, es winselt der Hund;
it rattles on the shutter (it) whines the dog

Nun ziehet mein Schäfer den Riegel - ei schau!
now draws my   shepherd the bolt   oo look

Da   stehen zwei Störche, der Mann   und die Frau.
there stand two storks   the husband and the wife

Das Pärchen,   es machet ein schön   Kompliment,
the (little) pair it makes a   beautiful bow

Es möchte   gern reden,   ach wenn es nur
it would like gladly to speak oh   if   it only
    könnt!
    could

Was will mir   das Ziefer? - ist so   was
what want to me the vermin   is such (a) thing
    erhört?
    heard of

Doch ist mir   wohl   fröhliche Botschaft beschert?
but is to me perhaps joyful   tidings   bestowed upon

30. THE STORKS'
    MESSAGE

There's a
shepherd's hut,
that stands on
two wheels, high
up on the heath
all day and all
night. Many would
be glad of such
an abode – a
shepherd would
never change
beds with a king!

And even if
the strangest
things happen at
night, he just
mutters a prayer
and buries his
head in the
pillow. Spirits,
hobgoblins and
misty wraiths may
knock at his door
– but he takes no
notice.

Once, however,
things went really
too far; the
shutters rattle,
the dog whines;
the shepherd
draws back the
bolt – Oo look!
Two storks stand
there, a husband
and wife.

The quaint
couple solemnly
bows and curtseys;
they've something
to say – oh, if
only they could!
What can these
creatures want?
It's unheard of!
But perhaps
they're bringing
me good news?

Ihr seid wohl   dahinten   zu Hause am   Rhein?
you are perhaps behind there at home on the Rhine

Ihr habt wohl   mein Mädel gebissen ins   Bein?
you have perhaps my   girl   bitten   in the leg

Nun weinet das Kind und die Mutter noch mehr,
now cries the child and the mother still more

Sie wünschet den Herzallerliebsten   sich
she wishes   the dearest of her heart to herself
  her.
  near

Don't you
live down there
on the Rhine?
Perhaps you've
been to see my
sweetheart? Oh,
the baby's crying,
and the mother
still more – how
she wishes her
heart's delight
were there!

Und wünschet daneben die Taufe   bestellt:
and wishes   besides the christening arranged

Ein Lämmlein,   ein Würstlein,   ein Beutelein
a   (little) lamb a   (little) sausage a   little purse
Geld?
gold

So sagt nur, ich käm'   in zwei Tag oder drei,
so say only I   might come in two days or   three

Und grüsst mir   mein Bübel   und rührt ihm
and greet to me my   little boy and stir to him
  den Brei!
  the gruel

And she
wishes, too, that
the christening
were fixed – with
lamb, and
sausage, and a
little purse of
gold? Just tell
her I'll be there
in two or three
days – and
greetings to my
little boy, and
stir up his gruel!

Doch halt! warum stellt ihr zu   Zweien euch
but stop why   present you in(a) twosome yourselves
  ein?
  -

Es werden doch, hoff' ich nicht Zwillinge sein?
it will   indeed hope I   not   twins   to be

Da   klappern die Störche im   lustigsten Ton,
then clatter the storks in the merriest   fashion

Sie nicken und knixen und fliegen davon.
they nod   and curtsey and fly   away

But wait! Why
are there two of
you here? There
aren't – I hope –
twins? At this the
storks clap their
wings in the
merriest
fashion. They nod,
and they curtsey
and fly away.

31. *BEI EINER TRAUUNG*
   AT A   WEDDING-CEREMONY

31. AT A
   WEDDING-CEREMONY

Eduard Mörike

Vor   lauter hochadligen Zeugen
before only   aristocratic witnesses

Kopuliert man ihrer   zwei;
united   one of them two

Die Orgel hängt voll Geigen,
(the organ hangs full violins)

Der Himmel nicht, mein Treu!
the Heaven not   my   honour

Seht doch! Sie weint ja   greulich,
see but   she weeps indeed dreadfully

Er macht ein Gesicht abscheulich!
he makes a   face   horrible

Before witnesses
of high and noble
blood, a pair of
them were married:
The expectations of
all were great, those
of Heaven were not, in
truth! Just see – *she*
is weeping dreadfully,
while *he* makes a
frightful face – for
of course, of course,
no love at all was
there.

Denn leider   freilich, freilich,
for   unfortunately of course of course

Keine Lieb' ist nicht dabei.
no   love is   not   there

32. *SELBSTGESTÄNDNIS*   32. SELF-CONFESSION
    SELF-CONFESSION

Eduard Mörike

Ich bin meiner Mutter einzig Kind,   I am my mother's
I   am of my mother only   child   only child, and
                                                    because the others
Und weil   die andern ausblieben sind,   were lacking – who
and because the others absent   are   knows how many, six
                                                    or seven – I came in
Was weiss ich wieviel, die sechs oder sieben,   for everything! I
what know I   how many the six   or seven   had to consume enough
                                                    love, devotion and
Ist eben   alles   an mir hängen blieben; goodness for a whole
is certainly everything on me to hang left   half dozen, and I'll
                                                    never forget it all
Ich hab' müssen   die Liebe, die Treue, die Gute the days of my life.
I   have to have to the love the loyalty the goodness I'm sure it would have
                                                    been better for me, if
Für ein ganz halb Dutzend allein aufessen,   I'd also received the
for a   whole half dozen   alone to eat up   cuffs for all six.

Ich will's mein Lebtag   nicht vergessen.
I   will it my   life's-day(s) not   to forget

Es hätte mir aber noch wohl   mögen frommen,
it had   me but still perhaps (might) to profit

Hätt' ich nur auch Schläg für Sechse bekommen.
had   I   only also blows for six   received

33. *ABSCHIED*
   FAREWELL

33. FAREWELL

Eduard Mörike

Unangeklopft   ein Herr   tritt abends   bei
without knocking a   gentleman steps in the evening at
   mir   ein:
   (my home) into

"Ich habe die Ehr'   ihr Rezensent zu sein!"
I   have the honour your critic   to to be

Sofort   nimmt er das Licht   in   die Hand,
at once takes he the candlestick into the hand

Besieht   lang meinen Schatten an der Wand,
examines long my   shadow   on the wall

Rückt nah und fern: "Nun, lieber junger Mann,
moves near and far   now dear   young man

Sehn sie doch gefälligst   'mal Ihre Nas' so von   der
look you (do) if you please once your nose so from the
   Seite an!
   side at

Sie geben zu, dass das ein Auswuchs is."
you agree   that it an outgrowth is

- "Das? Alle Wetter - gewiss!
   that all weathers undoubtedly

Ei Hasen! Ich dachte nicht,
oh hares I   thought not

All' mein Lebtage   nicht,
all my   life-days not

Dass ich so   eine Weltsnase führt im   Gesicht!!"
that I such a   world-nose bore in the face

Der Mann sprach noch Verschied'nes hin   und her,
the man   spoke still various things thither and hither

Ich weiss, auf meine Ehre, nicht mehr;
I   know on my   honour not more

Meinte vielleicht, ich sollt' ihm   beichten.
thought perhaps   I   should to him to confess

Zuletzt stand er auf; ich tat ihm   leuchten.
at last stood he up   I   did to him to light

Wie wir nun an der Treppe sind,
as we now at the stairs are

Da   geb' ich ihm, ganz froh gesinnt,
there give I   him quite gaily disposed

Einen kleinen Tritt,
a   small kick

Nur so von hinten aufs Gesässe, mit -
just so from behind on the seat   with

Alle Hagel!   ward das ein Gerumpel,
all hail(stones) was that a   rumbling

Ein Gepurzel,   ein Gehumpel!
a   somersaulting a   hobbling

One evening, unannounced, a gentleman steps into my room. 'I have the honour to be your critic, sir!' At once he takes the candlestick in his hand, and moving to and fro, he carefully examines my shadow on the wall. 'Now, my dear young man, just take one look at your nose from the side, if you please! You must admit, it's grotesque!' 'Indeed? Good heavens – so it is! Jumping Jacks! Never in all my days did I realise I had such a distinguished nose on my face!'

The man went on to speak of this and that – for the life of me I can't remember what. Perhaps he meant me to make some sort of confession to him? At last he stood up, and I lit the way for him. Then, as we reach the stairs, I give him, quite amiably, just a gentle kick from behind. By thunder! What a rumbling, a somersaulting and a tumbling there was! In all my days I've never seen the like – someone going downstairs quite so fast!

Dergleichen hab' ich nie   gesehn,
the like   have I   never seen

All' mein Lebtage   nicht gesehn,
all   my   life-days not   seen

Einen Menschen so rasch   die Trepp' hinabgehn!
a   man   so quickly the stairs to go down

34. *DER FREUND*
    THE FRIEND

                                                    34. THE FRIEND

Joseph von Eichendorff

Wer auf den Wogen schliefe,
who on the waves would sleep

Ein sanft gewiegtes Kind,
a   gently rocked   child

Kennt nicht des   Lebens Tiefe,
knows not   of the life   depth

Vor süssem Träumen blind.
with sweet dreaming blind

    He who would
sleep on the waves
like a gently
cradled child, his
vision dimmed by
sweet reveries –
he cannot know life's
deeps.

Doch wen die Stürme fassen
but whom the storms seize

Zu wildem Tanz und Fest,
for wild   dance and feast

Wen hoch auf dunklen Strassen
whom high on dark   streets

Die falsche Welt verlässt:
the false   world forsakes

    But he who enjoys
in the storm his
wildest revels, and
forsakes the false
world for ways high
and dark –

Der lernt sich   wacker   rühren,
he learns himself valiantly to act

Durch Nacht und Klippen hin
through night and reefs   thither

Lernt der das Steuer führen
learns he the helm   to steer

Mit sichrem, ernstem Sinn.
with safe   stern   feeling

he is a man who acts
with valour, who
steers the helm
unerringly amongst
the rocks by night.

Der ist von echtem Kerne,
he is of true   core

Erprobt zu Lust und Pein,
tried   to joy and pain

Der glaubt an Gott und Sterne,
he believes in God and stars

Der soll mein Schiffman sein!
he shall my   ship-mate to be

    He is stout of
heart, well-tried in
joy and sorrow, with
faith in God and the
stars – he shall be
my shipmate!

35. *DER MUSIKANT*
   THE MUSICIAN

Joseph von Eichendorff

Wandern lieb ich für mein Leben,
to roam love I   for my   life

Lebe eben, wie ich kann,
live just as I   can

Wollt ich mir   auch Mühe   geben,
wanted I   to me even trouble to give

Passt   es mir   doch gar   nicht an.
would suit it to me yet at all not   –

Schöne alte Lieder weiss ich;
lovely old   songs know I

In der Kälte, ohne   Schuh,
in the cold   without shoe

Draussen in die Saiten reiss ich,
outside in the strings pull I

Weiss nicht, wo   ich abends   ruh!
know not   where I in the evening rest

Manche Schöne   macht wohl   Augen,
many a pretty one makes perhaps eyes

Meinet, ich gefiel ihr sehr,
thinks I   please her very much

Wenn ich nur was   wollte taugen,
if   I   only something wanted to be worth

So ein armer Lump   nicht wär!
so a   poor fellow not   would be

Mag dir   Gott ein'n Mann   bescheren,
may to you God a   husband to give

Wohl   mit Haus und Hof versehn!
perhaps with house and home to provide

Wenn wir zwei zusammen wären,
when we two   together were

Möcht mein Singen mir   vergehn.
might my   singing to me to vanish

35. THE MINSTREL

    I love a life of
roaming, just living
as I can. Even if I
took the trouble to
work, it wouldn't
suit me at all.

    My songs are old
and lovely; out in
the cold, barefoot, I
pluck my strings, and
never know where I'll
sleep at night!

    Many a pretty
girl makes eyes at
me, thinking I might
please her, if only
I chose to make
something of myself,
and wasn't such a
poor fellow.

    May God give you
a husband, and
provide a house and
home! If we two were
together, perhaps
I'd sing no more.

36. VERSCHWIEGENE LIEBE
KEPT-SILENT LOVE

36. SILENT LOVE

Joseph von Eichendorff

Über Wipfel   und Saaten
over (tree-)tops and corn

Over tree-tops
and cornfields,
drawn towards the
splendour - who can
guess them? Who can
catch them? Thoughts
are lulled; the
night keeps silent,
thoughts wander
freely.

In   den Glanz   hinein -
into the gleaming (into)

Wer mag sie erraten,
who may them to guess

Wer holte   sie ein?
who might overtake them -

Gedanken sich   wiegen,
thoughts themselves lull

Die Nacht ist verschwiegen,
the night is   silent

Gedanken sind frei.
thoughts are free

Errät   es nur Eine,
might guess it only one

If only she could
guess who was
thinking of her,
when the trees
rustle in the wood,
when nothing is awake
but the drifting
clouds; my love is
silent, and lovely
as the night.

Wer an   sie gedacht,
who about her thought

Beim   Rauschen der   Haine,
by the rustling of the wood

Wenn niemand mehr wacht,
when no one more is awake

Als die Wolken, die   fliegen,
but the clouds that fly

Mein Lieb ist verschwiegen
my   love is silent

Und schön wie die Nacht.
and lovely as the night

37. DAS STÄNDCHEN
THE SERENADE

37. SERENADE

Joseph von Eichendorff

Auf die Dächer zwischen blassen
on the roofs between pale

From pale clouds
the moon glimmers
over the roof tops;
there in the street
a student sings at
his sweetheart's
door.

Wolken scheint der Mond herfür,
clouds shines the moon forth

Ein Student dort auf der Gassen
a   student there on the street

Singt vor   seiner Liebsten Tür.
sings before of his beloved door

Und die Brunnen rauschen wieder
and the springs rush   again

Durch   die stille Einsamkeit,
through the quiet   solitude

Und der Wald vom   Berge   nieder,
and the wood from the mountain down

Wie in alter, schöner Zeit.
as in old   fair   time

So in meinen jungen Tagen
so in my   young   days

Hab' ich manche Sommernacht
have I   many a summer-night

Auch die Laute hier geschlagen
also the lute here struck

Und manch lust'ges Lied erdacht.
and many a gay   song devised

Aber von der stillen Schwelle
but from the silent threshold

Trugen sie mein Lieb zur   Ruh' -
carried they my   love to the rest

Und du, fröhlicher Geselle,
and you merry   fellow

Singe, sing' nur immerzu!
sing   sing just always

The springs
murmur in the quiet
solitude, and the
woods rustle on the
mountain slopes, as
in fairer days of
old.

Here, too, in my
youth on summer
nights I sang many
a gay serenade to
the sound of my
lute.

But over the
silent threshold
they carried my dear
one to her rest - oh,
sing on, my merry
friend, sing on!

38. NACHTZAUBER
    NIGHT-MAGIC

38. NIGHT MAGIC

Joseph von Eichendorff

Hörst du nicht die Quellen gehen
hear you not   the springs to go

Zwischen Stein und Blumen weit
amongst stone and flowers far

Nach den stillen Waldesseen,
to   the silent   forest-lakes

Wo   die Marmorbilder   stehen
where the marble-statues stand

In der schönen Einsamkeit?
in the lovely   solitude

Von den Bergen   sacht hernieder,
from the mountains softly down

Weckend   die uralten Lieder,
awakening the age-old songs

Steigt die wunderbare Nacht,
climbs the wonderful night

Und die Gründe glänzen wieder,
and the valleys gleam   again

Do you not hear
the streams, flowing
through the stones
and flowers to
far-off silent
forest lakes, where
marble statues
stand in a lovely
solitude? Softly
down from the
mountains, awakening
age-old melodies,
the wondrous night
descends, and the
valleys gleam as so
often in your dreams.

Wie du's   oft   im   Traum gedacht.
as you it often in the dream thought

Kennst die Blume du, entsprossen
know   the flower you out in bud

In dem mondbeglänzten Grund?
in the moon-lit   valley

Aus der Knospe, halb erschlossen,
from the bud   half opened

Junge Glieder blühend   sprossen,
young limbs   blossoming sprang

Weisse Arme, roter Mund.
white arms red   mouth

Und die Nachtigallen schlagen,
and the nightingales sing

Und rings hebt   es an zu klagen,
and around begins it – to to lament

Ach, vor Liebe todeswund,
ah   for love mortally wounded

Von versunken schönen Tagen –
of lost   lovely days

Komm, o komm zum   stillen Grund!
come O come to the quiet   valley

          Do you know the
       flower unfolding in
       the moon-lit valley?
       From the half-open
       bud young limbs
       blossom, white arms,
       red lips. The
       nightingales sing,
       and all around rises
       a lament, a lament
       of mortally wounded
       love, and lovely,
       long-lost days.
       Come, O come to the
       quiet valley!

39. HEIMWEH
   HOMESICKNESS

Joseph von Eichendorff

Wer in   die Fremde   will   wandern,
who into the unknown place wishes to wander

Der muss mit der Liebsten gehn,
he must with the beloved to go

Es   jubeln und lassen die andern
(it) rejoice and leave the others

Den Fremden alleine stehn.
the stranger alone   to be

Was wisset ihr, dunkle Wipfel,
what know   you dark   (tree)-tops

Von der alten, schönen Zeit?
of the old   lovely time

Ach, die Heimat   hinter den Gipfeln,
oh   the homeland behind the mountain-peaks

Wie liegt sie von hier so weit!
how lies it from here so far

39. HOMESICKNESS

          He who journeys
       in far-off lands
       must take with him
       his beloved; there
       each is content on
       his own pleasure,
       and leaves the
       stranger alone.

          What do you
       dark tree-tops know
       of the old, sweet
       days? Oh, how far
       beyond the mountain
       peaks lies my native
       land!

Am   liebsten   betracht' ich die Sterne,
(at the) most gladly look at   I   the stars

Die schienen, wie ich ging zu ihr,
they shone   as   I   went to her

Die Nachtigall hör' ich so gerne,
the nightingale hear I   so gladly

Sie sang vor   der   Liebsten Tür.
she sang before of the dearest door

          I most love to
watch the stars, that
shone as I last went
to her. How gladly I
hear the nightingale
that sang before her
door.

Der Morgen, das ist meine Freude!
the morning that is my   joy

Da   steig' ich in stiller Stund'
then climb I in still   hour

Auf den höchsten Berg   in die Weite,
on the highest mountain into the distance

Grüss dich, Deutschland, aus   Herzensgrund!
greet you   Germany   from the heart's-bottom

          The morning is
my joy, for then,
when all is still,
I climb the highest
far-off peak; then
with my whole heart
I greet you, Germany!

40. *DER RATTENFÄNGER*
THE RAT-CATCHER

40. THE RAT-CATCHER

Johann Wolfgang von Goethe
(also set by Schubert)

Ich bin der wohlbekannte Sänger,
I   am the well-known   singer

Der vielgereiste   Rattenfänger,
the much-journeyed rat-catcher

Den diese altberühmte Stadt
whom this long-famous town

Gewiss besonders nötig   hat.
certainly specially necessary has

          I'm the
well-known minstrel,
the rat-catcher who
journeys everywhere –
and this long-famous
town certainly needs
me!

Und wären's Ratten noch so viele,
and were it rats   still so many

Und wären Wiesel mit im   Spiele,
and were weasel with in the game

Von allen säub'r ich diesen Ort,
of all   clean I   this   place

Sie müssen miteinander   fort.
they must   with one another away

          However many rats
there are, however
many weasles, I can
rid the place of them
all – they'll all be
led away!

Dann ist der gut gelaunte Sänger
then is the good-humoured singer

Mitunter   auch ein Kinderfänger,
occasionally also a   children-catcher

Der selbst die wildesten bezwingt,
who even   the wildest   subdues

Wenn er die gold'nen Märchen   singt.
when he the golden   fairy-tales sings

          I'm a
light-hearted
minstrel and a
child-catcher, too –
even the most unruly
ones are tamed by
my golden
fairy-tales!

Und wären Knaben noch so trutzig,
and were boys   still so defiant

Und wären Mädchen noch so stutzig,
and were girls   still so startled

In meine Saiten greif' ich ein,
in my   strings strike I   -

Sie müssen alle hinterdrein.
they must   all   after (me)

Dann ist der vielgewandte Sänger
then is the versatile   singer

Gelegentlich ein Mädchenfänger;
occasionally a   girl-catcher

In keinem Städtchen   langt   er an,
in no   (little) town arrives he -

Wo   er's nicht mancher angetan.
where he it not   to some bewitched

Und wären Mädchen noch so blöde,
and were girls   still so stupid

Und wären Weiber noch so spröde,
and were women still so coy

Doch allen wird   so liebebang
but   to all becomes so anxious with love

Bei Zaubersaiten und Gesang.
by magic-strings and song

However naughty
the boys, however
shy the girls, I've
only to start
playing, and they
all follow me.

I'm a minstrel
of many skills -
and a girl-catcher,
too! When I reach a
little town I never
fail to catch them.

However timid
the girls, however
coy the women, they
all become love-sick
at the sound of my
magic strings, and
my songs.

41. *KOPHTISCHES LIED I*
    COPTIC   SONG

41. COPTIC SONG I

Johann Wolfgang von Goethe

Lasset Gelehrte   sich   zanken   und streiten,
let   of learning (themselves) to wrangle and to dispute

Streng und bedächtig   die Lehrer   auch sein!
severe and hard thinking the teachers also to be

Alle die Weisesten aller der   Zeiten
all the wisest men of all of the times

Lächeln und winken und stimmen mit   ein:
smile   and nod   and agree   with (them) -

Töricht, auf Bessrung   der   Toren zu harren!
foolish on improvement of the fools to to wait for

Kinder   der   Klugheit, o habet
children of the cleverness 0 (have) (i.e. make)

  die Narren
   the fools

Eben zu   Narren auch, wie sich's   gehört.
just into fools also as itself it is proper

Let pedants
dispute and wrangle;
let scholars be
astute and severe!
The wisest men of all
times nod their
heads with a knowing
smile and agree: it
is foolish to wait
for fools to become
wise! O children of
wisdom make fools
of fools, as is right
and proper.

Merlin der Alte,   im   leuchtenden Grabe,
Merlin the old one in the shining   grave

Wo   ich als Jüngling gesprochen   ihn habe,
where I   as   youth   spoken   (to)him have

Hat mich mit ähnlicher Antwort belehret:
has me   with similar   answer   instructed

Töricht, auf Bessrung   der   Toren zu haren!
foolish on improvement of the fools to to wait for

Kinder der   Klugheit, o habet   die Narren
children of the cleverness 0 (have) (make) the fools

Eben zu   Narren auch, wie sich's   gehört.
just into fools also   as itself it is proper

Und auf den Höhen der   indischen Lüfte
and on the peaks of the Indian   breezes

Und in den Tiefen ägyptischer Grüfte
and in the depths of Egyptian tombs

Hab ich das heilige Wort nur gehört:
have I   the divine word only heard

Töricht, auf Bessrung   der   Toren zu harren!
foolish on improvement of the fools to to wait for

Kinder der   Klugheit, o habet   die Narren
children of the cleverness 0 (have) (make) the fools

Eben zu   Narren auch, wie sich's   gehört.
just into fools also   as itself it is proper

In my youth I
sought Old Merlin
in his shining
cavern. And he gave
me the same counsel:
it is foolish to
wait for fools to
become wise! O
children of wisdom,
make fools of fools,
as is right and proper.

On the wind-swept
peaks of India, and
in the depths of
Egyptian tombs, I
have heard all the
oracles say: it is
foolish to wait for
fools to become wise!
O children of
wisdom, make fools of
fools, as is right
and proper.

42. *KOPHTISCHES LIED II*
   COPTIC   SONG II

42. COPTIC SONG II

Johann Wolfgang von Goethe

Geh! gehorche meinem Winken,
go   obey   to my hints

Nutze deine jungen Tage,
use   your young days

Lerne zeitig klüger sein:
learn in time wiser to be

Auf des   Glückes grosser Waage
on of the fortune great   scales

Steht   die Zunge selten ein;
stands still the tongue seldom -

Du musst steigen oder sinken,
you must to rise or   to sink

Du musst herrschen und gewinnen,
you must to rule   and to win

Oder dienen   und verlieren,
or   to serve and to lose

Leiden   oder triumphieren,
to suffer or   to triumph

Amboss oder Hammer sein.
anvil or   hammer to be

Now! Take my
advice: let your
youth be well-spent.
Learn in good time
to be wise! On the
great scales of
Fortune the finger
is seldom still; you
must rise or you
must fall; you must
win and be master, or
lose and be a slave.
You must suffer or
triumph, be the
anvil or the hammer.

43. EPIPHANIAS
   EPIPHANY

43. EPIPHANY

Johann Wolfgang von Goethe

Die heiligen drei König' mit ihrem Stern,
the holy   three kings with their star

Sie essen, sie trinken und bezahlen nicht gern;
they eat   they drink   and pay   not   gladly

Sie essen gern, sie trinken gern,
they eat   gladly they drink   gladly

Sie essen, trinken und bezahlen nicht gern.
they eat   drink   and pay   not   gladly

The three Wise
Men with their star
like eating and
drinking, but they
don't like paying.

Die heil'gen drei König' sind kommen allhier,
the holy   three kings   are   come   all-here

Es sind ihrer drei und sind nicht ihrer vier:
there are of them three and are not   of them four

Und wenn zu dreien   der vierte wär,
and when to threesome the fourth were

So wär   ein heil'ger Drei-König mehr.
so would be one holy   three-king more

Here come the
three Wise Men, there
are three of them,
not four – and if
a fourth were added
to the three, there
would be one more
Wise Man.

Ich erster bin der weiss und auch der schön,
I first am the white and also the handsome

Bei Tage solltet ihr erst mich sehn!
by day should you first me   to see

Doch ach, mit allen Spezerein,
but oh   with all   spices

Werd ich sein Tag   kein Mädchen mir   erfrein.
will I   its day(s) no   girl   to me to marry

I am the first,
who is handsome and
fair. You should
just see me by day!
But for all my
spices, none of the
girls will ever wed
me.

Ich aber bin der braun und bin der lang,
I but am the brown and am the tall

Bekannt bei Weibern wohl und bei Gesang.
known   by women   well and by song

Ich bringe Gold statt   Spezerein,
I bring gold instead of spices

Da   werd ich überall   willkommen sein.
then will I everywhere welcome   to be

I am the one who
is tall and dark,
well-known for my
ways with women and
song. I bring gold
instead of spices,
so I'll be welcome
everywhere.

Ich endlich bin der schwarz und bin der klein,
I finally am the black   and am the small

Und mag auch wohl   einmal recht lustig sein.
and like also indeed once   very merry to be

Ich esse gern, ich trinke gern,
I eat gladly I drink gladly

Ich esse, trinke und bedanke mich   gern.
I eat   drink   and thank   (myself) gladly

I'm the last one,
black and small. I'd
like to be merry and
gay for once! I like
eating and drinking,
and I thank people
gladly.

Die heiligen drei König' sind wohlgesinnt,
the holy   three kings are well-disposed

Sie suchen die Mutter und das Kind;
they seek   the mother and the child

Der Joseph fromm   sitzt auch dabei,
the Joseph devoutly sits also there

Der Ochs und Esel liegen auf der Streu.
the ox   and ass lie   on the straw

The three Wise Men are in good humour; they're looking for the Mother and her Child; with Joseph sitting devoutly there, and the ox and ass lying on the straw.

Wir bringen Myrrhen, wir bringen Gold,
we bring myrrh   we bring gold

Dem Weihrauch   sind die Damen hold;
to the frankincense are the ladies well-disposed

Und haben wir Wein von gutem Gewächs,
and have we wine of good vintage

So trinken wir drei so gut als ihrer sechs.
so drink   we three so well as of you six

We bring myrrh, and gold, and ladies always like frankincense. And if we're given good wine, we three'll drink like six of you!

Da wir nun hier schöne Herrn   und Fraun,
as we now here fine   gentlemen and ladies

Aber keine Ochsen und Esel schaun,
but no   oxen   and ass see

So sind wir nicht am   rechten Ort,
so are we not in the right place

Und ziehen unseres Weges weiter fort.
and move   our   way   further on

Now, as we can see only gentlefolk here, but no ox and ass, we can't be in the right place, and will go on our way.

44. *GENIALISCH   TREIBEN*
GIFTED WITH GENIUS DOINGS

44. DOINGS OF A GENIUS

Johann Wolfgang von Goethe

So wälz   ich ohne   Unterlass,
so trundle I   without ceasing

Wie Sankt Diogenes, mein Fass.
like Saint Diogenes my   barrel

Bald ist es Ernst,   bald ist es Spass;
now is it seriousness now is it fun

Bald ist es Lieb, bald ist es Hass;
now is it love now is it hate

Bald ist es dies, bald ist es das;
now is it this now is it that

Es ist ein Nichts, und ist ein Was.
it is a   nothing and is a   something

So wälz   ich ohne   Unterlass,
so trundle I   without ceasing

Wie Sankt Diogenes, mein Fass.
like Saint Diogenes my   barrel

I trundle my barrel about all the time, like the good Diogenes. Sometimes grave, sometimes gay; sometimes loving, sometimes hating; now it's this, now it's that; now it's something, now it's nothing. I trundle my barrel about all the time, like the good Diogenes.

45. *BLUMENGRUSS*
FLOWER-GREETING

45. FLOWER GREETING

Johann Wolfgang von Goethe

Der Strauss, den ich gepflücket,
the nosegay that I   gathered

Grüsse   dich viel tausendmal!
let greet you many thousand-times

Ich habe mich   oft   gebücket,
I   have myself often bent down

Ach, wohl   eintausendmal,
ah   indeed a thousand times

Und ihn ans   Herz gedrücket
and him to the heart pressed

Wie hunderttausendmal!
how hundred-thousand-times

With this
nosegay I have
gathered, I send you
a thousand greetings!
Often have I stooped
down - oh, a thousand
times, and pressed
the flowers to my
heart; how many
hundred thousand
times!

46. *DIE SPRÖDE*
THE COY ONE

46. THE PERT
SHEPHERDESS

Johann Wolfgang von Goethe

An dem reinsten Frühlingsmorgen
on the clearest spring-morning

Ging   die Schäferin   und sang,
walked the shepherdess and sang

Jung und schön und ohne   Sorgen,
young and pretty and without cares

Dass es durch   die Felder klang,
that it through the fields rang

So la-la! le-ral-la-la!
tra-la-la le-ral-la-la

On a fair spring
morning, a pretty
young ,shepherdess
went her carefree
way, singing through
the fields,
tra-la-la, ra-la-la!

Thyrsis bot   ihr   für ein Mäulchen
Thyrsis offered to her for a   kiss

Zwei, drei Schäfchen gleich   am   Ort,
two   three lambs   instantly on the spot

Schalkhaft blickte sie ein Weilchen;
roguishly looked she a   little while

Doch sie sang und lachte fort:
but she sang and laughed on

So la-la! le-ral-la-la!
tra-la-la le-ral-la-la

Thyrsis came and
offered her two or
three lambs for a
kiss. She looked at
him artfully for a
while, but went on
singing and
laughing, tra-la-la,
ra-la-la!

Und ein andrer bot   ihr Bänder,
and another   offered her ribbons

Und der dritte bot   sein Herz;
and the third offered his   heart

Doch sie trieb mit Herz und Bändern
but she made with heart and ribbons

So wie mit den Lämmern   Scherz,
so as with the little lambs jest

Nur la-la! le-ral-la-la!
only la-la   le-ral-la-la

And another
offered her ribbons,
and a third his
heart, but she
laughed at the
ribbons and at his
heart, as she had
laughed at the
lambs, just
tra-la-la, ra-la-la!

---

47. DIE BEKEHRTE
THE CONVERT

47. THE SHEPHERDESS
BEWITCHED

Johann Wolfgang von Goethe

Bei dem Glanz der   Abendröte
in the gleam of the sunset

Ging   ich still   den Wald entlang,
walked I   silently the wood through

Damon sass und blies die Flöte,
Damon sat and blew the flute

Dass es von den Felsen klang,
that it from the rocks rang

So la-la! ral-la-la!
tra-la-la ral-la-la

In the red glow
of sunset, I passed
silently through the
wood. Damon sat
playing his flutè,
so it echoed from
the rocks, tra-la-la,
ra-la-la!

Und er zog mich zu sich   nieder,
and he drew me   to himself down

Küsste mich so hold,   so süss,
kissed me   so charmingly so sweetly

Und ich sagte: "blase wieder!"
and I   said   blow again

Und der gute Junge blies,
and the dear youth played

So la-la! ral-la-la!
tra la-la ral-la-la

And he drew me
down to him, and
gently, sweetly
kissed me. Then I
said, 'Play again!'
And the tender youth
played, tra-la-la,
ra-la-la!

Meine Ruh   ist nun verloren,
my   peace is now lost

Meine Freude floh davon,
my   joy   fled away

Und ich hör vor   meinen Ohren
and I   hear before my   ears

Immer nur den alten Ton,
always only the old   sound

So la-la, ral-la-la!
tra-la-la ral-la-la

Now my peace is
gone, my joy has
fled, and in my ears
I only hear the old
melody, tra-la-la,
ra-la-la!

48. *FRÜHLING ÜBERS JAHR*
SPRING   OVER THE YEAR

48. SOVEREIGN SPRING

Johann Wolfgang von Goethe

Das Beet,   schon   lockert
the flower-bed already loosens

Sichs   in die Höhe!
itself it - upwards -

Da   wanken Glöckchen,
there wave   little bells

So weiss wie Schnee;
so white as snow

Safran entfaltet
saffron unfolds

Gewaltge Glut,
intense glow

Smaragden keimt   es
emerald   springs up it

Und keimt   wie Blut;
and springs up like blood

Primeln stolzieren
primroses flaunt

So naseweis,
so saucily

Schalkhafte Veilchen,
roguish   violets

Versteckt mit Fleiss;
hidden   with diligence

Was auch noch alles
what also still everything

Da   regt und webt,
there stirs and weaves

Genug, der Frühling,
enough the spring

Er wirkt und lebt.
it works and lives

The flower-bed
is swelling up with
life! Little bells
tremble, as white as
snow; saffron unfolds
a glowing radiance;
emerald shoots
spring forth, and
buds blood-red;
primroses flaunt
their saucy heads,
and roguish violets
diligently hide.
Indeed everything
around is stirring
and growing - spring
is at work and alive!

Doch was im   Garten
yet what in the garden

Am   reichsten blüht,
(at) the richest   blossoms

Das ist des   Liebchens
that is of the beloved

Lieblich Gemüt.
sweet   disposition

Da   glühen Blicke
there glow   glances

Mir immerfort,
to me continually

Erregend Liedchen,
stirring little songs

But the richest
blossom in the
garden is my sweet
beloved. My heart
is warmed by her
glances, her gay
little songs, her
cheering words. An
ever-open,
blossoming spirit,
serious but smiling,
innocent in jest.
Summer may bring
roses and lilies, but
it vies in vain with
my beloved.

Erheiternd Wort.
cheering   word

Ein immer offen,
an always open

Ein Blütenherz,
a   blossom-heart

Im   Ernste   freundlich
in the earnestness cheerful

Und rein im   Scherz,
and pure in the jest

Wenn Ros und Lilie
when rose and lily

Der Sommer bringt,
the summer brings

Er doch vergebens
he yet in vain

Mit Liebchen ringt.
with sweetheart struggles

49. *ANAKREONS GRAB*   49. ANACREON'S GRAVE
    ANACREON'S GRAVE

Johann Wolfgang von Goethe

Wo   die Rose hier blüht, wo   Reben um   Lorbeer
where the rose here blooms where vines round laurel

sich   schlingen, wo   das Turtelchen
themselves wind   where the (little) turtle-dove

lockt, wo   sich   das Grillchen   ergötzt, welch
coaxes where (himself) the little cricket delights what

ein Grab ist hier, das alle Götter mit Leben
a   grave is here that all gods   with life
 schön
 beautifully

bepflanzt und geziert? Es ist Anakreons Ruh.
planted   and adorned it is Anacreon's resting-place

Frühling, Sommer und Herbst genoss der glückliche
spring   summer and autumn enjoyed the fortunate

Dichter; vor   dem Winter hat ihn endlich der
poet   against the winter has him finally the

Hügel geschützt.
hillock sheltered

Here where roses
bloom and vines cling
to the laurels, where
turtle-doves call,
and the little
cricket plays –
whose grave is this,
so beautifully
adorned with life by
the gods? It is
Anacreon's resting
place. Spring, summer
and autumn delighted
this most favoured of
poets, until this
hillock finally gave
him shelter from
winter.

50. *PROMETHEUS*
PROMETHEUS

50. PROMETHEUS

Johann Wolfgang von Goethe
(also set by Schubert)

Bedecke deinen Himmel, Zeus,
cover   your   sky   Zeus

Mit Wolkendunst
with clouds-haze

Und übe,   dem   Knaben gleich,
and practice to the boy   like

Der Disteln köpft,
who thistles beheads

An Eichen dich   und Bergeshöhn;
to oaks   (yourself) and mountain-tops

Musst mir   meine Erde
must to me my   earth

Doch   lassen stehn
indeed to let to stay

Und meine Hütte, die du nicht gebaut,
and my   hut   that you not   built

Und meinen Herd,
and my   hearth

Um   dessen Glut
about whose glow

Du mich beneidest.
you me   envy

Cover your heavens
with a haze of clouds,
O Zeus, and try your
strength on oak trees
and mountain tops,
like a boy knocking off
thistle heads! But
leave my world
untouched! Leave my
dwelling, that your
hands did not build,
and my hearth whose
warmth you envy!

Ich kenne nichts   Ärmeres
I   know - nothing more wretched -

Unter der Sonn', als euch, Götter!
under the sun   than you gods

Ihr nähret kümmerlich
you feed   pityfully

Von Opfersteuern
from sacrifice-dues

Und Gebetshauch
and prayer's-breath

Eure Majestät
your majesty

Und darbtet,   wären
and would starve were

Nicht Kinder   und Bettler
not   children and beggars

Hoffnungsvolle Toren.
hopeful   fools

I know of nothing
under the sun so
wretched as you gods!
Pitifully you feed
your majesty on
sacrificial offerings
and the breath of
prayers, and you
would starve, if
children and beggars
were not such hopeful
fools.

Da   ich ein Kind war,
when I   a   child was

Nicht wusste, wo   aus noch ein,
not knew   (where) outs nor ins

Kehrt' ich mein verirrtes Auge
turned I   my   bewildered eye

Zur   Sonne, als wenn drüber wär'
to the sun   as if   beyond were

Ein Ohr, zu hören   meine Klage,
an ear to to hear my   lament

Ein Herz wie meins,
a   heart like mine

Sich des   Bedrängten   zu erbarmen.
itself of the afflicted one to to pity

    When I was a child,
not knowing which way
to turn, I gazed
bewildered towards the
sun, as if there beyond
were someone to hear
my cry, a heart like
mine to pity me in my
distress.

Wer half   mir
who helped me

Wider   der   Titanen Übermut?
against of the Titans arrogance

Wer rettete vom   Tode mich,
who saved from the death me

Von Sklaverei?
from slavery

Hast du nicht alles   selbst vollendet,
have you not   everything yourself accomplished

Heilig glühend Herz?
holy   glowing heart

Und glühtest jung   und gut,
and glowed   youthfully and well

Betrogen, Rettungsdank
deceived saving-thank(s)

Dem   Schlafenden da   droben?
to the sleeping-one there above

    But who came to my
aid against the
arrogant Titans? Who
saved me from death
and slavery? Was it
not my own divine fire
that accomplished all
this? And yet in its
delusion did my pure
young heart not glow
with gratitude to the
sleeper up above for
my deliverance?

Ich dich ehren? Wofür?
I   you honour what for

Hast du die Schmerzen gelindert
have you the pains   allayed

Je des   Beladenen?
ever of the burdened one

Hast du die Tränen gestillet
have you the tears   soothed

Je des   Geängsteten?
ever of the frightened one

    I honour you? For
what? When did you
ever relieve the
anguish and the burdens
of men? When did you
ever dry their
frightened tears?

Hat nicht mich zum Manne geschmiedet
has not   me to the man   forged

Die allmächtige Zeit
the almighty   time

Und das ewige   Schicksal,
and the everlasting destiny

Meine Herrn und deine?
my   masters and yours

    Was I not forged
into manhood by
almighty Time and
everlasting Destiny –
my masters, and yours?

Wähntest du etwa,
thought you perhaps

Ich sollte das Leben hassen,
I should the life to hate

In Wüsten fliehen,
in wildernesses to flee

Weil nicht alle
because not all

Blütenträume reiften?
blossom-dreams matured

Hier sitz' ich, forme Menschen
here sit I form men

Nach meinem Bilde,
after my image

Ein Geschlecht, das mir gleich sei,
a race that to me similar be

Zu leiden, zu weinen,
to to suffer to to weep

Zu geniessen und zu freuen sich,
to to enjoy and to to rejoice itself

Und dein nicht zu achten,
and of you not to respect

Wie ich!
as I

Perhaps you thought
I would grow to hate
life, and flee into
the wilderness,
because not all my
dreams were fulfilled?

Here I sit, making
men in my own image;
a race of people who
like me shall suffer
and weep, rejoice and
be happy - despising
you as I do!

51. *GRENZEN DER MENSCHHEIT*
LIMITATIONS OF THE MANKIND

51. LIMITATIONS OF
MANKIND

Johann Wolfgang von Goethe
(also set by Schubert)

Wenn der uralte.
when the ancient

Heilige Vater
Holy Father

Mit gelassener Hand
with patient hand

Aus rollenden Wolken
from rolling clouds

Segnende Blitze
blessing flashes of lightning

Über die Erde sät,
over the earth sows

Küss' ich den letzten
kiss I the extreme

Saum seines Kleides,
hem of his robe

Kindliche Schauer
childlike awe

When the Eternal
Father, with his slow
and patient hand,
scatters his lightning
flashes from rolling
clouds in blessing
over the earth, I kiss
the lowest hem of his
garment with a
childlike awe, faith
in my heart.

Treu in der Brust.
true in the breast

Denn mit Göttern
for with gods

                                                       Let no man measure
himself against the
gods! If he reaches up
to touch the stars,
his unsure feet find
no hold, and he
becomes the plaything
of the winds and
clouds.

Soll sich   nicht messen
shall himself not   to measure

Irgendein Mensch.
any   man

Hebt er sich   aufwärts
rises he (himself) upwards

Und berührt
and touches

Mit dem Scheitel   die Sterne,
with the crown (of his head) the stars

Nirgends haften dann
nowhere cling then

Die unsichern Sohlen,
the unsure   soles

Und mit ihm spielen,
and with him play

Wolken und Winde.
clouds and winds

Steht er mit festen
stands he with firm

                                                       But if he stands
fast and secure on the
firm, enduring earth,
his meagre stature
cannot even compare
with that of the oak
or the vine.

Markigen Knochen
marrow bones

Auf der wohlgegründeten
on the well-founded

Dauernden Erde,
lasting   earth

Reicht er nicht auf,
reaches he not   up

Nur mit der Eiche
only with the oak

Oder der Rebe
or   the vine

Sich   zu vergleichen.
himself to to compare

Was unterscheidet
what distinguishes

                                                       What distinguishes
gods from men? Before
the gods, unceasing
waves roll on in
never-ending
succession. But we are
tossed by the waves;
we are swallowed up
and founder.

Götter von Menschen?
gods   from men

Dass viele Wellen
that many waves

Vor   jenen wandeln,
before those go

Ein ewiger Strom:
an eternal stream

Uns hebt die Welle,
us raises the wave

Verschlingt die Welle,
devours   the wave

Und wir versinken.
and we founder

Ein kleiner Ring   Our life is bound
a   little ring   by a little ring. And
                                                      countless generations
Begrenzt unser Leben,   succeed each other,
bounds   our   life   mere links in the
                                                      endless chain of their
Und viele Geschlechter   existence.
and many generations

Reihen sich   dauernd
rank   themselves continuously

An ihres   Daseins
in of their being

Unendliche Kette.
unending   chain

52. From *SPANISCHES LIEDERBUCH*   52. From SPANISH SONGBOOK
         SPANISH   SONGBOOK

Translations of Spanish folksongs into German
by Emmanuel Geibel and Paul Heyse

From *Geistliche Lieder*   From Sacred Songs
      sacred   songs

   iii.   iii.

(Der heilige Joseph singt:)   (Joseph sings:)
 the holy   Joseph sings   Let us keep on,
                                                    Mary, let us keep on.
Nun wandre Maria,   Already the cock is
Now go   Mary   crowing and the little
                                                    town is near.
Nun wandre nur fort.
now go   only on

Schon   krähen die Hähne,
already crow   the cocks

Und nah ist der Ort.
and near is the town

Nun wandre, Geliebte,   Let us keep on, my
now go   love   love, my treasure, and
                                                    soon we shall be in
Du Kleinod mein.   Bethlehem. There you
you treasure my   will find sweet rest
                                                    and sleep. Already
Und balde wir werden   the cock is crowing
and soon 'we shall   and the little town is
                                                    near.
In Bethlehem sein.
in Bethlehem to be

Dann ruhest du fein
then rest   you well

Und schlummerst dort.
and slumber   there

Schon   krähen   die Hähne
already are crowing the cocks

Und nah ist der Ort.
and near is the town

Wohl   seh ich, Herrin,
indeed see I   lady

Die Kraft   dir   schwinden;
the strength to you to vanish

Kann deine Schmerzen,
can your pains

Ach, kaum   verwinden.
ah   scarcely to overcome

Getrost!   Wohl finden
(be) of good cheer surely find

Wir Herberg dort.
we shelter there

Schon   krähen die Hähne
already crow the cocks

Und nah ist der Ort.
and near is the town

I see your strength
fading, dear wife; oh,
I can hardly bear to
see your pain. Take
courage! We will surely
find shelter there.
Already the cock is
crowing, and the little
town is near.

Wär erst bestanden
were only passed through

Dein Stündlein,   Marie,
your (little) hour Mary

Die gute Botschaft,
the good message

Gut lohnt   ich sie.
well would repay I her

Das Eselein   hie
the (little) ass here

Gäb   ich drum   fort!
would give I for that away

Schon krähen   die Hähne,
already are crowing the cocks

Komm! Nah ist der Ort.
come near is the town

If only your time
were over, Mary – I
would give much for
good tidings. I
would gladly give this
little ass! Already the
cock is crowing. Come!
The little town is
near.

iv.

iv.

Die ihr schwebet
who you hover

Um   diese Palmen
round these palms

In Nacht und Wind,
in night and wind

Ihr heil'gen Engel,
you holy   angels

Stillet die Wipfel!
hush   the tree-tops

Es   schlummert mein Kind.
(it) slumbers my   child

You angels,
hovering around the
palm trees in the
night wind – hush
the rustling leaves,
for my Child is
sleeping!

Ihr Palmen von Bethlehem
you palms of Bethlehem

In   Windesbrausen,
in the winds-blustering

Wie mögt   ihr heute
how are able you today

So zornig sausen!
so angrily to sough

O rauscht nicht also!
Oh rustle not   so

Schweiget, neiget
be silent bow

Euch   leis' und lind;
yourselves softly and gently

Stillet die Wipfel!
hush   the tree-tops

Es   schlummert mein Kind.
(it) slumbers   my   child

Der Himmelsknabe
the Heaven's-boy

Duldet Beschwerde,
bears burden

Ach, wie so müd' er ward
oh how so weary he was

Vom   Leid   der   Erde.
of the sorrow of the earth

Ach nun im   Schlaf ihm
oh now in the sleep to him

Leise gesänftigt
softly mitigated

Die Qual zerrint,
the pain disappears

Stillet ihr Wipfel!
hush   you tree-tops

Es   schlummert mein Kind.
(it) sleeps   my   child

Grimmige Kälte
fierce   cold

Sauset   hernieder;
blows hard down

Womit   nur deck' ich
with what only cover I

Des   Kindleins Glieder!
of the child   limbs

O all ihr Engel,
O all you angels

Die ihr geflügelt
who you winged

Wandelt im   Wind,
wander in the wind

You palms of
Bethlehem, how can you
sway so angrily in the
blustering wind on
this day. Oh, please
do not rustle! Be
still, and lean gently,
quietly down. Hush
the rustling leaves,
for my Child is
sleeping!

The Son of Heaven
has such grief to
bear. Oh, how weary
he is of the sorrowing
world. But now this
pain is eased in
quiet sleep – hush
the rustling leaves,
for my Child is
sleeping!

Cold winds blow
fiercely – with what
can I cover my
Child's limbs? O all
you winged angels
soaring on the wind –
hush the rustling
leaves, for my
Child is sleeping!

Stillet die Wipfel!
hush   the tree-tops

Es   schlummert mein Kind.
(it) slumbers   my   child

        vi.   vi.

Ach, des   Knaben Augen sind   Oh, this boy's
oh   of the boy   eyes   are   eyes are so clear and
                                          lovely, and they have
Mir   so schön und klar erschienen,   a strange radiance
to me so lovely and clear appeared   that wholly wins my
                                          heart.
Und ein Etwas   strahlt aus ihnen,
and a   something radiates from them

Das mein ganzes Herz gewinnt.
that my   whole   heart wins

Blickt' er doch mit diesen süssen   If with those
looked he but with these sweet   sweet eyes he should
                                          look into mine, and
Augen nach den meinen hin!   see his image there,
eyes to   the mine thither   would he then give me
                                          a loving smile?
Säh'   er dann sein Bild darin,
would see he then his image therein

Würd er wohl   mich liebend grüssen.
would he perhaps me   lovingly to greet

Und so geb' ich ganz   mich   hin,   And so I give my
and so give I   wholly myself up   very soul to follow
                                          and serve those eyes,
Seinen Augen nur zu dienen,   for they have a
his   eyes only to to serve   strange radiance, that
                                          wholly wins my heart.
Denn ein Etwas   strahlt aus ihnen,
for a   something shines from them

Das mein ganzes Herz gewinnt.
that my   whole   heart wins

        ix.   ix.

Herr, was trägt der Boden hier,   Lord, what will
Lord what bears the soil here   this soil bear
                                          watered by your bitter
Den du   tränkst so bitterlich?   tears? 'Thorns, dear
that you water   so bitterly   heart, for me, and to
                                          adorn you, flowers.'
"Dornen, liebes Herz für mich,
thorns dear   heart for me

Und für dich der   Blumen Zier."
and for you of the flowers adornment

Ach, wo   solche Bäche rinnen,   Oh, can a garden
oh   where such brooks flow   thrive, where such
                                          streams are flowing?
Wird ein Garten da   gedeihn?   'Yes, do you see —
will a   garden then to thrive   there they will twine
                                          crowns and garlands,
"Ja, und wisse! Kränzelein   of such different
yes and know   little garlands   kinds.'

Gar verschiedne, flicht man drinnen."
very different   twines one in there

O mein Herr, zu wessen Zier
O my   Lord to whose adornment

Windet man die Kränze? Sprich!
twines one the garlands say

"Die   von Dornen sind für mich,
"those of thorns are for me

Die   von Blumen reich ich dir."
those of flowers give I   to you

O my Lord, say
for whose adornment
do tney twine the
garlands and wreaths?
'Those of thorns are
for me — I'll give you
those of flowers.'

From *Weltliche Lieder*
    secular   songs

Secular Songs

i.

i.

Klinge, klinge mein Pandero,
sound   sound my tambourine

Doch an   andres   denkt mein Herz.
but about something else thinks my   heart

    Sound, sound, my
tambourine — but my
thoughts are elsewhere.

Wenn du, muntres Ding,   verständest,
if   you merry creature would understand

Meine Qual   und sie empfändest,
my   torment and her would feel

Jeder Ton, den du entsendest,
every note that you send off

Würde klagen   meinen Schmerz.
would to lament my   sorrow

    If you who are so
merry could
understand my torment,
every note you played
would be a sad lament.

Bei des   Tanzes Drehn   und Neigen
to of the dance   twirling and bowing

Schlag ich wild   den Takt zum   Reigen,
beat I   wildly the time to the dance

Dass nur die Gedanken schweigen,
that only the thoughts are silent

Die mich mahnen an den Schmerz.
that me   remind of the grief

    I beat the wild
rhythm of the
sweeping, twirling
dances to silence the
thoughts that remind
me of my grief.

Ach, ihr Herrn,   dann will im   Schwingen
ah   you gentlemen then wants in the whirling round

Oftmals mir   die Brust zerspringen,
often   to me the breast to break

Und zum   Angstschrei wird mein Singen,
and to the cry of anguish becomes my   singing

Denn an   andres   denkt mein Herz.
for about something else thinks my   heart

    Oh, you fine folk,
so often in your
whirling dance my
heart could break,
and my song becomes
a cry of anguish —
for my thoughts are
elsewhere.

ii.

ii.

In dem Schatten meiner Locken
in the shadow of my locks

Schlief   mir mein Geliebter ein.
fell asleep to me my   lover   —

Weck ich ihn nun auf? Ach nein!
wake I   him now up   oh no

    In the shadow of
my locks my lover fell
asleep. Shall I wake
him? Oh, no!

Sorglich strählt ich meine krausen
carefully combed I my curly

Locken täglich in der Frühe,
locks daily in the early morning

Doch umsonst ist meine Mühe,
but for nothing is my trouble

Weil die Winde sie zerzausen.
because the winds them dishevel

Lockenschatten, Windessausen
locks'-shadow wind's-blustering

Schläferten den Liebsten ein.
lulled to sleep the dearest —

Weck ich ihn nun auf? Ach nein!
wake I him now up oh no

Hören muss ich, wie ihn gräme,
to hear must I how him grieved

Dass er schmachtet schon so lange,
that he languishes already so long

Dass ihm Leben geb und nehme
that to him life gave and took

Diese meine braune Wange,
this my brown cheek

Und er nennt mich seine Schlange,
and he calls me his serpent

Und doch schlief er bei mir ein.
and yet fell asleep he near me —

Weck ich ihn nun auf? Ach nein!
wake I him now up oh no

Early each morning
I comb my locks so
carefully, but all for
nothing, for the wind
only tousles them. The
shadow of my locks,
and the soughing of
the wind have lulled
my dearest one to
sleep. Shall I wake
him? Oh, no!

I have to hear
how much he pines, how
long he has
languished, how my
brown cheeks are life
and death to him. And
he calls me a
serpent — yet he falls
asleep beside me!
Shall I wake him? Oh,
no!

v.

Auf dem grünen Balkon mein Mädchen
on the green balcony my girl

Schaut nach mir durchs Gitterlein.
looks at me through the (little) lattice

Mit den Augen blinzelt sie freundlich,
with the eyes twinkles she in a friendly way

Mit dem Finger sagt sie mir: Nein!
with the finger says she to me no

Glück, das nimmer ohne Wanken
fortune that never without wavering

Junger Liebe folgt hienieden,
to young love follows here below

Hat mir eine Lust beschieden,
has me a joy given

Und auch da noch muss ich schwanken.
and also there still must I to waver

Schmeicheln hör' ich oder Zanken,
caressing hear I or quarrelling

Komm' ich an ihr Fensterlädchen.
come I to her (little) window-shutters

Immer nach dem Brauch der Mädchen
always after the custom of the girls

v.

From her green
balcony my
sweetheart peeps at
me through the lattice.
Her twinkling eyes
encourage me, but her
finger says no!

Fortune, that
never lets young
love follow a smooth
path, has favoured
me, and yet has given
me doubts. I hear
caresses and quarrels
when I come to her
shuttered window. It's
always so with girls —
the happiness is
always tinged a little
with pain. Her
twinkling eyes
encourage me, but her
finger says no!

Träuft ins Glück ein bisschen Pein:
drips into the happiness a little bit pain

Mit den Augen blinzelt sie freundlich,
with the eyes twinkles she in a friendly way

Mit dem Finger sagt sie mir: Nein!
with the finger says she to me no

Wie sich   nur in ihr vertragen
how (themselves) only in her agree

Ihre Kälte, meine Glut?
her coldness my passion

Weil in ihr mein Himmel ruht,
because in her my heaven rests

Seh' ich Trüb und Heil sich jagen.
see I gloom and happiness themselves to pursue

In den Wind gehn meine Klagen,
into the wind go my laments

Dass noch nie die süsse Kleine
that as yet never the sweet little one

Ihre Arme schlange um meine;
her arms entwined about mine

Doch sie hält mich hin so fein –
indeed she holds me off so well

Mit den Augen blinzelt sie freundlich,
with the eyes twinkles she in a friendly way

Mit dem Finger sagt sie mir: Nein!
with the finger says she to me no

However can they
be reconciled in her –
my hot passion and her
coldness? Because she
is my heaven, I see a
despondency and
happiness pursue each
other. Away on the wind
is borne my lament
that the arms of my
little one never
entwined me. She holds
me off so artfully –
her twinkling eyes
encourage me, but her
finger says no!

  vi.   vi.

Wenn du zu den Blumen gehst,
when you to the flowers go

Pflücke die schönsten, dich zu schmücken.
pluck the most beautiful yourself to to adorn

Ach, wenn du in dem Gärtlein stehst,
oh when you in the (little)garden are

Müsstest du dich selber pflücken.
would have to you – yourself – to pluck

When you walk
amongst the flowers,
pluck the loveliest
for your adornment.
Oh, if you were in the
garden, you would be
the one to be plucked!

Alle Blumen wissen ja,
all flowers know indeed

Dass du hold bist ohne gleichen.
that you lovely are without equal

Und die Blume, die dich sah –
and the flower that you saw

Farb' und Schmuck muss ihr erbleichen.
colour and adornment must to her to grow pale

Wenn du zu den Blumen gehst,
when you to the flowers go

Pflücke die schönsten, dich zu schmücken.
pluck the most beautiful yourself to to adorn

Ach, wenn du in dem Gärtlein stehst,
oh when you in the (little garden) are

Müsstest du dich selber pflücken.
would have to you – yourself – to pluck

All the flowers
can see that you are
lovely beyond compare;
any flower looking at
you must fade and
lose her lustre. When
you walk amongst the
flowers... etc.

Lieblicher als Rosen sind
lovelier   than roses are

Die Küsse, die dein Mund verschwendet,
the kisses that your mouth lavishes

Weil   der Reiz der   Blumen endet,
because the charm of the flowers ends

Wo   dein Liebreiz erst beginnt.
where your charm   just begins

Wenn du zu den Blumen gehst,
when you to the flowers go

Pflücke die schönsten,   dich   zu schmücken.
pluck the most beautiful yourself to to adorn

Ach, wenn du in dem Gärtlein   stehst,
oh   when you in the (little) garden are

Müsstest   du dich selber pflücken.
would have to you – yourself – to pluck

Lovelier than
roses are the kisses
lavished by your lips;
the charm of flowers
ends where yours is
just beginning. When
you walk amongst the
flowers... etc.

xiii.

Mögen alle bösen   Zungen
may   all malicious tongues

Immer sprechen was beliebt,
always to say   what pleases (them)

Wer mich liebt, den lieb ich wieder,
who me loves him love I   in return

Und ich lieb und bin geliebt.
and I   love and am loved

All those
spiteful tongues may
say what they please;
I love him, and he
loves me – I love and
am loved.

Schlimme, schlimme Reden flüstern
wicked   wicked   words whisper

Eure Zungen schonungslos,
your tongues pitilessly

Doch ich weiss es, sie sind lüstern
but I   know it they are lustful

Nach unschuld'gem Blute bloss.
for innocent   blood only

Nimmer soll es mich bekümmern,
never shall it me   to trouble

Schwatzt so viel es euch   beliebt;
gossip   so much it to you pleases

Wer mich liebt, den lieb ich wieder,
who me   loves him love I   in return

Und ich lieb und bin geliebt.
and I   love and am loved

Pitilessly your
tongues whisper such
wicked, wicked words.
But I know you only
lust for innocent
blood. However much
you like to gossip,
it will never
trouble me; I love
him, and he loves
me – I love and am
loved.

Zur   Verleumdung sich   verstehet
to the slander   (himself) understands well

Nur, wem   Lieb und Gunst   gebrach,
only to whom love and affection lacked

Weil's   ihm   selber elend   gehet
because it to him himself wretchedly goes

Und ihn niemand minnt und mag.
and him no one loves and likes

Slander only
comes from those who
know no kindness and
affection, and no one
loves or wants them.
I am proud of the love
that they despise; I
love him, and he
loves me – I love and
am loved.

Darum   denk ich, dass die Liebe,
therefore think I   that the love

Drum   sie schmähn, mir Ehre   gibt;
about that they despise to me honour gives

Wer mich liebt, den lieb ich wieder,
who me   loves him love I   in return

Und ich lieb und bin geliebt.
and I   love and am loved

Wenn ich wär aus   Stein und Eisen,
if   I   were out of stone and iron

Möchtet   ihr darauf bestehn,
would like you thereon to insist

Dass ich sollte von mir weisen
that I   should from me to direct

Liebesgruss   und Liebesflehn.
love's greeting and love's-entreating

Doch mein Herzlein   ist nun leider
but my   (little) heart is now unfortunately

Weich, wie's Gott uns Mädchen gibt,
tender how it God to us girls   gives

Wer mich liebt, den lieb ich wieder,
who me   loves him love I   again

Und ich lieb und bin geliebt.
and I   love and am loved

If I were made
of stone and iron,
you would expect me
to turn away love's
entreaties and
caresses; but my
heart is tender –
tender as God makes
a maiden's heart. I
love him, and he
loves me – I love and
am loved.

xxi.

Alle gingen, Herz, zur   Ruh,
all went   heart to the rest

Alle schlafen, nur nicht du.
all sleep   only not you

Denn der hoffnungslose Kummer
for the hopeless   grief

Scheucht   von deinem Bett den Schlummer,
frightens away from your bed the slumber

Und dein Sinnen   schweift in stummer
and your thinking strays   in silent

Sorge seiner Liebe zu.
sorrow to its love (to)

xxi.

All things have
gone to their rest,
my heart; all sleep
but you.

For hopeless
grief drives slumber
from your bed, and
your thoughts stray
in quiet sorrow to
your love.

xxiv.

Bedeckt mich mit Blumen,
cover   me   with flowers

Ich sterbe   vor Liebe.
I   am dying of love

Dass die Luft mit leisem Wehen
that the breeze with gentle blowing

Nicht den süssen Duft mir   entführe,
not   the sweet scent to me may carry away

Bedeckt mich!
cover   me

xxiv.

Cover me with
flowers, for I am
dying of love!

So the gently
blowing breeze does
not carry the sweet
scent away, cover
me!

Ist ja   alles   doch   dasselbe,
is indeed everything (indeed) the same

Liebesodem   oder Düfte
love's-breath or   scents

Von Blumen.
of flowers

Are they not
indeed the same,
breath of love, or
scent of flowers?

Von Jasmin und weissen Lilien
of jasmine and white   lilies

Sollt ihr hier mein Grab bereiten,
shall you here my   grave to prepare

Ich sterbe.
I   am dying

Prepare my
grave here with
jasmine and white
lilies, for I am
dying.

Und befragt ihr mich: Woran?
and question you me   what of

Sag ich: unter süssen Qualen
say I   under sweet   torments

Vor Liebe.
of love

And if you ask,
of what? I will say,
of the sweet pangs of
love!

xxxiv.

xxxiv.

Geh', Geliebter, geh' jetzt!
go   darling   go   now

Sieh, der Morgen dämmert.
see   the morning dawns

Go, my darling,
go now - see the
dawn is breaking!

Leute gehn schon durch die Gasse,
people walk already through the street

Und der Markt wird   so belebt,
and the market is becoming so bustling

Dass der Morgen wohl, der blasse,
that the morning indeed the pale (one)

Schon die weissen Flügel hebt.
already the white   wings lifts

Und vor   unserm Nachbarn bin ich
and before our   neighbours am I

Bange, dass du Anstoss gibst;
afraid that you shock   give

Denn sie wissen nicht, wie innig
for they know   not   how fervently

Ich dich lieb' und du mich liebst.
I   you love and you me   love

People are
already in the
street, and the
market begins to
bustle. The pale
morning already lifts
its white wings, and
I am afraid the
neighbours will be
shocked. They cannot
know how deeply I
love you, and you
love me.

Drum,   Geliebter, geh' jetzt!
therefore beloved   go   now

Sieh, der Morgen dämmert.
see   the morning dawns

Therefore, my
darling, go now -
see the dawn is
breaking!

Wenn die Sonn' am   Himmel scheinend
when the sun   in the sky   shining

Scheucht vom   Feld die Perlen klar,
scares   from the field the pearls clear

Muss auch ich die Perle weinend
must also I   the pearl weeping

Lassen,   die mein Reichtum war.
part with that my   wealth   was

Was als Tag den   andern funkelt,
what as day to the others sparkles

Meinen Augen dünkt es Nacht,
to my eyes seems it night

Da die Trennung   bang   mir   dunkelt,
as the separation afraid to me grows dark

Wenn das Morgenrot erwacht.
when the dawn   awakes

Geh', Geliebter, geh' jetzt!
go   darling   go   now

Sieh, der Morgen dämmert.
see   the morning dawns

Fliehe denn aus meinen Armen!
flee   then from my   arms

Denn versäumest du die Zeit,
for   let slip   you the time

Möchten für ein kurz Erwarmen,
would   for a   short warming

Wir ertauschen langes Leid.
we to exchange long   sorrow

Ist in Fegefeuersqualen
is in purgatory's-torments

Doch ein Tag schon   auszustehn,
yet   one day already to to endure

Wenn die Hoffnung fern in Strahlen
when the hope   afar in rays

Lässt des   Himmels Glorie sehn.
lets of the heaven   glory to see

Drum   Geliebter, geh' jetzt!
therefore darling   go   now

Sieh, der Morgen dämmert.
see   the morning dawns

When the bright
sun in the sky
chases the clear
pearls from the
fields, must I,
weeping, give up my
pearl too, that was
my treasure.

What to others
is radiant daylight,
to my eyes seems as
night; for when the
dawn awakes, our
separation makes me
darkly anxious.

Go my darling,
go now – see the
dawn is breaking!

Flee then from
my arms! For if you
let the time slip
by, a short tender
hour would become a
long time of sorrow.
Can we endure one
single day in the
torments of
purgatory, when a
distant glimpse of
hope shows us
Heaven's glory?

Therefore, my
darling, go now –
see, the dawn is
breaking!

53. *ITALIENISCHES LIEDERBUCH*
   ITALIAN   SONG-BOOK

53. ITALIAN
   SONG-BOOK

(Italian poems translated
into German by Paul Heyse)

i.

i.

Auch kleine Dinge   können uns entzücken,
even little things can   us to delight

Auch kleine Dinge   können teuer   sein.
even little things can   precious to be

Bedenkt, wie gern   wir uns   mit Perlen schmücken;
consider how gladly we ourselves with pearls adorn

Sie werden schwer bezahlt   und sind nur   klein.
they are   heavily paid for and are   only small

Bedenkt, wie klein ist die Olivenfrucht,
consider how little is the olive-fruit

Und wird um ihre Güte   doch gesucht.
and is   for her goodness yet sought for

Denkt an die Rose nur, wie klein sie ist,
think of the rose only how little she is

Und duftet   doch so lieblich, wie ihr wisst.
and sends forth scent yet so sweetly   as you know

Even little
things can delight
us, even little
things can be
precious. Think how
gladly we adorn
ourselves with
pearls; their price
is high, yet they
are only small. Think
how small is the
olive, yet how sought
for its goodness.
Only think of the
rose, how small it
is - and yet, as you
know, its scent is
so sweet.

ii.

ii.

Mir   ward gesagt, du reisest in   die Ferne.
to me was told   you journey into the distant place

Ach, wohin   gehst du, mein geliebtes Leben?
oh   whither go   you my beloved   life

Den Tag, an dem   du scheidest, wüsst'   ich gerne;
the day in which du depart   would know I   gladly

Mit Tränen will ich deinen Weg befeuchten –
with tears will I   your   path to moisten

Mit Tränen will ich das Geleit dir   geben.
with tears will I   the escort to you to give

Gedenk' an mich, und Hoffnung wird mir   leuchten!
think of me   and hope   will to me to glimmer

Mit Tränen bin ich bei dir allerwärts –
with tears am I   with you everywhere

Gedenk' an mich, vergiss es nicht, mein Herz!
think of me   forget it not   my   heart

They told me
you journey far away.
Oh, where are you
going, my dearest
life? If I but knew
the day of your
leaving! I would go
with you and water
your path with my
tears, but think of
me, and hope will
glimmer. My tears
are with you
everywhere. Think of
me – do not forget,
dear heart!

iii.

Ihr seid die Allerschönste weit und breit,
you are the fairest of all far and wide

Viel schöner als im   Mai der Blumenflor.
much fairer than in the May the flower-blossoming

Orvietos Dom   steigt so voll Herrlichkeit,
Orvieto's cathedral rises so full splendour

Viterbos grösster Brunnen nicht empor.
Viterbo's greatest fountain not   upwards

So   hoher Reiz und Zauber   ist dein eigen,
such high grace and enchantment is your own

Der Dom   von Siena muss sich   vor   dir neigen.
the cathedral of Siena must himself before you to bow

Ach, du bist so an Reiz und Anmut reich,
oh   you are so in charm and grace rich

Der Dom   von Siena selbst ist dir   nicht gleich
the cathedral of Siena himself is to you not   equal

iii.

You are the
fairest far and
wide, fairer than
the blossoming in
May! Neither
Orvieto's cathedral,
nor Viterbo's greatest
fountain surpass such
great beauty; such
grace and enchantment
are yours alone – even
Siena's cathedral must
bow before you. Oh,
you are so rich in
charm and grace, even
Siena's cathedral is
not your equal!

iv.

Gesegnet sei, durch   den die Welt entstund;
Blessed be   through whom the world began

Wie trefflich schuf er sie nach allen Seiten!
how admirably created he her on   all   sides

Er schuf   das Meer mit endlos   tiefem Grund,
he created the ocean with endlessly deep   bottom

Er schuf   die Schiffe, die   hinübergleiten,
he created the ships   which glide across

Er schuf   das Paradies mit ew'gem Licht,
he created the Paradise with eternal light

Er schuf   die Schönheit und dein Angesicht.
he created the beauty   and your face

iv.

Blessed be He
through whom the world
began; how admirably
He made it on every
side! He made the
ocean with its
endless deeps; He
made the ships which
glide across it; He
made Paradise with its
eternal light; He made
beauty – and your
face.

v.

Selig   ihr Blinden,   die ihr nicht zu schauen
blessed you blind people who you not   to to see

Vermögt die Reize, die uns   Glut   entfachen;
are able the charms that to us passion kindle

Selig   ihr Tauben,   die ihr ohne   Grauen
blessed you deaf people who you without horror

Die Klagen der   Verliebten könnt verlachen;
the laments of the in love ones can   to laugh at

Selig   ihr Stummen,   die ihr nicht den   Frauen
blessed you dumb people who you not   to the women

Könnt eure Herzensnot   verständlich machen;
can   your heart's-misery intelligible to make

Selig   ihr Toten,   die man hat begraben!
blessed you dead ones who one has buried

Ihr sollt vor Liebesqualen   Ruhe haben.
you shall from love's-torments peace to have

v.

Blessed are the
blind, who cannot see
the charms that kindle
our passions; blessed
are the deaf, who can
fearlessly laugh at
the laments of lovers;
blessed are the dumb,
who cannot tell
women of their hearts'
misery; blessed are
the dead in their
graves, for they shall
have peace from the
torments of love.

vi.

Wer rief   dich denn? Wer hat dich herbestellt?
who called you   then   who has you   sent for

Wer heiss dich kommen, wenn es dir   zur   Last?
who bade   you to come   if   it to you to the burden

Geh zu dem Liebchen, das dir mehr gefällt,
go to the sweetheart who you more pleases

Geh dahin, wo   du die Gedanken hast.
go thither where you the thoughts have

Geh nur, wohin   dein Sinnen   steht und Denken!
go only whither your thinking is   and thinking

Dass du zu mir kommst, will ich gern   dir
that you to me come   will I   willingly to you
  schenken.
  to let off

Geh zu dem Liebchen, das dir mehr gefällt!
go to the sweetheart who you more pleases

Wer rief   dich denn? Wer hat dich herbestellt?
who called you   then   who has you   sent for

Who called you?
Who sent for you?
Who told you to come,
if it's such a
trouble to you? Go to
the sweetheart who
pleases you more –
go where you mind is
wandering! Just go
where your thoughts
and fancies lie! You
can keep your coming
here, with pleasure!
Go to the sweetheart
who pleases you more!
Who called you? Who
sent for you?

vii.

Der Mond hat eine schwere Klag'   erhoben
the moon has a   grave   complaint raised

Und vor   dem Herrn die Sache kund gemacht;
and before the Lord the thing known made

Er wolle nicht mehr stehn   am   Himmel droben,*
he   wants not   more to stand in the sky   there above

Du habest ihn um seinen Glanz   gebracht.
you have   him - his   splendour caused to lose

Als er zuletzt   das Sternenheer gezählt,
as he the last time the star-host   counted

Da   hab' es an der vollen Zahl gefehlt;
there has it in the full   count been missing

Zwei von den schönsten   habest du entwendet:
two of the most beautiful have   you stolen

Die beiden Augen dort, die mich verblendet.
the both   eyes there that me   dazzled

The moon has made
a grave complaint, and
made it known to the
Lord; he will no
longer stand there in
the sky, for you have
robbed him of his
splendour. When last
he counted the host of
stars, the number was
not complete. You have
stolen two of the
loveliest: those two
eyes there, that
dazzle me.

*The moon is masculine in German.

viii.

Nun lass uns Frieden schliessen, liebstes Leben,
now let us peace   to make   dearest life

Zu lang ist's schon, dass wir in Fehde liegen.
too long is it already that we in feud lie

Wenn du nicht willst, will ich mich dir   ergeben;
if   you not   will   will I   me   to you to yield

Wie könnten wir uns auf den Tod   bekriegen?
how could   we us unto the death make war

Es   schliessen Frieden Könige und Fürsten,
(it) make   peace   kings and princes

Und sollten Liebende nicht darnach   dürsten?
and should lovers   not   towards that to thirst

Es   schliessen Frieden Fürsten und Soldaten,
(it) make   peace   princes and soldiers

Und sollt'es zwei Verliebten wohl missraten?
and should it two lovers   thus to fail

Meinst du, dass, was so grossen Herrn   gelingt,
think you that what so to great gentlemen succeeds

Ein Paar zufriedner Herzen nicht vollbringt?
a   pair of contented hearts not   achieves

viii.

Now let us make our peace, my dearest life, our feud has lasted far too long. If you will not give way, I will yield to you; how could we fight to the death? Kings and princes, they make peace – should lovers then not crave it? Princes and soldiers make peace – can two lovers be defeated? Do you think, that where great men succeed, two contented hearts can fail?

ix.

Dass doch gemalt all' deine Reize wären,
that yet painted all   your charms were

Und dann der Heidenfürst das Bildnis fände.
and then the pagan-prince the portrait found

Er würde dir   ein gross' Geschenk verehren,
he would to you a   great   gift   to bestow

Und legte   seine Kron in deine Hände.
and would lay his   crown in your hands

Zum   rechten Glauben müsst'   sich
to the right   faith   would have to (itself)
  bekehren
  to become converted

Sein ganzes Reich, bis an sein fernstes Ende.
his whole   kingdom even to its furthest end

Im   ganzen Lande würd'   es ausgeschrieben,
in the whole land would be it proclaimed

Christ   soll ein jeder werden   und dich lieben.
Christian shall everyone to become and you to love

Ein jeder Heide   flugs   bekehrte   sich
– every – heathen at once would convert himself

Und würd'   ein guter Christ   und liebte   dich.
and would become a   good Christian and would love you

ix.

If only all your charms were painted, and a pagan prince should find the portrait! He would bestow great gifts upon you, and lay his crown in your hands. His whole kingdom, to its farthest ends would be converted to the true faith. Throughout the land it would be proclaimed: everyone shall be Christian, and adore you! Everyone at once would be converted, would become a good Christian, and worship you.

x.

Du denkst mit einem Fädchen   mich zu fangen.
you think with a   little thread me to to catch

Mit einem Blick schon   mich verliebt zu machen?
with one glance already me   in love to to make

Ich fing schon andre, die sich   höher schwangen,
I caught already others who themselves higher soared

Du darfst mir ja   nicht trau'n, siehst du mich
you must me indeed not   to trust see   you me
  lachen.
  to laugh

Schon andre fing ich, glaub' es sicherlich.
already others caught I   believe it certainly

Ich bin verliebt, doch eben nicht in dich.
I   am in love   but just not   in you

    You think you
can catch me with a
tiny thread, and
make me fall in love,
with just one glance?
I've caught others
before, who aimed
higher. You really
shouldn't trust me,
when you see me
laughing! I've caught
others before,
believe me. I am in
love – but not with
you!

xi.

Wie lange schon   war immer mein Verlangen:
how long already was always my   yearning

Ach, wäre doch ein Musikus mir   gut!
ah were but a   musician to me kind

Nun liess der Herr mich meinen Wunsch erlangen
now let   the Lord me   my   wish   to attain

Und schickt mir einen, ganz wie Milch und Blut.
and sends   me one   wholly like milk and blood

Da   kommt er eben her mit sanfter Miene,
there comes he just here with gentle mien

Und senkt den Kopf und spielt die Violine.
and lowers the head and plays the violin

    Oh, how long have
I yearned to be loved
by a musician! Now
the Lord has granted
me my wish, and sent
me one, all milk and
roses. Here he comes
now, with gentle
mien; he bows his
head, and plays the
violin.

xii.

Nein, junger Herr, so treibt   man's nicht, fürwahr;
no   young sir   so carries on one it not   truly

Man sorgt   dafür, sich schicklich zu betragen.
one takes care about it oneself properly   to to behave

Für alltags bin ich gut genug, nicht wahr?
for every day am I   good enough not   true

Doch bessre suchst du dir   an   Feiertagen.
yet better look for you to you on high days and holidays

Nein, junger Herr, wirst du so weiter sünd'gen,
no   young sir   will you so further to sin

Wird dir   den Dienst dein Alltagsliebchen
will to you the post   your everyday sweetheart
  künd'gen.
  to give notice

    Oh no, young sir,
you can't carry on
like this – you must
try and behave
properly! I'm good
enough for weekdays,
aren't I? But you
look for something
better on Sundays. Oh
no, young sir, if you
go on like this,
your weekday
sweetheart'll give
you her notice!

xiii.

                                                 xiii.

Hoffärtig seid Ihr, schönes Kind, und geht
haughty   are you pretty child and go

Mit Euren Freiern um   auf stolzem Fuss.
with your suitors about on proud   foot

Spricht man Euch an, kaum   dass Ihr Rede steht,
speaks one you to scarcely that you - answer -

Als kostet' Euch zuviel ein holder Gruss.
as would cost you too much a   pleasant greeting

Bist keines Alexanders Töchterlein,
are no   Alexander's (little) daughter

Kein Königreich wird deine Mitgift sein,
no   kingdom   will your dowry to be

Und willst du nicht das Gold, so nimm das Zinn;
and want   you not   the gold so take the tin

Willst du nicht Liebe, nimm   Verachtung hin.
want   you not   love   put up with contempt -

You are so proud, my fine one, so high and mighty with your suitors! If one speaks to you, you hardly answer, as if a pleasant greeting cost too much. You're no Alexander's daughter – you'll have no kingdom for your dowry. If you don't want gold, take tin instead! If you don't want love, take contempt!

         xiv.

                                                 xiv.

Geselle, woll'n wir uns in Kutten hüllen,
brother will   we us in cowls to wrap

Die Welt dem   lassen, den sie mag ergötzen?
the world to him to leave whom she may to please

Dann pochen wir an Tür um   Tür im Stillen:
then knock we on door after door - quietly -

Gebt einem armen Mönch um Jesu willen.'
give to a poor monk for Jesus sake

- O lieber Pater, du musst später kommen,
O dear   father you must later to come

Wenn aus   dem Ofen wird das Brot genommen.
when out of the oven is   the bread taken

O lieber Pater, komm nur später wieder,
O dear   father come but later again

Ein Töchterlein   von mir liegt krank darnieder.
a   little daughter of me lies ill   -

- Und ist sie krank, so lass mich zu ihr gehen,
and is she ill   so let me   to her to go

Dass sie nicht etwa   sterbe   unversehen.
that she not   perhaps might die by chance

Und ist sie krank, so lass mich nach ihr schauen,
and is she ill   so let me   at   her to look

Dass sie mir ihre Beichte mag vertrauen.
that she to me her confession may to confide

Schliesst Tür und Fenster, dass uns keiner störe,
shut   door and window that us no one might disturb

Wenn ich des   armen Kindes Beichte   höre!
when I of the poor child confession hear

Come, brother, let us put on monks' robes, and leave the world to those who can enjoy it! Then we will steal from door to door, and knock, 'Give alms to a poor monk for Jesus' sake!' 'O you must come later, dear father, when the bread is taken from the oven. O come back later, dear father, for my little daughter lies sick!' 'But if she is sick, let me go to her, for she may suddenly die! If she is sick, let me see her, that she may confess to me – and close the door and window, so no one disturbs us as I hear the poor child's confession!'

xv.

Mein Liebster   ist so klein, dass ohne   Bücken
my   sweetheart is so small that without stooping

Er mir   das Zimmer fegt   mit seinen Locken.
he to me the room   sweeps with   his   locks

Als er ins   Gärtlein   ging, Jasmin
when he into the (little) garden went   jasmine
  zu pflücken,
  to to gather

Ist er von einer Schnecke sehr erschrocken.
is he by a   snail   very frightened

Dann setzt'   er sich   ins   Haus um
then went and sat down he himself into the house in order
  zu verschnaufen,
  to recover breath

Da   warf ihn eine Fliege übern   Haufen;
there threw him a   fly   (over the heap)

Und als er hintrat   an mein Fensterlein,
and when he stepped up to my (little) window

Stiess eine Bremse   ihm den Schädel ein.
knocked a   horsefly him the skull   into

Verwünscht sei'n alle Fliegen, Schnaken, Bremsen
cursed   be   all flies   gnats   horseflies

Und wer ein Schätzchen   hat aus den Maremmen!
and who a   little sweetheart has from the Maremma

Verwünscht sei'n alle Fliegen, Schnaken, Mücken
cursed   be   all flies   gnats   midges

Und wer sich,   wenn er küsst, so tief muss bücken!
and who (himself) when he kisses so deep must to stoop

My sweetheart is
so small, that even
without stooping he
sweeps the room with
his hair. When he
went into the garden
to gather jasmine, he
was badly frightened
by a snail. He went
and sat down indoors
to get his breath,
but a fly knocked him
over backwards. When
he stepped up to my
window, a horsefly
bumped into his head.
A curse on all flies
and gnats, and all
those with sweethearts
from Maremma! A curse
on all flies and
midges and all who
have to stoop so low
to kiss!

xvi.

Ihr jungen Leute, die ihr zieht ins   Feld
you young   people who you march into the field

Auf meinen Liebsten sollt ihr Achtung geben.
to my   dearest shall you care   to give

Sorgt,   dass er tapfer sich   im   Feuer hält;
take care that he bravely himself in the fire holds

Er war noch   nie im   Kriege all sein Leben.
he was as yet never in the   war   all his life

Lass nie ihn unter freiem Himmel schlafen;
let never him under free   sky   to sleep

Er ist so zart,   es möchte sich   bestrafen.
he is so delicate it might itself to punish

Lasst mir   ihn ja   nicht schlafen unterm
let   to me him on no account not   to sleep under the
  Mond;
  moon

Er ginge drauf, er ist's ja   nicht gewohnt.
he might perish he is it really not   used

You young lads
marching off to war,
take care of my
sweetheart! See that
he's brave under
fire - he was never
in his life in a
battle! Don't let
him sleep in the
open - he's so
delicate, he might
catch his death!
Don't let him sleep
under the moon - it'd
be the end of him,
he's not used to it!

xvii.

Und willst du deinen Liebsten sterben sehen,
and want   you your   dearest to die to see

So trage nicht dein Haar gelockt, du Holde.
so wear   not   your hair curled   you lovely one

Lass von den Schultern frei   sie niederwehen;
let from the shoulders freely them to flutter down

Wie Fäden   sehn sie aus von purem Golde.
like threads look they – of pure gold

Wie goldne Fäden, die der Wind bewegt,
like golden threads that the wind moves

Schön sind die Haare, schön ist, die sie trägt!
lovely are the hairs lovely is   who them wears

Goldfäden,   Seidenfäden   ungezählt –
gold-threads silken-threads uncounted

Schön sind die Haare, schön ist, die sie strählt!
lovely are the hairs lovely is   who them combs

And if you would
see your sweetheart
die of love, my fair
one, do not bind up
your hair! Let it
flow freely round
your shoulders, like
threads of pure gold,
like golden threads
stirred by the breeze.
Your hair is lovely,
and lovely is she who
wears it! Golden
threads, silken
threads without
number – your hair
is lovely, and lovely
is she who combs it!

xviii.

Heb' auf dein blondes Haupt und schlafe nicht,
raise up your fair   head and sleep   not

Und lass dich   ja   vom   Schlummer nicht
and let yourself on no account from the slumber   not
   betören.
   to be fooled

Ich sage dir   vier Worte   von Gewicht,
I   say to you four sayings of weight

Von denen darfst du keines   überhören.
of which may   you not one to miss

Das erste: dass um dich mein Herze bricht,
the first that for you my   heart is breaking

Das zweite: dir   nur will ich angehören,
the second to you only want I   to belong

Das dritte: dass ich dir   mein Heil   befehle,
the third that I   to you my   happiness entrust

Das letzte: dich allein liebt meine Seele.
the last   you alone loves my   soul

Raise your fair
head, and sleep no
more – do not let
slumber bemuse you! I
have four weighty
things to say, and
not one must you miss.
The first: for you my
heart is breaking; the
second: only to you
would I belong; the
third: to you I
entrust my whole
happiness; and the
last: my soul loves
you alone.

xix.

Wir haben beide lange Zeit geschwiegen,
we have both long time been silent

Auf   einmal kam uns nun die Sprache wieder.
(all) at once came to us now the speech again

Die Engel, die herab vom   Himmel fliegen,
the angels who down from the heaven fly

Sie brachten nach dem Krieg den Frieden wieder.
they brought after the war   the peace   again

Die Engel Gottes sind herabgeflogen,
the angels of God are flown down

Mit ihnen ist der Frieden eingezogen.
with them is the peace   entered

We were silent a
long time – all at
once our speech
returned. Angels flew
down from heaven and
after our hostility
brought peace again.
God's angels flew
down and with them
came peace. Angels of
love came in the
night, and brought
peace to my heart.

Die Liebesengel   kamen über Nacht
the love's-angels came over night

Und haben Frieden meiner Brust   gebracht.
and have peace   to my breast brought

xx.

Mein Liebster singt am   Haus im   Mondenscheine,
my   dearest sings by the house in the moonlight

Und ich muss lauschend hier im   Bette liegen.
and I   must listening here im the bed   to lie

Weg von der Mutter wend' ich mich   und weine,
away from the mother turn I   myself and weep

Blut sind die Tränen, die   mir   nicht versiegen.
blood are the tears   which to me not   are exhausted

Den breiten Strom am   Bett hab' ich geweint,
the broad   stream by the bed have I   wept

Weiss nicht vor Tränen, ob der Morgen scheint.
know not   for tears   if the morning appears

Den breiten Strom am   Bett weint' ich vor Sehnen;
the broad   stream by the bed wept I   for longing

Blind haben mich gemacht die blut'gen Tränen.
blind have me   made   the bloody   tears

My beloved sings
by the house in the
moonlight, and I must
lie listening here in
bed. I turn away from
my mother, and weep;
the tears are my
blood, tears that I
cannot stem. I have
wept a broad stream
of them by my bed; I
cannot see for tears
if it is day. In my
longing I have wept
a broad stream by
my bed; the tears of
my blood have blinded
me.

xxi.

Man sagt mir, deine Mutter woll' es nicht;
one told me   your mother wants it not

So bleibe weg, mein Schatz,   tu' ihr den Willen.
so stay away my   sweetheart do her the wish

Ach Liebster, nein! tu ihr den Willen nicht,
ah dearest   no   do her the wish   not

Besuch' mich doch,   tu's ihr zum   Trotz,
visit   me   yes (do) do it her to the spite
im stillen!
 - secretly -

Nein, mein Geliebter, folg' ihr nimmermehr,
no   my   beloved   follow her never more

Tu's ihr zum   Trotz, komm öfter   als bisher!
do it her to the spite come oftener than till now

Nein, höre   nicht auf sie, was sie auch sage;
no   listen not   to her what-she-ever might say

Tu's ihr zum   Trotz, mein Lieb, komm alle Tage!
do it her to the spite my   love come every day

They tell me your
mother is against it,
so stay away, my
darling - do as she
bids! Oh no, dearest,
no! Don't do as she
bids - do visit me,
defy her secretly!
No, my beloved, don't
obey her any more -
defy her, come more
often than before!
No, don't listen to
her, whatever she may
say - defy her, my
love, come every day!

xxii.

xxii.

Ein Ständchen Euch   zu bringen kam ich her,
a   serenade to you to to bring came I   here

Wenn es dem   Herrn vom   Haus nicht ungelegen.
if   it to the master of the house not   inconvenient

Ihr habt ein schönes Töchterlein.   Es wär'
you have a   pretty (little) daughter it were

Wohl   gut, sie nicht zu   streng   im   Haus zu
perhaps good her not   too strictly in the house to

hegen.
to enclose

Und liegt sie schon im   Bett, so bitt' ich sehr,
and lies she already in the   bed   so beg   I   very much

Tut es zu wissen   ihr von meinetwegen,
(do) it to to let know her of my sake

Dass ihr Getreuer hier vorbeigekommen,
that her true love here passed by

Der Tag und Nacht sie in den Sinn genommen,
who day and night she in the mind received

Und dass am   Tag, der   vierundzwanzig zählt,
and that in the day which twenty-four   numbers

Sie fünfundzwanzig Stunden lang mir   fehlt.
she twenty-five   hours   long to me is missing

I have come to sing you a serenade, if the master of the house does not object. You have a pretty daughter – it would be as well if you were not strict in keeping her in. And if she is already asleep, then I beg you for my sake to tell her that her true love passed by; he thinks of her day and night, and of the twenty-four hours each day, he misses her for twenty-five.

xxiii.

xxiii.

Was für   ein Lied soll dir   gesungen werden,
what kind of a   song shall to you sung   to be

Das deiner würdig sei?   Wo   find' ich's nur?
that of you worthy would be wher- find I it -ever

Am   liebsten grüb'   ich es tief aus   der Erden,
most preferably would dig I   it deep out of the earth

Gesungen noch von keiner Kreatur.
sung   still by no   creature

Ein Lied, das weder Mann noch Weib bis heute
a   song that neither man nor woman till today

Hört' oder sang, selbst nicht die ält'sten Leute.
heard or   sang even   not   the oldest   people

What kind of song can I sing that is worthy of you? Wherever can I find it? I should most like to dig it from deep in the earth, as yet unsung by any creature; a song that no man or woman has ever heard or sung until today – not even the very oldest.

xxiv.

Ich esse nun mein Brot   nicht trocken mehr,
I   eat now my   bread not   dry   more

Ein Dorn ist mir   im   Fusse stecken blieben.
a   thorn is to me in the foot to stick stayed

Umsonst nach rechts und links blick' ich umher,
in vain to   right and left look   I   around

Und keinen find' ich, der mich möchte lieben.
and no one find I   who me   might to love

Wenn's doch   auch nur ein altes Männlein   wäre,
if it indeed even only an old   little man might be

Das mir erzeigt' ein wenig Lieb' und Ehre.
who me showed   a   little love and respect

Ich meine nämlich   so ein wohlgestalter,
I   mean of course so a   handsome

Ehrbarer   Greis, etwa von meinem Alter.
respectable old man about of my   age

Ich meine, um   mich ganz zu offenbaren,
I   mean   so as me   quite to to reveal

Ein altes Männlein   so von vierzehn Jahren.
an old   little man so of fourteen years

I can't eat my
bread any more
without weeping;
there's a thorn
stuck in my foot. I
look in vain all round
me, and find no one
who'll love me. If
there were just one
little old man who
showed a bit of love
and respect! I mean,
of course, a fine
upstanding old man,
about my own age. I
mean, to be quite
frank, a little old
man about fourteen.

xxv.

Mein Liebster   hat zu Tische mich geladen
my   sweetheart has to table me   invited

Und hatte doch kein Haus mich zu empfangen,
and had   yet no   house me   to to receive

Nicht Holz noch Herd zum   Kochen und zum   Braten,
not   wood nor hearth to the boiling and to the baking

Der Hafen   auch war längst   entzwei gegangen.
the earthen pot even was long since in two gone

An einem Fässchen   Wein gebrach es auch,
of a   (little) cask wine lacked it also

Und Gläser hat er gar   nicht im   Gebrauch;
and glasses has he at all not   in the use

Der Tisch war schmal, das Tafeltuch   nicht besser,
the table was narrow   the table-cloth not   better

Das Brot   steinhart und völlig   stumpf das Messer.
the bread stone-hard and completely blunt the knife

My sweetheart
asked me to supper,
and yet he had no
house – no wood, no
hearth to boil and
bake, and even the
pot had long been
in two pieces! There
was no cask of wine,
no glasses to fill;
the table was mean,
the cloth no better;
the bread like stone
and the knife quite
blunt!

xxvi.   xxvi.

Ich liess mir   sagen und mir   ward erzählt,   They tell me
I   let   to me to say and to me was   told   handsome Toni starves
                                                          himself to death.
Der schöne   Toni hungre sich   zu Tode;   Since he has suffered
the beautiful Toni starves himself to death   so from love, he eats
                                                          only seven loaves per
Seit ihm so überaus   die Liebe quält,   tooth. After a meal,
since him so exceedingly the love   torments   to strengthen his
                                                          digestion, he
Nimmt er auf einen Backzahn   sieben Brote.   consumes a sausage
takes he for a   molar-tooth seven loaves   and seven more loaves,
                                                          and if Tonina doesn't
Nach Tisch, damit   er die Verdauung stählt,   ease his pangs,
after table so that he the digestion steels   there'll soon be
                                                          famine and inflation!
Verspeist er eine Wurst   und sieben Brote,
consumes he a   sausage and seven loaves

Und lindert nicht Tonina seine Pein,
and eases   not Tonina his   pain

Bricht nächstens Hungersnot und Teurung   ein.
sets   very soon famine   and inflation in

  xxvii.   xxvii.

Schon   streckt' ich aus im   Bett die müden Glieder,   As I stretched my
already stretched I   out in the bed the weary limbs   weary limbs in bed,
                                                           your image, my
Da   tritt   dein Bildnis vor   mich hin, du Traute.   darling, rose before
then appears your image   before me   there you beloved me. At once I spring
                                                           up, put on my shoes
Gleich spring' ich auf, fahr' in   die Schuhe wieder   again, and wander
at once spring I   up   slip into the shoes again   through the town
                                                           with my lute. The
Und wandre durch   die Stadt mit meiner Laute.   street echoes to my
and wander through the town with my   lute   singing and playing;
                                                           many listen, but soon
Ich sing' und spiele, dass die Strasse schallt;   I am gone. Many a girl
I   sing and play   that the street resounds   is touched by my song,
                                                           as the wind bears the
So manche   lauscht – vorüber bin ich bald.   singing and playing
so many a one listens   gone by am I   soon   away.

So manches Mädchen hat mein Lied gerührt,
so many a girl   has my   song touched

Indes der Wind schon   Sang und Klang entführt.
while the wind already song and sound carries off

xxviii.

Du sagst mir, dass ich keine Fürstin sei;
you tell me   that I   no   princess be

Auch du bist nicht auf Spaniens Thron entsprossen.
also you are not   on Spain's throne sprung from

Nein, Bester   stehst du auf bei Hahnenschrei,
no   my dear fellow get   you up at cock-crow

Fährst du aufs Feld und nicht in Staatskarossen.
ride   you to the field and not   in state-coaches

Du spottest mein   um meine Niedrigkeit,
you jeer   (of) me for my   lowliness

Doch Armut tut dem Adel   nichts zuleid.
but poverty does to the nobility nothing harm

Du spottest, dass mir Krone fehlt   und
you mock   that to me crown is wanting and
  Wappen,
  coat of arms

Und fährst doch selber nur mit Schusters Rappen.
and go   yet yourself only with cobbler's black horse

You tell me I'm no princess, but neither did you spring from the Spanish throne! No, my lad, when you get up at cock-crow, you go off to the fields – and not in a state coach! You may jeer at my low station, but even the great are not shamed by poverty. You jeer because I have no crown, nor coat of arms – but you yourself just go on Shanks's pony!

xxix.

Wohl kenn' ich Euern Stand, der nicht gering.
well know I   your station which not mean

Ihr brauchtet nicht so tief herabzusteigen,
you need   not so low to to descend

Zu lieben solch ein arm und niedrig Ding,
to to love such a   poor and humble thing

Da sich   vor Euch die Allerschönsten neigen.
as themselves before you the fairest of all bow down

Die schönsten   Männer leicht besiegtet Ihr,
the most handsome men easily conquer   you

Drum   weiss ich wohl, Ihr treibt nur Spiel
therefore know I   well you carry on only play
  mit mir.
  with me

Ihr spottet mein, man hat mich warnen wollen,
you mock   (of) me one has me   to warn to want

Doch ach, Ihr seid so schön! Wer kann Euch
but ah you are so lovely who can you
  grollen?
  to be angry with

I know full well your station is no mean one; you didn't have to stoop so low and love such a poor humble creature, for the finest of the fine bow down to you. You conquer so easily the most handsome men, so I know you're only trifling with me. You make fun of me – they've tried to warn me. But you are so lovely! Who could be angry with you?

xxxx.

Lass sie nur gehn, die so die Stolze   spielt,
let her just to go who so the haughty one acts

Das Wunderkräutlein   aus dem Blumenfeld.
the little wonder-plant from the flower-field

Man sieht, wohin   ihr blankes Auge zielt,
one sees   whither her shining eye   aims

Da Tag um Tag ein andrer ihr gefällt.
as day by day another   her pleases

Sie treibt   es grade wie Toscanas Fluss,
she carries on it just like Tuscany's river

Dem   jedes Berggewässer   folgen   muss.
to which each   mountain-water to follow must

Sie treibt   es wie der Arno, will mir   scheinen:
she carries on it like the Arno will to me to seem

Bald hat sie viel Bewerber, bald nicht einen.
now has she many suitors   now not   one

xxx.

Let her go then,
if she acts so
haughtily, the
fairest flower in the
field! You can see
what catches her
bright eye, for every
day another takes her
fancy. She carries on
like Tuscany's river,
that every mountain
stream must follow.
It seems to me, she
carries on like the
Arno; one moment she
has many followers,
the next not one.

xxxi.

Wie soll ich fröhlich sein und lachen   gar,
how shall I   gay   to be and to laugh even

Da du mir   immer zürnest   unverhohlen?
when you to me always are angry openly

Du kommst nur einmal alle hundert Jahr,
you come   only once every hundred years

Und dann, als hätte man dir's   anbefohlen.
and then as had   one to you it ordered

Was kommst du, wenn's die Deinen ungern   sehn?
why come   you when it the yours not like to see

Gib frei mein Herz, dann magst du weitergehn.
give free my heart then may you to go on

Daheim mit deinen Leuten leb' in Frieden,
at home with your   people live in peace

Denn was der Himmel will,   geschieht   hienieden.
for what the heaven desires comes to pass here below

Halt Frieden mit den Deinigen zu Haus,
keep peace   with the yours   at home

Denn was der Himmel will,   das bleibt
for what the heaven desires that fails to appear
  nicht aus.
  not   –

xxxi.

How can I be gay
and laughing, when
you're always so
openly vexed with
me? You come but
once in a hundred
years, and then as if
it were by order. Why
do you come if your
family frowns upon
it? Set my heart
free, then you can
go your way. Live in
peace at home with
your family – what
heaven ordains will
come to pass. Keep
the peace at home
with your family –
what heaven ordains,
will always be.

xxxii.

Was soll der Zorn, mein Schatz, der dich erhitzt?
what means the rage my   treasure that you inflames

Ich bin mir   keiner Sünde ja   bewusst.
I   am to me of no sin   indeed conscious

Ach, lieber nimm ein Messer wohlgespitzt
oh   rather take a   knife well-sharpened

Und tritt zu mir, durchbohre mir   die Brust.
and approach me pierce   to me the breast

Und taugt ein Messer nicht, so nimm ein Schwert,
and serves a   knife not   so take a   sword

Dass meines Blutes Quell   gen   Himmel fährt.
that of my blood fountain towards heaven goes

Und taugt ein Schwert nicht, nimm des   Dolches Stahl
and serves a   sword not   take of the dagger steel

Und wasch' in meinem Blut all meine Qual.
and wash in my   blood all my   torment

   xxxiii.

Sterb' ich, so hüllt in Blumen meine Glieder;
die   I   so cover in flowers my   limbs

Ich wünsche nicht, dass ihr ein Grab mir   grabt.
I   wish   not   that you a   grave to me dig

Genüber jenen Mauern legt mich nieder,
opposite these walls lay me   down

Wo   ihr so manchmal mich gesehen habt.
where you so often   me   seen   have

Dort legt mich hin, in Regen oder Wind;
there lay me   down in rain or   wind

Gern sterb' ich, ist's um dich, geliebtes Kind.
gladly die   I   is it for you beloved   child

Dort legt mich hin in Sonnenschein und Regen;
there lay me   down in sunshine   and rain

Ich sterbe lieblich, sterb' ich deinetwegen.
I   die   sweetly   die   I   because of you

---

xxxii.

Why this rage,
my love, that so
inflames you? I know
of no wrong I have
done. Oh, rather
take a sharpened
knife, and come and
plunge it in my
breast! If a knife
is of no avail, then
take a sword, and let
the fountain of my
blood well up to
heaven! If a sword
is of no avail, take
a steel dagger, and
let my blood wash
away my torment!

xxxiii.

If I should die,
then cover my limbs
with flowers! I do
not wish that you
should dig a grave
for me. Lay me down
beside those walls,
where you have so
often seen me. There
let me be laid in
rain and wind; gladly
I would die for you,
dear love. There let
me be laid in
sunshine and rain;
dying for me is
sweet, if I die for
you!

xxxiv.

Und steht Ihr früh am   Morgen auf vom   Bette,
and get   you early in the morning up from the bed

Scheucht Ihr vom   Himmel alle Wolken fort,
scare away you from the sky   all   clouds away

Die Sonne lockt Ihr auf die Berge   dort,
the sun   lure you on the mountains there

Und Engelein   erscheinen um die Wette
and little angels appear   - in rivalry -

Und bringen Schuh und Kleider Euch   sofort.
and bring   shoe and clothes to you at once

Dass, wenn Ihr ausgeht in   die heil'ge Mette,
that when you go out into the holy   Mass

So zieht Ihr alle Menschen mit Euch fort,
so draw you all people   with you along

Und wenn Ihr naht der benedeiten Stätte,
and when you near the blessed   place

So zündet Euer Blick die Lampen an.
so kindles your glance the lamps -

Weihwasser nehmt Ihr, macht des   Kreuzes Zeichen
holy water take   you make of the cross   sign

Und netzet Eure weisse Stirn sodann
and moisten your white brow   then

Und neiget Euch   und beugt die Knie ingleichen -
and bow   (yourself) and bend the knee also

O wie holdselig   steht Euch alles   an!
O how most charmingly becomes you everything -

Wie hold   und selig   hat Euch Gott begabt,
how graciously and blessedly has you God endowed

Die Ihr der   Schönheit Kron' empfangen habt!
who you of the beauty   crown received have

Wie hold   und selig   wandelt Ihr im   Leben;
how gracious and blessed go   you in the life

Der   Schönheit Palme ward an Euch gegeben.
of the beauty   palm was to you given

xxxv.

Benedeit   die sel'ge Mutter,
blessed be the blissful mother

Die so lieblich dich geboren,
who so sweetly you gave birth

So an   Schönheit auserkoren,
so as to beauty   most favoured

Meine Sehnsucht fliegt dir zu!
my   longing   flies you to

Du so lieblich von Gebärden,
you so lovely   of bearing

Du die Holdeste   der   Erden,
you the most gracious of the earth

Du mein Kleinod, meine Wonne,
you my   treasure my   delight

xxxiv.

And when you rise early from your bed, you chase all the clouds from the sky, lure the sun to the mountains, and cherubs vie with each other to bring your shoes and clothes. Then, when you go to Mass, all men are drawn to follow you, and when you approach the sanctuary the very lamps are kindled by your glance. You take holy water and moisten your brow, make the sign of the cross, then bow your head and kneel. Oh, with what charm it becomes you! What gracious and blessed gifts God has bestowed upon you - you who received the crown of beauty! Gracious and blessed you go through life - to you the palm of beauty was given!

xxxv.

Blessed be the mother, who bore you in sweetness and joy; you, who are favoured with such beauty - how my longing flies to you!

You, so beautiful of bearing, you, most gracious one on earth; you, my treasure, my delight - how sweet and blessed are you!

Süsse, benedeit bist du!
sweet blessed are you

Wenn ich aus der Ferne schmachte
when I from - afar - languish

Und betrachte deine Schöne,
and behold   your beauty

Siehe wie ich beb' und stöhne,
see how I quiver and groan

Dass ich kaum es bergen kann!
that I hardly it to hide can

Und in meiner Brust gewaltsam
and in my   breast violently

Fühl' ich Flammen sich   empören,
feel I flames (themselves) to rage

Die den Frieden mir zerstören,
that the peace   to me to destroy

Ach, der Wahnsinn fasst mich an!
ah the madness seizes me   -

When far from you
I languish, reflecting
on your beauty, how
I tremble and sigh –
I can hardly conceal
it!

I feel my heart
to be on fire, the
raging flames destroy
my peace – ah, I am
gripped by madness!

   xxxvi.

xxxvi.

Wenn du, mein Liebster, steigst zum Himmel auf,
when you my dearest ascend to the heaven -

Trag' ich mein Herz dir in der Hand entgegen.
bear I my heart to you in the hand towards

So liebevoll umarmst du mich darauf,
so lovingly embrace you me thereupon

Dann woll'n wir uns dem Herrn zu Füssen legen.
then want we us to the Lord to feet to lay

Und sieht der Herrgott unsre Liebesschmerzen,
and sees the Lord God our   love's-sorrows

Macht er ein Herz aus zwei verliebten Herzen,
makes he one heart out of two in love   hearts

Zu einem Herzen fügt er zwei zusammen,
to one heart joins he two together

Im   Paradies, unglänzt von Himmelsflammen.
in the Paradise surrounded by heaven's-flames

When you, my
beloved, go up to
heaven, I will meet
you, my heart in my
hand. Then you will
lovingly embrace me,
and we will lay
ourselves at the feet
of the Lord. And when
He sees the anguish
of our love, He will
make our two loving
hearts as one; the
Lord God will join
our two hearts as
one in Paradise, in
the glorious radiance
of Heaven.

xxxvii.

Wie viele Zeit verlor ich, dich zu lieben!
how much   time lost   I   you to to love

Hätt' ich doch Gott geliebt in all der   Zeit.
had   I   but God loved in all of the time

Ein Platz im   Paradies wär'   mir   verschrieben,
a   place in the Paradise would be to me ordered

Ein Heil'ger sässe   dann an meiner Seit'.
a   saint   would sit then at my   side

Und weil   ich dich geliebt, schön frisch Gesicht,
and because I   you loved   lovely fresh face

Verscherzt' ich mir des   Paradieses Licht,
lost foolishly I to me of the Paradise   light

Und weil   ich dich geliebt, schön Veigelein,
and because I   you loved   lovely little bird

Komm' ich nun nicht ins   Paradies hinein.
come   I   now not   in the Paradise into

xxxvii.

   How much of my
life has been
wasted in loving
you! If only I had
loved God all this
time, a place in
Paradise would be
reserved for me,
with a saint to sit
by my side. But
because I have
loved you and your
lovely young face, I
have foolishly lost
the light of Heaven,
and because it is you
I have loved, little
bird, I shall now
never enter
Paradise.

xxxviii.

Wenn du mich mit den Augen streifst und lachst,
when you me   with the eyes brush   and laugh

Sie senkst, und neigst das Kinn zum   Busen dann,
them lower   and bow   the chin to the bosom then

Bitt' ich, dass du mir erst ein Zeichen machst,
beg   I   that you me first a   sign   make

Damit ich doch mein Herz auch bänd'gen kann,
so that I indeed my   heart also subdue can

Dass ich mein Herz mag bänd'gen, zahm und still,
that I   my   heart may subdue   tame and still

Wenn es vor grosser Liebe springen will,
when it for great   love to leap wants

Dass ich mein Herz mag halten in der Brust,
that I   my   heart may to keep in the breast

Wenn es ausbrechen will vor grosser Lust.
when it to burst forth wants for great   joy

xxxviii.

   When you caress
me with a glance and
laugh, lower your
eyes, and bow your
head, I beg you for
a warning sign, that
I may subdue my
heart, and keep it
tame and quiet, when
it would leap for
love so great; that
I may keep my heart
within my breast,
when it would burst
forth for sheer joy!

xxxix.

Gesegnet sei das Grün und wer es trägt!
blessed be the green and who it wears

Ein grünes Kleid will ich mir   machen lassen.
a green dress will I to me to make to let

Ein grünes Kleid trägt auch die Frühlingsaue,
a green dress wears also the spring-meadow

Grün kleidet sich   der Liebling meiner Augen.
green dresses himself the darling of my eyes

In Grün sich   kleiden ist der   Jäger   Brauch,
in green himself to dress is of the hunter custom

Ein grünes Kleid trägt mein Geliebter auch;
a green dress wears my   loved one too

Das Grün steht   allen Dingen lieblich   an,
the green becomes all   things charmingly –

Aus   Grün wächst jede schöne Frucht heran.
out of green grows each lovely fruit   –

xl.

O wär' dein Haus durchsichtig wie ein Glas,
O were your house transparent as a   glass

Mein Holder, wenn ich mich   vorüberstehle!
my   love   when I   myself steal by

Denn säh'   ich drinnen dich ohn'   Unterlass,
then would see I within you without ceasing

Wie blickt'   ich dann nach dir mit ganzer Seele!
how would look I then at   you with all   soul

Wie viele Blicke schickte   mir dein Herz,
how many glances would send me your heart

Mehr als da   Tropfen hat der Fluss im   März!
more than there drops has the river in the March

Wie viele Blicke schickt' ich dir   entgegen,
how many glances would send I to you towards

Mehr als da   Tropfen niedersprühn im   Regen!
more than there drops scatter down in the rain

xli.

Heut' nacht erhob ich mich   um Mitternacht,
today night rose I   myself at midnight

Da   war mein Herz mir   heimlich fortgeschlichen.
there was my   heart to me secretly stolen away

Ich frug: Herz, wohin   stürmst du so mit Macht?
I asked heart whither rage   you so with might

Es sprach: Nur Euch zu sehn, sei es entwichen.
it said   only you to to see is it escaped

Nun sieh, wie muss es um   mein Lieben stehn:
now see   how must it with my   loving to stand

Mein Herz entweicht der   Brust, um   dich zu sehn!
my   heart escapes   of the breast so as you to to see

xxxix.

Blessed be green
and those who wear
it! I'll have a
dress made in green
– the meadows too
wear green in
spring, and the
darling of my eyes
wears green. To
dress in green is
the hunter's custom,
and my love too
wears green.
Everything looks
charming in green,
each lovely fruit
grows out of green.

xl.

If only your
house were
transparent as
glass, my love,
when I steal by!
Then I could
always see you
within – how I would
gaze at you with all
my soul! How many
glances your heart
would send me –
more than all the
drops in a river
in March! How many
glances I would
send to you – more
than all the drops
of falling rain!

xli.

Last night I
rose at midnight,
and found my heart
had stolen secretly
away. I asked:
Heart, where are
you rushing so
impetuously? It said
it was escaping,
just to see you.
Now you see what
kind of love it is
– my very heart
escapes my breast,
to see you!

xlii.

Nicht länger kann ich singen, denn der Wind
not   longer can I to sing for the wind

Weht stark   und macht dem Atem   was   zu schaffen.
blows strongly and gives the breath something to to work

Auch fürcht' ich, dass die Zeit umsonst   verrinnt.
also fear   I   that the time to no purpose runs away

Ja wär' ich sicher, ging'   ich jetzt nicht schlafen.
yes were I sure   would go I now not to sleep

Ja wüsst' ich was,   würd' ich nicht heimspazieren.
yes knew I something would I not   to go home

Und einsam diese schöne Zeit verlieren.
and alone this lovely time to lose

I can sing no longer, for the wind is strong and takes my breath away. I fear, too, that I am wasting my time. If I were only sure, I would not go off to bed; if I had but one sign, I would not go home and waste this lovely night alone.

xliii.

Schweig' einmal still,   du garst'ger Schwätzer dort!
be silent once   (silent) you detestable babbler   there

Zum   Ekel   ist mir   dein verwünschtes Singen.
to the disgust is to me your cursed   singing

Und triebst du es bis morgen   früh   so fort,
and carried you it till tomorrow morning so on

Doch würde dir   kein schmuckes Lied gelingen.
yet would to you no   pretty   song succeed

Schweig' einmal still und lege dich   aufs Ohr!
be silent once   and lay yourself on the ear

Das Ständchen eines Esels zög'   ich vor.
the serenade of a donkey would prefer I   -

Be quiet there, you garrulous wretch! I am sick of your cursed singing, and even if you carried on till morning, you wouldn't come out with a single decent song. Be quiet once and for all, and go to bed! I'd rather have a donkey's serenade!

xliv.

O wüsstet du, wie viel ich deinetwegen,
O if knew you how much I because of you

Du falsche Renegatin, litt   zur   Nacht,
you false renegade   suffered at the night

Indes du im   verschlossnen Haus gelegen
while you in the locked   house lain

Und ich die Zeit im   Freien zugebracht.
and I the time in the open spent

Als Rosenwasser diente mir der Regen,
as rose-water served me the rain

Der Blitz   hat Liebesbotschaft mir   gebracht;
the lightning has love's-message to me brought

Ich habe Würfel mit dem Sturm gespielt,
I have dice with the storm played

Als unter deinem Dach ich Wache hielt.
as under your roof I watch kept

Mein Bett war unter deinem Dach bereitet,
my   bed was under your roof made ready

Der Himmel lag als Decke drauf gebreitet,
the sky   lay as blanket on it spread out

If you only knew how much I've suffered each night for your sake, you fickle one! While you lay behind locked doors, I spent the night in the open. The rain was my rosewater, lightning brought me messages of love; I played at dice with the storm, as I kept watch beneath your eaves. There I made my bed; the sky spread overhead was my blanket, your doorstep served me for a pillow — oh, most miserable of men, what I must endure!

Die Schwelle deiner Tür, das war mein Kissen –
the threshold of your door that was my   pillow

Ich Ärmster,   ach, was hab' ich aussteh'n müssen!
I   most miserable alas what have I   to endure to have to

xlv.

Verschling' der Abgrund meines Liebsten Hütte,
let devour   the abyss   of my   lover   hut

An ihrer Stelle schäum' ein See zur   Stunde.
in her   place let foam a   lake at the hour (now)

Bleikugeln soll der Himmel drüber   schütten,
lead-bullets shall the sky   over there to pour out

Und eine Schlange hause   dort im   Grunde.
and a   serpent let dwell there in the ground

Drin   hause   eine Schlange gift'ger   Art,
therein let dwell a   serpent of poisonous kind

Die ihn vergifte,   der mir   untreu ward.
who him would poison who to me untrue was

Drin   hause   ein Schlange, giftgeschwollen,
therein let dwell a   serpent   swollen with poison

Und bring' ihm   Tod, der mich verraten wollen!
and bring to him death who me   to betray to wish

xlv.

   May my lover's
hovel be engulfed
by the earth, and
a lake swirl there
in its place! May
bullets rain on it
from the heavens,
and a serpent dwell
there under the
ground! Let the
serpent who dwells
there be poisonous,
and poison him who
was untrue to me!
Let the serpent who
dwells there be
swollen with poison,
and bring death to
him who thought to
betray me!

xlvi.

Ich hab' in Penna einen Liebsten wohnen,
I   have in Penna a   lover   to live

In der Maremmeneb'ne einen andern,
in the Maremma plain – an-other –

Einen im   schönen Hafen   von Ancona,
one   in the lovely harbour of Ancona

Zum   vierten muss ich nach Viterbo wandern;
to the fourth   must I   to Viterbo to go

Ein andrer   wohnt in Casentino dort,
– an-other – lives in Casentino there

Der nächste lebt mit mir am   selben Ort,
the next   lives with me in the same   place

Und wieder einen hab' ich in Magione,
and again one   have I   in Magione

Vier in La Fratta, zehn in Castiglione.
four in La Fratta ten in Castiglione

xlvi.

   I have a lover
who lives in Penna,
another in the
Maremma plain; one
in the lovely port
of Ancona, for the
fourth I have to go
to Viterbo; another
lives in Casentino,
the next lives in
my own village;
I've yet another in
Magione, four in
La Fratta – ten in
Castiglione!

54. *TRETET EIN, HOHER KRIEGER*   54. ENTER, PROUD
    ENTER   PROUD WARRIOR   WARRIOR

Gottfried Keller

Tretet ein, hoher Krieger,   Enter, proud
enter (in) proud warrior   warrior! You have
                                          given your heart to
Der sein Herz mir   ergab!   me! Lay down your
who his heart to me yielded   scarlet cloak and
                                          golden spurs.
Legt den purpurnen Mantel
lay the crimson   cloak

Und die Goldsporen   ab.
and the golden-spurs down

Spannt das Ross in den Pflug,   Harness your
harness the steed in the plough   steed to the plough
                                          in homage to my
Meinem Vater zum   Gruss!   father, and give
to my father to the greeting   me your
                                          saddle-cloth with
Die Schabrack   mit dem Wappen   its coat of arms as
the saddle-cloth with the coat-of-arms   a rug for my feet.

Gibt 'nen Teppich meinem Fuss.
gives a   rug   to my foot

Euer Schwertgriff muss lassen   Give me the
your sword-hilt   must to part with   gold and gems from
                                          the hilt of your
Für mich Gold und Stein,   sword, and let the
for me   gold and stone   flashing blade
                                          serve me as a
Und die blitzende Klinge   poker.
and the flashing blade

Wird ein Schüreisen sein.
will a   poker   to be

Und die schneeweisse Feder   And the
and the snow-white   feather   snow-white feather
                                          on your blood-red
Auf dem blutroten Hut   cap will make a
on the blood-red cap   fan to cool me in
                                          the summer.
Ist zu 'nem kühlenden Wedel
is to a   cooling   fan

In der Sommerszeit gut.
in the summer-time good

Und der Marschall muss lernen   The marshall
and the marshall must to learn   must learn how to
                                          bake white bread,
Wie man Weizenbrot backt,   and at Christmas
how one white bread bakes   make sausages and
                                          stuffing.
Wie man Wurst   und Gefüllsel
how one sausage and stuffing

Um die Weihnachtszeit hackt.
at the Christmas-time chops

Nun befehlt eure Seele
now commend your soul

Dem   heiligen Christ!
to the Holy   Christ

Euer Leib ist verkauft,
your body is sold

Wo   kein Erlösen   mehr ist!
where no   redeeming more is

And now
commend your soul
to Christ our
Lord! You've sold
yourself, and
cannot be redeemed!

55. MORGENSTIMMUNG
  MORNING-MOOD

55. MORNING MOOD

Robert Reinick

Bald ist der   Nacht ein End gemacht,
soon is of the night an end made

Schon   fühle ich Morgenlüfte   wehen.
already feel I   morning-breezes to blow

Der Herr, der spricht: "Es werde   Licht!"
the Lord he says   it let become light

Da   muss, was dunkel ist, vergehen.
then must what dark is   to vanish

Soon the night
will be at an end;
already I feel the
freshness of the
morning breeze.
The Lord says, 'Let
there be light.'
And then all
darkness must
vanish.

Vom   Himmelszelt   durch   alle Welt
from the Heaven's-vault through all   world

Die Engel   freudejauchzend fliegen;
the angels exulting   fly

Der   Sonne Strahl durchflammt   das All.
of the sun   ray   flames through the universe

Herr, lass uns kämpfen, lass uns siegen!
Lord let us   to strive let us to conquer

Angels from the
vaults of Heaven
fly over all the
earth, singing in
exultation; the
fiery rays of the
sun flood the
universe. O Lord,
let us strive, let
us conquer!

Gustav Mahler
(1860-1911)

<table>
<tr><td>

1. LIEDER EINES FAHRENDEN GESELLEN
   SONGS OF A - WAYFARER -

</td><td>

1. SONGS OF A
   WAYFARER

</td></tr>
</table>

Gustav Mahler

i.   i.

Wenn mein Schatz   Hochzeit macht,
when my   sweetheart wedding makes

Hab' ich meinen traurigen Tag!
have I   my   sad   day

Geh' ich in   mein Kämmerlein, dunkles Kämmerlein,
go   I into my little room dark   little room

Weine! Wein! um meinen Schatz,   um meinen lieben
weep   weep for my   sweetheart for my   dear
  Schatz!
  sweetheart

The day my
sweetheart gaily
weds will be a sad
one for me! I'll go
into my little room,
my dark little room,
and weep for my
sweetheart, my dear
sweetheart!

Blümlein   blau! Verdorre nicht!
little flower blue wither   not

Vöglein   süss! Du singst auf grüner Heide!
little bird sweet you sing on green heath

Ach! Wie ist die Welt so schön!   Ziküth!
oh   how is the world so beautiful chirrup

Little blue
flower, do not
wither! Sweet little
bird, singing on the
green heath - 0
how beautiful is the
world! Chirrup!

Singet nicht! Blühet nicht! Lenz   ist ja   vorbei!
sing   not   blossom not   spring is indeed over

Alles Singen ist nun aus!
all   singing is now ended

Des   Abends, wenn ich schlafen geh',
of the evening when I   to sleep go

Denk' ich an mein Leid! An mein Leide!
think I of my   grief of my   grief

Sing no more,
bloom no more -
spring is over now!
All the singing is at
an end. Each night
when I go to bed, I
think of my grief.

ii.

Ging   heut' Morgen über's   Feld,
walked today morning over the field

Tau noch auf den Gräsern hing,
dew still on the grasses hung

Sprach zu mir der lust'ge Fink:
spoke to me the merry finch

"Ei, du! Gelt?   Guten Morgen! Ei, gelt?   Du!
 hey you isn't it good morning oh isn't it you

Wird's nicht eine schöne   Welt? schöne   Welt?
is it not   a   beautiful world beautiful world

Zink! Zink! Schön und flink!
chink chink fair and bright

Wie mir doch   die Welt gefällt!"
how me   indeed the world pleases

Auch die Glockenblum' am   Feld
also the harebell   in the field

Hat mir lustig, guter   Ding',
has me gaily   of good things (i.e. spirits)

Mit den Glöckchen   klinge, kling,
with the little bells tinkle tinkle

Ihren Morgengruss   geschellt:
her   morning-greeting rung

"Wird's nicht ein schöne   Welt? schöne   Welt?
 is it not   a   beautiful world beautiful world

Kling! Kling! Schönes   Ding!
tinkle tinkle beautiful thing

Wie mir doch   die Welt gefällt! Heia!"
how me   indeed the world pleases hey ho

Und da   fing im   Sonnenschein
and then began in the sunshine

Gleich die Welt zu funkeln an;
at once the world to sparkle –

Alles,   alles   Ton und Farbe gewann! Im
everything everything tone and colour gained in the
 Sonnenschein!
 sunshine

Blum' und Vogel, gross und klein!
flower and bird   great and small

"Guten Tag! Guten Tag! Ist's nicht eine schöne   Welt?
 good day good day is it not   a   beautiful world

Ei, du! Gelt? Schöne   Welt!
hey you isn't it beautiful world

Nun fängt auch mein Glück   wohl   an?
now begins also my   happiness perhaps –

Nein! Nein! Das ich mein', mir   nimmer blühen   kann!
no   no   that I   think to me never to blossom can

---

ii.

This morning I
walked in the fields,
dew still hung on the
grass. The merry
chaffinch called to
me, 'Hey, you there!
Isn't it a good
morning! Oh, isn't
it? You there! Isn't
the world beautiful,
beautiful? Chink!
Chink! Bright and
fair! O how I love
the world!'

The harebell too
in the field, in gay
and happy mood, rang
out her morning
greeting to me on
her little bells:
tinkle, tinkle,
'Isn't the world
beautiful, beautiful?
Tinkle, tinkle!
Beautiful! How I love
the world! Hey ho!'

And in the
sunshine the world
at once began to
sparkle. Everything
grew bright in the
sunshine; flowers and
birds, both great
and small. 'Good day,
good day! Isn't the
world beautiful?
Hey, you there, isn't
it? A beautiful
world!'

Now will my
happiness begin as
well? Oh no, I
believe that mine
can never blossom!

iii.

Ich hab' ein glühend Messer, ein Messer in meiner Brust.
I have a glowing knife a knife in my breast

O weh! O weh!
O alas O alas

Das schneid't so tief in jede Freud' und jede
that cuts so deeply into every joy and every

   Lust, so tief!
   pleasure so deeply

Ach! was ist das für ein böser Gast!
ah what is that for an evil guest

Nimmer hält er Ruh', nimmer hält er Rast,
never keeps he quiet never keeps he rest

Nicht bei Tag, nicht bei Nacht, wenn ich schlief!
not by day not by night when I slept

O weh! O weh!
O alas O alas

Wenn ich in den Himmel seh',
when I into the sky look

Seh' ich zwei blaue Augen steh'n!
see I two blue eyes to stand

O weh! O weh!
O alas O alas

Wenn ich im gelben Felde geh',
when I in the yellow field walk

Seh' ich von fern das blonde Haar im Winde weh'n!
see I from afar the fair hair in the wind to blow

O weh! O weh!
O alas O alas

Wenn ich aus dem Traum auffahr'
when I from the dream start up

Und höre klingen ihr silbern Lachen,
and hear to sound her silvery laugh

O weh! O weh!
O alas O alas

Ich wollt', ich läg' auf der schwarzen Bahr'
I would I might lie on the black bier

Könnt nimmer die Augen aufmachen!
could never the eyes to open

iv.

Die zwei blauen Augen von meinem Schatz,
the two blue eyes of my treasure

Die haben mich in die weite Welt geschickt.
they have me in the wide world sent

Da musst' ich Abschied nehmen vom allerliebsten
then had to I farewell to take of the most loved of all

   Platz!
   place

iii.

I feel a knife burning in my breast, alas, alas! It cuts so deep into every joy and pleasure. Oh, what an evil guest it is, never quiet, never at rest by day or night, even when I sleep, alas, alas!

When I look up at the sky, I see two blue eyes, alas, alas! When I walk through the yellow corn fields, I see from afar her fair hair blowing in the wind, alas, alas!

When I start up from a dream, and hear her silvery laugh, alas, alas! I wish I were lying in a black coffin, and would never open my eyes again!

iv.

My dear love's two blue eyes have driven me out into the world. I had to bid farewell to the place I love the best. O blue eyes, why did you look at me? Now pain and grief will be with me for ever!

O Augen blau! Warum habt ihr mich angeblickt?
O eyes blue why have you me   looked at

Nun hab' ich ewig   Leid und Grämen!
now have I   for ever pain and grieving

Ich bin ausgegangen in stiller Nacht,
I am gone out   in still   night

In stiller Nacht wohl   über die dunkle Heide.
in still   night indeed over the dark   heath

Hat mir   niemand ade   gesagt, ade!
has to me no one farewell said   farewell

Mein Gesell' war Lieb' und Leide!
my   companion was love and grief

Auf der Strasse stand ein Lindenbaum,
in the road   stood a   linden-tree

Da   hab' ich zum   erstenmal im   Schlaf geruht!
there have I   for the first time in the sleep rested

Unter dem Lindenbaum, der hat
under the linden tree that has

Seine Blüten   über mich geschneit,
his   blossoms over me   snowed

Da   wusst' ich nicht, wie das Leben tut,
there knew I   not   how the life does

War alles, ach alles wieder gut!
was all   ah all   again well

Alles! Alles! Lieb' und Leid,
all   all   love and grief

Und Welt und Traum!
and world and dream

I went out into
the still night over
the dark heath. No
one said farewell,
my only companions
were love and grief.
By the road was a
linden tree, and
there for the first
time I found rest
and sleep.

The linden tree
shed its blossoms on
me like snow, and I
forgot what life can
do - all, oh all was
well again! All -
love and grief, and
world and dream!

2. WER HAT DIES LIEDLEIN   ERDACHT?
WHO HAS THIS LITTLE SONG DEVISED

(From *Des   Knaben Wunderhorn,*
       of the boy magic-horn
folk poems published by
Achim von Arnim and Clemens Brentano)

2. WHO THOUGHT UP
   THIS LITTLE SONG?

Dort oben am   Berg in dem hohen Haus,
there above on the hill in the tall house

Da   gucket ein fein's, lieb's Mädel heraus.
there peeps a   fine   dear maid out

Es ist nicht dort daheime!
it is not   there at home

Es ist des   Wirts   sein Töchterlein!
it is of the inn-keeper his little daughter

Es wohnet auf grüner Heide!
it lives on green heath

Up there on the
hill, a sweet pretty
maid peeps out of a
tall house. She
doesn't live there -
she's the inn-keeper's
daughter, and lives
on the green heath!

Mein Herzle   ist wund!
my   (little) heart is   sore

Komm, Schätzle,   mach's g'sund!
come (little) sweetheart make it well

Dein schwarzbraune Äuglein   die hab'n mich
your dark brown   (little) eyes they have me
 verwund't!
  wounded

Dein rosiger Mund macht Herzen gesund,
your rosy   mouth makes hearts well

Macht Jugend verständig, macht Tote   lebendig,
makes youth   wise   makes dead persons alive

Macht Kranke gesund, ja   gesund!
makes invalid well   indeed well

My heart is sore
– come, sweetheart,
make it well! Your
dark brown eyes have
wounded me! Your rosy
lips mend broken
hearts, make youth
wise, give life to
the dead, and health
to the sick.

Wer hat denn das schön schöne Liedlein   erdacht?
who has then the lovely lovely little song devised

Es   haben's drei Gäns' übers   Wasser gebracht.
(it) have it three geese over the water   brought

Zwei graue und eine weisse!
two grey and a   white

Und wer das Liedlein   nicht singen kann,
and who the little song not   to sing can

Dem   wollen sie es pfeifen! Ja.
to him will   they it to whistle yes

Who thought up
this pretty little
song? Three geese
brought it over the
water – two greys
and a white one! And
if you can't sing
this little song,
they'll whistle it
for you!

3. RHEINLEGENDCHEN
   RHINE LEGEND

(From *Des   Knaben Wunderhorn,*
       of the boy   magic-horn
folk poems published by
Achim von Arnim and Clemens Brentano)

Bald   gras' ich am   Neckar, bald   gras' ich
sometimes graze I   by the Neckar sometimes graze I
 am   Rhein,
 by the Rhine

Bald   hab' ich ein Schätzel, bald   bin ich
sometimes have I   a   sweetheart sometimes am I
 allein!
 alone

Was hilft mir   das Grasen, wenn d'Sichel   nicht
what use   to me the grazing if   the sickle not
 schneid't,
 cuts

Was hilft mir   ein Schätzel, wenn's bei mir nicht
what use   to me a   sweetheart if it with me not
 bleibt!
 stays

Sometimes I make
hay by the Neckar,
sometimes I make hay
by the Rhine.
Sometimes I have a
sweetheart, sometimes
I'm alone. What use
is it haymaking if the
scythe is blunt –
what use is a
sweetheart who doesn't
stay by me!

So soll   ich denn grasen   am   Neckar, am   Rhein;
so should I   then to graze by the Neckar by the Rhine

So werf' ich mein goldenes Ringlein   hinein!
so throw I   my   golden   (little)ring in there

Es fliesset im   Neckar und fliesset im   Rhein,
it flows   in the Neckar and flows   in the Rhine

Soll schwimmen hinunter ins   Meer tief hinein.
must to swim   down   into the sea deep (into)

Und schwimmt es, das Ringlein,   so frisst es ein
and swims   it the (little)ring so devours it a
  Fisch!
  fish

Das Fischlein   soll kommen auf's Königs sein Tisch!
the (little)fish shall to come on the king's his table

Der König tät   fragen, wem's   Ringlein
the king would(do) to ask to whom the (little)ring
  sollt' sein?
  should to be

Da   tät   mein Schatz   sagen: "Das Ringlein
then would(do) my   sweetheart to say the (little) ring
  g'hört mein!"
  belongs of me

Mein Schätzlein tät   springen bergauf und bergein,
my   sweetheart would(do) to run   up-hill and down-hill

Tät   mir wied'rum bringen das Goldringlein   fein!
would me again   to bring the little gold ring fine

Kannst grasen am   Neckar, kannst grasen   am
can   to graze by the Neckar can   to graze by the
  Rhein!
  Rhine

Wirf du mir   nur immer dein Ringlein   hinein!
throw you to me only always your (little)ring in there

So whenever I
make hay by the
Neckar or the Rhine,
I throw my gold ring
into the water! It
sweeps along the
Neckar, and it sweeps
along the Rhine, and
it swims right into
the deep sea.

     And as it swims a
fish swallows it up,
the fish that must
come to the table of
the king! The king
will ask, 'Whose ring
is this?' And my
sweetheart will say,
'The ring is mine!'

     Then my
sweetheart will run
up-hill and
down-dale to bring
back my fine
golden ring to me!
So if you make hay
by the Neckar, or
make hay by the Rhine,
all you must do is to
throw in your ring!

4. *KINDERTOTENLIEDER*
   CHILDREN'S DEATH SONGS

4. SONGS ON THE DEATH
   OF CHILDREN

Friedrich Rückert

i.

i.

Nun will die Sonn' so hell   aufgeh'n,
now will the sun   so brightly to rise

Als sei kein Unglück   die Nacht gescheh'n.
as were no   misfortune the night happened

Das Unglück   geschah nur mir   allein,
the misfortune happened only to me alone

Die Sonne, sie scheinet allgemein!
the sun   she shines   universally

Du musst nicht die Nacht in dir verschränken,
you must not   the night in you to enclose

Musst sie ins   ew'ge   Licht versenken!
must her in the eternal light to sink

Ein Lämplein   verlosch in meinem Zelt,
a   little lamp went out in my   tent

Heil sei dem   Freudenlicht der   Welt!
hail be to the light of joy of the world

Soon the sun will
rise again, as
brightly as if the
night had brought no
sudden grief. But this
grief was mine alone,
and the sun shines on
everyone. You must not
enclose the night
within yourself, but
let it merge in the
Eternal Light. A
tiny lamp went out in
my small dwelling –
blessed be the
joyous Light of the
world!

ii.

ii.

Nun seh' ich wohl, warum so dunkle Flammen
now see I   indeed why   so dark   flames

Ihr sprühtet mir   in manchem Augenblicke,
you flashed to me in many a   moment

O Augen!
O eyes

Gleichsam um   voll in einem Blicke
as if   in order full in a   glance

Zu drängen eure ganze Macht zusammen.
to to press your whole might together

Doch ahnt'   ich nicht, weil   Nebel mich umschwammen,
but suspected I   not   because mist me   swam about

Gewoben vom   verblendenden Geschicke,
woven   from the deluding   Fate

Dass sich   der Strahl bereits zur   Heimkehr
that himself the ray   already to the return home
  schicke,
  might send

Dorthin, von wannen alle Strahlen stammen.
thither from whence all rays   spring

Ihr wolltet mir   mit eurem Leuchten sagen:
you wanted to me with your shining to say

Wir möchten   nah. dir   bleiben gerne,
we would like near to you to stay (gladly)

Doch ist uns   das vom   Schicksal abgeschlagen.
but is to us that by the fate   refused

Now I understal.
why the flames in
your eyes that you
sometimes flashed at
me were so dark, as if
you would press your
whole strength into a
single glance.
Deluding Fate
shrouded me in its
mists, so I did not
suspect that this one
bright ray was ready
to return home to the
Source of all light.
You wanted in your
shining to say: we
would gladly stay with
you, but Fate will not
allow it. Look at us
now, for soon we shall
be far away! What
today you see as eyes,
in nights to come will
only be stars.

Sieh' uns nur an, denn bald sind wir dir   ferne!
look us   only at for soon are we to you far away

Was dir   nur Augen sind in diesen Tagen,
what to you only eyes are in these days

In künft'gen Nächten sind es   dir   nur Sterne.
in coming   nights   are (it) to you only stars

iii.

Wenn dein Mütterlein
when your (little) mother

Tritt zur   Tür herein,
comes to the door in

Und den Kopf ich drehe,
and the head I   turn

Ihr entgegensehe,
her look towards

Fällt auf ihr Gesicht
falls on her face

Erst der Blick mir   nicht,
first the glance to me not

Sondern auf die Stelle
but   on the place

Näher nach der Schwelle,
nearer to   the threshold

Dort wo   würde dein
there where would your

Lieb Gesichtchen sein,
dear little face to be

Wenn du   freudenhelle
if   you bright with joy

Trätest mit   herein
walked with (her) in here

Wie sonst,   mein Töchterlein.
as formerly my   little daughter

Wenn dein Mütterlein
when your (little) mother

Tritt zur   Tür herein
walks to the door in here

Mit der Kerze Schimmer,
with the candle glimmer

Ist es mir, als immer
is it to me as always

Kämst du mit   herein,
came you with (her) in here

Huschtest hinterdrein
slipped   behind

Als wie sonst   ins   Zimmer!
as (as) formerly into the room

iii.

When your dear
mother comes in at
the door, and I turn
my head to look at
her, my first glance
falls not on her face,
but on the place
nearer the threshold
where your dear little
face would be, if you
were at her side,
bright and happy as
you used to be, little
daughter.

When your dear
mother comes in at
the door with a
flickering candle, it
seems as if you were
with her, slipping
after her into the
room as you used to
do.

O du, des   Vaters Zelle,
O you of the father cell

Ach, zu schnelle
ah   too quickly

Erloschner   Freudenschein!
extinguished light of joy

    iv.

Oft   denk' ich, sie sind ausgegangen!
often think I   they are gone out

Bald werden sie wieder nach Hause   gelangen!
soon will   they again - homewards - to reach

Der Tag ist schön! O sei nicht bang!
the day is lovely O be not   anxious

Sie machen nur einen weiten Gang!
they make   only a   long   walk

Jawohl,   sie sind nur ausgegangen
yes indeed they are only gone out

Und werden jetzt nach Hause   gelangen!
and will   now   - homewards - to reach

O sei nicht bang,   der Tag ist schön!
O be not   anxious the day is lovely

Sie machen nur den Gang zu jenen Höhn!
they make   only the walk to those hills

Sie sind uns   nur vorausgegangen
they are to us only gone ahead

Und werden nicht wieder nach Haus   verlangen!
and will   not   again - homewards - to desire

Wir holen   sie ein auf jenen Höh'n
we catch (with) them up on those hills

Im   Sonnenschein!
in the sunshine

Der Tag ist schön auf jenen Höh'n.
the day is lovely on those hills

O you of your
father's seed - a
light of joy, alas,
too quickly
extinguished.

    iv.

    I sometimes think
they have just gone
out, and will soon be
coming home again. It
is a lovely day, do
not be anxious - they
have only gone for a
long walk. Yes, of
course, they have
just gone out, and
will soon be coming
home. O do not be
anxious, it is a
lovely day! They have
only gone for a walk
to the hills. They
have just gone on
ahead of us, and will
not want to come
home again. We will
catch up with them
there on the hills in
the sunshine. It is a
lovely day up there
on the hills.

v.

In diesem Wetter, in diesem Braus,
in this   weather in this   raging

Nie hätt' ich gesendet die Kinder hinaus!
never would have I sent   the children out

Man hat sie hinaus getragen,
one has them out   taken

Ich durfte nichts dazu sagen!
I was allowed nothing to that to say

In diesem Wetter, in diesem Saus,
in this   weather in this   storm

Nie hätt' ich gelassen die Kinder hinaus,
never would have I let   the children out

Ich fürchtete, sie erkranken,
I was afraid they might fall ill

Das sind nun eitle Gedanken.
that are now vain thoughts

In diesem Wetter, in diesem Graus,
in this   weather in this   horror

Nie hätt' ich gelassen die Kinder hinaus,
never would have I let   the children out

Ich sorgte, sie stürben morgen,
I was afraid they might die next day

Das ist nun nicht zu besorgen.
that is now not to to be anxious about

In diesem Wetter, in diesem Saus, in diesem Braus,
in this   weather in this   storm in this   tumult

Sie ruhn als wie in der Mutter Haus,
they sleep as though in of the mother house

Von keinem Sturme erschrecket,
by no   storm frightened

Von Gottes Hand bedecket.
by God's hand sheltered

Sie ruhn als wie in der Mutter Haus.
they sleep as though in of the mother house

v.

In such weather, in such a storm, I would never have sent the children out. But they were taken out, and I could say nothing about it. In such weather, in such a gale, I would never have let the children go out. I was afraid they might fall ill – but these are vain thoughts. In such weather, in such a dreadful tumult, I would never have let the children go out. I was afraid they might soon die – but now there is nothing to fear. In such weather, in such a gale, in such a raging tumult, they sleep as in their mother's house – frightened no more by storms, sheltered by God's hand.

5. FÜNF RÜCKERT LIEDER
FIVE RÜCKERT SONGS

Friedrich Rückert

i.

Ich atmet' einen linden Duft.
I breathed a   gentle fragrance

Im Zimmer stand
in the room   was

Ein Zweig der Linde
a   twig of the lime-tree

5. FIVE SONGS BY RÜCKERT

i.

I breathed a gentle fragrance. In the room was a sprig of lime, a gift from your dear hand. How lovely was the scent of the lime!

Ein Angebinde
a   gift

Von lieber Hand.
from dear   hand

Wie lieblich war der Lindenduft!
how lovely   was the lime-scent

Wie lieblich ist der Lindenduft!
how lovely   is the lime-scent

Das Lindenreis
the linden-sprig

Brachst du gelinde;
broke   you gently

Ich atme   leis'
I   breathe softly

Im   Duft der   Linde
in the scent of the lime

Der   Liebe linden Duft.
of the love gentle fragrance

How lovely is the
scent of the lime!
You broke the sprig
so gently; I softly
breathe the scent of
the lime, the gentle
fragrance of love.

ii.

Liebst du um   Schönheit, o nicht mich liebe!
love   you (about) beauty   O not   me   love

Liebe die Sonne, sie trägt ein goldnes Haar!
love   the sun   she wears (a) golden hair

Liebst du um   Jugend, o nicht mich liebe!
love   you (about) youth O not   me   love

Liebe den Frühling, der   jung ist jedes Jahr!
love   the spring   which young is each year

Liebst du um   Schätze, o nicht mich liebe!
love   you (about) treasure O not   me   love

Liebe die Meerfrau, sie hat viel Perlen klar!
love   the mermaid   she had many pearls clear

Liebst du um   Liebe, o ja - mich liebe!
love   you (about) love O truly me   love

Liebe mich immer, dich lieb ich immerdar!
love   me   always you love I   always

ii.

If you love
beauty, then do not
love me - love the
sun, with its
golden hair!

If you love
youth, then do not
love me - love the
spring, which is young
every year!

If you love
treasure, then do not
love me - love the
mermaid with her many
shining pearls!

If it is love you
love - O then love me!
Love me always, as I
will always love you!

iii.

Blicke mir   nicht in die Lieder!
look   to me not   at the songs

Meine Augen schlag' ich nieder,
my   eyes cast   I   down

Wie ertappt auf böser Tat.
as caught in bad   deed

Selber darf ich nicht getrauen,
myself may I   not   to trust

Ihrem Wachsen zuzuschauen,
their growing to to watch

iii.

Do not look at my
songs as I write! I
lower my eyes, as
though caught in a
shameful deed. I
cannot even trust
myself to watch their
growing - but your
curiosity is betrayal.

Deine Neugier   ist Verrat.
your   curiosity is betrayal

Bienen, wenn sie Zellen bauen,
bees   when they cells build

Lassen auch nicht zu sich   schauen,
let   also not   to themselves to watch

Schauen selber   auch nicht zu.
watch   themselves also not   –

Wenn die reichen Honigwaben
when the rich   honeycombs

Sie zu Tag   befördert haben,
they to day(light) dispatched have

Dann vor   allen nasche du!
then before all   nibble you

When the bees
build their cells,
they too let no one
watch them, they do
not even watch
themselves. When they
have brought their
rich honeycombs to the
light of day, only
then may you enjoy
them!

iv.

Ich bin der   Welt abhanden gekommen,
I   am of the world lost   got

Mit der   ich sonst   viele Zeit verdorben;
with which I formerly much time spoilt

Sie hat so lange nichts von mir vernommen,
she has so long nothing from me heard

Sie mag wohl   glauben,   ich sei gestorben.
she may perhaps to believe I   am dead

Es ist mir   auch gar   nichts daran   gelegen,
it is to me also at all nothing thereon concerned

Ob   sie mich für gestorben hält.
whether she me   for dead   takes

Ich kann auch gar   nichts sagen dagegen,
I   can also at all nothing to say against that

Denn wirklich bin ich gestorben der   Welt.
for really   am I dead   to the world

Ich bin gestorben dem   Weltgetümmel
I   am dead   to the world-turmoil

Und ruh' in einem stillen Gebiet.
and rest in a   still   sphere

Ich leb' allein in meinem Himmel,
I   live alone in my   heaven

In meinem Lieben, in meinem Lied.
in my   love   in my   song

iv.

I am lost to the
world, where once I
wasted so much time.
It has heard nothing
of me for so long, it
may even think me
dead.

It is nothing to
me if it thinks me
dead; indeed I cannot
deny it, for truly I
am dead to the world.

I am dead to the
world's turmoil, and
rest in a quiet place;
alone I dwell in my
own heaven, in my
love, and in my song.

v.

Um Mitternacht
at midnight

Hab ich gewacht
have I   been awake

Und aufgeblickt zum   Himmel;
and looked up   at the sky

Kein Stern vom   Sterngewimmel
no   star of the star-busy throng

v.

At midnight I was
awake, and looked up
at the sky; not one
of the busy throng of
stars smiled at me,
at midnight.

Hat mir   gelacht
has to me laughed

Um Mitternacht.
at midnight

Um Mitternacht
at midnight

Hab ich gedacht
have I   thought

Hinaus in   dunkle Schranken;
out   into dark   enclosures

Es   hat kein Lichtgedanken
(it) has no   light-thoughts

Mir   Trost gebracht
to me comfort brought

Um Mitternacht.
at midnight

At midnight, my
thoughts reached out
into the enclosing
darkness; no ray of
light came into my
mind to bring me
comfort, at midnight.

Um Mitternacht
at midnight

Nahm ich in   acht
took I   (into) heed

Die Schläge meines Herzens;
the beats   of my heart

Ein einz'ger Puls des   Schmerzens
a   single   pulse of the pain

War angefacht
was kindled

Um Mitternacht.
at midnight

At midnight, I
took heed of the
beating of my heart;
a single pulse of
pain hotly throbbed,
at midnight.

Um Mitternacht
at midnight

Kämpft ich die Schlacht,
fought I   the battle

O Menschheit, deiner Leiden;
O mankind   of your suffering

Nicht konnt ich sie entscheiden
not   could I   her to resolve

Mit meiner Macht
with my   might

Um Mitternacht.
at midnight

At midnight, I
fought the battle of
your suffering, O
mankind; with all my
might I could not
resolve it, at
midnight.

Um Mitternacht
at midnight

Hab ich die Macht
have I   the might

In   deine Hand gegeben:
into your hand given

Herr über Tod und Leben,
Lord over death and life

Du hältst die Wacht
you keep   the watch

Um Mitternacht!
at midnight

At midnight, I
gave my whole strength
into your hands. O
Lord, you keep watch
over life and death,
at midnight!

Richard Strauss
(1864-1949)

1. DEDICATION

1. ZUEIGNUNG
DEDICATION

Hermann von Gilm

Ja, du weisst es, teure Seele,
yes you know   it   dear   soul

    Yes, you know,
dear heart, that far
from you I am
tormented. Love makes
the heart sick – for
this I thank you!

Dass ich fern von dir mich   quäle,
that I   far   from you myself torment

Liebe macht die Herzen krank,
love makes the hearts sick

Habe Dank.
have thanks

Einst hielt ich, der   Freiheit Zecher,
once held I   of the freedom   reveller

    Once, revelling in
liberty, I raised high
a goblet of amethyst,
and you blessed the
draught – for this I
thank you!

Hoch den Amethysten-Becher
high the amethyst   goblet

Und du   segnetest den Trank,
and you blessed   the draught

Habe Dank.
have thanks

Und beschworst darin   die Bösen,
and exorcised   therein the evil

    And you banished
the evil away, till I
was purified as never
before, and sank on
to your breast – for
this I thank you!

Bis   ich, was ich nie   gewesen,
until I   what I   never been

Heilig, heilig an's Herz dir   sank,
hallowed hallowed on the heart to you sank

Habe Dank.
have thanks

2. *DIE NACHT*
   THE NIGHT

2. NIGHT

Hermann von Gilm

Aus   dem Walde tritt die Nacht,
out of the wood   treads the night

Aus   den Bäumen schleicht sie leise,
out of the trees   steals   she softly

Schaut sich um   in weitem Kreise,
looks   her about in wide   circle

Nun gib acht.
now give heed

Night is creeping
out of the wood,
stealing softly from
among the trees,
peering around in
widening circles.
Now, take care!

Alle Lichter dieser Welt,
all lights of this world

Alle Blumen, alle Farben
all flowers all colours

Löscht sie aus und stielt die Garben
blots she out and steals the sheaves

Weg vom   Feld.
away from the field

She blots out all
light on this earth -
all flowers, all
colours - and steals
the sheaves away from
the field.

Alles   nimmt sie, was   nur hold,
everything takes she -whatsovever- lovely

Nimmt das Silber weg des   Stroms,
takes the silver away from the river

Nimmt vom   Kupferdach des Doms
takes from the copper roof of the cathedral

Weg das Gold.
away the gold

She seizes all
that is lovely; the
silver from the
river, and from the
copper on the dome,
the gold.

Ausgeplündert steht der Strauch,
stripped   stands the bush

Rücke näher, Seel' an Seele;
move nearer soul to soul

O die Nacht, mir   bangt, sie stehle
O the night to me afraid she might steal

Dich mir   auch.
you to me too

Stripped stands
the bush - edge
nearer, soul to soul.
Oh, I fear the night
will steal you from
me too.

3. *ALLERSEELEN*
   ALL SOULS

3. ALL SOULS

Hermann von Gilm

Stell' auf dem Tisch die duftenden   Reseden,
lay   on the table the sweet-smelling mignonette

Die letzten roten Astern trag' hierbei,
the last   red   asters carry hereby

Und lass uns wieder von der Liebe reden,
and let us again of the love to speak

Lay on the table
the fragrant
mignonette and the
last red asters, and
let us speak again of
love, like once in
May!

Wie einst im   Mai.
like once in the May

Gib mir   die Hand, dass ich sie heimlich drücke,
give to me the hand that I   her secretly may press

Und wenn man's sieht, mir   ist es einerlei,
and if   one it sees to me is it all the same

Gib mir   nur einen deiner süssen Blicke,
give to me only one   of your sweet glances

Wie einst im   Mai.
like once in the May

Give me your hand, that I may press it secretly – and if anyone should see, what matter? Then give me just one sweet glance, like once in May!

Es blüht   und duftet   heut' auf jedem Grabe
it blossoms and is fragrant today on each grave

Ein Tag im   Jahr ist ja   den Toten   frei,
one day in the year is indeed the dead one free

Komm an mein Herz, dass ich dich wieder habe,
come to my heart that I   you again have

Wie einst im   Mai.
like once in the May

Today each grave is fragrant with flowers, for one day in the year the dead are free. Come to my heart that I may hold you again, like once in May!

4. STÄNDCHEN
   SERENADE

4. SERENADE

Adolf Friedrich von Schack

Mach' auf, mach' auf, doch leise, mein Kind,
– open – – open – but softly my   child

Um   keinen vom   Schlummer zu wecken.
so as no one from the slumber   to to wake

Kaum murmelt der Bach, kaum zittert im   Wind
hardly murmurs the brook hardly trembles in the wind

Ein Blatt an den Büschen und Hecken.
a   leaf on the bushes and hedges

D'rum   leise, mein Mädchen, dass nichts sich
therefore softly my   girl   that nothing (itself)
  regt,
  stirs

Nur leise die Hand auf die Klinke gelegt.
just softly the hand on the latch laid

Open the door, but softly my child, so no one awakens from sleep. The brook barely murmurs, and the leaves hardly tremble on bush and hedge. So softly, my love, that nothing stirs, just lay your hand gently on the latch.

Mit Tritten   wie Tritte   der   Elfen so sacht,
with footsteps like footsteps of the elves so light

Um   über die Blumen zu hüpfen,
so as over the flowers to to skip

Flieg' leicht hinaus in   die Mondscheinnacht,
fly \ nimbly out   into the moonlight-night

Zu mir in   den Garten zu schlüpfen.
to me into the garden to to slip

Rings schlummern die Blüten am   rieselnden Bach
around slumber   the flowers by the rippling   brook

With steps light as elfin steps skipping over the flowers, fly nimbly out into the moonlit night, slip out to me in the garden. Flowers slumber by the rippling brook, sending forth their fragrance as they sleep; only love keeps watch.

Und duften   im   Schlaf, nur die Liebe
and send forth fragrance in the sleep   only the love

  ist wach.
  is awake

Sitz' nieder, hier dämmert's   geheimnisvoll
sit   down   here grows dusk it mysteriously

Unter den Lindenbäumen,
under the linden-trees

Die Nachtigall uns   zu   Häupten soll
the nightingale to us at (our) heads   shall

Von uns'ren Küssen träumen
of our   kisses to dream

Und die Rose, wenn sie am   Morgen erwacht,
and the rose when she in the morning awakens

Hoch   glühn von den Wonneschauern   der   Nacht.
highly to glow from the rapture-shuddering of the night

Sit here, where
dusk mysteriously
gathers under the
linden trees; the
nightingale above us
will dream of our
kisses, and the rose,
awakening in the
morning, will
fervently glow with
the quivering
rapture of the night.

5. WIE SOLLTEN WIR GEHEIM SIE HALTEN
   HOW SHOULD WE   SECRET HER KEEP

5. SECRET RAPTURE

Adolf Friedrich von Schack

Wie sollten wir geheim   sie halten,
how should we   secretly her keep

Die Seligkeit, die uns erfüllt?
the bliss   that us fills

Nein, bis in   seine tiefsten Falten
no   till into its   deepest folds

Sei allen unser Herz enthüllt!
be to all our   heart revealed

How can we keep
secret this rapture
that fills us? No,
the deepest corners of
our hearts are
revealed to the world!

Wenn zwei in Liebe sich   gefunden,
when two in love themselves found

Geht Jubel   hin   durch die Natur,
goes rejoicing thither through the nature

In längern   wonnevollen Stunden
in lengthier blissful   hours

Legt sich   der Tag auf Wald und Flur.
settles (itself) the day on wood and meadow

The whole of
nature rejoices, when
two beings find
themselves in love.
The day in ever
lengthening hours of
bliss settles over
wood and meadow.

Selbst aus der   Eiche morschem Stamme,
even   from of the oak   rotten   trunk

Die ein Jahrtausend   überlebt,
that a   thousand years survived

Steigt neu des   Wipfels   grüne Flamme
rises new of the (tree-)top green flame

Und rauscht von Jugendlust   durchbebt.
and rustles with youth(ful)-delight quivered through

Even from the
trunk of the
rotting oak, that has
endured a thousand
years, a new green
shoot flames high in
its branches,
rustles and trembles
with youthful joy.

Zu höherm Glanz   und Düfte brechen
to higher splendour and scents burst

Die Knospen auf beim   Glück   der   Zwei,
the buds   open at the happiness of the two

Und süsser rauscht es in den Bächen
and sweeter murmurs it in the streams

Und reicher blüht   und reicher glänzt der Mai.
and richer blossoms and richer shines the May

The buds burst
open with a
heightened fragrance
and splendour at the
joy of the two lovers;
even sweeter murmur
the streams, even
richer blossoms the
radiant month of May.

6. ALL MEIN GEDANKEN
  ALL MY   THOUGHTS

6. ALL MY THOUGHTS

Felix Dahn

All mein Gedanken, mein Herz und mein Sinn,
all my   thoughts   my heart and my   mind

Da, wo   die Liebste ist, wandern sie hin.
there where the beloved is   wander they thither

Gehn ihres Weges trotz   Mauer und Tor,
go   their way   in spite of wall and gate

Da   hält kein Riegel, kein Graben nicht vor,
there holds no   bolt   no   moat   not out

Gehn wie die Vögelein   hoch durch   die Luft,
go   like the (little)birds high through the air

Brauchen kein Brücken über Wasser und Kluft,
need   no   bridges over water and ravine

Finden das Städtlein   und finden das Haus,
find •the (little)town and find   the house

Finden ihr Fenster aus allen heraus,
find   her window from all   out

Und klopfen und rufen;
and knock   and call

Mach auf lass uns ein,
- open - let us in

Wir kommen vom   Liebsten
we come   from the beloved

Und grüssen dich fein,
and greet   you fine

Mach auf, mach auf, lass uns ein.
- open - - open - let us in

All my thoughts,
my heart and mind,
stray to my beloved.
They go their way in
spite of wall and
gate; no bolt can
hold them, no moat
can keep them out.
They soar like birds
high in the air; they
need no bridges over
water or ravine. They
find her town, they
find her house, and
find her window
amongst all others.

And there they knock
and call, 'Open and
let us in! We come
to greet you from
your beloved - open,
open, and let us in!'

7. *DU MEINES HERZENS KRÖNELEIN*
   YOU OF MY HEART   LITTLE CROWN

7. LITTLE JEWEL OF
   MY HEART

Felix Dahn

Du meines Herzens Krönelein,
you of my heart   little crown

Du bist von lautrem Golde,
you are of pure   gold

Wenn andere daneben sein,
when others close by should be

Dann bist du noch viel holde.
then are you still much love(lier)

Little jewel of
my heart, you are of
pure gold. When
others are close at
hand, you appear
even lovelier.

Die Andern tun so gern   gescheit,
the others act so gladly clever

Du bist gar sanft und stille,
you are very gentle and quiet

Dass jedes Herz sich   dein   erfreut,
that each heart (itself) of you takes pleasure

Dein Glück   ist's, nicht dein Wille.
your happiness is it not   your wish

Others like to
put on airs, but you
are gentle and still.
You cannot but bring
joy to every heart;
it is your own sweet
gift.

Die andern suchen Lieb und Gunst
the others seek   love and favour

Mit tausend falschen Worten,
with thousand false   words

Du ohne   Mund- und Augenkunst
you without mouth- and eyes-artifice

Bist wert an allen Orten.
are valued in all   places

Others seek love
and favour, with a
thousand false words,
but you, without
artful speech or
glances, are beloved
everywhere.

Du bist als wie die Ros' im   Wald,
you are as like the rose in the wood

Sie weiss nichts von ihrer Blüte,
she knows nothing of her   bloom

Doch jedem, der vorüber wallt,
yet to each who past   wanders

Erfreut sie das Gemüte.
delights she the feelings

You are like the
rose in the wood,
unaware of her own
beauty, who yet
delights the heart
of all who pass.

8. *RUHE, MEINE SEELE*
   REST MY   SOUL

8. REST, MY SOUL

Karl Henckell

Nicht ein Lüftchen   regt sich   leise,
not a (little) breeze stirs (itself) quietly

Sanft entschlummert   ruht der Hain;
gently fallen into slumber rests the wood

Durch der   Blätter dunkle Hülle
through of the leaves dark   covering

No breath of air
is stirring, the
wood has gently
fallen into slumber;
bright sunshine steals
through the dark
covering of leaves.

Stiehlt sich   lichter Sonnenschein.
steals (himself) bright   sunshine

Ruhe, ruhe, meine Seele,
rest rest my   soul

Deine Stürme gingen wild,
your   storms went   fiercely

Hast getobt und hast gezittert,
have raged and have shuddered

Wie die Brandung, wenn sie schwillt!
like the surf   when she swells

Diese Zeiten sind gewaltig,
these times are   violent

Bringen Herz und Hirn in   Not —
bring   heart and brain into misery

Ruhe, ruhe, meine Seele,
rest rest my   soul

Und vergiss, was dich bedroht!
and forget   what you menaces

> Rest, rest my
> soul; fierce were
> your storms, that
> raged and shuddered
> like the heaving of
> breaking waves!

> These times are
> violent, they bring
> misery to heart and
> mind. Rest, rest my
> soul, and forget
> what threatens you!

9. *CÄCILIE*
     CECILIA

9. CECILIA

Heinrich Hart

Wenn du es wüsstest, was träumen heisst
if   you it knew   what to dream means

Von brennenden Küssen, von Wandern   und Ruhen   mit
of burning   kisses of wandering and resting with
  der Geliebten,
  the beloved

Aug' in   Auge und kosend   und plaudernd,
eye into eye and caressing and talking

Wenn du es wüsstest, du neigtest dein Herz!
If   you it knew   you would bow your heart

Wenn du es wüsstest, was bangen   heisst,
if   you it knew   what to be anxious means

In einsamen Nächten, umschauert   vom Sturm,
in solitary nights   shuddered about by the storm

Da   niemand tröstet milden   Mundes die kampfmüde
when no one   comforts of gentle mouth the strife-weary
  Seele,
  soul

Wenn du es wüsstest, du kämest   zu mir.
if   you it knew   you would come to me

> If you knew what
> it is to dream of
> burning kisses, of
> wandering with your
> sweetheart, and
> resting then, gazing
> into each other's
> eyes, and speaking
> loving words - if you
> but knew, your heart
> would change!

> If you knew what
> it is to spend
> anxious, solitary
> nights, surrounded by
> shuddering storms,
> with no gentle lips
> to comfort the strife-
> weary soul - if you
> but knew, you would
> come to me!

Wenn du es wüsstest, was leben heisst,
if   you it knew   what to live means

If you knew what it is to live, to feel the divine

Umhaucht   von der   Gottheit weltschaffendem Atem
breathed about by of the Deity   world-creating breath

Breath of the Creator and to soar up,

Zu schweben empor, lichtgetragen, zu seligen Höh'n,
to to soar upwards lightly borne to blissful heights

lightly borne to Elysian heights – if you but knew, you

Wenn du es wüsstest, du lebtest   mit mir.
if   you it knew   you would dwell with me

would dwell with me!

10. HEIMLICHE AUFFORDERUNG
SECRET   INVITATION

10. SECRET INVITATION

John Henry Mackay

Auf, hebe die funkelnde Schale empor zum   Mund,
up   raise the sparkling vessel up   to the mouth

Raise the sparkling vessel to your lips, drink and cheer your heart at the feast! And when you raise it, give me a sign in secret, that I may smile and silently drink like you...

Und trinke beim   Freudenmahle dein Herz gesund.
and drink at the feast   your heart sound

Und wenn du sie hebst, so winke mir   heimlich zu,
and when you her raise so wave to me secretly (to)

Dann lächle ich und dann trinke ich still   wie du...
then smile I   and then drink I   silently like you

Und still   gleich mir betrachte um   uns das Heer
and silently like me watch   about us the host

Silently like me, watch this crowd of drunken babblers – only do not be too harsh in your disdain. No, raise the shining vessel filled with wine, and let them be merry at their carousing!

Der   trunknen Schwätzer - verachte sie nicht zu sehr.
of the drunken babblers   disdain them not too much

Nein, hebe die blinkende Schale, gefüllt mit Wein,
no   lift the shining   vessel filled with wine

Und lass beim   lärmenden Mahle sie glücklich sein.
and let by the noisy   banquet them happy   to be

Doch hast du das Mahl genossen, den Durst gestillt,
but have you the meal enjoyed   the thirst quenched

But when you have enjoyed the feast, and quenched your thirst, leave your noisy comrades in their gay and festive scene, and wander out into the garden, and there by the rose-bush I'll await you as of old.

Dann verlasse der   lauten Genossen festfreudiges Bild
then leave   of the noisy comrades feast-merry picture

Und wandle hinaus in   den Garten zum Rosenstrauch,
and wander out   into the garden to the rose-bush

Dort will ich dich dann erwarten nach altem Brauch.
there will I   you then to await after old   custom

Und will an die Brust dir   sinken, eh' du's
and want on the breast to you to sink before you it
  gehofft,
  hoped

Sooner than you dare to hope, I'll sink into your arms, and drink your kisses as I used to do, and entwine the roses in your hair in all their splendour. O come, wonderful night for which I long!

Und deine Küsse trinken, wie ehmals oft,
and your kisses to drink as of old often

Und flechten in   deine Haare der   Rose Pracht.
and entwine into your hairs of the rose splendour

O komm, du wunderbare, ersehnte Nacht!
O come you wonderful   longed for night

11. *MORGEN*
   TOMORROW

11. TOMORROW

John Henry Mackay

Und morgen   wird die Sonne wieder scheinen
and tomorrow will the sun   again   to shine

Und auf dem Wege, den   ich gehen werde,
and on the path   which I   to go shall

Wird uns, die Glücklichen, sie wieder einen
will to us the happy ones   she again   to unite

Inmitten   dieser sonnenatmenden Erde...
in the midst of this sun-breaking   earth

Und zu dem Strand, dem weiten, wogenblauen,
and to the shore   the wide   waves'-blue

Werden wir still   und langsam niedersteigen,
shall we quietly and slowly descend

Stumm   werden wir uns in   die Augen schauen,
silently shall we us into the eyes to look

Und auf uns sinkt des   Glückes   stummes Schweigen...
and on us   falls of the happiness mute   silence

And tomorrow the
sun will shine again,
and on the path which
I shall take, it will
again unite us, the-
blessed ones, in the
midst of this
sun-breaking earth...

And quietly and
slowly we will go
down to the wide
blue-waved shore;
silently we will gaze
into each other's
eyes, and upon us will
fall the mute
stillness of joy...

12. *TRAUM DURCH   DIE DÄMMERUNG*
    DREAM THROUGH THE TWILIGHT

12. DREAM IN THE
    TWILIGHT

Otto Julius Bierbaum

Weite   Wiesen   im   Dämmergrau;
distant meadows in the twilight-grey

Die Sonne verglomm,   die Sterne ziehn,
the sun ceased glowing the stars advance slowly

Nun geh ich hin   zu der schönsten Frau,
now go I   there to the fairest   woman

Weit über Wiesen im   Dämmergrau,
far over meadows in the twilight-grey

Tief in   den Busch von Jasmin,
deep into the bush of jasmine

Durch Dämmergrau   in   der   Liebe Land;
through twilight-grey into of the love   land

Ich gehe nicht schnell, ich eile   nicht;
I walk not   fast   I   hasten not

Mich zieht·ein weiches samtenes Band
me   draws a   soft   velvety ribbon

Durch Dämmergrau   in   der   Liebe Land,
through twilight-grey in of the love land

In   ein blaues, mildes Licht.
into a   blue   gentle light

Distant meadows
in the twilight grey;
the sun extinguished,
the stars slowly
appearing. Now I go
to my fairest one,
far over the meadows
in the twilight grey,
deep among the
jasmine;

through the
twilight grey to the
land of love. I walk
without haste, drawn
by a soft velvety
ribbon, through the
twilight grey into
the gentle blue light
of the land of love.

13. *SCHLAGENDE HERZEN*
    BEATING   HEARTS

Otto Julius Bierbaum

Über Wiesen und Felder ein Knabe ging;
over meadows and fields a   boy   walked

Kling klang, schlug ihm   das Herz,
bing bang   beat   to him the heart

Es glänzt ihm   am   Finger von Golde ein Ring,
it shone to him on the finger of gold   a   ring

Kling klang, schlug ihm   das Herz!
bing bang   beat   to him the heart

O Wiesen, o Felder, wie seid ihr schön!
O meadows O fields how are you lovely

O Berge,   o Täler   wie schön!
O mountains O valleys how fair

Wie bist du gut, wie bist du schön,
how are you good how are you lovely

Du gold'ne Sonne in Himmelshöhn!
you golden sun   in heaven's heights

Kling klang, schlug ihm   das Herz.
bing bang   beat   to him the heart

Schnell eilte   der Knabe mit fröhlichem Schritt,
fast   hurried the boy   with merry   step

Kling klang, schlug ihm   das Herz.
bing bang   beat   to him the heart

Nahm manche lachende Blume mit;
took many a laughing flower with(him)

Kling klang, schlug ihm   das Herz.
bing bang   beat   to him the heart

Über Wiesen und Felder weht Frühlingswind,
over meadows and fields blows spring's-wind

Der treibt zu dir mich leise, lind.
that drives to you me   softly gently

Kling klang, schlug ihm   das Herz.
bing bang   beat   to him the heart

Zwischen Wiesen und Feldern ein Mädel stand,
among   meadows and fields   a   girl stood

Kling, klang, schlug ihr   das Herz,
bing bang   beat   to her the heart

Hielt über die Augen zum   Schauen die Hand,
held over the eyes to the seeing the hand

Kling klang, schlug ihr   das Herz.
bing bang   beat   to her the heart

"Über Wiesen und Felder, über Berge   und Wälder,
over meadows and fields over mountains and woods

Zu mir schnell kommt er her,
to me   quickly comes he here

O wenn er bei mir nur, bei mir schon   wär".
O if   he with me only with me already were

Kling klang, schlug ihr   das Herz.
bing bang   beat   to her the heart

13. BEATING HEARTS

A boy walked over
the meadows and
fields. (Bing bang
beat his heart.) On
his finger shone a
golden ring. (Bing
bang beat his heart.)
'O meadows, O fields,
how lovely you are!
O mountains, O
valleys, how fair!
How good you are, how
lovely you are, O
golden sun high in the
sky!' (Bing bang beat
his heart.) The boy
hurried along with a
merry step. (Bing
bang beat his heart.)
He took many gay
flowers with him.
(Bing bang beat his
heart.) 'A spring
breeze blew over the
meadows and fields,
and blew right into
my heart; softly,
gently, it sends me
to you!' (Bing bang
beat his heart.) A
girl stood in the
meadows and fields.
(Bing bang beat his
heart.) She shaded
her eyes with her
hand to see. (Bing
bang beat her heart.)
'He hurries to me over
meadows and fields,
over mountains and
through woods. Oh, if
only he were already
here with me!' (Bing
bang beat her heart.)

14. *FÜR FUNFZEHN PFENNIGE*
   FOR FIFTEEN PFENNIGS

14. FOR FIFTEEN PENCE

(From *Des   Knaben Wunderhorn*,
      of the boy   magic-horn
folk poems published by
Achim von Arnim and Clemens Brentano)

Das Mägdlein will ein' Freier habn,
the girl   wants a   suitor to have

Und sollt sie'n aus   der Erde grabn,
and must she him out of the earth to dig

Für funfzehn Pfennige.
for fifteen pfennigs

The girl wants a
lover; she'll have to
dig him out of the
earth – for fifteen
pence.

Sie grub wohl   ein, sie grub wohl   aus
she dug indeed in   she dug indeed out

Und grub nur einen Schreiber heraus
and dug only a   clerk   out

Für funfzehn Pfennige.
for fifteen pfennigs

She digs down,
she digs up, and only
digs a clerk out –
for fifteen pence.

Der Schreiber hatt des   Gelds zu viel,
the clerk   had of the money too much

Er kauft dem   Mädchen was sie will
he buys to the girl   what she wants

Für funfzehn Pfennige.
for fifteen pfennigs

The clerk has too
much money, and he
buys the girl
anything she wants –
for fifteen pence.

Er kauft ihr einen Gürtel schmal,
he buys her a   girdle narrow

Der starrt   von Gold wohl   überall,
that bristles of gold indeed all over

Für funfzehn Pfennige.
for fifteen pfennigs

He buys her a
narrow girdle
bristling all over
with gold – for
fifteen pence.

Er kauft ihr einen breiten Hut,
he buys her a   wide   hat

Der wär   wohl für die Sonne gut,
that would be indeed for the sun good

Für funfzehn Pfennige.
for fifteen pfennigs

He buys her a
broad brimmed hat,
that's good for the
sun – for fifteen
pence.

Wohl   für die Sonn, wohl   für den Wind,
indeed for the sun indeed for the wind

Bleib du bei mir, mein liebes Kind
stay you with me my dear child

Für funfzehn Pfennige.
for fifteen pfennigs

Good for the sun,
and good for the wind.
Stay with me, dear
love – for fifteen
pence.

15. *HAT GESAGT - BLEIBT'S   NICHT DABEI*   15. PROMISES - WITH
    HAS SAID   REMAINS IT NOT   BY IT   NOTHING TO THEM

(From *Des   Knaben Wunderhorn,*
      of the boy   magic-horn
 folk poems published by
 Achim von Arnim and Clemens Brentano)

Mein Vater hat gesagt,   My father says I
my   father has said   must rock the baby to
                                                   sleep; then this
Ich soll das Kindlein wiegen,   evening he'll boil
I   must the baby   to rock   me three eggs. But if
                                                   he boils three for me,
Er will mir auf den Abend   he'll eat two of
he will me in the evening   them - and I'm not
                                                   going to rock the
Drei Gaggeleier   sieden;   baby for a single
three chicken's-eggs to boil   egg!

Siedt er mir   drei,
boils he to me three

Isst er mir   zwei,
eats he to me two

Und ich mag nicht wiegen
and I   like not   to rock

Um ein einziges Ei.
for a   single   egg

Mein Mutter hat gesagt,   My mother says I
my   mother has said   must tell on the
                                                   maid; then this
Ich soll das Mägdlein   verraten,   evening she'll roast
I   must the maid servant to betray   me three birds. But
                                                   if she roasts three
Sie wollt mir   auf den Abend   for me, she'll eat
she would to me in the evening   two of them - and
                                                   for a single bird
Drei Vögelein   braten, ja braten;   I'm not going to tell
three (little)birds to roast yes to roast   on anyone!

Brat   sie mir   drei,
roasts she to me three

Isst sie mir   zwei,
eats she to me two

Um ein einzig Vöglein
for a   single (little)bird

Treib' ich kein Verräterei.
practise I   no   treachery

Mein Schätzlein   hat gesagt,   My sweetheart says
my   (little)sweetheart has said   I must think of him,
                                                   then this evening
Ich soll sein   gedenken,   he'll give me three
I   must of him to think   kisses. He'll give me
                                                   three, and it won't
Er wollt mir   auf den Abend,   stop at that - what
he would to me in the evening   do I care about
                                                   birds or eggs!
Drei Küsslein   auch   schenken;
three (little)kisses (indeed) to give

Schenkt er mir drei,
gives   he me three

Bleibt's nicht dabei,
stays it not   by that

Was kümmert mich's Vöglein,
what concerns me the (little)bird

Was schiert mich das Ei.
what concerns me   the egg

16. *MEINEM KINDE*
    TO MY CHILD   16. TO MY CHILD

Gustav Falke

Du schläfst   und sachte neig' ich mich   You are sleeping
you are sleeping and softly lean I   (myself)   softly. I lean over
                                                 your cot and give you
Über dein Bettchen   und segne dich.   my blessing. Each
over your (little)bed and bless you   gentle breath is a
                                                 soaring flight to
Jeder behutsame Atemzug   Heaven, a far-flung
each careful   breath   search for a star,
                                                 where from its pure
Ist ein schweifender Himmelsflug,   brightness love
is a   roving   Heaven's-flight   itself might pluck a
                                                 happy flower, and fly
Ist ein Suchen   weit umher,   down with it to lay
is a   searching far - and wide -   on your white
                                                 coverlet.
Ob   nicht doch   ein Sternlein   wär,
whether not   indeed a   (little)star were

Wo   aus eitel Glanz   und Licht
where from sheer brightness and light

Liebe sich   ein Glückskraut   bricht,
love herself a   happiness-plant plucks

Das sie geflügelt hernieder trägt
that she winged   down   carries

Und dir   auf's weisse Deckchen   legt.
and to you on the white (little)coverlet lays

17. *WIEGENLIED*
    CRADLE-SONG   17. CRADLE SONG

Richard Dehmel

Träume, träume du, mein süsses Leben,   Dream, my sweet
dream   dream you my   sweet life   life, dream of
                                                 heaven that brings
Von dem Himmel, der die Blumen bringt.   the flowers.
of the heaven that the flowers brings   Blossoms shimmer
                                                 there, trembling with
Blüten   schimmern da, die beben   the song your mother
blossoms shimmer   there that tremble   sings.

Von dem Lied, das deine Mutter singt.
from the song that your mother sings

Träume, träume, Knospe meiner Sorgen,
dream   dream   bud   of my   sorrows

Von dem Tage, da   die Blume spross,
of the day   when the flower budded

Von dem hellen Blütenmorgen,
of the bright blossom-morning

Da   dein Seelchen   sich   der   Welt erschloss.
when your little soul itself to the world opened

Träume, träume, Blüte   meiner Liebe,
dream   dream   blossom of my   love

Von der stillen, von der heil'gen Nacht,
of the silent of the holy   night

Da   die Blume   seiner Liebe
when the flower of his love

Diese Welt zum   Himmel mir   gemacht.
this   world to the heaven to me made

Dream, little
bud of my sorrows,
dream of the day when
the flower first
appeared, and of the
bright blossoming
morning, when your
little soul opened to
the world.

Dream, little
blossom of my love,
dream of the silent
and hallowed night,
when the flowering
of his love made this
world for me into
heaven.

18. *MUTTERTÄNDELEI*
    MOTHER-DALLYING

18. MOTHER'S
    CROONING

Gottfried August Bürger

Seht mir   doch mein schönes Kind,
look to me (do) my   lovely child

Mit   den gold'nen Zottellöckchen,
with the golden   shaggy-little curls

Blauen Augen, roten Bäckchen!
blue   eyes   red   little cheeks

Leutchen,   habt ihr auch so eins?
(little)people have you also so one

Leutchen,   nein, ihr habt keins!
(little)people no   you have none

Seht mir   doch mein süsses Kind,
look to me (do) my   sweet child

Fetter als   ein fettes Schneckchen,
fatter than a   fat   little snail

Süsser als   ein Zuckerweckchen!
sweeter than a   sugar-roll

Leutchen,   habt ihr auch so eins?
(little)people have you also so one

Leutchen,   nein, ihr habt keins!
(little)people no   you have none

Just look at my
lovely child with
her long golden curls,
her blue eyes and
little red cheeks!
Have you good people
got one like this! No,
you haven't, good
people!

Just look at my
sweet child, plumper
than a plump little
snail, sweeter than a
sugar bun! Have you
good people got one
like this? No, you
haven't, good people!

Seht mir   doch mein holdes Kind,
look to me (do) my   lovely child

Nicht zu mürrisch, nicht zu wählig!
not   too sullen   not   too hard to please

Immer freundlich, immer fröhlich!
always cheerful   always merry

Leutchen,   habt ihr auch so eins?
(little)people have you also so one

Leutchen,   nein, ihr habt keins!
(little)people no   you have none

Just look at my lovely child, never sulky, never hard to please; always so sweet and merry. Have you good people got one like this? No, you haven't, good people!

Seht mir   doch mein frommes Kind!
look to me (do) my   innocent child

Keine bitterböse Sieben,
no   very wicked vixen

Würd' ihr Mütterchen   so lieben.
would her(little)mother   so to love

Leutchen,   möchtet   ihr so eins?
(little)people would like you so one

O, ihr kriegt gewiss   nicht meins!
O you get   certainly not   mine

Just look at my innocent child! No wicked little vixen could love her mother as much. Would you good people, like one like this? Oh, you certainly won't get mine!

Komm'   einmal ein Kaufmann her!
let come once   a   merchant here

Hunderttausend   blanke Taler,
hundred-thousand shining talers

Alles Gold der   Erde zahl'   er!
all   gold of the earth would pay he

O, er kriegt gewiss   nicht meins!
O he gets   certainly not   mine

Kauf' er sich   woanders eins!
let buy he himself elsewhere one

If a buyer came here with a hundred thousand shining shillings, or all the gold in the world! Oh, he certainly wouldn't get mine – he'd have to buy elsewhere!

19. FREUNDLICHE VISION
    FRIENDLY   VISION

19. A FRIENDLY VISION

Otto Julius Bierbaum

Nicht im   Schlafe hab ich das geträumt,
not   in the sleep   have I   that dreamed

Hell am   Tage sah ich's schön vor   mir:
bright in the day saw I it lovely before me

Eine Wiese voller Margeritten;
a   meadow full of daisies

Tief ein weisses Haus in grünen Büschen;
deep a   white   house in green bushes

Götterbilder   leuchten aus dem Laube.
god-like forms glimmer   from the leaves

Und ich geh'   mit Einer, die mich lieb hat,
and I   am walking with one   who me   - loves -

Ruhigen Gemütes   in die Kühle
quiet   of spirit in the coolness

Dieses weissen Hauses, in   den Frieden,
of this white   house   into the peace

Der   voll   Schönheit wartet, dass wir kommen.
which full(of) beauty   waits   that we come

Und ich geh'   mit Einer, die mich lieb hat,
and I   am walking with one   who me   - loves -

In den Frieden voll Schönheit!
in the peace   full beauty

It was not in
sleep or in dreams,
but in bright day that
I saw it, lovely
before me; a meadow
full of daisies, and
a white house deep in
green bushes, where
god-like figures
glimmer among the
leaves. And serene in
spirit I am walking
with one who loves
me into the coolness
of the white house,
where peace full of
beauty awaits our
coming. I am walking
with one who loves me,
in the full beauty of
its peace.

20. EINERLEI
    SAMENESS

20. SWEET SAMENESS

Achim von Armin

Ihr Mund ist stets der selbe,
her mouth is always the same

Sein Kuss mir   immer neu,
his kiss to me always new

Ihr Aug noch das selbe,
her eye still the same

Sein freier Blick mir   treu;
his open   glance to me true

O du liebes Einerlei,
O you dear   sameness

Wie wird   aus   dir so mancherlei!
how becomes out of you so many things

Her lips are ever
the same; his kiss
ever new. Her eyes
ever the same, his
open glances ever
true.

O sweet sameness,
how many things are
born of you!

21. SCHLECHTES WETTER
    BAD   WEATHER

21. BAD WEATHER

Heinrich Heine

Das ist ein schlechtes Wetter,
that is a   bad   weather

Es regnet und stürmt und schneit;
it rains   and storms and snows

Ich sitze am   Fenster und schaue
I   sit   at the window and look

Hinaus in   die Dunkelheit.
out   into the darkness

What terrible weather! There's a raging storm, and rain, and snow. I'm sitting at the window, looking out into the darkness.

Da   schimmert   ein einsames Lichtchen,
there is shimmering a   solitary little light

Das   wandelt langsam fort:
which goes   slowly   away

Ein Mütterchen mit dem Laternchen
a   little dame with the (little) lantern

Wankt   über die Strasse dort.
totters over the street   there

A solitary little light is glimmering, and moving slowly away across the street. A motherly little woman totters along with her lantern.

Ich glaube, Mehl und Eier
I   think   flour and eggs

Und Butter kaufte sie ein;
and butter bought she -

Sie will einen Kuchen backen
she wants a   cake   to bake

Für's   grosse Töchterlein.
for the big   (little) daughter

I think she's been buying some flour and eggs and butter to bake a cake for her big spoilt daughter.

Die liegt   zu Haus im   Lehnstuhl
she is lying at home in the easy chair

Und blinzelt schläfrig ins   Licht;
and blinks   sleepily into the light

Die goldenen Locken wallen
the golden   curls fall in waves

Über das süsse Gesicht.
over the sweet face

She's lying at home in the easy chair, blinking sleepily at the light. Her golden curls fall luxuriantly over her sweet face.

22. *VIER LETZTE LIEDER*
    FOUR LAST   SONGS

   i. Beim   Schlafengehen
      by the going to bed

Hermann Hesse

Nun der Tag mich müd' gemacht,
now the day me   weary made

Soll   mein sehnliches Verlangen
shall my   yearning   desire

Freundlich die gestirnte Nacht
kindly   the starry   night

Wie ein müdes Kind empfangen.
like a   tired child to receive

Hände, lasst von allem Tun,
hands desist from all   doing

Stirn, vergiss du alles Denken,
brow   forget you all   thinking

Alle meine Sinne   nun
all my   senses now

Wollen sich   in   Schlummer senken.
want (themselves) into slumber   to sink

Und die Seele unbewacht,
and the soul   unguarded

Will in freien Flügen schweben,
longs in free   flights to float

Um   im   Zauberkreis der   Nacht,
so as in the magic-circle of the night

Tief   und tausendfach zu leben.
deeply and thousandfold to to live

   ii. September
       September

Hermann Hesse

Der Garten trauert,
the garden mourns

Kühl sinkt in   die Blumen der Regen.
cool sinks into the flowers the rain

Der Sommer schauert
the summer shivers

Still   seinem Ende entgegen.
quietly his   end towards

22. FOUR LAST SONGS

i. Whilst falling
   asleep

   The day has made
me weary, and my
yearning desire will
be gently received
like a tired child by
the starry night.

   Hands, rest from
all doing; brow,
cease from all
thinking, for now all
my senses would sink
into slumber.

   And my unguarded
soul longs to move
in flight unfettered –
to live deeply,
thousandfold, in the
magic circle of the
night.

ii. September

   The garden mourns;
rain falls cool upon
the flowers. The
summer quietly shivers
towards its close.

Golden tropft Blatt um Blatt
golden drips leaf by leaf

Nieder vom   hohen Akazienbaum.
down from the tall acacia-tree

Sommer lächelt erstaunt   und matt
summer smiles astonished and spent

In   den sterbenden Gartentraum.
into the dying   garden-dream

Lange noch bei den Rosen
long still by the roses

Bleibt er stehen, sehnt sich   nach Ruh.
remains he to stand yearns (himself) for rest

Langsam tut   er die (grossen)*
slowly closes he the (large)

Müdgewordnen Augen zu.
tired-become eyes   -

            Leaf after leaf
            drips golden from the
            tall acacia tree.
            Summer, astonished
            and spent, smiles on
            the dying garden
            dream.

            It tarries long
            among the roses,
            yearning for rest,
            and slowly closes
            eyes grown (large and)
            weary.

    iii. Frühling
      Spring

iii. Spring

    Hermann Hesse

In dämmrigen Grüften träumte ich lang
in dusky   vaults dreamt I   long

Von deinen Bäumen und blauen Lüften,
of your   trees and blue   breezes

Von deinen Duft   und Vogelgesang.
of your   fragrance and bird-song

Nun liegst du erschlossen in Gleiss und Zier,
now lie   you opened out in glitter and finery

Von Licht übergossen wie ein Wunder vor   mir.
by light poured over like a   miracle before me

Du kennst mich wieder, du lockst mich zart,
you know me again   you entice me   tenderly

Es   zittert durch   all meine Glieder
(it) quivers through all my   limbs

Deine selige Gegenwart!
your blessed presence

            As in a gloomy
            vault, I dreamt so
            long of your trees
            and blue breezes, of
            your fragrance and
            the songs of your
            birds.

            Now like a
            miracle you lie
            unfolded before me
            in lustrous
            adornment, flooded
            with light. You know
            me of old; you draw
            me to you tenderly,
            and your blessed
            presence sends a
            quivering through my
            every limb!

*omitted in the song

iv. Im   Abendrot
    in the evening glow

iv. In the evening
    glow

Joseph von Eichendorff

Wir sind durch   Not   und Freude
we are through misery and joy

Gegangen Hand in Hand;
gone   hand in hand

Vom   Wandern   ruhen wir (beide)*
from the wandering rest we   (both)

Nun überm   stillen Land.
now above the still   countryside

Through joy and
sorrow we have gone
hand in hand; now we
(both) rest from our
wanderings, here
above the still
countryside.

Rings sich   die Täler   neigen,
around (themselves) the valleys slope

Es   dunkelt   schon   die Luft,
(it) grows dark already the air

Zwei Lerchen nur noch steigen
two   larks   only still rise

Nachtträumend   in   den Duft.
dreaming of night into the scent

Around us the
valleys slope away,
the air already
darkens; only two
larks dreaming of
the night, rise up in
the haze.

Tritt her und lass sie schwirren,
step here and let   them to hover

Bald ist es Schlafenszeit,
soon is it sleep-time

Dass wir uns nicht verirren
that we us   not   go astray

In dieser Einsamkeit.
in this   solitude

Come, and leave
them hovering; it will
soon be time to sleep,
and we must not stray
in this solitude.

O weiter, stiller Friede!
O wide   still   peace

So tief im   Abendrot
so deep in the evening glow

Wie sind wir wandermüde –
how are we wandering-weary

Ist dies etwa   der Tod?
is this perhaps the death

O wide, still
peace! Deep in the
twilight, how weary
we are of wandering
– can this be death?

*omitted in the song

Index of titles and first lines

Titles of song cycles appear in italics